THE LISTENING EXPERIENCE

ELEMENTS, FORMS, AND STYLES IN MUSIC

❖ ❖ ❖

JAMES P. O'BRIEN

UNIVERSITY OF ARIZONA

SCHIRMER BOOKS
A Division of Macmillan, Inc.
NEW YORK

Collier Macmillan Publishers
LONDON

Copyright © 1987 by Schirmer Books
        A Division of Macmillan, Inc.

Schirmer Books
A Division of Macmillan, Inc.
866 Third Avenue, New York, N.Y. 10022

Collier Macmillan Canada, Inc.

Library of Congress Catalog Card Number: 86-23695

Printed in the United States of America

printing number
    2 3 4 5 6 7 8 9 10

Library of Congress Cataloging-in-Publication Data

O'Brien, James Patrick.
  The listening experience.

  Includes index.
    1. Music—Analysis, appreciation.   2. Music—Manuals,
text-books, etc.   I. Title.
MT6.03 1987   780'.1'5   86-23695
ISBN 0-02-872130-6 (pbk.)

To S. O. B., L. B., and B. O. B.

CONTENTS

CHAPTER EIGHTEEN   NON-WESTERN MUSICAL STYLES   **487**

LISTENING SELECTIONS

A NOTE ON THE LISTENING SELECTIONS

Almost all of the listening examples discussed and charted in this text have been included on the record set, and are designated within the text as *listening selections*. The only exceptions are the following compositions, which should be readily available in a music library or private collection. They are referred to in the text as *supplemental listening*.

Selection	Composer	Suggested Recording
Overture, Hornpipe and Bourrée from Suite no. 1 in F major (*Water Music*)	Handel	Angel 36173 Bach Festival Orchestra Yehudi Menuhin, Conductor
Presto (Scherzo, Symphony no. 7 in A, op. 92)	Beethoven	Columbia Masterworks ML 5404 Columbia Symphony Orchestra Bruno Walter, Conductor
The Moldau	Smetana	Columbia Masterworks ML 6375 The Cleveland Orchestra George Szell, Conductor
Allegro Vivace (Symphony no. 4 in A, op. 90, *Italian*)	Mendelssohn	Columbia Masterworks ML 6375 The Cleveland Orchestra George Szell, Conductor
Allegro energico e passionato, più allegro (Symphony no. 4 in e, op. 98)	Brahms	Odyssey U32313 Columbia Symphony Orchestra Bruno Walter, Conductor
Allegro (*Brandenburg* Concerto no. 4 in G, BWV 1049)	J. S. Bach	Epic LC 3605 Bach Netherlands Chamber Orchestra Szymon Goldberg, Conductor
Fêtes (*Nocturnes*)	Debussy	Angel 35977 Philharmonia Orchestra Carlo Maria Giulini, Conductor
"Alabama"	Coltrane	Impulse AS-50; also The Smithsonian Collection of Classic Jazz P 6 11891 John Coltrane, tenor sax McCoy Tyner, piano Jimmy Garrison, bass Elvin Jones, drums
Benedicamus Domino *O Maria Maris Stella* *Vetus Abit Littera*	Perotin anonymous anonymous	Telefunken Das Alte Werk STE LP 074-925 *Ars Antiqua: Organum — Motette — Conductus*
"Serenade to a Soul Sister"	Silver	Blue Note (Liberty Records) BST 84277 The Horace Silver Quintet

PREFACE

Music listening is an acquired skill. Although people may listen to music on many levels without guidance, the premise of *The Listening Experience* is that enjoyment can be enhanced if the listener has a conceptual framework for perceiving and understanding musical events. In order to provide such a framework, and augment the pleasures to be found from informed perception of all kinds of music, the book and its accompanying recordings systematically develop listening and appreciation skills in four basic areas.

Section I, Listening Skills, provides an overview of the entire course of study, sampling the range of music to be encountered—from classical to jazz—and emphasizing the "attentive" style of music listening. As in the rest of the book, each chapter opens with an outline of the main topic headings to be discussed.

Section II, Musical Elements, is a systematic study of the essential musical ingredients such as rhythm, dynamics, timbre, pitch and melody, harmony, and tonality. Each concept is amply illustrated with pertinent recorded musical examples that are diagramed and timed to direct the listener to the major musical events. This section is arranged to begin with the musical ideas most accessible to the non-musician, and then adds layers of complexity chapter by chapter until the student has at least a working knowledge of all the factors that contribute to a richly structured musical work.

Section III, Musical Forms, takes the elements studied in the preceding section and shows the various ways they can be combined to form a complete work. Separate chapters are devoted to single-movement works, multi-movement compositions, and pieces in various genres. In addition to a quantity of new listening examples, works already examined are re-introduced to demonstrate the interplay of elements in creating overall form.

Section IV, Musical Styles, provides a historical overview, noting the continuity of the previously examined elements and forms over the course of the varied historical periods of composition, and devoting extended separate chapters to the history and styles of jazz, and to music in the non-Western world. The increasingly familiar listening examples are now shown in their historical context, with further selections added to round out the attentive listener's perception of the musical universe.

Throughout the book, key terms in the textual discussion are pointed up with marginal callouts. Boxed inserts in every chapter provide biographies of major composers, adjunct discussions of matters of style, and descriptions of unique instrumental families. Musical illustrations are used where relevant, in a manner intended to reinforce or underscore descriptive material. Photographic illustrations are distributed generously, showing composers, instruments, and, especially in Section IV, works of art and architecture that are related either in time or spirit to the musical explication.

Each chapter ends with a concise summary, as well as Study Guidelines including lists of key terms and concepts, exercises and questions for chapter review, musical chronologies, and suggestions for further listening. In addition, every elements and forms chapter concludes with a table relating the topic under discussion to various style periods, and an organizational guide to perception presented in convenient flow-chart form. A Glossary at the end of the book supplies definitions of every term that might be unfamiliar to the non-musician reader.

The six recordings that accompany the book (on records or cassettes) contain almost every musical example cited and analyzed within the text, and are an essential part of the process of cultivating the attentive listener.

The Listening Experience is designed for a basic music appreciation course ranging in length from one quarter or semester to a full school year. For the shorter period, the instructor may wish to accelerate some of the material according to personal preference, or to make selective use of the chapters on style. Conversely, the longer period could be enhanced by the addition of several of the recordings suggested at the end of each chapter.

This book has been developed from the author's involvement with college music appreciation courses, and he wishes to thank the more than 10,000 students who have enrolled in his music appreciation course at the University of Arizona since 1975. They have truly been the inspiration and catalyst that motivated the writing of this book.

Finally, the author would like to express his appreciation to the staff of Schirmer Books, whose care and attention to detail helped bring this project to fruition. Senior editor Maribeth Anderson Payne and former editorial assistant Ronald Gabriel have been helpful throughout, but thanks are especially due associate editor Michael Sander, whose inquiring mind and editorial perception have proved invaluable.

James P. O'Brien

The premise of this book is that enjoyment and appreciation of music can be enhanced if one listens attentively. Although each individual may not choose to do so all the time, developing the skill provides the listener with an alternative to bathing in sound, to associating music with extra-musical stories or pictures, or to debating the quality of the performance. The guidelines in this text, if practiced and refined, will lead the listener to heightened perception, enjoyment, and appreciation of music.

The book is divided into four sections:

Section I: Listening Skills
Section II: Musical Elements
Section III: Musical Forms
Section IV: Musical Styles

Each section is designed to enhance the reader's ability to hear music, perceive its elements, and gain meaning by relating its details to the whole experience. Only by understanding how to listen attentively can one begin to explore and process musical detail. This first section, which contains one chapter only, is therefore the foundation for the remainder of the book.

LEARNING TO LISTEN

❖

LISTENING TO MUSIC

What do people hear in music? What does it mean to listen? In our fast-paced lives we seldom listen attentively, whether to music, conversation, or messages. Listening has become a peripheral and casual activity. With so much to hear, we listen to less. This helps reduce the complexity around us and probably makes life easier to deal with. Unfortunately, this filtering process does not foster good habits in music listening. Learning to listen to music is an acquired skill that frequently has to be cultivated and practiced. Fortunately, the skill can be developed and refined at any point in one's life.

As a first listening encounter we will sample music of a different culture, which may provide a fresh experience. Listen to *Murat Music of North Borneo (listening selections)*. What do you hear in this selection? Can you discern how the music is organized? Does it have an emotional or physical effect on you?

Selection no. 1

This example is relatively easy to comprehend since only two musical events are occurring: the men chant on one tone while their feet pound the hollow wooden floor of a hut, thus providing a steady, percussive accompaniment.

The music comes from the Semambu tribe on the island of Borneo. It is simpler than the music to which the contemporary

3

listener might be accustomed, but it does compel a person to listen, if only momentarily, because of its stark simplicity. The predictability of its form provides little interest for a listener after the structure becomes apparent. For the Semambus, however, the music probably has a ceremonial function and is not intended for listening alone. Music intended purely for listening, regardless of its culture, must contain some variety beyond sheer repetition. Otherwise, people would not listen to music for any length of time.

WAYS TO LISTEN

Entertainment
In reality, people listen to music in many ways and for a variety of reasons. Some listen to music merely as a form of entertainment; they enjoy hearing music that they define as "pleasant," with an agreeable sound.

Listen to Handel's "Hornpipe" *(supplemental listening)*. How does

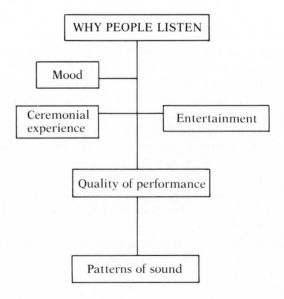

this compare with the selection from Borneo? Does it have a "pleasant" sound? Is there any variety?

This selection comes from a larger orchestral work by George Frideric Handel. It is considered a *movement*, which is defined as a **MOVEMENT** musically complete section of a longer composition. A movement is like a chapter of a book, since it stands on its own but also relates to other movements of the composition. Handel provides variety in this movement by alternating two musical ideas, which we can picture as □ and ○, two sets of instruments, strings and woodwinds, and two levels of loudness, soft and loud, in this manner:

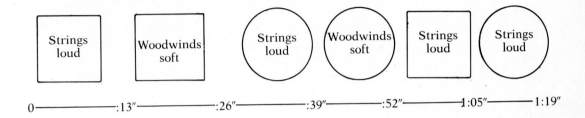

Although this provides contrast and variety, the music still has unity because ideas and instruments are repeated. Music for listening needs both *unity* and *variety* to be interesting. When you hear a composition **UNITY** like this, development of good listening habits requires that you keep **AND** track of the main musical ideas. The more complex the music, the **VARIETY** greater the concentration that is necessary. It is important to remember what has been repeated in the music (the unity) as well as to hear what is different (the variety).

Mood
Some people listen for the overall mood of music and then relate this to their own emotional state. If they are depressed, they may want to hear music that will give them a lift. If they are nervous or upset, they may seek music that has a calming effect. Music is often an effective evoker of sentiments or sensations.

Listen to "Flowers on Brocade" *(listening selections)*. The overall   Selection no. 2 mood is of peace and tranquility, often typical of the music of China. How is this peaceful quality achieved?

The composition uses two instruments, the *cheng*, a string instru-   **CHENG** ment, and the *hsiao*, a wind instrument. The cheng, which has sixteen   **HSIAO** strings stretched over a long, hollow frame, dates from the Ch'in dynasty (221–206 B.C.). The hsiao is a bamboo flute played in a forward (vertical) position much like the clarinet. These instruments play a simple melody in unison, its rise and fall providing some variety but certainly no great degree of tension.

Cheng, Chinese
16-stringed zither
with bridges.

Photo by K.H. Han. Northern Illinois University.

Cheng
Hsiao

TEMPO

The steady speed or *tempo* also contributes to the feeling of tranquility. As with many Chinese instrumental pieces, "Flowers on Brocade" describes a representation of the beauty of nature—in this case, woven flowers on a piece of tapestry. The melody is a Northern Chinese folk tune that was popular in the sixteenth century.

Quality of Performance

SOUND
REPRODUCTION

Listening for mood contrasts with listening for sound quality, either in characteristics of performance or in sound reproduction. Stereo aficionados pride themselves on owning equipment that reproduces sound with the least distortion, enabling them to listen for the accuracy and the interpretation of the artist.

Hsiao, Chinese
notched vertical flute.

Photo by K.H. Han. Northern Illinois University.

Quality of performance can also refer to distinctive individual traits. List to "Rainy Day Blues" *(listening selections)*. Lightnin' Hopkins is the artist in this selection. He was not formally trained as a musician, but learned his art by observing other performers and then experimenting on his own. Hopkins made a living as a street musician in Texas, creating songs, such as "Rainy Day Blues," that reflected his mood, the weather, or contemporary events.

The quality of the Hopkins performance is certainly different from that of a trained opera singer accompanied by a professional orchestra performing in a formal auditorium. But the validity of this musical event is not diminished by its vocal quality. Musicians like Lightnin' Hopkins are able to project a feeling in music as honestly as can any trained singer. "Rainy Day Blues," with its raspy singing and twangy guitar, can be enjoyable to a listener. Although training and skill may enable one to perform a wider variety of music, much of it complex, folk singers without formal training are still able to convey a musical experience to listeners. A good performance, then, is more than merely sophisticated music and refined playing techniques.

INDIVIDUAL TRAITS
Selection no. 3

Lightnin' Hopkins, blues singer.

Courtesy of the New York Public Library.

Patterned Sound

Many persons listen to music for patterned sound—how notes are combined into longer units, and how sections are joined to form movements and longer musical structures. The frequent definition of music as "organized sound" implies pattern and structure. Some compositions are as rigidly organized and symmetrically arranged as a classical painting, while other scores are like mobiles, their design dependent upon the aural and physical environment in which they are heard. Listening for the design of music, its structure and logic, its pattern of sound, can enhance one's appreciation and understanding.

Selection no. 4   Listen to Chopin's Etude no. 12 in c minor, op. 10 *(listening selections)*. The design is a basic one, with only three sections. The first and third are almost identical (unity), but the second is different and therefore provides contrast or variety.

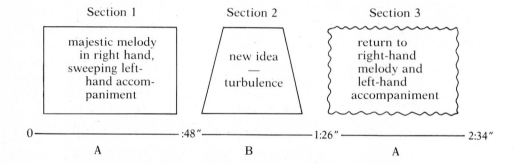

Unity and variety can be achieved in music by the composer's use of *three-part form,* a musical design that literally has three distinct parts. The composer typically uses one idea, such as a pattern of durations or pitches, in section one but provides a contrasting idea in the second section, leading the listener to anticipate the return of the original idea. The return does then occur in the third section, when the original idea reappears in a slightly more elaborate version. This particular structure is called *ABA,* a design followed by most three-part forms.

THREE-PART FORM

ABA
ETUDE

This composition is called an *etude,* which means a "study." Although etudes had previously been little more than technical exercises, Chopin's virtuosity as a composer elevated them into viable recital pieces. This work is nicknamed the "Revolutionary Etude" because the Polish Chopin is said to have written it in commemoration of the Poles on the sad occasion of a Russian invasion of his homeland. The *opus* marking (opus 10) represents the place of the composition within an approximate chronology of publication, assigned by either the composer himself or by his publisher. Opus numbers were not used extensively by composers until about 1800, so earlier works generally do not include such designations.

OPUS

Frédéric Chopin.
Photo by Institute of Frédéric Chopin, Warsaw. Courtesy of the New York Public Library.

Frédéric Chopin (1810–1849) was born near Warsaw. His mother was Polish and his father was an expatriate Frenchman who made his living as a tutor. Since he was a musical child, Frédéric was sent to study at the Warsaw Conservatory. Because of political unrest in Poland he moved in 1831 to Paris, where he achieved great acclaim as a piano virtuoso and earned his living by concertizing and teaching. In Paris Chopin became part of a circle that included many of the artistic and cultural leaders of the nineteenth century: the composers Liszt, Mendelssohn, and Berlioz, the poet Heine, the painter Delacroix, and the novelist George Sand. Chopin's lengthy amorous liaison with Sand, who changed her name from Aurore Dudevant in order to gain acceptance in a literary atmosphere hostile to women, brought him into contact with the salon society of the city. His numerous piano pieces became favorites of this social set. Chopin's tumultuous affair with Sand, full of turmoil and heartache, lasted almost until his death at the age of thirty-nine.

Most of Chopin's compositions are for the piano, either solo or with orchestra. He also was responsible for some chamber works, pieces written for small instrumental ensembles, originally intended to be performed in relatively intimate surroundings. One of his major contributions to the craft of composition is his use of harmonies, forms, rhythms, and melodic figures derived from the influences of Polish folk music. Chopin wrote 54 mazurkas, 19 nocturnes, 24 etudes, 26 preludes, 13 waltzes, 4 ballades, 4 fantasias, and 11 polonaises.

TYPES OF LISTENER

Which manner of listening is best? Each person develops a unique approach for hearing and understanding various types of music. This is why listening to music can be a joyous experience providing hours of worthwhile pursuit. Although there are numerous approaches to music appreciation, most persons listen in one of the following four manners.

Sensuous

First there is the *sensuous* listener, who bathes in sound and uses music as aural wallpaper. This person delights in the presence of sound

TYPES OF LISTENER

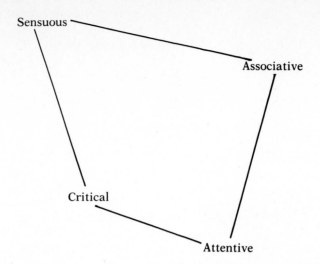

and often surrounds him/herself with it. Whether they are highly conscious of the sound or merely relegate it to the background, music is like a security blanket to such people. It makes them "feel good."

Associative

The second type of listener uses music as a springboard for memories and associations. This is the *associative* listener: "That reminds me of our walk on the beach." "They're playing *our* song!" "I remember when we saw that opera in Rome." We all develop associations through music. "The Star-Spangled Banner" probably evokes images of flags, the Fourth of July, and red, white, and blue, while a lullaby brings back fond memories of home and loving parents.

PROGRAM AND ABSOLUTE MUSIC

Music in which the composer provides a narrative or description, or suggests either in the title, is called *program music*. Associations are to be expected in such compositions. Some music, however, is *absolute*, that is, it has no story or description, and associative listening is probably not as appropriate. Absolute music is intended by the composer to be sufficient unto itself. The listener must then look directly to the music to find meaning while listening.

Selection no. 5

Listen to Bach's Toccata in d minor *(listening selections)*. This composition has been used on stage and film to accompany images depicting phantoms and monsters, and it is difficult to hear it without making these associations. In reality, it was never intended to be program music because it depicts nothing extramusical. It is an example of absolute music.

TOCCATA

A *toccata*, a keyboard piece written for organ, piano, or harpsichord, especially displays the technical skill of the performer. Toccatas are therefore often flamboyant and showy, and this one is no exception. The work begins dramatically and then builds by using runs, skips, and other flourishes on the keyboard. Many toccatas have a free feeling, as if they are being created or improvised on the spot.

Critical

A third type of listener, the *critical listener,* is concerned with the quality of the performance. Do the performers convey the intent of the composer and the mood of the music? Is their performance valid? Is their stage presence acceptable? This person monitors musical in-

Johann Sebastian Bach.
Engraved by C. Cook from a painting by L. Sichlong. Courtesy of the New York Public Library.

Johann Sebastian Bach (1685–1750), master of composition and gifted organist, was born in Eisenach, Thuringia, a region now part of the German Democratic Republic. Bach hailed from a family of professional musicians, and received systematic musical training from his brother, Johann Christoph, with whom he was sent to live after his parents died in 1694. As a choir boy at Lüneberg, he studied violin, clavichord, and organ, later winning organist positions at Arnstadt and Mühlhausen.

Although many of Bach's artful works established laws and became models of Baroque composition, his works also reflect extraordinary vision into the future. Bach's choral music includes about 200 church cantatas, a Mass in B minor and two Passions. His orchestral works include the *Brandenburg Concertos,* masterpieces of the Baroque period, and four orchestral suites, while his keyboard music includes the French and English suites and *The Well-Tempered Clavier.*

Composers of Bach's time earned their living by working for a church or secular court. His professional appointments included Weimar, where he served as organist for nine years, and Cöthen, where he directed a secular orchestra of eighteen performers. Professional appointments influenced the type music a composer produced, so it is hardly surprising that Bach composed numerous organ pieces earlier in his career, and composed orchestral and chamber works while employed at Cöthen. His final appointment was at Leipzig, where his responsibilities included playing organ for the church services, teaching Latin and music to school boys, and writing and directing music for church services. Accordingly, Bach wrote his greatest sacred works, while at Leipzig including the *St. John Passion* and the *Christmas Oratorio.*

terpretation. Has the conductor followed tradition? How is the tuning? The balance? Were the notes accurate? Critical listeners seek the ultimate in performance. They do not want technical limitations or improper interpretation to mar the music. Anything short of perfection constitutes a poor performance to them. When they listen to recordings, they insist on excellent equipment to reproduce the sound. They take meticulous care of their records and tapes since scratches and static buildup ruin the music for them.

Certainly all listeners want a quality performance, since this will present the music most favorably, and indeed the level of most professional public performances *is* very high. Unfortunately, our expectations for live music are formed from a steady diet of recordings that are usually edited to correct errors. We accept this perfection as the norm, but it cannot be maintained at all times in live performance with fallible *human* performers. Even though live music can never be flawless, a few mistakes do not make a performance totally bad.

Selection no. 6   Listen to "Navajo Hoop Dance" *(listening selections)*. This example was recorded at an actual Indian ceremonial and has not been modified by modern electronic techniques. The purpose of the dance is for the performers to display their skill in dancing with hoops, but the accompanying song has a deeper meaning. In Navajo culture, a singer is effective not only because of how he or she sounds but because the song creates a desired effect, which suggests a magical or mystical intent. Medicine songs, important in Navajo healing ceremonies, are effective if they heal the sick person. For this reason, many Navajo are not willing to share their songs since this would weaken the medicine.

The standards for a "correct" performance vary in each culture, even within subcultures. The Navajo standard of excellence is different from that of a concert pianist. Jazz aficionados look for something

Photo by Michael Lloyd. Courtesy of *The Oregonian*, Portland, Oregon.

Navajo Hoop Dancer.

different from those who listen to chamber music. Ultimately, however, each seeks perfection in a unique way.

Attentive

The *attentive* type of listener embodies and improves on the other three. This person enjoys sound and is often surrounded by music. Although he or she may draw associations with past events, these usually have some musical connection. A symphony of Mozart may remind the attentive listener of the last time the work was heard or of other works by Mozart. The attentive listener will also be keenly aware of the quality of the performance. Since the attentive listener will probably gain in the understanding of a composition with each repeated hearing, he or she will tend to associate listening to music with feelings of accomplishment through increased musical recognition.

In addition to responding to the feeling of the music, a quality shared with both the sensuous and the associative listener, the attentive listener goes a step further and analyzes why the music conveys the feeling it does. If the music is spirited, why? What techniques has the composer utilized? Is the music fast or slow? Does the speed change? How? Is it soft or loud? What instruments are used? Is the sound massed or spread out thinly? The attentive listener works at listening by returning to compositions that are difficult to comprehend instead of seeking immediate satisfaction and pleasure (and subsequent boredom) with the obvious. The attentive listener reads about music, trying to discover and hear its structure. Music listening is an end in itself and not merely something to be done while performing more important tasks. This listener is not concerned with liking a musical composition on the first few hearings, since many compositions take time to understand and appreciate, nor are her or his mind and ears closed to any valid musical experience.

Listen to the Kyrie eleison *(listening selections).* This may be a new listening experience for many listeners. What do you hear in the music? What can you notice that is different from the types of music you are used to hearing?

This is an example of *Gregorian chant,* once the official music of the Catholic Church. It is usually sung entirely by men and is almost always unaccompanied. The Kyrie Eleison, a religious plea for God to have mercy, is the opening movement of the Ordinary of the Mass, the Catholic sacrament celebrated with the bread and wine (body and blood) of Christ. Three statements of Kyrie eleison are followed by three Christe eleisons, and then three additional Kyrie eleisons.

Kyrie eleison (Lord, have mercy)
Christe eleison (Christ have mercy)
Kyrie eleison (Lord, have mercy)

Selection no. 7

KYRIE

The overall effect is of deep religiosity and tranquillity. The music almost floats and generally unfolds without hurry or care. An attentive listener can appreciate Gregorian chant by listening carefully to its structure and noting the techniques used to achieve its desired effect.

No one can be an attentive listener all of the time. Most people who have this skill will listen less intently at times, with variations in focus and attention even during a single concert. One who has developed skills as an attentive listener can easily listen in other ways, but will probably choose to listen attentively most of the time. This is the most rewarding way to listen, and leads to heightened awareness and appreciation of music. Understanding a musical composition is probably essential before one can make an intelligent, informed decision as to whether or not one likes it.

FACTORS IN LISTENING

Why does listening to music require special skills? Part of the reason is the nature of sound itself. It is heard in passing and then it is gone. Unlike painting or sculpture, where the viewer sees the entire product

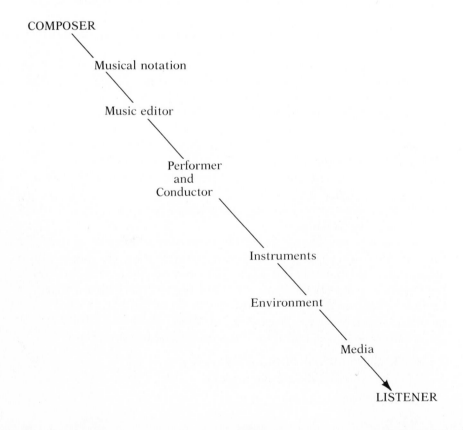

of the artist, music is recreated each time it is performed. Since it is heard in segments, the attentive listener must reconstruct the whole from the aural components. As the listener formulates this mental construct, certain factors affect his or her perception.

Musical Notation

Musical notation, the writing down of the notes and performance instructions that comprise a musical composition, is one of these factors. In music of earlier periods, the *composer*, who was often the performer as well, did not notate music as precisely as is now the norm. Specific notes and expression marks were frequently omitted. Modern performers may not understand the intent of a composer who lived four hundred years ago, since notation, like words in language, changes in meaning with the passage of time, and research may be necessary to decipher the true intentions of the composer. Even today, musical notation does not reflect everything the composer intends. Although composers are now quite specific in their scores, it is still impossible to indicate all the nuances that are possible in performance and that affect the listening experience.

COMPOSER

Courtesy of the New York Public Library.

Aaron Copland,
American composer.

Music Editor

The *music editor* therefore strives to clarify the composer's written intentions. The editor often takes a manuscript written in an earlier notation and translates the notes into contemporary notation so musicians can read them. This may include adding or deleting notes, and even suggesting musical directions. The earlier the music, the greater the task. During the nineteenth century composers began to be more specific in their compositions. In recent times, some electronic composers have eliminated both the musical score and performer by working directly on magnetic tape, thus giving themselves total control over musical interpretation.

Performer

The *performer*, another factor in the listening process, learns music from the notated and edited copy. Like the historian who reads several different accounts of a past event in the attempt to find the truth, the performer may consult several editions before deciding on an interpretation. He or she is then able to perform the music based on the best information that is available. The performance that results is derived from individual interpretation, so it may still be unique; renditions of the same composition by two equally qualified performers are often quite different.

CONDUCTOR   The *conductor* is a special performer who interprets the music of a composer by using the entire symphony orchestra, choir, or band as his or her instrument. Research and rehearsal are tools needed by the conductor as much as by any performer to arrive at a valid performance.

Instruments

A further factor in the listening process is the wide variety of *instruments*. Compositions written with a nine-foot grand piano in mind sound different on a spinet. Works for pipe organ are not the same when performed on a small electronic model. Sounds actually heard in performances may differ in varying degrees from the composer's original idea. Music of earlier times certainly was not performed on instruments of today, and many musicians prefer authentic "period" instruments (such as the fortepiano, harpsichord, and recorder) for the performance of music of earlier periods.

Environment

The acoustical *environment* in which we hear music is another factor in music listening. Compositions written to be performed in a small

The conductor of an orchestra not only beats time (rhythm) for the performers, but elicits the correct feeling and expressive shading of the composition being performed from all the musicians. Music Director Zubin Mehta conducts the New York Philharmonic.

Photo by David Rentas. Courtesy the New York Philharmonic.

room will not be the same if performed in a large concert hall. Ambient sounds, such as noise and people coughing and talking, can vary from one performance to the next in the same concert hall. All of these factors may make it difficult to be attentive to the music.

Media

The availability of music on records, tapes, radio, and television is another factor to consider. We lose the true sound of music when it is presented in these media, regardless of the quality of the sound reproduction equipment. Live performance has more vitality than recorded sound because it includes the human factor, the interaction between listener and performer. An attentive listener recognizes the importance of using both live performance and recordings in the development of good listening habits. Recordings enable the listener to repeat a work until it becomes familiar, and television performances

Although string instruments (foreground) often dominate in the orchestra, wind (background) and percussion instruments are also an integral part.

Photo by Tim Fuller.

allow the viewer to see the performers' fingerings, techniques, and gestures much closer than would be possible in a concert hall. But a balance of live performances and recordings is still necessary to develop good listening habits.

All of these factors—the notation, the music editor, the performer, the conductor, the environment, the instruments, and the media—can but do not necessarily inhibit the development of attentive listening. The seasoned listener may never be aware of the contributory nature of these factors, but to the novice struggling to be attentive, a scratchy record or flamboyant performer may distract from hearing the music.

ATTENTIVE LISTENING

Concentration

Enjoyment, understanding, and appreciation of music can be enhanced if one listens attentively. Attentive listening requires *concentration* and should not be attempted while reading a book or carrying on a conversation. Many listeners find the best way of listening to recordings is with headphones, since attention is enhanced when extraneous sights and sounds are reduced. Concentrating during a live performance is somewhat more difficult, of course, because one can easily be distracted by the atmosphere that surrounds live performance. The lights are usually dimmed in a concert hall to facilitate concentration and provide focus on the performance. Whether the music is live or recorded, the attentive listener strives to concentrate on the sound.

Repetition

Attentive listening also requires *repetition* of the music. Good music rarely reveals itself on one hearing, and it behooves the listener to play a recording several times in order to grasp the overall design as well as many of its details. This is also a useful preparation for attending a live concert at which the composition will be performed.

Technical Understanding

Attentive listening requires some *technical understanding* of music as well as historic perspective. A good listener should eventually be able to describe his or her musical experiences with an appropriate musical vocabulary. This vocabulary can be developed from studying critical and analytical writings and reading music reviews in newspapers and magazines, descriptions on record jackets, and notes in concert programs.

Broad Perspective

The attentive listener develops *broad perspective* in musical taste and has little concern about "liking" or "disliking" a composition or judging whether the work is "good" or "bad." Rather it is more important that the music is valid and can be understood. It is rarely possible to determine this validity after hearing a piece only once or twice, no matter whether the music is old or new. Appreciation comes from listening several times and realizing that music does not need to be beautiful, relaxing, or even inoffensive. It does not need to convey a message. But it does need to be organized somehow, even if this organization is not obvious and can be understood only with some endeavor. The attentive listener thus seeks and accepts validity despite personal preference. Although this book will provide various ways in which one can respond to music, the reader will ultimately develop his or her own modes for dealing with the musical experience. There is no "one" correct way to appreciate music.

AWARENESS OF STYLE

The attentive listener develops an awareness of various musical styles and understands that music is often created for diverse purposes and by many types of people. Therefore all music is not heard with an identical set of expectations. *Folk music,* for example, is composed by untrained musicians and is usually relatively simple. In some examples, each succeeding generation has added its own interpretation and the composer is really an entire community. Since folk music is usually not notated and is passed along through oral tradition, it is subject to change and variation with the passage of time. *Art music,* on the other hand, is generally developed and written down by trained musicians, so it has an "official" version and changes relatively little over a period of time. Folk music may be easily accessible to listeners while art music may require greater concentration, since its design is not always easily revealed. Whereas folk music is often vocal, art music can be either vocal or instrumental.

FOLK MUSIC

ART MUSIC

The dividing line between folk and art music, of course, is not rigid and there is some music that could justifiably be classified as either. Jazz, for example, has characteristics that make classification difficult. The musicians who play it are typically virtuosos on their instruments, but most jazz is not written down. The same observation may be made of East Indian music. In reality, folk and art music, if definitions can be drawn, are much more alike than dissimilar and the attentive listener can enjoy either as a valid experience.

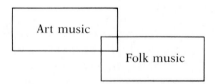

Two listening examples will clarify some of the similarities and differences between art and folk music. Listen to "Lost Your Head Blues" *(listening selections). Blues* is an early type of jazz that is considered a folk idiom. In blues, the singer improvises the lyrics as

Selection no. 8
BLUES

well as the tune, following a modification of a standard poetic form, the *couplet*.

COUPLET

VERSE ONE

I was with you, baby, when you didn't have
    a dime.
I was with you, baby, when you didn't have
    a dime.
Now since you got plenty money you have
    throwed your good gal down.

A couplet in poetry is two lines that rhyme, but in blues, the words of the first line are repeated, making a total of three musical lines. Each couplet, in turn, becomes one verse of the blues. The succeeding four couplets are variations on the first verse, a *variation* in any musical form being simply an elaboration of a basic musical idea.

VARIATION

Bessie Smith.
Courtesy of CBS Records.

Bessie Smith (c. 1894–1937) was born in Chattanooga, Tennessee. Since she never had a certificate, the exact date of birth is not known. Her singing career began in tent shows and speakeasies and eventually led to sound recordings in the 1920s. Along with singers Mamie Smith and "Ma" Rainey, Bessie Smith established the vocal blues style and demonstrated that its popularity could extend beyond a strictly black audience. This was due in part to her strong and compelling voice, which could project even with the rather anemic recording devices of her time. Her inherent mastery of the blues style featured interesting rhythmic and melodic improvisations. Bessie was able to convey a convincing message through her vocal inflections that appealed to both black and white audiences.

Her first recording was made in 1923, her fame peaking between 1924 and 1929 when she appeared in a feature Hollywood film, *St. Louis Blues*, and continued on the vaudeville circuit. During the depression years of the 1930s, the blues faded in popularity and Bessie found diminishing audiences for her music. She turned to alcohol and died as a result of medical neglect after an automobile crash.

Verse two	One saint for always . . .
Verse three	When you were lonesome . . .
Verse four	I goin' leave, baby . . .
Verse five	Days are lonesome . . .

The instrumentalists play a somewhat standardized accompaniment for the singer. In this example the singer is Bessie Smith, who improvised both the words and melody. The music has not been written down and every rendition of "Lost Your Head Blues" differs, even if performed by the same musicians. This is partly the nature of folk music, and attentive listeners know there is thus no official version of the piece.

Selection no. 9
GAVOTTE

Now listen to Stravinsky's "Gavotta con due Variazioni" (gavotte with two variations) from the *Pulcinella* Suite *(listening selections)*. A *gavotte* is a French dance that originated in the seventeenth century, although this is a twentieth-century version by Igor Stravinsky that includes two *variations* (defined above). This composition is clearly an example of art music. It is scored for flutes, oboes, bassoons, and horns, and, since it is notated, the Gavotte with two variations is similar each time it is heard. Although blues variations are usually improvised, those in art music are specifically notated.

TWO-PART
FORM

The form of the gavotte is *two-part,* and each variation, therefore, follows the same form. (Although there are exceptions, variations generally take the same form as the initial musical statement.) Follow this graph as you listen.

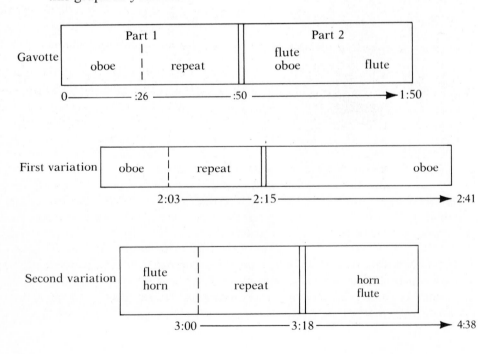

Igor Stravinsky.
Courtesy of the New York Public Library.

Igor Stravinsky (1882–1971) was born in Russia, then lived in Paris and Switzerland for some years before settling in the United States prior to World War II. One of the dominant and most-performed figures in twentieth-century art music, Stravinsky was often inspired by dance in his compositions. Some of his earliest orchestral works, the ballet scores *The Firebird* (1910), *Petrouchka* (1911), and *The Rite of Spring* (1913), demonstrate his neo-romantic nationalism, employing a large orchestra, driving rhythms, and striking dissonance. All of these were written for the ballet impresario Diaghilev, and the orchestral suites derived from them proved as powerful and influential in the concert hall as they had been as accompaniments for the dance.

Stravinsky subsequently changed his compositional style to one of classic restraint and smaller performing groups, a shift in emphasis due both to economic conditions of the time and the composer's belief that classical balance and objectivity were not dead. The Pulcinella Suite (1919–1920) began this Neo-Classic period, which continued during Stravinsky's residence in Paris and Switzerland (1921–1930) and lasted until the 1950s. The melodies in the Pulcinella Suite are derived from works by Pergolesi, an eighteenth-century composer, but the harmonies and instrumental writing are Stravinsky's. Other major works from Stravinsky's Neo-Classic period include *The Soldier's Tale* (1918) and Octet for wind instruments (1923).

In his late works Stravinsky began to write atonally. Many of his major compositions, such as *In Memoriam Dylan Thomas* (1954), *Canticum Sacrum* (1955–1956), and *Variations: Aldous Huxley, In Memoriam* (1963–1964), exhibited a common thread of religiosity. Through all his changes of style Stravinsky remained a premier composer, and is today considered an undisputed giant of twentieth-century music.

This composition is somewhat more complex than the blues, requiring concentration to grasp its structure. It would probably be difficult for a beginning listener to hear the form without the aid of the graph, but an experienced listener should recognize the overall design after hearing it a few times.

What is the meaning of the music? Since the basic form of the gavotte is a type of dance, the message, if any needs to be assigned, is in the ear of the beholder. Grasping the overall design is probably sufficient "meaning" in itself. This is typical of both folk and art music. The attentive listener would probably not try to assign any meaning beyond this.

STUDY GUIDELINES

KEY TERMS AND CONCEPTS

Absolute music
Art music
Blues
Etude
Factors in Listening
  Composer
  Conductor
  Environment
  Instruments
  Media
  Music editor
  Musical score
  Notation
  Performer
Folk music

Movement
Program music
Tempo
Toccata
Two-part form
Types of Listener
  Associative
  Attentive
  Critical
  Sensuous
Unity/variety
Variations

EXERCISES

1. Describe your listening habits. What kind of listener are you?
2. Listen to one of the following compositions and write a paragraph on how each of the four types of listener would probably describe or react to the music.

Selection no. 59   "Old Monk Sweeping the Buddhist Temple"

Selection no. 57   Mussorgsky—Selection from *Pictures at an Exhibition,* "Samuel Goldenberg and Schmuyle"

Selection no. 31   Vivaldi—Concerto in a minor, movement I, for flute, two violins and continuo

3. Listen to one of the following compositions *twice*. Each time, keep track of when your mind wanders from the music by making a √ on the line indicated. Does your score change on the repetition? Why? How could you improve your score on further repetitions?

  First hearing
    Begin _____ End   Total √s = _____
  Second hearing
    Begin _____ End   Total √s = _____

Compositions
  Handel—"Bourrée" from *Royal Fireworks Music*
  Hampton— *"When Lights Are Low"*
  Dowland—*"Orlando Sleepeth"*

Supplemental
Selection No. 13
Selection No. 11

4. Describe an ideal environment for yourself that would enable you to listen to music attentively. What things would you like to know about the music first? Why?

5. Which of the listening selections in this chapter are folk music? Art music? Which seem to be a bit of both? Why?

6. Which of the factors involved in attentive listening apply to folk music? Art music?

CHAPTER REVIEW

Match items in the two columns. Answers in Appendix.

1. _____ Mass movement
2. _____ a musical study
3. _____ music that is usually based on oral tradition
4. _____ two poetic lines
5. _____ early vocal jazz
6. _____ seventeenth-century French dance
7. _____ music that is usually notated
8. _____ music without a story
9. _____ keyboard composition
10. _____ musical speed
11. _____ complete section of a musical composition
12. _____ music with a story
13. _____ listens for mistakes
14. _____ listens to fill silence
15. _____ listens for the story
16. _____ listens for feeling of music, then analyzes

A. sensuous listener
B. art music
C. critical listener
D. blues
E. attentive listener
F. etude
G. program
H. absolute
I. toccata
J. Kyrie
K. movement
L. folk music
M. tempo
N. associative listener
O. couplet
P. gavotte

FOR FURTHER LISTENING

Absolute Music
  Bach, J. S.   *Brandenburg Concerto* no. 5 in D major
                           Chromatic Fantasy and Fugue

Barber	*Adagio for Strings*
Chopin	Ballade no. 3 in A♭ major, op. 47
	Nocturne in E♭ major, op. 9, no. 2
Franck	*Symphonic Variations*
Handel	Sonata no. 4 in D major for violin and harpsichord, op. 1, no. 13.
Haydn	Quartet in E♭ major, op. 33, no. 2
Milhaud	Sonatina
Mozart	*Eine kleine Nachtmusik*, K. 525
Poulenc	Trio for piano, oboe and bassoon
Prokofiev	*Classical Symphony* in D major
	Toccata in d minor
Rachmaninoff	Concerto no. 2 in c minor for piano and orchestra
Ravel	Concerto in G major for piano and orchestra
Shostakovitch	Symphony no. 5
Sibelius	Symphony no. 1 in e minor
Tchaikovsky	Concerto in D major for violin and orchestra

Program Music

Beethoven	Symphony no. 6 in F major (*Pastorale*)
Borodin	*On the Steppes of Central Asia*
Copland	*Appalachian Spring*
Debussy	*La Mer*
Grofé	*Grand Canyon Suite*
Holst	*The Planets*
Mussorgsky	*Pictures at an Exhibition*
Respighi	*The Fountains of Rome*
	The Pines of Rome
Saint-Saëns	*Carnival of the Animals*
Sibelius	*Finlandia*
	The Swan of Tuonela
Strauss, Richard	*Don Quixote*
Tchaikovsky	*1812 Overture*
	Romeo and Juliet Overture-Fantasy

Examples of both program and absolute music may be found in the following.

Country-Western
The Best of Country (Columbia House P5S 5914)

Jazz
The Smithsonian Collection of Classic Jazz (Columbia Special Products P611891)

Non-Western Music
Music of the World's Peoples (Four Volumes), Folkways Records FE4504, FE4505, FE4506, FE4507

MUSICAL ELEMENTS

◆

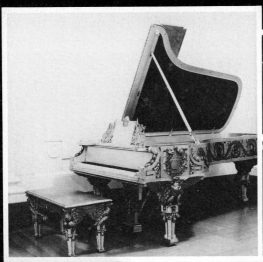

Attentive listening involves more than merely being aware of ways to listen and of the factors involved in aural perception. There must be details to grasp or the experience becomes so generalized that listening will be cursory. The numerous musical details are grouped into six areas in this section:

Rhythm: the time element of music

Dynamics: the level of volume of sound

Timbre: the tone color or unique sounds that are heard

Pitch and Melody: the horizontal highs and lows of music

Harmony: the vertical combinations of music that serve to provide a background for a melody

Tonality: the arrangement of pitches, melody, and harmony to give a feeling of pitch center or focus

These details or elements are interrelated and are separated here only to provide clearer models for study purposes. The reader should continually try to relate each element, each detail, to the wholeness of the music, just as one's appreciation of a great building would imply perceiving such details as a fireplace, a light fixture, or a staircase and continually relating them to the beauty of the whole structure. Similarly, these musical elements must be processed and interrelated, ultimately to find one's individual meaning in the music.

CHAPTER TWO

RHYTHM

❖

MUSIC AND RHYTHM

Music is an art that occurs in passing time. It begins, it exists, and then it ends. Although a painting's entirety can be perceived in one glance, music is heard in segments. We never grasp the entire image until the composition is finished, and there is little opportunity to ponder detail. The attentive listener must therefore keep in mind the details of a musical composition until the end, when all the pieces can be assembled into a whole.

Language

Listening to music is similar to listening to spoken language. One may suspend judgment until the meaning becomes evident, weighing and deciding what is important along the way. Some compositions may offer few surprises but the attentive listener learns to develop expectations while listening, even when the title has provided all the necessary cues. What *has* happened? What *may* happen next? What *does* happen next? What is significant? What was expected? Although music is a type of language, as is all art, the language is not universal. If it were, music listening would neither have to be taught nor learned, and music would communicate the same message to all listeners, which it rarely does. Perhaps it is better to consider that music is a universal need and expression that has no international meaning or message. What music conveys is music, and what makes it unique among the arts is that it exists in a temporal span, the time dimension.

Rhythmic regularity
and accent can
be observed in the
visual arts.
Rectangles, I. Rice
Pereira, American,
1940, oil on canvas.

University of Arizona Museum of Art, gift of Leonard Pfeiffer.

Rhythm

Rhythm refers to the temporal span of music. All music has rhythm.
There would be no music without a time span, a length, a duration.
Rhythm, however, involves more than the length of a composition. One
musical selection may last five minutes, another fifty, but the listener
will not necessarily perceive the first as short and the second as long.
Actual time, measured by a clock, is only part of rhythm. One's
perception of duration, *psychic time,* is a more important consideration, since it is subjective. In everyday life, time sometimes seems to
"fly" and at other times to "drag." A fifty-minute lecture may seem
long to some students, short to others. Musical time is similar to this.
A composer can expand the sense of time and give listeners the feeling
of a drawn-out experience. Conversely, he or she can condense time

ACTUAL
AND
PSYCHIC TIME

32

and make listeners feel as if a great deal has happened in a short duration. Rhythm could be called the determining factor in perception of musical duration. Rhythm is a composite musical element that includes the tempo, pulse, accented beat, and rhythm patterns actually used in a composition.

TEMPO

A composition may unfold gradually, that is, have a slow *tempo* in which musical events are developed gradually. Another may be busy, in which case it can be said to have a fast tempo. A composition may even change, moving from slow to fast and perhaps back again.

Listen to the Prelude to Act III of Richard Wagner's *Lohengrin* *(listening selections)*. The tempo throughout is brisk and there is a feeling that time is passing quickly. Although the first section is loud, variety is provided by a softer middle section, followed by the return of a loud section.

Selection no. 10

	loud	soft	loud	
0	1:10	1:56		2:35

Listen to John Dowland's (1562–1626) "Orlando Sleepeth" *(listening selections)*. Compared to the *Lohengrin* Prelude this composition moves slowly. The piece seems much longer than its 1:37 minutes because the tempo is slower. Musical events seem to unfold gradually, with the slowness helping to create a tranquil feeling.

Selection no. 11

Listen to Chopin's Mazurka no. 24 in C Major, op. 33, no. 3 *(listening selections)*. This piano piece is ABA in form, with the B section marked off from the others largely by a change in tempo.

Selection no. 12

A Section 1	B Section 2	A Section 3
soft lilting moderate tempo	louder more forceful slightly faster	soft lilting moderate tempo

0	:24	:49	1:22

An opera is a large dramatic work written for soloists and chorus accompanied by orchestra. In opera, singers portray characters who converse in song while performing on stage, often with lavish sets and costumes. Prelude to Act III is from the opera *Lohengrin* by Richard Wagner, written between 1845–1848 and derived from a medieval legend. Lohengrin, a knight of the Holy Grail, miraculously appears in a swan-drawn boat to defend Elsa, a maiden accused of murdering her brother. In the course of the opera, they wed following the famous wedding processional known familiarly as "Here Comes the Bride," and Elsa promises that she will never question Lohengrin's true identity. But she persists in her curiosity to find his origin and he eventually returns to Montsalvat, the home of the Grail. The opera ends as Lohengrin departs in a boat pulled by the white dove of the Holy Grail.

Two scenes from Wagner's *Lohengrin.* Right, Teresa Zylis-Gara and Siegfried Jerusalem as Elsa and Lohengrin; below, the wedding scene.

Photographs by James Heffernan. Courtesy of the Metropolitan Opera Association.

D.C. AL
FINE
(DA CAPO)

The third section of a composition in ABA form is often not written out if the repeat is exact. Written instructions in the following form tell the performer to repeat the first section: at the conclusion of section B, the composer writes *D.C. al Fine (da capo al fine)*, which means return to the "capo" or "head" (beginning of the A section) of the music and repeat until "fine" or the "finish" is indicated, usually at the end of the A section. Notational shorthand such as *D.C. al Fine* is common in music in which the composer wants to have a section repeated.

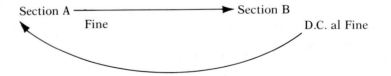

Section A ⟶ Section B
Fine   D.C. al Fine

Tempo Markings

Tempo is indicated in music with *Italian terms* used as tempo indicators; in the following chart, reading from left to right, the terms represent a progression from slow to fast:

Slower	Moderate	Faster

← Largo   Lento   Adagio   Andante   Moderato   Allegretto   Allegro   Presto   Prestissimo →

Each term represents a relative rather than an absolute speed. For example, *andante* is a slow, walking tempo, while *moderato* is close to a normal heartbeat. *Allegro* means a quick tempo, *presto* a very fast one. In addition, each term indicates the overall character of the music; whereas *largo* may be somber, *allegro* is cheerful.

ITALIAN
TERMS

Composers also use qualifying terms in conjunction with these tempo markings: *meno* (less); *piu* (more); *poco a poco* (little by little); *assai* (very); and *non troppo* (not too much). *Allegro assai*, for example, means "very quick" while *allegro non troppo* means "not too fast."

QUALIFYING
TERMS

Performers naturally need to know the tempo and character suggested by each Italian term, but these implications are also important for the listener, since some compositions and movements are titled generically as "Allegro" or "Largo." The attentive listener who is aware of these Italian terms is thus able to anticipate the tempo of a composition.

Listen to the Overture to Handel's *Water Music* (Suite no. 1 in F

Lute by Uldrich Dieffopruchar (?), Venice, before 1693.

Smithsonian Institution Photo #72729.

The lute is a pear-shaped string instrument with a flat top and rounded back. Like the guitar, it has an extended fingerboard divided by frets used to change the pitch of each string. The peg mechanism for tuning its eleven strings is at a right angle to the fingerboard, giving the lute a unique shape. Lutes intricately decorated and inlaid with fine wood were popular during the Renaissance, a musical stylistic period (1450–1600). They later lost favor as a solo instrument to the simpler guitar.

The mazurka is a Polish dance form with a specific rhythmic pattern that Chopin used extensively in his piano compositions. As a social dance, it was popular in the eighteenth and nineteenth centuries and resembled the polka. The mazurka, performed either fast or slowly, is danced by four couples and characterized by the heavy accent on a weak beat. Although written in triple time where the first beat is normally accented, as in the waltz, the accent in a mazurka is placed on the weaker second or third beat.

OVERTURE   major) *(supplemental listening)*. An *overture* is an introduction to a longer work, such as an opera or a suite. The composition is marked *Maestoso* (majestically), *Allegro* (quick and lively), and *Adagio e staccato* (slow and detached), suggesting these three sections.

Maestoso slow pompous	Allegro fast	Adagio slow

0 ———————— 2:30 ———————— 4:46 ———————— 7:00

Perception of Time

Tempo can affect the perception of time in a musical composition. *Largo* can provide the effect of a slow passage of time, while the opposite may be true with *Presto*. Slow tempos do not always result in slow psychic time, however, nor is the reverse always true, since perception of time also depends on the receptivity of the listener. If one is eager to listen, time may be perceived as passing quickly; conversely, if one is not receptive to music, time may seem to crawl by.

A suite, as observed in Stravinsky's *Pulcinella* Suite on page 22, is an instrumental piece with several movements based on dance rhythm and form. The exact date for the composition of Handel's *Water Music* is not known, and the entire suite did not appear in print until 1733. Some claim it was used for festivities in 1717 to accompany the English royal family as they sailed down the River Thames. The king's boat was said to be followed by a barge on which a fifty-piece orchestra played most of Handel's score.

BEAT (PULSE)

The regular pulse in a composition is called a *beat*, and it is like the ticking of a mechanical clock, evenly spaced and regular. In fast tempos there are many beats per minute, in slower tempos, fewer beats.

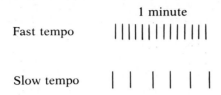

A moderate tempo is usually considered between 80 and 100 beats per minute.

Direct Beat

When the beat is audible, that is, when it is played by an instrument, it is called *direct*.

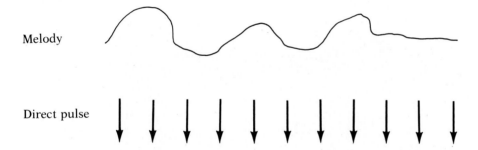

Although any instrument can play the beat, the job is frequently given to bass drum, tuba, or string bass. In a solo piano composition, the performer's left hand can maintain a direct beat while the right hand plays the melody. In orchestras and bands, the beat is often played by the percussion section, which includes drums and cymbals.

Listen to Lionel Hampton's performance of "When Lights Are Low" *(listening selections)*. This piece is an example of a 1930s jazz style called *swing*. A steady, direct beat is typical, maintained throughout this composition by the rhythm section, that is guitar, drums, piano, and bass. At only one point, indicated in the chart by an asterisk (*), is the beat silent.

Selection no. 13
SWING

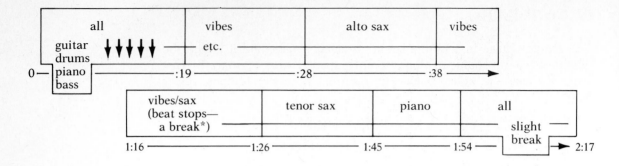

all	vibes	alto sax	vibes
guitar drums ↓↓↓↓↓ —	etc.		
0 — piano bass	:19	:28	:38 →

vibes/sax (beat stops— a break*)	tenor sax	piano	all
			slight break
1:16	1:26	1:45	1:54 → 2:17

VIBRAHARP
VIBRAPHONE

Solos by various instruments, especially the *vibraharp* or *vibraphone* (vibes), an amplified metal-type of xylophone, occur over the direct beat. There is no deviation in the tempo set at the beginning; since swing was played primarily for ballroom dancing, a steady beat was necessary.

Selection no. 14

Listen to Domenico Scarlatti's Sonata in C, L.454 (K.309) *(listening selections)*. It is possible to provide a direct pulse with a solo instrument as well as with a group. The instrument here is a *harpsichord*, a keyboard instrument in which the strings are plucked by a quill or *plectrum*, activated when the key is depressed.

HARPSICHORD
PLECTRUM

A direct beat is played consistently throughout in the performer's left hand while a melody is heard in the right.

Vibraphone, known interchangeably as the vibraharp.

Courtesy of the Slingerland Drum Co.

Left, harpsichord by Ionnes Daniel Dulcken, Antwerp, 1745, an instrument with two manuals (keyboards) covering a five-octave range (FF to f₃); below, model of harpsichord action showing plectrum of jack (on left of photo) about to pluck the string.

Smithsonian Institution Photos #56314 and #811314.

Right hand

Left hand

A *sonata* is a composition for instruments, whether solo or accompanied. Although typically in three or four movements, Scarlatti's keyboard sonatas are usually in one movement, and each addresses a singular keyboard technique, including the playing of wide leaps, runs, or other musical figures. Each is also in two-part form, referred to as *binary form*.

SONATA

BINARY
FORM

Part 1	Part 2

0————————:51————————▶1:44

Indirect Beat

Not all music has an audible beat. The beat may be felt rather than heard. In this case, it is referred to as being *indirect*, which means the beat is internalized by both performer and listener.

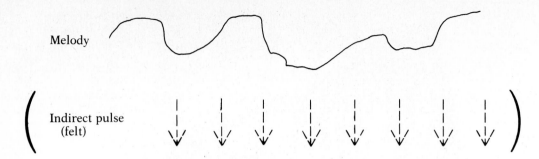

Melody

Indirect pulse
(felt)

Listen to the J. S. Bach *Gavotte en Rondeau* from Partita no. 3 in E major for violin (S.1006) *(listening selections)*. The pulse here is generally indirect.

PARTITA
RONDO

Gavotte en Rondeau is one movement of a *partita*, another name for a suite. The gavotte is in *rondo* form, a musical design in which the main melody, A, keeps returning after each of numerous contrasting sections. The form of the rondo by sections is AABACADAEA.

A	A	B ↓ ↓ ↓ (some feeling of beat)	A	C	A	D	A	E	A

Indirect (↓ ↓ ↓ ↓)
beat

0————:13——:26————:40——:54—1:20—1:34—2:00—2:15——2:47——▶3:03

Most compositions do not have a direct beat throughout, unless the purpose of the music is to accompany dancing or marching. Music, of course, does not have to have a beat, either direct or indirect, to have rhythm. The measuring of time may not be by the beat. Such music can still be said to have rhythm, however, since musical events exist and move within a time frame. Music without a beat may use actual time to cue events, or one sound may begin when a prior sound has died away.

MUSIC
WITHOUT
A BEAT

Selection no. 16

Listen to Pauline Oliveros's *Sound Patterns* (listening selections). There is no apparent beat, direct or indirect, in this composition. Sounds unfold unpredictably on first hearing. They begin, grow, and end, are sometimes long, sometimes short, detached or sustained, high or low, loud or soft; they seem not to be measured by a beat since it is virtually impossible to tap one's foot to this composition.

Pauline Oliveros, an American composer, wrote *Sound Patterns* in 1961. She explored the expressive potential of the human voice without using singing, with results often startling to listeners. Although there is no *apparent* beat, in reality, the conductor is guided by an inaudible pulse with which to cue the performers. That is, musical time is

Pauline Oliveros
(playing
piano-accordion).

Photo © Becky Cohen, 1981. Used by permission.

measured strictly with an indirect pulse. It is simply not obvious to the listener. A look at the music itself reveals the disciplined underlying organization of the rhythm.

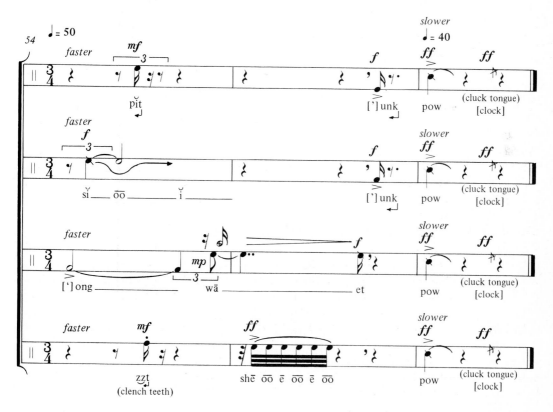

DEVIATIONS FROM THE BEAT

In music in which there is a discernible beat, rarely does the listener find that beat inflexible. Music moving strictly in time could become extremely dull, while deviations from the beat can provide heightened interest.

Rubato

Rubato is a term used to describe a "give and take" in the basic beat. This word is the Italian for "robbed" and it is fitting since the beat is "robbed" at one point, but "paid back" at another.

Although the specifics of rubato may be marked in the score, they are more generally left to the discretion of performers or conductor.

Selection no. 17   Listen to the Brahms *Ballade* in g minor, op. 118 *(listening selections)*.
BALLADE   A ballade is a musical piece that opposes two ideas, a dramatic (A) and lyric (B), like two characters in an English ballad. Rubato occurs to some degree in each of the three sections of this ballade. In the first and last sections, slight tempo surges are followed by an equally slight pulling back, but the most noticeable use of rubato occurs in the slow middle section.

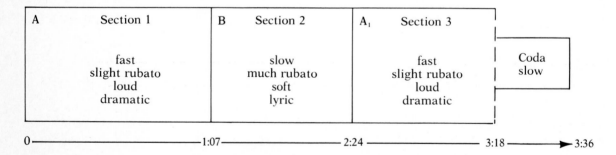

A Section 1	B Section 2	A₁ Section 3	
fast slight rubato loud dramatic	slow much rubato soft lyric	fast slight rubato loud dramatic	Coda slow

0 —————————————— 1:07 ———————— 2:24 ———————— 3:18 ———→ 3:36

Since rubato is a subtle deviation in the tempo and beat, it is most often observed in solo piano works such as this ballade, one of the last compositions Brahms wrote for solo piano in 1892–93. Brahms exploits the tonal possibilities of the piano in many of his works. The form here is
TERNARY   *ternary*, represented by letters ABA₁ since the final A is slightly varied.
CODA   This is followed by a brief musical extension or *coda* that alludes to the B section before concluding the work. The ternary form is typical of many ballades.

Accelerando

Another deviation from a steady beat is *accelerando*, which means a gradual increase in the tempo. Such a change from the normal beat

can generate tension and excitement in music, often signaling a climax or the end of the composition. Since it would be physically impossible for performers to continue playing faster and faster if the composition continues beyond the accelerando, it is necessary for the composer to indicate where it should end. A musical "brake" is applied when the composer writes *a tempo*, which means to return to the original tempo.

A TEMPO

Selection no. 18

Listen to Edvard Grieg's *In the Hall of the Mountain King (listening selections)*. *In the Hall of the Mountain King* is a movement from the *Peer Gynt Suite*, incidental music composed by Grieg in 1875 for Henrik Ibsen's epic drama. Peer Gynt is a Scandinavian hero, and the work describes his wanderings to exotic places. This movement depicts his encounter with a band of trolls, mountain gnomes, who menace him while they dance faster and faster. The accelerando is coupled with a gradual increase in loudness, a musical device called *crescendo*. A brief coda then terminates the short movement.

CRESCENDO

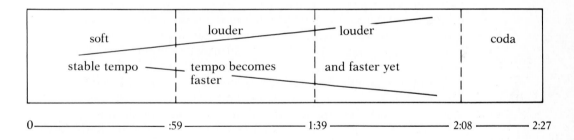

Ritardando

Ritardando, a third type of deviation from a steady beat, is used on its own and is sometimes used to conclude an accelerando. It is also called a *rallentando* or simply *ritard.* and generally appears at the end of an important idea or of the entire composition. The ritardando is a signal to the listener that an important musical idea or section has just been completed.

Edvard Grieg (1843–1907), the son of a British consul, was born in the Norwegian city of Bergen. Receiving his first instruction in music from his mother, by the age of twenty-five Grieg established himself as a major composer of his time through the pronounced nationalism of his music. Basing his compositions on Nordic stories and tunes, he recreated the melodic and rhythmic flavor of his

Edvard Grieg.
Reproduction of a photo from life by Elliot and Fry of London. Courtesy of the New York Public Library.

country's folk songs. Grieg composed the incidental music for *Peer Gynt* in 1875, and arranged from this music two *Peer Gynt* suites that later became extremely popular. In addition to these, the Concerto in A Minor for Piano and Orchestra is one of his most frequently performed concert pieces. Grieg's use of ornaments, scales, and rhythm gives his music a uniquely Norwegian quality.

Selection no. 19
ART SONG
LIEDER

Listen to Franz Schubert's *Gretchen am Spinnrade* (Gretchen at the Spinning Wheel) *(listening selections)*. *Gretchen am Spinnrade* is an *art song*, a short piece for solo voice and piano. Art songs in German are known as *lieder* (singular, *lied*); they are written in other languages as well, notably French, Spanish, Italian, and English. The art song form was particularly popular during the Romantic era (nineteenth century). Texts of art songs are generally taken from the existing works of great poets, in this case Goethe's *Faust*. Since the musical setting is intended as much as possible to echo the natural inflections of the speaking voice, lieder are seldom sung in translations from the original language.

In this example, Faust, the ill-famed doctor, has seduced Gretchen, leaving her to despair as she spins and sings. The voice tells the story while the piano sets the mood and accompanies the drama. The piano provides the illusion of a spinning wheel, speeding up and slowing down as the maiden Gretchen narrates her tale. The musical flow is frequently interrupted by ritardandos. Some are slight, as at the end

QUATRAIN

of each *quatrain* (four lines). As the story develops, there is an accelerando followed by an extensive ritardando on the words "Und ach, sein Kuss!" There is another accelerando near the end of the composition as well as a final ritardando. The accelerandos provide drama and excitement as the tension increases, while the ritardandos heighten the feeling of desperation and at the same time offer punctuation.

> *Meine Ruh ist hin,*　　My peace is gone,
> *Mein Herz ist schwer,*　　my heart is heavy;
> *Ich finde sie nimmer*　　never, never again
> *Und nimmermehr.*　　will I find rest.

slight
ritard.

Wo ich ihn nicht hab,
Ist mir das Grab,
Die ganze Welt
Ist mir vergällt.

Where I am not with him
I am in my grave,
the whole world
turns to bitter gall.

Mein armer Kopf
Ist mir verrückt,
Mein armer Sinn
Ist mir zerstückt.

My poor head
is in a whirl,
my poor thoughts
are all distracted.

slight
ritard.

Meine Ruh ist hin,
Mein Herz ist schwer,
Ich finde sie nimmer
Und nimmermehr.

My peace is gone,
my heart is heavy,
never, never again
will I find rest.

slight
ritard.

Nach ihm nur schau ich
Zum Fenster hinaus,
Nach ihm nur geh' ich
Aus dem Haus.

I seek only him when I look
out of the window,
I seek only him when I leave
the house.

Sein hoher Gang,
Sein' edle Gestalt,
Seines Mundes Lächeln,
Seiner Augen Gewalt,

His noble walk,
His fine stature,
the smile of his lips,
the power of his eyes,

Und seiner Rede
Zauberfluss,
Sein Händedruck,
Und ach, sein Kuss!

and the magic flow
of his speech,
the pressure of his hand,
and oh, his kiss!

full
ritard.

Meine Ruh ist hin,
Mein Herz ist schwer,
Ich finde sie nimmer
Und nimmermehr.

My peace is gone,
my heart is heavy;
never, never again
will I find rest.

slight
acceler-
ando

Mein Busen drängt
Sich nach ihm hin;
Ach dürft' ich fassen
Und halten ihn,

My bosom yearns
towards him.
If only I could seize him
and hold him

Und küssen ihn,
So wie ich wollt',
An seinen Küssen
Vergehen sollt!

and kiss him
to my heart's content—
under his kisses
I should die!

ritard.

Meine Ruh ist hin,
Mein Herz ist schwer . . .

My peace is gone,
My heart is heavy. . . .

full
ritard.

Franz Schubert, after a copy of a watercolor by A.W. Rider.

Photograph by Hans Makart. Courtesy of the New York Public Library.

Franz Schubert (1797–1828) is credited with writing more than 600 lieder.

Schubert was one of thirteen children born to a schoolmaster in a Austrian village near Vienna. As a child he played the violin and studied music with the famous court composer, Salieri. He began to compose when very young, writing symphonies, Masses, string quartets, and some of his most famous lieder, including *Gretchen am Spinnrade*, between 1813–1816. He became a teacher in his father's school, but soon left to devote his life to music, composing nine symphonies, twenty-two piano sonatas, six Masses and numerous chamber works before he died at the age of thirty-one. Schubert had a gift for writing beautiful melodies that, linked with poetry, typified the musical expressiveness of the German Romantic era. In 1815 alone, Schubert wrote 144 lieder, basing many on texts from poems by German poets of the period: Goethe, Müller, Heine, and Mörike. It is generally agreed that through his lieder he provided inspiration to other nineteenth-century composers.

ACCENTED BEATS (METER)

The beats in a musical composition are rarely of equal stress. Some seem stronger than others, thus establishing a metric pattern of accented beats. Typical arrangements are:

Strong weak — duple

Strong weak weak — triple

Strong weak weak weak — quadruple

DUPLE TIME
TRIPLE TIME

QUADRUPLE TIME

Selection no. 20
RAGTIME

In the first example, the beats are grouped into two's, an arrangement known as *duple time* (duple meter), since every other beat is stressed. When every third pulse is accented, the pulses are in three's, *triple time* (meter). If every fourth pulse is stressed, the pulses are in four's, which is *quadruple time* (meter). Whereas a waltz is usually in triple time, a march is duple or quadruple.

Listen to Scott Joplin's *Euphonic Sounds (listening selections)*. This is an example of *ragtime* and it is in duple meter. *Rags*, an early type of jazz for solo piano, were popular in America between 1890 and 1910.

The characteristic sound is of a pianist beating out duple time with the left hand while a syncopated melody occurs in the right.

Syncopation refers to a rhythm that occurs off the normal metric pattern, a quality noticeable in *Euphonic Sounds*. The overall form is:

SYNCOPATION

Introduction	A	A	B	B	A	C	C	A
				grows loud			softens	

0 ——————— :07 —— :36 ——— 1:02 ——— 1:32 — 1:56 ——— 2:24 —— 2:50 ——— 3:18 ➡ 3:56

The recurrence of A gives a rondolike feeling to this composition. The A section is simple and straightforward, the B section dramatic, and the C section provides a quiet contrast before the final return of A. *Euphonic Sounds*, a late work (1909) within the span of ragtime's popularity, is considered a somewhat complex piece.

Listen to the Allegretto grazioso from Dvořák's Symphony no. 8 in G major (third movement) *(listening selections)*, which premiered in 1890. There is a dancelike quality in this movement. Except for the coda in duple meter, the movement is in triple meter throughout. There are frequent ritardandos, particularly at the end of the three large sections. This movement is the third in Dvořák's symphony, and

Selection no. 21

Scott Joplin.
Courtesy of the New York Public Library.

Scott Joplin (1868–1917) popularized ragtime in this country. Born in Texarkana, Texas, he began formal piano lessons at age eleven, and at seventeen left home to earn his living playing piano in St. Louis. He became an itinerant pianist, allowed only to play in speakeasies and brothels because he was black. He undoubtedly became a master at improvising rags. As an adult, he studied at George Smith College in Sedalia, Missouri, and learned to notate his compositions. The *Maple Leaf Rag* was one of Joplin's early compositions and is the most famous of all piano rags. Named after a local dance hall, the Maple Leaf Club, the piano rag sold so well Joplin was able to devote himself exclusively to composition. He continued to write piano rags, operas, waltzes, and marches, but in his last years lamented failing to achieve the recognition he felt his music merited. He became insane and died broken and bankrupt, obsessed with becoming known and respected as a serious composer.

it is common for the third movements of eighteenth- and nineteenth-century symphonies to be in triple time.

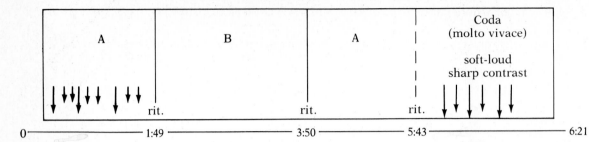

A	B	A	Coda (molto vivace) soft-loud sharp contrast

0————————1:49————————3:50————————5:43————————6:21

Selection no. 22   Listen to John Philip Sousa's *Hands Across the Sea (listening selections)*, written in 1899. Marches are almost always in quadruple time, which can be Strong–weak–weak–weak or Strong–weak–strong–weak. Since the secondary strong beat is not quite as heavy as the first strong, it is difficult to tell the difference between quadruple and duple time. The distinction is not important for listeners, since it is almost impossible to differentiate a secondary accent on the "3" of a quadruple grouping from a downbeat of "1" in duple, and it is typical for a conductor to beat the time in two.

The form of this march is as follows:

Introduction	A	A	B	B	C C Trio (soft)	D	C	D	C

0————:04——:20——:35——:52——1:08—1:24——1:40—1:56—2:12—2:30—2:51

Anton Dvořák (1841–1904) is the most celebrated of Czech national composers. His music exhibits a folklike quality, but the melodies are usually his own invention, not derived from folk songs. Dvořák's music, characterized by spontaneous melodies, intense harmonies, and rhythmic variety, became popular in Germany, England, and the United States. He was invited to serve as head of the National Conservatory of Music in New York for three years, and during his stay in America wrote the famous symphony *From the New World* no. 9 in E minor. The symphony features melodies reminiscent of those found in black spirituals and Indian chants.

Anton Dvořák.
Courtesy of the New York Public Library.

John Philip Sousa.
Photo by Apeda. Courtesy of the New York Public Library.

John Philip Sousa (1854–1932) was born in Washington, D.C. Instead of studying music in Europe, as was common at this time, he received his training in America, studying violin and several wind instruments. At age thirteen, Sousa enlisted in the Marine Corps and earned a chair in the Marine band. Before forming his own band in 1892, Sousa conducted the U.S. Marine Band and com-posed his most famous marches, including *Semper Fidelis, Thunderer,* and *The Stars and Stripes Forever.* He also composed musical comedies, light opera, and 136 *concert marches,* many with a form similar to *Hands Across the Sea.* Although he did not invent the military concert march, his band made it popular and with a world tour introduced it to other countries.

The time patterns conductors use with musical groups normally reflect the meter played by performers. The basic conducting patterns are: **CONDUCTING PATTERNS**

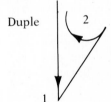

Duple

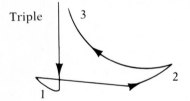

Triple

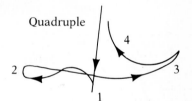

Quadruple

The strong downbeat is the *one* of each group and the last beat of each group is generally up.

Not all music moves in duple, triple, or quadruple time. The music of India is often grouped into sevens and eights (among an infinite number of possibilities), with subdivisions occurring within the pattern. A seven might be divided as: **MUSIC OF INDIA**

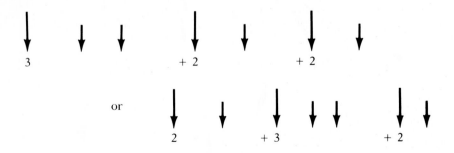

An eight might be divided as:

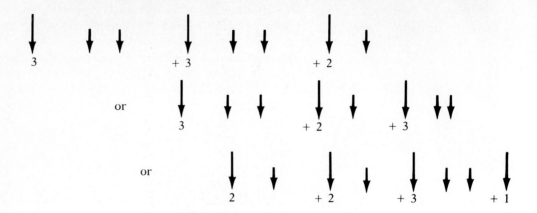

or

or

These are called *asymmetric meters.*

Selection no. 23   Listen to *Rága Simhendra-Madhyamam (listening selections).* The music of India springs from a cultural base that is among the world's oldest dating back as far as 2000 years in a similar form. Contemporary compositions reflect the same principles observed in some of the earliest reported performances, following an unbroken oral tradition. This piece is based on two principles: a melody (*raga*) and a rhythm (*tala*). Indian compositions are not notated; rather, musicians choose an appropriate raga and tala upon which to improvise. The choice is made from the traditional musical system developed over centuries. This composition is binary, since there are basically two sections.

RAGA

TALA

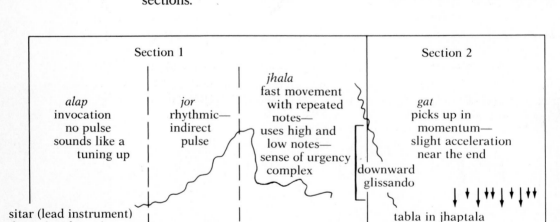

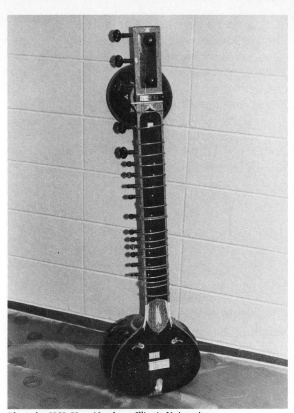

Sitar.

Photo by K.H. Han. Northern Illinois University.

In section one, the main instrument is a *sitar*, a string instrument, which introduces and explores the raga, accompanied by the *tamboura*. This simpler instrument with four strings provides the *drone* or repeated sound. The raga is gradually developed in the *alap*, an introductory sub-section. An indirect beat is introduced in the *jor* and the music becomes increasingly involved in the *jhala*, the third sub-section. A downward sweep of pitches, a *glissando*, ends section one, and section two, the *gat*, then begins. Two hand drums, collectively called *tabla*, play a rhythmic cycle with a set pattern of accents. An Indian time cycle is called a *tala* and this one has 10 beats,

SITAR
TAMBOURA
DRONE

GLISSANDO

TABLA

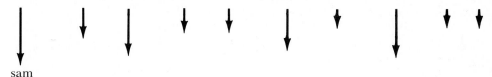

sam

subdivided into 2 + 3 + 2 + 3. The sitar and tabla then improvise within the established foundation of raga while the tamboura provides a drone accompaniment.

An Indian composition has no set length. Rather, duration is up to the performers, and proficient musicians may develop the two basic sections of the compositions as long as they wish. The gat provides increasing excitement but also tests the musicians' ability to maintain musical control within the structural bounds of raga and tala. Each performance, like jazz improvisation, varies.

Selection no. 24

Listen to "Unsquare Dance" by the Dave Brubeck Quartet *(listening selections)*. Brubeck's piece is constructed on an underlying seven beats, played by bass and hand claps. The subdivision is 2 + 2 + 3, which is thus asymmetric.

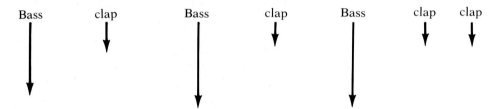

This pattern is repeated six times to equal one *chorus*, with eleven resulting choruses in the entire work.

Rhythm	Piano	Rhythm	Piano	Piano
1 chorus	2 choruses	6 choruses	1 chorus	1 chorus

0———————:11——————————:33————————1:38————————1:50————————▶2:01

Although the piano provides variety in choruses two and three as well as the final two, most of the composition is rhythmic only.

In the twentieth century, composers of art music began to explore new or previously unexplored rhythmic organizations. One such phenomenon is called *mixed* or *changing* meters.

MIXED
METER

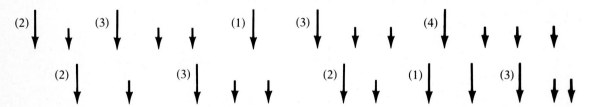

In both asymmetrical and mixed accented beats, regularity occurs over a longer time cycle than with simple duple, triple, or quadruple time. It takes more beats to complete the typical rhythmic pattern. In addition, composers can superimpose two or more groupings simultaneously,

Jazz of the 1950s and 1960s was no longer just for dancing. It had become an art form, influenced by the structures, timbres, and rhythms of contemporary art music studied by jazz musicians in conservatories and universities. The musicians adapted to jazz the twentieth-century meters and accent groupings heard in the music of Stravinsky and other modern composers. The new styles of jazz—including Bop, Cool, and Progressive—evolved from the frenzied dance orientation of the 1930s' Swing Era and moved to a sophisticated concert style. Rock 'n' roll and country/western sounds replaced jazz as the preferred forms of popular music.

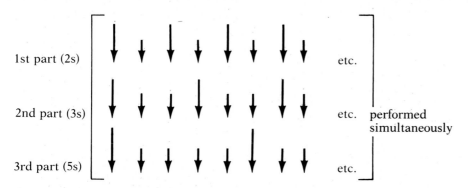

1st part (2s)   etc.

2nd part (3s)   etc.   performed simultaneously

3rd part (5s)   etc.

a phenomenon called *polyrhythms*.

POLYRHYTHM

Listen to Charles Ives's *Putnam's Camp* from *Three Places in New England (listening selections).* This composition uses polyrhythms, leading some listeners to observe that it sounds like two signals competing for the same frequency on a radio dial. Since this is program

Selection no. 25

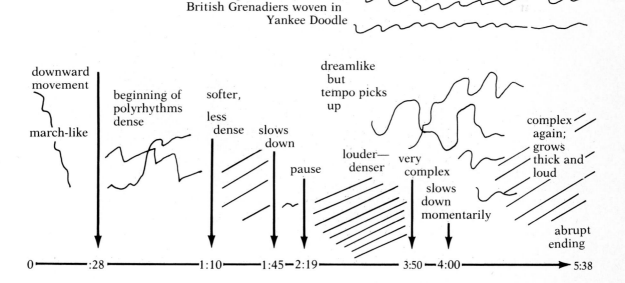

Folk Songs
British Grenadiers woven in
Yankee Doodle

downward movement

march-like

beginning of polyrhythms dense

softer, less dense

slows down

pause

dreamlike but tempo picks up

louder—denser

very complex

slows down momentarily

complex again; grows thick and loud

abrupt ending

0 ———:28 ——————— 1:10—— 1:45—2:19 ————————— 3:50 — 4:00 ———————➤ 5:38

music, as well as being the second movement of a symphonic work, knowledge of the story is a prerequisite to understanding the music.

A child has gone to a Fourth of July picnic celebration near Redding, Connecticut, the location of a Revolutionary Memorial for General Israel Putnam's soldiers who quartered here in the winter of 1778–79. The child wanders to the old campsite, and his imagination is stirred by the fireplaces of stone that have remained from Colonial times. He falls asleep and in a dream sees the Goddess of Liberty, pleading with the Revolutionary soldiers to keep the war effort going. They ignore her, marching out of the camp to music of fife and drum. Suddenly General Putnam returns, accompanied by another band. The soldiers joyously return and are rallied to the war cause; the Revolutionary spirit is saved. But the little boy awakens, discovers it was all a dream, and runs back to his family.

Three faces of Liberty. *Sisters,* Edwin Howland Blashfield, American, 1917, oil on canvas.

University of Arizona Museum of Art, anonymous donor.

Charles Ives (1874–1954) is a singular figure in American music. The Yankee son of a Civil War bandmaster who promoted musical experimentation, Ives gained exposure to unconventional musical sounds at an early age. He became a church organist at age thirteen and later studied music at Yale University, but did not become a professional musician in his adult life; instead he managed an insurance company and devoted his leisure time to musical composition. Incorporating complex rhythms and tonal patterns, his music

Charles Ives.
Photo by Frank Gerratana, Bridgeport *Herald.* Courtesy of the New York Public Library.

was so out of the mainstream and ahead of its time that Ives found it virtually im-

possible to get his compositions published or performed unless he did so at his own expense. Among his innovations, Ives wove folk songs and hymn tunes into the complex design of his music, supporting the simple melodies with brooding and dissonant countermelodies. The greatness of his music was realized slowly, and only after his health had deteriorated and he stopped composing. The belated recognition of his work was evidenced in 1947 when Ives received the Pulitzer Prize for his Third Symphony, composed in 1911.

PREDOMINANT PATTERNS

Tempo, beat, deviations, and accented beats all refer to the temporal organization of music at a basic level; the attentive listener usually perceives these elements as *background*. It is the rhythm of patterns occurring over this foundation that stands out as *foreground* for the listener, perceived and measured against the background of the beat and meter.

BACKGROUND
FOREGROUND

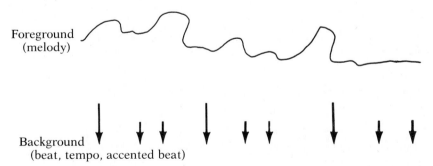

Foreground
(melody)

Background
(beat, tempo, accented beat)

Within the foreground, patterns move with or against the pulse in varying ways. Some rhythm patterns move exactly with the pulse, that is, they are divided over it.

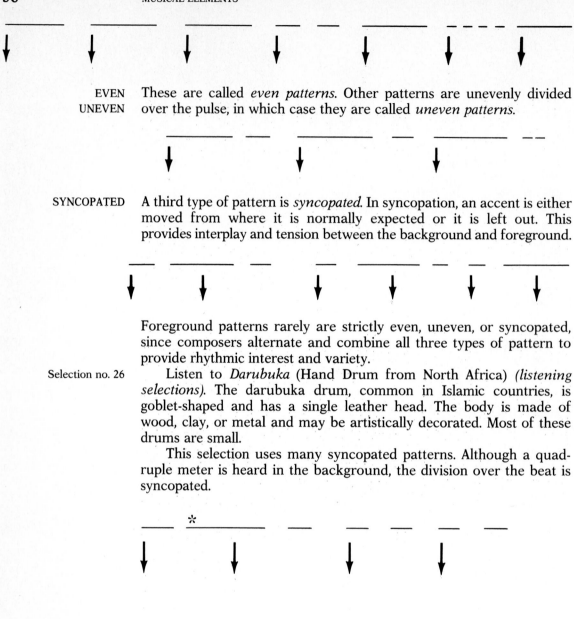

Selection no. 26

EVEN
UNEVEN
These are called *even patterns*. Other patterns are unevenly divided over the pulse, in which case they are called *uneven patterns*.

SYNCOPATED
A third type of pattern is *syncopated*. In syncopation, an accent is either moved from where it is normally expected or it is left out. This provides interplay and tension between the background and foreground.

Foreground patterns rarely are strictly even, uneven, or syncopated, since composers alternate and combine all three types of pattern to provide rhythmic interest and variety.

Listen to *Darubuka* (Hand Drum from North Africa) *(listening selections)*. The darubuka drum, common in Islamic countries, is goblet-shaped and has a single leather head. The body is made of wood, clay, or metal and may be artistically decorated. Most of these drums are small.

This selection uses many syncopated patterns. Although a quadruple meter is heard in the background, the division over the beat is syncopated.

The longest duration (marked by *) occurs *after* the expected strong first downbeat, giving a feeling of excitement and movement to this selection.

NOTATION OF RHYTHM

Note Values

In music with a regular pulse, a given note is typically designated as the *beat*. The note chosen as this basic duration is generally the *half note* ♩, the *quarter note* ♩, or the *eighth note* ♪. If an eighth note is chosen, the performers are mentally tapping or counting to the constant flow of eighth notes.

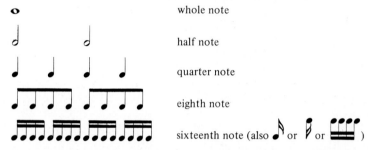

All durations are proportional to the basic beat.

𝅝	whole note
𝅗𝅥 𝅗𝅥	half note
♩ ♩ ♩ ♩	quarter note
♫♫ ♫♫	eighth note
♬♬♬♬	sixteenth note (also ♬ or ♬ or 𝅘𝅥𝅲𝅘𝅥𝅲𝅘𝅥𝅲𝅘𝅥𝅲)

Thus if a quarter note is designated as the basic beat, all patterns are measured by a beat of quarter notes. A whole note would then equal four beats, a half note, two, an eighth note only half of a beat. Conversely, if the eighth note is taken as one beat, a quarter note equals two beats, a half note, four, and a whole note, eight. In a given composition or movement, the note chosen for the basic beat generally remains the same.

If	♩	=	1 beat,		If	♪	=	1 beat,
Then	♪	=	½ beat		Then	♩	=	2 beats
	𝅗𝅥	=	2 beats			𝅗𝅥	=	4 beats
	𝅝	=	4 beats			𝅝	=	8 beats

In measuring patterns above the beat, a *dot* can be added to any note to lengthen that note's duration by one-half.   DOT

$$𝅝. = 𝅝 + 𝅗𝅥$$
$$𝅗𝅥. = 𝅗𝅥 + ♩$$
$$♩. = ♩ + ♪$$

Electric (left) and mechanical (right) metronomes. The higher the weight on the mechanical metronome's pendulum, the slower the tempo sounded.

Metronome marks are used by composers to designate tempo. The metronome is a mechanical or electronic device that sounds a set number of beats or pulses per minute, and can be adjusted to indicate various musical speeds. Although it was invented by Dietrich Nikolaus Winkel of Amsterdam c. 1812, its name comes from Johannes Maelzel, the person who marketed and received credit for Winkel's invention. Beethoven was one of the first composers to use the new invention to notate tempos in his compositions.

Maelzel's Metronome (M.M.) ♪ = 120 indicates there will be 120 pulsations of ♪ in one minute. M.M. ♩ = 100 means there will be 100 pulsations of ♩ in one minute, and M.M. ♩ = 90 means there will be 90 pulsations of ♩ in one minute. The tempo may also be indicated by traditional tempo markings such as Allegro, Moderato, or Adagio.

TIE   Similarly, *ties* are used to add the note value of a following note to the original.

$$\text{♩ ⌣ ♩ = ♩.}$$

$$\text{♩. ⌣ ♩ = 𝅝}$$

$$\text{♩ ⌣ ♩ = ♩}$$

REST   When a composer wants silence in the foreground, *rests* are used, each of which corresponds to a basic note value.

- ▬   whole rest   (𝅝)
- ▬·   dotted half rest (♩.)
- ▬   half rest   (♩)
- 𝄽   quarter rest   (♩)
- 𝄾   eighth rest   (♪)
- 𝄿   sixteenth rest   (♬)

Complete units in the metric pattern of accented beats are divided in music by a *bar line*| . Bar lines mark off *measures*.

BAR LINE
MEASURE

Meter Signatures

Accented beats are indicated in music by *meter signatures*, such as $\frac{3}{4}$ or $\frac{4}{4}$.

$\frac{3}{4}$ = ♩ ♩ ♩   or equivalent per measure

$\frac{4}{4}$ = ♩ ♩ ♩ ♩   or equivalent per measure

The top number in a meter signature generally represents the number of beats per measure (duple = 2, triple = 3, quadruple = 4), while the bottom number is the note that is counted as the pulse (2 = ♩, 4 = ♩, 8 = ♪).

$\frac{4}{2}$ = ♩ ♩ ♩ ♩ $\frac{3}{8}$ = ♫♫♫

Meters are termed *simple* when the top number shows the actual accented beat, such as 2, 3, or 4. All of these are simple meters.

SIMPLE
METER

2	2	2	3	3	3	4	4	4
2	4	8	2	4	8	2	4	8

In simple meters, the beat is normally divided into two equal parts, or by multiples of 2 (4, 8, etc.). If composers want to divide the beat into three equal parts, instead of this two-to-one proportion, they use a *compound* meter. The activity over the beat is thus normally 3 to 1. Compound meters with a top number of 6 have a duple feeling:

COMPOUND
METER

$\frac{6}{8}$ = ♫♫♫ ♫♫♫
            1   2

those with 9, triple:

$\frac{9}{4}$ = ♩ ♩ ♩ ♩ ♩ ♩ ♩ ♩ ♩
        1   2   3

and with 12, quadruple:

$\frac{12}{8}$ = ♫♫♫ ♫♫♫ ♫♫♫ ♫♫♫
        1   2   3   4

The true metric feeling of a compound meter can always be found by dividing the top number by 3 (6÷3=2, 9÷3=3, 12÷3=4). A listener can usually tell whether the music is written in a simple or compound meter by observing whether the beat is divided into twos (simple) or threes (compound).

ASYMMETRICAL METER

Asymmetrical groupings are notated with a meter signature that reflects the subdivision:

MIXED METERS

Mixed meters have a new signature in each measure in which there is a change:

MUSIC WITHOUT A BEAT

In music in which there is no beat, it is difficult to generalize how rhythm may be notated. Some electronic music does not require notation, since sounds are composed directly onto magnetic tape. In other cases, time is measured against the clock, that is, by actual time. A composer may indicate, for example, that every inch on the musical score represents five seconds of sound, or that every measure equals ten seconds. When live music is performed in conjunction with a prerecorded tape, the tape becomes the foundation of time. Events are cued and measured by what is occurring on the tape.

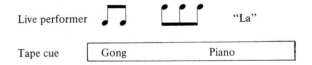

In some compositions a conductor may simply signal to performers **SOUND** when to begin and to end a sound; in other cases, *sound decay* may be the **DECAY** basis of duration, one sound beginning when another has completely died away.

Many very recent compositions combine traditional rhythmic notation with one or more of these newer techniques, and it is not unusual for performers of such pieces to have to learn a new system of notation.

SUMMARY

Music, by definition, moves in time. Consequently, all music has rhythm. Time is perceived somewhat differently by each listener, a phenomenon known as psychic time.

The perception of time in music depends upon many factors: tempo, the speed of the music; the presence or absence of a beat, whether direct or indirect; deviations from a steady pulse, such as rubato, accelerando, or ritardando; accented beats, whether duple, triple, or quadruple, or asymmetrical or mixed; and rhythm patterns, including even, uneven, and syncopated, that occur over and against the pulse.

Rhythmic notation is usually represented with a pulse assigned to a half, quarter, or eighth note. Dots add one-half of a given note's value to it, whereas ties create longer sounds by adding each note's value within the tie to the original note. Meter signatures, whether for simple or compound meters, are written instructions reflecting the accented beats. Non-traditional music may use a similar type of rhythmic notation or depend upon actual time, electronic cuing, or sound decay to sequence sounds.

STUDY GUIDELINES

**Guide to Perceiving Rhythm
(Rhythm—Time Elements)**

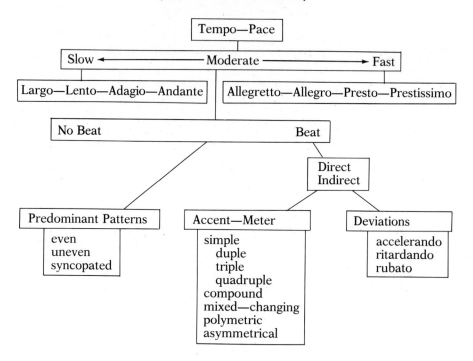

KEY TERMS AND CONCEPTS

Accented beat
  Asymmetrical
  Duple
  Mixed (changing)
  Quadruple
  Triple
Actual time
Background
Bar line |
Beat (pulse)
Coda
Crescendo
Da capo (D.C.) al Fine

Deviations
  Accelerando
  A tempo
  Ritardando (rallentando)
  Rubato
Direct pulse (beat)
Dot (•)
Foreground
Harpsichord
Indirect pulse (beat)
Italian tempo terms
  Adagio
  Andante

Allegretto
Allegro
Largo
Lento
Moderato
Prestissimo
Presto
Lied (lieder)
Measure
Meter signatures
  Compound
  Simple
Note value
  Eighth note ♪ rest ♩
  Half note ♩ rest ▬
  Quarter note ♩ rest ⅊
  Sixteenth note ♪ rest ⅋
  Whole note ○ rest ▬
Polyrhythm

Psychic Time
Pulse (beat)
Qualifying Terms
  Assai
  Meno
  Non troppo
  Più
  Poco a poco
Rhythm
Rhythm pattern
  Even
  Syncopated
  Uneven
Sound Decay
Suite
Tala
Tempo
Tie

EXERCISES

1. Listen to several short musical selections and outline the following
   components briefly for each in the accompanying chart. (See page
   62 for help.)

Selection	Tempo (fast, medium slow, changing, etc.)	Beat or no beat	If beat, direct or indirect	Deviations from beat
Number 1 (Name, composer, group, etc.)				
Number 2				
Number 3				

2. Listen to several short musical selections and outline the following components briefly for each in the accompanying charts. (See page 62 for help.)

Selection	Beat or no beat	If beat, direct or indirect	Accented beats (2,3,4, asymmetrical, mixed)
1.			
2.			
3.			

3. Listen to several short musical selections and outline the following components for each in the accompanying chart. (See page 62 for help.)

Selection	Accented beat (meter)	Predominant patterns
1.		
2.		
3.		

4. At a play, film, or ballet, graph the pace or tempo from beginning to end using the chart on page 65 as a model.

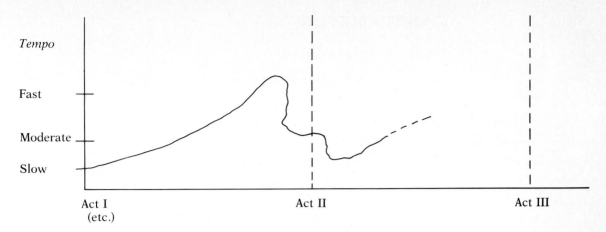

How was the pace changed? Why? What effect did it have on the overall feeling of the work?

5. In an hour of listening to a classical music radio station, jot down all expressions the announcers use to refer to tempo.

6. In a musical review in a local newspaper, jot down all terms used by the reviewer to refer to rhythm. (See page 62 for help.)

7. Sit in on a rehearsal of a musical group in your school or community. Jot down all the terms used by the conductor that refer to rhythm.

8. Listen to a selection from each of the following:
    Easy Listening station
    Muzak
    Rock
    Jazz
    Folk
    Symphonic
   What generalizations, if any, can you make for each musical category regarding:
    Beat/no-beat
    Direct or indirect pulse
    Deviations from the beat/tempo
    Tempo
    Accent groupings
    Patterns

9. What type of music has a fast psychic time for you? A slow psychic time? Listen to an example of both and discuss in a few short paragraphs what is happening with the rhythm to create those feelings for you.

10. What is happening with rhythm in a composition you consider
    happy?   sombre?
    sad?   majestic?

CHAPTER REVIEW

Tempos, Notes, and Meters

Match items in the two columns. Answers in Appendix.

1. ____ tempo	A.	fast but not too fast
2. ____ largo	B.	quarter note
3. ____ presto	C.	very slow
4. ____ moderato	D.	gradually speeding up
5. ____ allegro non troppo	E.	quadruple time
6. ____ rubato	F.	moderate tempo
7. ____ accelerando	G.	duple time
8. ____ ritardando	H.	off-beat
9. ____ a tempo	I.	half note
10. ____ syncopated	J.	sixteenth note
11. ____ andante	K.	"robbed" time
12. ____ 𝅝	L.	whole note
13. ____ 𝅗𝅥	M.	return to original tempo
14. ____ 𝅘𝅥 𝅘𝅥𝅮	N.	triple time
15. ____ 𝅘𝅥𝅯	O.	the speed
16. ____ 𝅘𝅥𝅮	P.	tie
17. ____ ⌣	Q.	very fast
18. ____ $\frac{3}{4}$	R.	eighth note
19. ____ $\frac{2}{4}$	S.	gradually slowing down
20. ____ $\frac{4}{4}$	T.	slow walking tempo

Terms and Concepts

Match items in the two columns. Answers in Appendix.

1. ____ lieder	A.	felt but not heard
2. ____ crescendo	B.	piano jazz of 1890–1910
3. ____ indirect bent	C.	ternary form
4. ____ suite	D.	partita
5. ____ ABA	E.	grow louder
6. ____ harpsichord	F.	jazz for dancing
7. ____ overture	G.	return to "the head" of the music
8. ____ swing	H.	tells story with voice and piano
9. ____ rag	I.	two-part form
10. ____ da capo	J.	curtain raiser
11. ____ binary	K.	keyboard instrument that plucks strings

Note Values and Meters

Complete each of the following rhythms with *one* note value or rest:

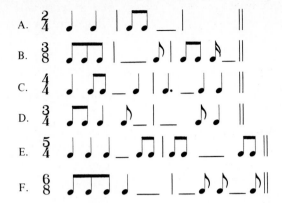

Supply the missing meter signature for each of the following:

FOR FURTHER LISTENING

Direct Beat
  Bach   *Brandenburg Concerto* no. 5 in D major

Indirect Beat
  Debussy   *Prélude à l'Après-midi d'un Faune*

Accelerando and Ritardando
  Chopin   Waltz in c♯ minor, op. 64, no. 2

  Honegger   *Pacific 231*
  Tchaikovsky   "Waltz of the Flowers" (final section) from *The Nutcracker* Suite

Duple and Quadruple Meter
  Albeniz   Tango in D major
  Prokofiev   March from *The Love of
                                             Three Oranges*

Triple Meter
  Chopin   Mazurka in A♭ major, op. 59,
                                             no. 2
                                             Waltz in D♭ major, op. 64,
                                             no. 1
  Tchaikovsky   "Arabian Dance," "Waltz of
                                             the Flowers" (*Nutcracker*
                                             Suite)

Asymmetrical and Changing Meter
  Copland   *Music for the Theater*
                                             (second movement)
  Golden Rain   Nonesuch Records H-72028
  (Balinese Music)
  Music of India—Morning and   Angel Records #35283
  Evening Ragas
  (Talas = 16 and 7)
  Stravinsky   *L'Histoire du Soldat*
  Tchaikovsky   Symphony no. 6 in b minor
                                             (second movement)
  Three Ragas   Capitol Records DT-2720
  (Talas = 7, 10)

Even Pattern
  Bach   Prelude in C major (*The Well-
                                             Tempered Clavier*, Vol. I)
  Ravel   *Bolero*

Syncopated Pattern
  Debussy   "Golliwog's Cakewalk" (from
                                             Children's Corner Suite)
  Gershwin   Preludes
  Haydn   Quartet in D major, op. 20,
                                             no. 4 (third movement)

CHAPTER THREE

DYNAMICS

❖

Dynamics refers to the overall loudness and softness of music as well as the change between one level of intensity and another. This is one of the most expressive elements of sound, since diverse changes between loud and soft in music can provide interest and variation. Changes in dynamics and the listener's perception of these depend on several factors, including the energy with which an instrument is played, the number of instruments heard, and the distance between performers and listener.

ENERGY

Dynamics in a solo instrument are usually changed by the pressure or force with which the performer plays. In wind instruments, for example, the performer increases the velocity of air to make a louder sound; the faster the air stream, the louder the sound. With percussion instruments, a hard blow results in a louder sound. In string instruments such as the violin, the pressure of the bow as well as its velocity affect the dynamics. Variations of loudness in electronic instruments are caused by changes in the electrical energy or voltage, in much the same way that we alter the volume when listening to a stereo broadcast or recording. This is why an electronic organ or synthesizer can sound louder or softer. Most modern musical instruments are sensitive to touch, pressure, and energy, and are therefore able to play a wide range of dynamic levels. *PRESSURE OR FORCE*

Listen to Claude Debussy's *Clair de Lune (listening selections).* Clair de lune means "moonlight" and this piano composition creates *Selection no. 27*

Piano by Johann Adolf Dulcken, Munich, 1795 (left); model of Viennese (German) piano action (below).

Smithsonian Institution Photos #56409 and #74283.

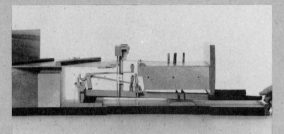

The piano was invented in 1709 by Bartolomeo Cristofori, a harpsichord maker of Florence. Early inventors attempted to manufacture a harpsichord that could play both loudly and softly, but used a mechanism that plucked the strings. Cristofori's instrument was the first to strike the strings with a hammer, allowing the pressure applied to the keys to control the dynamics. Because his instrument could play either softly (piano) or loudly (forte), it was called the pianoforte.

During the nineteenth century, many improvements were made in the instrument, including double-escapement (repetition action), double and triple stringing (two or three strings per key), a cast-iron frame to support greater string tension, and cross stringing (an arrangement of strings so the upper ones fan across the entire soundboard while the bass strings stretch over them). Pianos are now made in either a wing shape, ranging in size from the five-foot baby grand to the nine-foot concert grand, or a more compact upright model. Although the earliest pianos had only four or five octaves, the present-day piano typically has eighty-eight keys, just over seven octaves.

an impression of a nocturnal setting. The piano, which is sensitive to touch, conveys the feeling of moonlight partly because of the subtle changes between loud and soft. The only way for a piano to sound louder or softer, of course, is through the player's touch.

NUMBER OF INSTRUMENTS

GEOMETRIC INCREASE

Two violins will obviously sound louder than one. However, since intensity increases geometrically, two similar instruments playing in tandem do not double the sound of one. It would take almost ten violins to double the intensity of one. Nonetheless, the size of the musical group naturally determines the overall level of dynamics an attentive listener can expect. A symphony orchestra is going to sound louder than a string quartet. In practice, both the energy of the individual performer and the total number of players affect change of dynamics.

Listen to Handel's "For Unto Us a Child is Born" *(listening selections)*, a chorus that demonstrates both of these principles. The orchestra opens the work with a brisk tempo in $\frac{4}{4}$ time. Sopranos enter, followed by tenors, and the dynamics gradually become louder. Altos and basses enter, all voices interweave and then become very loud on the words:

Selection no. 28

> "Wonderful, Counselor, the Mighty God, the
> Everlasting Father, the Prince of Peace."

The entire chorus is an alternation between interweaving vocal sections at a medium dynamic level and massed voices at a loud level. These changes provide dramatic contrast. The orchestra accompanies throughout with a steady, direct pulse. With the exception of a few ritardandos, the tempo never deviates.

"For Unto Us a Child is Born" is from *Messiah* (1742), an *oratorio* by George Frideric Handel. Although an oratorio is similar in construction to an opera, it is unstaged and uncostumed. Singers do not act out their parts but perform "in concert." Musically, however, there are numerous parallels, including the solo songs and orchestral accom-

ORATORIO

Messiah (1742), an oratorio in three parts, is Handel's greatest work. Although Handel was well-known as a composer of opera, he turned to oratorio composition when his London opera company went bankrupt. Composed in only twenty-five days, the performance of *Messiah* takes two and a half hours. The first section tells of the advent of a Messiah, based on Old Testament prophecy found in Isaiah IX:6. The second section depicts the trial and

George Frideric Handel.

Engraving by J. Sartain. Printed by Hudson. Courtesy of the New York Public Library.

death of Christ, the third his Resurrection. Throughout, soloists convey the narrative and choruses summarize main points of prophecy. At the London premier on March 23, 1743, King George II rose to his feet at the closing of "Hallelujah," a chorus near the end of the first section of the work. Following his example, the audience rose and established a tradition observed to this day by listeners moved by the famous chorus.

paniment. Although oratorios have traditionally been based on quasi-religious subjects, they are not intended for liturgical purposes. Handel's works were performed during Lent when staged theatrical productions, including opera, were banned by the authorities in England. Oratorios are like choral dramas, each an epic in song. Other oratorios by Handel include *Israel in Egypt* (1737), *Judas Maccabaeus* (1746), and *Jephtha* (1751).

DISTANCE

Since intensity is perceived differently if a listener is near the performers, distance is a factor in dynamics. The farther the listener from the source, the softer the overall sound. The acoustics and resonance of concert halls, of course, are intended to minimize this distance factor. Although it is rare, some ensembles even use electronic amplification.

Distance is more of a concern out-of-doors. Since sound travels at 1,120 feet per second, what is perceived as loud and soft depends on the listener's position. Sound also seems to warp with distance and some instruments are perceived more clearly than others. Anyone who has heard a marching band in a parade has experienced this phenomenon.

Selection no. 29

Listen to *Der Trumpet* by Herman, Monk of Salzburg (1365–1396) *(listening selections)*. The four instruments here were considered *haut* ("loud") instruments during the Middle Ages and Renaissance since their volume made them suitable for performance out-of-doors. They differ from *bas* or "soft" instruments, which were principally used indoors.

In this selection there is a direct beat, with uneven rhythmic patterns in § meter predominating, as well as imitation among the instrument parts.

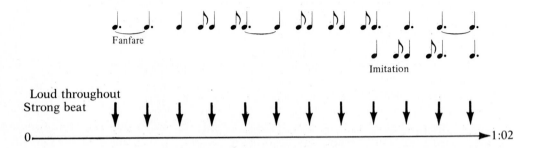

TABOR

The instruments in this selection are the *tabor,* a type of snare drum that is slung over the left shoulder and played with a stick held

in the right hand; the *shawm,* a woodwind instrument sounding like a   SHAWM
modern oboe; the *cornett,* an instrument with a cup-shaped mouth-   CORNETT
piece like a modern brass instrument; and the *slide* (or draw) *trumpet,*   SLIDE TRUMPET
a brass instrument that looked somewhat like a very small version of
a trombone. It appeared as early as the fourteenth century. These
Renaissance outdoor instruments did not have the wide dynamic
possibilities of modern brass, woodwind, and percussion instruments.
They simply played loud or *haut.*

MEASURING INTENSITY

Decibel Level

There are both scientific and musical ways to measure dynamics. A
common unit of scientific measurement is the *decibel,* with zero
decibels the threshold of hearing while 130 is the threshold of pain.
Few instruments are able to play softer than 20 decibels and, conversely, very few produce sounds above 100. Most instruments play at
medium level, considered to be between forty and eighty decibels.
Decibels are measured on a logarithmic scale in which a change from
70 to 73 decibels, for example, represents a doubling in intensity.

Notation of Dynamics

Although it might seem precise to indicate decibels in a musical score,
musicians do not use this type of notation. Rather, the composer
indicates loud by writing *forte,* soft by writing *piano.* These are the two   FORTE
most basic designations; the majority of other dynamic markings use   PIANO
qualifying designations in conjunction with these two terms.

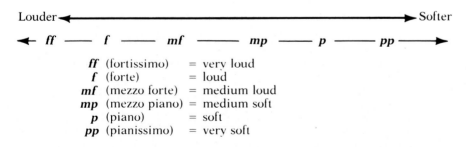

Louder ←————————————————————————→ Softer

← *ff* ——— *f* ——— *mf* ——— *mp* —— *p* —— *pp* →

ff (fortissimo)	=	very loud
f (forte)	=	loud
mf (mezzo forte)	=	medium loud
mp (mezzo piano)	=	medium soft
p (piano)	=	soft
pp (pianissimo)	=	very soft

How loud is forte? Forte is a relative level that depends upon how
soft piano is and can vary widely among musical compositions. Performers and conductors must make artistic judgments concerning
dynamic levels; these decisions are determined not only by the style of
the music and the environment in which it is performed, but also by

the skill and control of the performer. These are often purely intuitive choices, demonstrating why music is an art and not a science.

Other dynamic markings are used in addition to piano and forte. CRESCENDO A *crescendo,* which means to become louder, may occur either over a DECRESCENDO few notes or in longer passages. The opposite effect, *decrescendo,* means to become gradually softer. It is also called *diminuendo.*

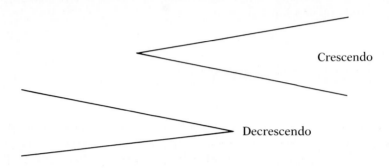

Crescendo

Decrescendo

Selection no. 30   Listen to Giovanni Salvatore's Toccata (c. 1600) *(listening selections)* and the Allegro from Vivaldi's (1678–1741) Concerto in a minor Selection no. 31 for flute, two violins, and continuo *(listening selections).* The *harpsichord* is heard in both listening examples. As noted earlier, the harpsichord is an instrument whose volume is not related directly to touch. A given amount of key pressure is needed for the string to be plucked, but any additional pressure has no effect on the degree of loudness.

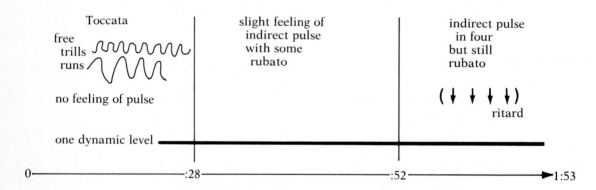

Harpsichords are sometimes built with several sets of strings, with at least two keyboards common in such instruments to control the different sets. An additional set of strings can be engaged by a stop COUPLER lever or *coupler,* thereby making the harpsichord appear to be playing louder. An instrument with four sets of strings also needs four sets of mechanisms for plucking, operated by the two keyboards. These pluck- JACK ing devices are called *jacks.* When all strings and jacks are engaged, the instrument is playing at its loudest. Dynamics in the harpsichord can change only in layers, as each separate set of strings is brought into play; the process is called *terraced dynamics*.

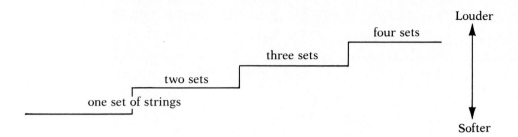

In the Allegro the harpsichord is heard with two violins, a flute, and a cello. All instruments in this selection are sensitive to pressure, except the harpsichord, and the range of dynamics is wider than it would be with a solo harpsichord. The flexible dynamics of the other instruments make it seem as if the harpsichord is also capable of getting louder or softer.

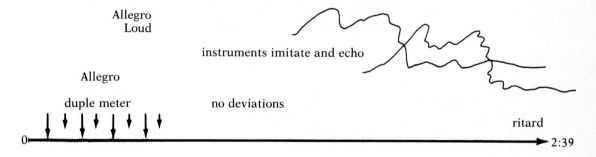

The soloists in this concerto are flute and violins. The harpsichord and cello provide a harmonic background and beat, a musical function referred to as the *continuo*. A *concerto* is an instrumental piece that exploits the contrast between solo and ensemble or between soloists, and there is thus a spirit of competition between the flute and violins.

Listen to the Presto from Beethoven's Symphony no. 7 in A major, op. 92, Movement III *(supplemental listening)*. The range of dynamics in an orchestral work can be quite wide. Beethoven's seventh symphony is considered a monument in the history of music. He began it in 1811, completed it one year later, and considered it one of his best works. It uses a large variety of instruments—strings, two flutes, two oboes, two clarinets, two bassoons, two horns, two trumpets, and tympani—and thus has a richer color and dynamic spectrum than is possible with a solo harpsichord.

Front and back of violin. The violin is one of the solo instruments heard in the Vivaldi Concerto.

Courtesy of Yamaha International Corporation.

This third movement uses two major ideas that are arranged ABABA. The markings are *Presto* (fast A section) and *Assai meno presto* (slower B section). The two sections are clearly delineated because of the contrast in dynamics.

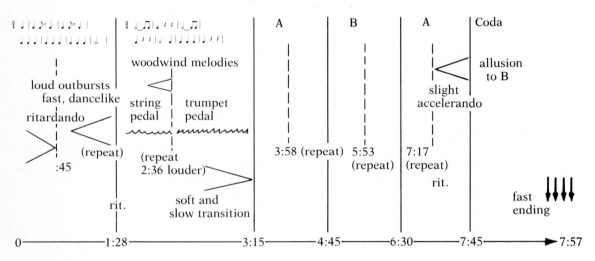

Ludwig van Beethoven (1770–1827) was a prodigious composer born in Bonn. He studied composition with Haydn as a young man and made his public debut as a pianist and composer in Vienna in 1795, when he was twenty-five years old. Soon after, he discovered he was losing his hearing. Although he consulted many doctors in search for a cure, he learned the hearing loss would progressively become complete.

Ludwig van Beethoven.
Courtesy of the New York Public Library.

Beethoven was temperamental in personality and his music often reflects the swing in his own life between contagious exhilaration and deep despair. In spite of his hearing loss, which was complete by 1812, Beethoven continued to compose and produced his most significant works after 1800, including most of his nine symphonies.

Symphonies of Beethoven's time were almost always in four movements: the first, moderately fast; the second, slow; the third, dance-like and moderately fast; and the fourth, very fast. Beethoven was specific in his notation of tempo and dynamics, one of the first composers to consistently use metronome markings. He favored a *return* form, a design in which a musical idea repeats after a contrasting section (ABA, ABABA, etc.) in his third movements.

Among Beethoven's works are sixteen string quartets, one opera, two Masses, thirty-two sonatas for piano, and five piano concertos. He stands as a monument to the musical style of the early nineteenth century, a period of transformation from the Classic heritage of Mozart and Haydn to the emotional tradition of the Romantic era.

Courtesy of The Selmer Company.

Closed-hole flute. The flute is heard in the Allegro from the Vivaldi Concerto.

ACCENTUATIONS

Closely related to dynamics is *accentuation.* Accented notes are stressed by being played with more pressure. This is marked in music as:

(sharp attack)   (lingering pressure)

SFORZATO   Musicians also find markings of *sforzato (sf, sfz)* and *forzato (fz)* under notes, both of which indicate a sudden loud attack followed by an immediate return to the original dynamic level.

sfz

Selection no. 32   Listen to John Coltrane's "Alabama" (recorded in New York in 1963) *(supplemental listening).* The melody incorporates frequent accents, that is, certain notes are emphasized by being played louder.

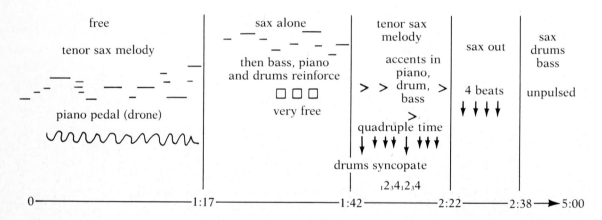

FREE-FORM   John Coltrane (1926–1967) created a jazz style in the late 1950s and early 1960s called *free-form.* In free-form, performers interact with one another to create their own improvised composition. Free-form jazz may be based on a known song, which becomes the springboard for variations that can go far afield from the original theme; it may also be created without a set tune in mind. The lead performer, such as the saxophone here, improvises a "new" melody while the accompanying musicians react, providing appropriate rhythm and harmony. Since the music is made up on the spot, no two free-form improvisations will be alike, even if inspired by the same material.

Coltrane and his quartet were moved emotionally by the deaths of several school children killed by a bomb explosion in Alabama during the Civil Rights era. They were inspired to create this work as a memorial, therefore endowing it with elements of meditation, prayer, and redemption. Several aspects of "Alabama" are associated with Indian music. There is a noticeable similarity between the piano drone here and that of the tamboura in *Raga Simhendra-Madhyamen* (see page 50). The section with rhythmic freedom followed by one in more structured time also parallels development in the Indian composition. Coltrane was a master of intricate improvisation, characterized by the hard accents heard in "Alabama."

INTENSITY AS AN EXPRESSIVE ELEMENT

Since the feeling brought to a performance depends so much upon the shadings of loud and soft, it would be impossible for a composer to notate dynamics precisely or to expect every performer to shape the dynamics in exactly the form the composer intended. The performer will seldom play all notes in a melody at the same dynamic level. Even when the melody is marked generally "piano" or "forte," musicians adjust their playing within this general level. If the melody rises, loudness, while remaining within the general dynamic level, may increase to emphasize the climax.

Present-day madrigal singers.

Courtesy of the University of Arizona School of Music.

Selection no. 33   Listen to Thomas Morley's "Now Is the Month of Maying" *(listening selections)*. This madrigal has much repetition, but the performers alter the dynamics each time to provide variety and interest.

A   Now is the month of Maying, When merry lads are playing, *mf*
           Fa la la la la la la, fa la la la la la la.

A   Now is the month of Maying, When merry lads are playing, *f*
           Fa la (etc.)

B   Each with his bonny lass, Upon the greeny grass. *f*
           Fa la (etc.)

B   Each with his bonny lass, Upon the greeny grass. *f*
           Fa la (etc.)

A   The Spring, clad all in gladness, Doth laugh at Winter's sadness, *mf*
           Fa la (etc.)

A   The Spring, clad all in gladness, Doth laugh at Winter's sadness, *mp*
           Fa la (etc.)

B   And to the bagpipes' sound The nymphs tread out the ground. *mf*
           Fa la (etc.)

B   And to the bagpipes sound The nymphs tread out the ground. *f*
           Fa la (etc.)

A   Fie, then, why sit we musing, Youth's sweet delight refusing? *f*
           Fa la (etc.)

A   Fie, then, why sit we musing, Youth's sweet delight refusing? *f*
           Fa la (etc.)

B   Say, dainty nymphs, and speak, Shall we play barley break? *f*
           Fa la (etc.)

B   Say, dainty nymphs, and speak, shall we play barley break? *f*
           Fa la (etc.)   rit.

MADRIGAL

RENAISSANCE

Morley (1557–1602), an Elizabethan composer, wrote many madrigals, mostly to texts dealing with love (often erotic), beauty, and pastoral themes. A *madrigal* is a secular vocal piece in a style popular during the *Renaissance* (1450–1600). Both Italian and English composers wrote madrigals as entertainment for nobles who considered the art of singing part of everyday life. Madrigals were written in three to five voice parts (this example is five-part). Both women and men joined in the singing, two or three persons on each part, thereby suggesting that the madrigals were sung by fifteen or fewer persons.

There are two musical sections in this work, which is in binary form (AABB), with the pattern repeated three times. The text and dynamic changes provide diversity and performance subtlety. It is of interest that the dynamic markings followed in this performance are not Morley's. It was not common practice in the Renaissance to furnish such musical directions, so these were added at a later date. Nonetheless, the examples illustrate how performers can supply dynamic contrast even in a work without specific instruction from the composer.

DYNAMICS AND STYLE PERIODS

Several historical style periods have been alluded to thus far and will be continually discussed throughout this text. Styles in music, as with all artistic endeavors, change over time because the consumers of art change their preferences. This results in audiences developing new tastes and expectations in what they hear. Musical styles have also changed in part because composers evolved new techniques and employed new technology, such as changes in musical instruments. Each style period has had a different way to treat dynamics. A brief outline of the historical periods, from the Renaissance to the present, may help clarify how composers have incorporated dynamics in their works. Note that many of the changes were gradual, so there is some overlap of the dates dividing the various periods.

Period	Dynamics	Examples
Renaissance 1450–1600	Dynamics are restrained. Use of haut and bas instruments. Formal and unemotional sounds are used. No extremes in dynamics.	Dowland—"Orlando Sleepeth" Morley—"Now Is the Month of Maying"
Baroque 1600–1750	Dynamics tend to be terraced—layered. Dramatic contrasts between loud and soft occur.	Handel—*Water Music;* "For Unto Us A Child Is Born" Bach—Toccata in d minor Vivaldi—Concerto in a minor
Classical 1750–1825	Use of $<$ and $>$. Use of modest louds and softs. Dynamics are logical, controlled, and restrained, and used to help achieve climaxes.	D. Scarlatti—Sonata in C major.
Romantic 1825–1900	Softer softs *(ppp)* and louder louds *(fff)* and use of all ranges in between. There are violent, sudden, and dramatic changes. Dynamics give goal to the music.	Dvořák—Allegretto grazioso Grieg—*In the Hall of the Mountain King* Brahms—Ballade in g Wagner—Prelude to Act III (*Lohengrin*) Beethoven—Presto (Symphony no. 7)
Impressionist 1885–1930+	Generally soft with brief loud outbursts. Dynamics are used to enhance the varied harmonies and timbres.	Debussy—*Clair de Lune*
Twentieth Century	All techniques of past periods are used. There is a wider range of contrasts. Composers give specific directions on how loud a note or passage should be.	Stravinsky—"Gavotte with Two Variations" Ives—*Putnam's Camp* Oliveros—*Sound Patterns*

SUMMARY

Intensity or dynamics is an expressive element of music that depends upon the energy to produce the sound. The number of performers also affects dynamics to a lesser extent, as does the distance between performer and listener. Dynamics are notated in music with Italian terms such as *piano* and *forte*. These represent a generalized indication that is adjusted for each group of instruments, performers, and environment. Levels of intensity can be explained scientifically through the use of decibels, but musicians respond to dynamics on an intuitive basis. Sensitive use of dynamic levels helps make a musical performance expressive and meaningful.

STUDY GUIDELINES

**Guide to Perceiving
Dynamics—Intensity**

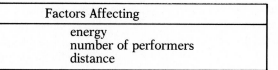

Factors Affecting
energy
number of performers
distance

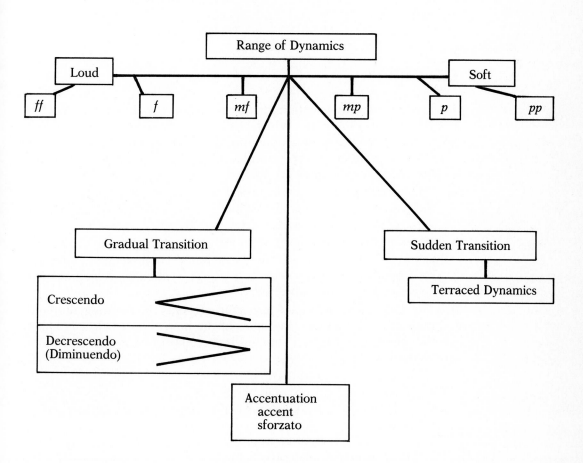

KEY TERMS AND CONCEPTS

Accentuation
  Accents
  Forzato *(fz)*
  Sforzato *(sf, sfz)*
Bas Instruments
Decibel
Dynamics
Factors Affecting Dynamics
  Distance
  Energy
  Number of performers
Forte
Haut Instruments
Intensity
Notation
  Crescendo

Decrescendo (Diminuendo)
Forte *(f)*
Fortissimo *(ff)*
Mezzo forte *(mf)*
Mezzo piano *(mp)*
Pianissimo *(pp)*
Piano *(p)*
Periods of Music History
  Baroque
  Classical
  Impressionist
  Renaissance
  Romantic
  Twentieth Century
Piano
Terraced Dynamics

EXERCISES

1. Listen to varying selections of music—art, jazz, rock—and discuss the changes in dynamics. Which groups have the greatest changes? Which have the widest dynamics levels? How are the changes in intensity created (energy, number of performers, or distance)? Are the changes sudden or gradual?

2. Compare the speaking voices of three friends, three professors, or three television personalities. Which is louder? Softer? Has the most variety? Which is the most interesting? Why?

3. Listen to *two* recordings of the *same* musical work by *two* different artists (i.e., two versions of the same song, symphony, piano sonata, etc.). What differences do you notice in dynamics? Which do you consider more expressive? Why?

4. The diagram at the top of page 85 represents the mapping of dynamics in a time frame. On copies of the blank chart below it, chart the intensity levels and changes for five minutes in at least two of the following:

  A. a musical composition
  B. noises you hear on a city street
  C. listening to a speaker (minister, professor, public orator)
  D. at a dramatic play
  E. watching a television program
  F. at a basketball or football game
  G. where you live in the evening

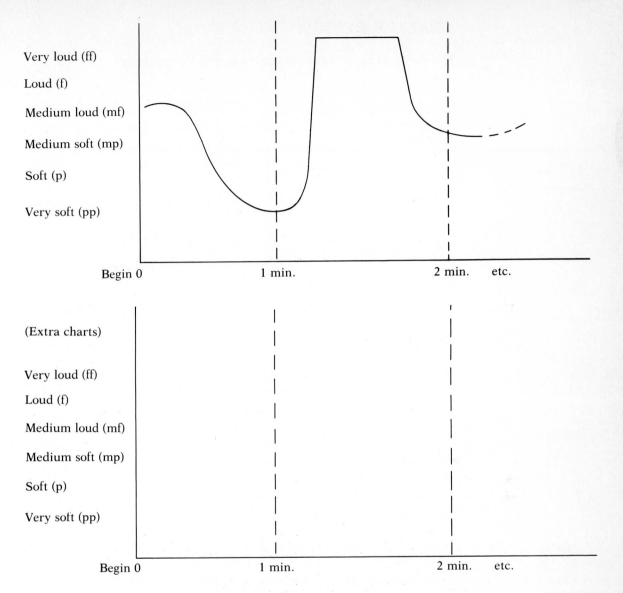

5. Copy the chart from number 4 and make a graph for ten minutes of music from each of the following:
   A. Classical music station
   B. Easy listening station
   C. Jazz station
   D. Rock music station
   E. Muzak
   What conclusions can you draw from your five charts?
6. Repeat your chart for one of the works from this chapter.

CHAPTER REVIEW

Match items in the two columns. Answers in Appendix.

1. _____ crescendo
2. _____ decrescendo
3. _____ fortissimo
4. _____ forte
5. _____ mezzo forte
6. _____ mezzo piano
7. _____ piano
8. _____ pianissimo
9. _____ decibels
10. _____ accent
11. _____ "haut"
12. _____ "bas"

A. scientific measurement of sound intensity
B. >
C. loud
D. soft indoor instruments
E. soft
F. ◁
G. loud outdoor instruments
H. medium loud
I. ▷
J. very loud
K. medium soft
L. very soft

FOR FURTHER LISTENING

Bach	*Brandenburg Concerto* no. 5 in D major (terraced dynamics)
Beethoven	Sonata no. 23 in f minor (*Appassionata*) First movement
Debussy	*Nocturnes:* "Fêtes"
Hadyn	Symphony no. 94 in G major (*Surprise*) Second movement
Saint-Saëns	*Dance Macabre*
Wagner	*Lohengrin:* Prelude to Act I

TIMBRE

◆

DEFINITION OF TIMBRE

Timbre is tone color in music, and it can be discussed at many levels. A symphony orchestra has a composite timbre since it consists of several instruments. A jazz ensemble has a composite timbre too, but since it consists of fewer instruments than the symphony orchestra, its timbre would be less complex. At another level, we can refer to the timbre of a single instrument, such as the trumpet, as well as various ways in which an individual trumpet can sound. Finally, we can even refer to the differences in tone color between two trumpets. All of these colors are timbre.

Why does one instrument sound different from another? Why does a clarinet sound different from an oboe? Why does a beginning violinist sound different from a professional? Vibration is the source of sound in every instrument. The plucking or bowing of a string or the striking of a drum head creates vibration. With wind instruments, the column of air inside must be set into vibration. Other instruments, such as cymbals, bells, or woodblocks, are self-vibrators. The vibrating string, air column, skin, metal, or wood produces a *fundamental* sound. However, the object also vibrates partially at various points. These *partial vibrations*, called *overtones* or *harmonics*, become part of the sound, but are not perceived separately from the basic tone, the fundamental.

Since different partials vibrate at varying degrees of loudness, the overtones for any given instrument are different from those of another. Factors contributing to this variation include the material in the instrument, the way the sound is produced, and the skill of the

VIBRATION

FUNDAMENTAL

OVERTONE

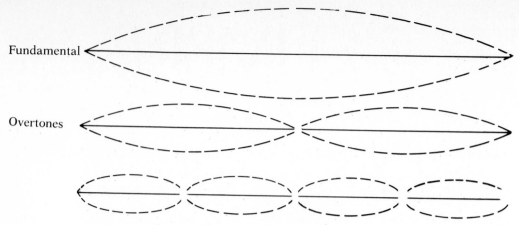

Fundamental

Overtones

person producing the sound. All clarinets sound somewhat alike because each one produces similar overtone structures, but a clarinet sounds different from an oboe because each has a different pattern of overtones. Similarly, the voice of one person is distinct from that of another because the overtones differ depending on the size and shape of the person's vocal cords, chest, throat, and sinus cavities. The beginning violinist does not sound like a professional because the former has not developed a stable overtone pattern on the instrument. Intuitively, the experienced musician knows what is a good tone quality and how to achieve it.

OSCILLOSCOPE

SINE WAVE

Sound waves can be shown on an *oscilloscope*, a device that has a cathode tube like a television. A fundamental tone would appear as a *sine wave*, a wave without overtones. The complete sound wave for

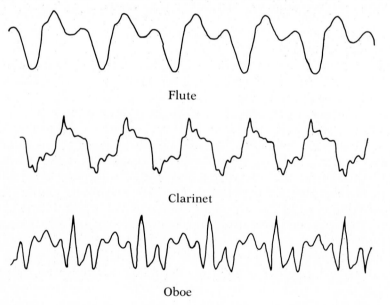

Flute

Clarinet

Oboe

any specific instrument is more complex than a sine wave because partial vibrations are a part of it. A clarinet not only sounds different from an oboe, but the wave it generates looks different. Electronic instruments, such as a synthesizer or an electronic organ, are able to duplicate timbres by producing an overtone structure similar to that of a given instrument.

BROAD CLASSIFICATIONS

Musical groups are broadly classified as being *vocal* or *instrumental.*

Vocal

The largest vocal group is called a *choir.* The *mixed* choir or chorus has both women's and men's voices, divided into soprano, alto, tenor, and bass sections. Choirs may also be all male or all female. They perform with orchestral or piano accompaniment or may be unaccompanied. An unaccompanied performance by any individual or ensemble is referred to as *a cappella* (without instrumental accompaniment).

CHOIR

A CAPPELLA

Listen to the Sanctus from *L'homme armé* mass by Josquin des Prez *(listening selections).* Since women were not permitted to sing the sacred music of the Catholic Church during the Renaissance, this choir is all male, the upper parts being taken by boy sopranos and altos. The

SANCTUS
Selection no. 34

Male singers in a chorus.

Courtesy of the University of Arizona School of Music.

Sanctus is the fourth movement of the Ordinary of the Mass; the words are:

Sanctus, sanctus, sanctus   (Holy, holy, holy)
Dominus Deus sabaoth   (Lord God of Sabaoth)

Josquin des Prez (c. 1440–1521), a Flemish composer, served as a musician to courts in Milan, Rome, France, and Ferrara. In addition to Masses he composed motets, vocal pieces that do not require the set text that is standard in the Mass, but can be composed to any sacred text. In Josquin's time it was common to incorporate secular tunes into sacred choral music, as this Mass demonstrates. *L'homme armé* (The armed man), a popular medieval tune, was used by several composers CANTUS in the late Middle Ages as a founding melody *(cantus firmus)* in Masses FIRMUS and motets. Josquin incorporated it into this Mass, which has tradition-ally been known as *L'homme armé*.

Use of an unaccompanied choir is typical of sacred music of the Renaissance. All vocal parts are equal in importance and imitation can be noted among the vocal lines. There is no strong metric feeling, the pulse is typically indirect, and the dynamics are quite restrained.

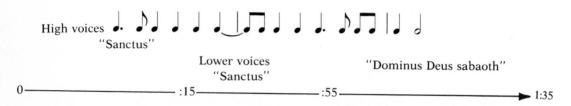

High voices

"Sanctus"

Lower voices
"Sanctus"

"Dominus Deus sabaoth"

0 —————————— :15 —————————— :55 —————————→ 1:35

Smaller vocal groups are sometimes called chamber choirs, imply-ing fewer persons in each section. Vocal groups, such as trios, quartets, and quintets, do exist, but not much art music has been created specifically for chamber-sized vocal organizations. Rather, such groups are usually heard within the context of a larger vocal assemblage, such as in a performance of a Mass.

Instrumental

Orchestras. One of the largest instrumental groups in music is the *symphony orchestra*. It consists of several families of instruments, including strings, winds, and percussion. Since the orchestra is large in size, it is usually directed by a conductor. Most orchestral sections have several performers per part, that is, ten violinists may all be playing the same music. The orchestra may be relatively small in size, twenty to thirty performers, or quite large, sixty to eighty or more, depending

Photo by Tim Fuller.

Most orchestral sections have several performers per part. Here is the cello section of a symphony orchestra.

on whose music is being performed. The orchestra is often presented by itself in a musical performance, but it is also used to accompany performances of dance and theater.

Chamber Groups.   Unlike the large orchestra, in which many musicians play the same part, *chamber groups* are musical organizations with only one or two performers on a musical part. Terminology for chamber groups is rarely standardized. *Trio,* of course, designates three performers, *quartet,* four, *quintet,* five, *sextet,* six, and *octet,* eight. A *string trio* is three string instruments, but a *piano trio* consists of piano, violin, and cello. The *string quartet* has two violins, one viola, and one cello. A *brass quartet* is two trumpets, one French horn, and a trombone. A *piano quintet* consists of one piano plus string quartet, a *clarinet quintet* substitutes the clarinet for the piano, but a *brass quintet* is a brass quartet plus tuba. A *wind* (or *woodwind*) *quintet* is flute, clarinet, oboe, bassoon, and French horn. Instrumentation is rarely standardized beyond the quintet. Sextets and octets may be all strings, woodwinds, brass, or any mixture thereof.

STRING
QUARTET

WIND
QUINTET

Johann Joachim Quantz (1697–1773), a famous German composer and flutist, wrote almost exclusively for the flute. He began his career playing oboe in the Dresden royal orchestra, but soon took up the flute, studying under European masters. In 1728 he played before Frederick the Great in Berlin, and so impressed the prince that he was hired to return twice annually to give lessons. When the prince later ascended the throne, he appointed Quantz chamber musician and court composer in Berlin and Potsdam, where Quantz served until death.

Quantz wrote more than three hundred concertos for the flute and many trio sonatas. Most of his compositions can be considered chamber music. Quantz observed and chronicled the historical period in which he lived. He wrote an important treatise on flute playing and musical taste in 1752, *Versuch einer Anweisung die Flöte traversière zu spielen* (On Playing the Flute), that offers this advice for listening:

Now, since music is the sort of art which must be judged, not according to our own fancy, but, like the other fine arts, according to good taste, acquired through certain rules and refined by much experience and exercise; since he who wishes to judge another ought to understand at least as much as the other, if not more; since these qualities are seldom met within those who occupy themselves with the judging of music; since, on the contrary, the greater part of these are governed by ignorance, prejudice, and passions which hinder correct judgement; many a one would do much better if he would keep his judgment to himself and listen with greater attention, if, without judging, he can still take pleasure in music.

Johann Joachim Quantz.

Drawing from the Joseph Miller Collection. Courtesy of the New York Public Library.

Selection no. 35
TRIO SONATA

Listen to the Larghetto from the Johann Joachim Quantz Trio in C major for flute, recorder, and continuo *(listening selections)*. This larghetto movement is one of four from a type of composition called a *trio sonata*. Trio sonatas were written during the Baroque period for four instruments. It may seem confusing to call a work with four performers a trio, but the *continuo*, the term referring to the harmony provided jointly by cello and harpsichord, constitutes a single part. With the flute and recorder, there are then only three parts, thus justifying use of the term "trio."

The flute and recorder take turns leading while the other imitates; the steady pulse in ¾ and harmony part are provided by the continuo.

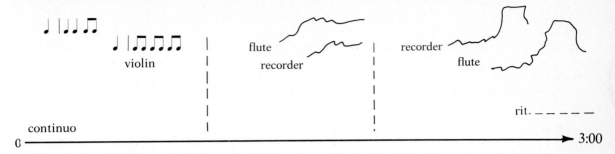

Chamber music is not limited to the Western world. The *Sankyoku* of Japan, which means three instruments, for example, consists of *samisen* and *koto,* both string instruments, and *shakuhachi,* a wind instrument, and is thus a trio.

SANKYOKU

Listen to Yatsuhashi Kengyo's *Rokudan No Shirabe (listening selections).* The main part is played by the samisen, an instrument with three strings. The samisen has a resonating body covered with animal skin, somewhat like an American banjo. It is held like a guitar and played with a large pick.

Selection no. 36
SAMISEN

The wind instrument is the shakuhachi, a vertically held flute made of bamboo, similar to the Chinese instrument called the *hsiao.*

SHAKUHACHI

Courtesy Embassy of Japan.

Shakuhachi, Japanese notched vertical flute.

Koto, 13-stringed
Japanese zither.

Courtesy Seka Bunka Photo.

This instrument was used by samurai warriors of seventeenth-century Japan who were forbidden from carrying weapons. They learned to play the shakuhachi and carried it with them, utilizing it to make music as well as wielding it as a billy club for defense when necessary.

KOTO   The third instrument is the koto, which is similar to the Chinese cheng. Although its adoption into Japan from China can be traced to the eighth century, it did not become well established in music there until the sixteenth century. The koto has thirteen strings, each tuned by a separate moveable bridge placed between the string and the body. The performer kneels before the instrument and plucks the strings with finger picks.

Unlike the Quantz trio, in which flute and violin carry the melody while the continuo plays the harmony, all instruments in sankyoku play the melody or a slight variation of it. Harmony is only incidental. The tempo is slow and the beat is indirect duple time.

VOCAL TIMBRES

SATB
RANGES/
QUALITY

A choir consists of *soprano, alto, tenor,* and *bass* voices, often abbreviated SATB in choral literature; the same designations are used for solo voices. The four voice types differ in both range and quality. The soprano voice is the highest, bass the lowest. Although each voice type has a distinct range, there is some overlapping. A soprano is able to sing the distance of about ten notes on the piano, from e_1 through f_1 $g_1 a_1 b_1 c_2 d_2 e_2 f_2 g_2 a_2$. An alto can sing some of the same notes, but is not able to go as high, reaching to d, which is five notes lower than the soprano's top. However, the alto can sing five notes lower than the soprano. Thus there is a difference of about a *fifth*—an interval of five tones—between each voice category. A bass can sing five pitches lower than the tenor, the tenor five notes lower than the alto, and so forth.

FIFTH

There are also voice designations between the soprano and alto range, called *mezzo-soprano*, as well as between tenor and bass, the *baritone*. Although range helps to classify voice types, it is really the *quality* that supplies the identifiable difference. Soprano and tenor qualities are bright, while *contralto*, another name for alto, and bass are darker, as are mezzo-soprano and baritone.

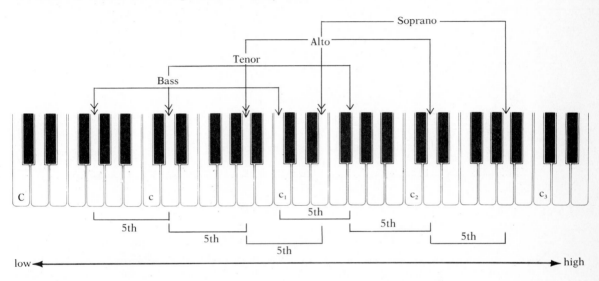

Contralto

The contralto, the lowest female voice, is usually cast in secondary roles, playing older characters, in operatic performances. The depth of the voice suggests greater age than higher, lighter sounds. Listen to "O Thou That Tellest Good Tidings" from Handel's *Messiah (listening selections)*. This *aria* is a solo for contralto voice. The text, which is partially found in Isaiah 60:1, describes the advent of a messiah. Since the emphasis in arias is on the music, rather than the words, repetition within the text is often a standard part of their makeup. Arias are often very complex and are found in *opera*, a musical drama that is staged, as well as *oratorio*, an unstaged vocal composition on a religious theme, of which *Messiah* is an example. In opera the dramatic action typically pauses while the soloist sings an aria, but in oratorios there is no stage action. In *Messiah*, arias are alternated with choruses, providing variety within the unfolding of the story. This example uses the low range of the contralto to bring authority and depth to the words of the aria.

Selection no. 37
ARIA

OPERA
ORATORIO

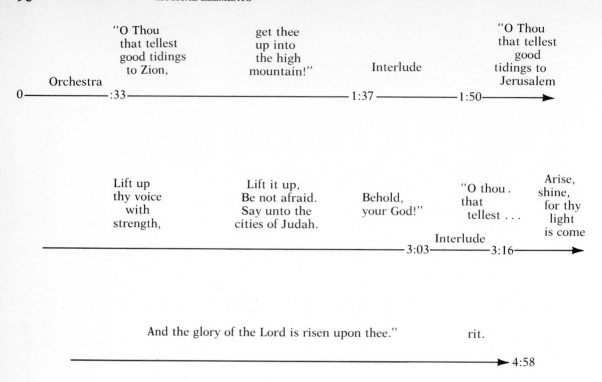

"O Thou that tellest good tidings to Zion,   get thee up into the high mountain!"   Interlude   "O Thou that tellest good tidings to Jerusalem

Orchestra

0 —————— :33 ———————————— 1:37 ————— 1:50 ————→

Lift up thy voice with strength,   Lift it up, Be not afraid. Say unto the cities of Judah.   Behold, your God!"   "O thou . that tellest . . .   Arise, shine, for thy light is come

Interlude

————————————————————— 3:03 ———— 3:16 ———→

And the glory of the Lord is risen upon thee."   rit.

————————————————————————————→ 4:58

Soprano

In opera and in operetta a less complicated form with more moderate vocal demands, the heroine and hero are generally composed for soprano and tenor, respectively, while contralto and bass play older characters, such as mothers and fathers, aunts and uncles, or priests and goddesses. This convention of casting allows the audience immediate identification of roles with vocal quality.

There are numerous types of sopranos. The classifications below are not rigid, and singers of one type will often be cast in roles usually played by those of another category. However, these are the divisions that usually apply in regard to the soprano voice. Those who specialize in singing elaborate vocal passage in the upper range are called COLORATURA *coloratura* sopranos. Listen to the Queen of the Night's aria from Selection no. 38 Mozart's opera, *The Magic Flute (listening selections)*. This role is played by a coloratura soprano who demonstrates elaborate vocal techniques in this selection, including runs, jumps, intricate figurations, and trills, all in a high vocal register.

> KONIGIN. Der Hölle Rache kocht in meinem Herzen;
> Tod and Verzweiflung; flammet um mich her!
> Fühlt nicht durch dich Sarastro Todesschmerzen,
> so bist du meine Tochter nimmermehr!

Verstoben sei auf ewig, verlassen sei auf ewig,
zertrümmert sei auf ewig alle Bande der Natur—
wenn nicht durch dich Sarastro wird erblassen!
Hört! Rachegötter! Hört der Mutter Schwur!

QUEEN. The vengeance of Hell boils in my heart;
    death and despair flame around me!
    If you do not cause Sarastro a painful death
    you will be my daughter no more!
    Outcast be forever, abandoned forever,
    destroyed forever be all ties of nature—
    If Sarastro be not blasted through you!
    Hear me, gods of vengeance! Hear a mother's vow!

Lyric sopranos, those with a pleasant, light, and smooth-flowing vocal style, are typically cast as young ladies or ingenues in opera and operetta. They do not usually sing as high as coloraturas. Listen to "Un Bel Di" from Giacomo Puccini's opera *Madama Butterfly* (1904) *(listening selections)*, the story of a young Japanese girl who falls in love with an American naval officer. Before she bears him a child out of wedlock he returns to America, promising to return to her. In this scene Cio-cio-san (Butterfly), a lyric soprano, has been chided by her female servant, Suzuki, who declares Lt. Pinkerton will never return. Cio-cio-

LYRIC

Selection no. 39

Photo by James Heffernan. Courtesy of the Metropolitan Opera Association.

Renata Scotto as Cio-cio-san in Puccini's *Madama Butterfly.*

san protests and then describes to Suzuki just how it will be in the aria, "Un Bel Di" (One Fine Day).

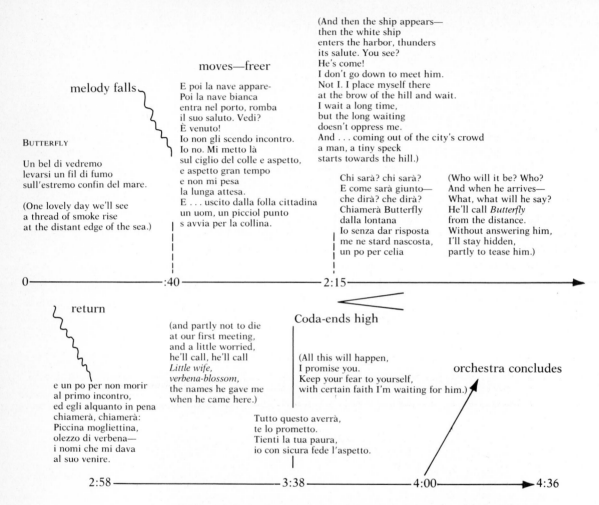

Pinkerton eventually does return, accompanied by his American wife, Kate, in order to claim the child. Butterfly, performing the only honorable act left to her, commits suicide as the opera ends.

DRAMATIC

MEZZO

Selection no. 40

Dramatic sopranos, who have more powerful voices than the lyrics or coloraturas, are cast as older heroines or in roles that require this stronger quality. This is true as well for *mezzo*-sopranos, who sing the lower portion of the range. They play mature characters or anti-heroines, such as *Carmen*. Listen to "Habanera" from Georges Bizet's opera, *Carmen* (1875) *(listening selections)*. This aria is sung by Carmen, a gypsy girl who trifles with men and then leaves them as her fancy dictates. In this scene she describes love as a "rebel bird that nobody can ever tame," a sentiment that aptly describes her relation-

Giacomo Puccini.

Courtesy of the New York Public Library.

Giacomo Puccini (1858–1924), a celebrated Italian composer, spent three years at the Milan Conservatory where serious study with Amilcare Ponchielli gave him a start in opera composition. While his first two operas met only moderate success, *Manon Lescaut* in 1893 brought him fame. With his next opera, *La Bohème,* Puccini's name spread throughout the world. His most dramatic work, *Tosca,* soon followed, and joined his two previous compositions as standards in the opera house repertoire. He wrote *Madama Butterfly* in 1903 while confined for eight months in a wheelchair after an auto accident. The opera at its premiere was hissed, prompting Puccini to withdraw and revise the work. The new version, released three months later, moved the audience to frenzied applause and established Puccini as the acknowledged ruler of the Italian opera. His last work, *Turandot,* followed a penchant for setting his operas in exotic places, in this case, China. Puccini, however, died before completing the last scene of *Turandot.* It was finished by Franco Alfano, an eminent Italian composer, though not Puccini's equal in skill and creativity.

Viorica Cortez as Carmen in Bizet's *Carmen.*

Photo by James Heffernan. Courtesy of the Metropolitan Opera Association.

ship to Don Jose, the corporal whose career is ultimately ruined by his obsessive love for her. Although he follows her into a life of crime and smuggling, at the conclusion of the opera, in a fit of jealousy, he murders Carmen.

$$0 \frac{\text{Introduction}}{\text{recitative}} :43 \qquad ♩. \;\; ♪♩ \;\; ♩ \;\; (\text{etc.})$$

:48   L'amour est un oiseau rebelle   Love, love is a rebel bird
que nul ne peut apprivoiser,   that nobody can ever tame,
et c'est bien en vain qu'on   and you call him quite in vain
    l'appelle,
s'il lui convient de refuser.   if it suits him not to come.
Rien n'y fait; menace ou prière,   Nothing helps, nor threat nor
                                        prayer.
l'un parle bien, l'autre se tait;   One man talks well, the other's
                                        mum;
et c'est l'autre que je préfère,   it's the other one that I prefer.
it n'a rien dit mais il me plaît.   He's silent, but I like his looks.
L'amour! l'amour! l'amour!   Love! Love! Love! Love!
    l'amour!

CIGARETTE GIRLS AND YOUNG MEN

1:15   L'amour est un oiseau rebelle   Love, love is a rebel bird
chorus and   que nul ne peut apprivoiser,   that nobody can ever tame,
solo overlap   et c'est bien en vain qu'on
     l'appelle,   and you call him quite in vain
s'il lui convient de refuser!   if it suits him not to come!

CARMEN

1:28   L'amour est enfant de Bohème,   Love, love is a gypsy child,
il n'a jamais, jamais connu de loi;   it has never, never known a law;
si tu ne m'aimes pas, je t'aime;   love me not, then I love you;
si je t'aime, prends garde à toi!   if I love you, you'd best beware!

CIGARETTE GIRLS AND YOUNG MEN

Prends garde à toi!   Beware!

CARMEN

Si tu ne m'aimes pas, je t'aime!   Love me not, then I love you!

CIGARETTE GIRLS AND YOUNG MEN

Prends garde à toi!   Beware! (FF)

CARMEN

Mais si je t'aime, prends garde
   à toi!

But if I love you, you'd best beware!

CIGARETTE GIRLS AND YOUNG MEN

L'amour est enfant de Bohème,
   etc.

Love, love is a gypsy child, *etc.*

CARMEN

Si tu ne m'aimes pas, je t'aime!

Love me not, then I love you!

CIGARETTE GIRLS AND YOUNG MEN

Prends garde à toi!

Beware!

CARMEN

2:07   L'oiseau que tu croyais surprende

battit de l'aile et s'envola;
l'amour est loin, tu peux l'attendre;
tu ne l'attends plus, il est là!
Tout autour de toi, vite, vite,
il vient, s'en va, puis il revient;
tu crois le tenir, il t'évite,
tu crois l'éviter, il te tient.

The bird you thought that you had
   caught
spreads its wings and flies away;
love stays away, you wait and wait;
when least expected, love appears!
All around you, swift, so swift,
it comes, it goes, and then returns;
you think you hold it fast, it flees!
You think you're free, it holds you
   fast.

2:35   L'amour! l'amour, l'amour,
   l'amour!

Love! Love! Love! Love!

CIGARETTE GIRLS AND YOUNG MEN

chorus and
solo overlap

Tout autour de toi, vite, vite,
il vient, s'en va, puis il revient;
tu crois le tenir, il t'évite;
tu crois l'éviter, il te tient!

All around you, swift, so swift,
it comes, it goes, and then returns;
you think you hold it fast, it flees!
You think you're free, it holds you
   fast.

CARMEN

2:48   L'amour est enfant de Bohème,
   etc.

Love, love is a gypsy child, *etc.*

CIGARETTE GIRLS AND YOUNG MEN

| Prends garde à toi! | Beware! |

CARMEN

| Si tu ne m'aimes pas, je t'aime. | Love me not, then I love you. |

CIGARETTE GIRLS AND YOUNG MEN

| Prends garde à toi! | Beware! |

CARMEN

| Mais si je t'aime, prends garde à toi! | But if I love you, you'd best beware! |

CIGARETTE GIRLS AND YOUNG MEN

| L'amour est enfant de Bohème, *etc.* | Love, love is a gypsy child, *etc.* |

CARMEN

| Si tu ne m'aimes pas, je t'aime. | Love me not, then I love you. |

CIGARETTE GIRLS AND YOUNG MEN

| Prends garde à toi! | Beware! |

CARMEN

4:00 | Mais si je t'aime, prends garde à toi! | But if I love you, you'd best beware! |

Tenor

LYRIC

Selection no. 41

The tenor is usually the leading man in opera. Those with a light, clear voice are called *lyric* and are cast opposite the lyric soprano. Listen to "Ecco Ridente," an aria from Rossini's opera, *The Barber of Seville* (1815) *(listening selections)*, based on a play by Beaumarchais. Count Almaviva, played by a lyric tenor, is in love with Rosina, a young girl. Since her guardian, Dr. Bartolo, refuses to let her see the Count, he sings this serenade beneath her window in the first scene. In the course of the opera, with the help of the barber Figaro, love eventually foils the strictness of Bartolo, and Almaviva and Rosina are united

Georges Bizet.
Courtesy of the New York Public Library.

Georges Bizet (1838–1875) was a student of the Paris Conservatory at the age of nine, and won the coveted Prix de Rome in 1857, allowing him to live and compose for three years in Italy. He wrote several one-act operas, but an orchestral suite composed for Daudet's play *L'Arlésienne* was the first of Bizet's works to win popular approval. Although modestly successful throughout his lifetime, his fame was truly established only after his death, three months following the premiere of *Carmen*. In spite of an unenthusiastic reception from critics who attacked the opera for its lurid subject, *Carmen* after its premiere became a worldwide success. This masterpiece, along with the orchestral suite *L'Arlésienne*, established his musical immortality.

Marilyn Horne as Rosina and Rockwell Blake as Count Almaviva from Rossini's *The Barber of Seville.*

Photo by James Heffernan. Courtesy of the Metropolitan Opera Association.

Introduction

guitar and
orchestra

steady tempo
duple time

(Aurora touches the sky with radiance,
yet my lady wakes not, she sleeps serenely on.
Arise, my love, my beloved,
let a ray from your dazzling eyes fall upon me.)

Erro ridente in cielo spunta la bella aurora,
E tu non sorgi ancora, e puoi dormie cosi?
Sorgi, mia dolce speme, vieni bell'idol mio.
Rendi men erudo, oh Dio! lo stral che mi teri.

tempo picks up
but there are pauses

very elaborate singing—
almost tenor coloratura

(Oh rise, let me look upon you—
have pity on me—that I could but see you—
an instant of rapture,
of divine happiness unequaled on earth!)

O sorte! già veggo quel caro sembiante:
Quest'aninia amante ottenne pietà!
Oh! istante d'amore! Felice momento!
Oh dolee contento, che equal, no non ha:

0————:56 ———————————————— 2:41 —————————————▶

orchestral Coda

————————▶ 4:31 ———————————▶ 4:49

Gioacchino Rossini
(1792–1868), master of the
Italian opera, wrote his first
at age 18 and became
known as a successful opera
composer by the age of
twenty-one. During his
lifetime Rossini composed
on average two operas a
year for nineteen years,
four being produced in one
year alone. Among his most
famous works are *Italian
Girl in Algiers* (1813), *Barber of Seville* (1815), *Cin-
derella* (1817), and *William
Tell* (1829). The French
Government of King Charles

Gioacchino Rossini.
Courtesy of the New York Public
Library.

X in 1829 guaranteed Ros-
sini a lifetime salary in
return for works composed
for the Paris Opera. He
wrote *William Tell* under
this arrangement, but one
year later stopped composing operas. The French
revolution of July 1830
dethroned the king and
made invalid Rossini's contract with the French
government. He continued
to compose numerous piano
pieces and instrumental
works, but never made
clear his motivation to cease
opera composition.

Other tenor types include the *dramatic,* who has a powerful quality preferred by some composers, and the *heroic (heldentenor),* called for in some German operas, especially those by Richard Wagner. The heldentenor voice combines ringing high notes with the depth of the lower baritonal range, thus lending it a particularly imposing quality.

DRAMATIC
HELDENTENOR

Baritone

Baritones, in the vocal range between tenor and bass, rarely play the lead, but they may be cast as a companion to the hero or as a villain. Listen to Franz Schubert's "Who is Sylvia?" *(listening selections).* The singer and piano salute Sylvia in this lied, the text of which is taken from Shakespeare's *Two Gentlemen of Verona.* There are three verses, alike musically except for dynamic shadings. The words change for each verse (strophe). The voice in this case is mezzo-soprano.

Selection no. 42

Unlike opera, in which the role usually determines whether a male or female voice is used, lieder allows some interchangeability of performer. If the lied tells a story, the narrator (singer) may be either male or female. However, if the text suggests a man singing about a woman, as here, logic suggests that a male voice, baritone normally used, be the performing instrument. This listening example is thus an exception to convention.

1. Was ist Sylvia, saget an,
     dass sie die weite Flur preist?
   Schön und zart seh' ich sie nah'n,
     auf Himmels Gunst und Spur weis't.
   dass ihr Alles unterthan,
   dass ihr Alles unterthan.

2. Ist sie schön und gut dazu?
     Reiz labt wie milde Kindheit;
   ihrem Aug' eilt Amor zu,
     dort heilt er seine Blindheit,
   und verweilt in süsser Ruh',
   und verweilt in süsser Ruh'.

3. Darum Sylvia tön', o Sang,
     der holden Sylvia Ehren!
   Jeden Reiz besiegt sie lang,
     den Erde kann gewähren:
   Kränze ihr und Saitenklang,
   Kränze ihr und Saitenklang.

1. Who is Silvia, what is she,
     That all our swains commend her?
   Holy fair, and wise is she;
     The heavens such grace did lend her,
   That she might admired be.

2. Is she kind as she is fair?
     For beauty lives with kindness.
   Love doth to her eyes repair
     To help him of his blindness,
   And, being helped, inhabits there.

3. Then to Silvia let us sing,
     That Silvia is excelling;
   She excels each mortal thing
     Upon the dull earth dwelling;
   To her let us garlands bring.

Bass

Bass roles are parallel to those assigned to the contralto, mature characters such as a god or father. Although the bass voice can provide authority, it is sometimes used as a vehicle for comedy as well. Listen to Mozart's "Madamina, Il Catalogo" (*listening selections*), a humorous aria from the opera *Don Giovanni* (1787). Don Giovanni's servant, Leoporello (bass), tells Donna Elvira, a woman jilted by the Don, that she was neither his first nor his last romantic conquest. There have been many—"one thousand and three in Spain." He then proceeds to enumerate the conquests listed in his catalogue. Preceding the aria is a short musical section called a *recitative*, the equivalent of dialogue or conversation in a play. Most of the physical action in opera takes place during the recitative. During the arias, action ceases, or at least lessens, and the emphasis is upon the music.

Selection no. 43

RECITATIVE

LEPORELLO

Eh, consolatevi!	Oh, console yourself!
Non siete voi, non foste e non	You aren't, weren't and won't be
sarete nè la prima, nè l'ultima.	either the first or the last.
Guardate questo non picciol libro;	Look at this book which isn't exactly
	small; it's all full up
è tutto pieno	
dei nomi di sue belle.	with the names of his lady-loves.
Ogni villa, ogni borgo, ogni paese	Every village, town and country
è testimon di sue donne che	is witness to the women whose
imprese.	conquest he's undertaken.

recitative (not heard)

0

aria

Madamina, il catalogo è questo	Pretty lady, this is the catalogue
delle belle, che amò il padron mio;	of the fair ladies my master has loved;
un catalogo egli è, che ho fatto io.	it's a catalogue I made myself.
Osservate, leggete con me.	Mark well, read with me.
In Italia seicento e quaranta,	In Italy six hundred and forty,
in Almagna duecento e trentuna,	in Germany two hundred and thirty-one,
cento in Francia, in Turchia novantuna,	a hundred in France, in Turkey ninety-one,
ma in Ispagna son già mille e tre!	but in Spain there are already one thousand and three!
V'han fra queste contadine,	Amongst them there are peasant girls,
cameriere, cittadine,	chambermaids, townswomen;
v'han contesse, baronesse,	there are countesses, baronesses,
marchesine, principesse,	marchionesses, princesses,
e v'han donne d'ogni grado,	and women of every degree,
d'ogni forma, d'ogni età.	

In Italia seicento e quaranta, *ecc.*
Nella bionda egli ha l'usanza
di lodar la gentilezza;
nella bruna la costanza;
nella bianca la dolcezza;
vuol d'inverno la grassotta,
vuol d'estate la magrotta;
è la grande maestosa,
la piccina è ognor vezzosa;
delle vecchie fa conquista
pel piacer di porle in lista.

Sua passion predominante

è la giovin principiante.
Non, si picca se sia ricca,
se sia brutta, se sia bella;
se sia ricca, brutta,
se sia bella;
purchè porti la gonnella,
voi sapete quel che fa! *ecc.*

every shape and every age!
In Italy six hundred and forty, *etc.*
In the blonde he is accustomed
to praise her kindness;
in the brunette her constancy;
in the white-haired her sweetness;
in winter he wants a plump one,
in summer a slim one;
the tall one is stately,
the small one is always charming;
he makes a conquest of the old
    ones for
the pleasure of adding them to the
    list.
His dominant passion
is the young beginner.
He doesn't care a fig if she's rich,
if she's ugly or if she's pretty,
if she's rich, ugly or pretty;
so long as she wears a skirt,
you know very well what he does!
    etc.

5:41

Photo by James Hefferman. Courtesy of the Metropolitan Opera Association.

The Catalog Aria from Mozart's *Don Giovanni*. Gabriel Bacquier as Leporello and Julia Varady as Donna Elvira.

Wolfgang Amadeus Mozart (1756–1791) was a prolific composer of both instrumental and vocal music. Able to work out musical designs in his mind more quickly than he could write them on paper, Mozart learned musical composition and theory from his father and at age seven began to write symphonies. Legends of his extraordinary musical talents spread, fueled by stories of his ability to improvise entire musical scores from a simple melody or musical idea. Playing clavier, organ, and violin, Mozart concertized throughout Europe between 1761 and 1770. Great Italian musicians frequently tested him. In 1781 Mozart moved from Salzburg to Vienna where he discovered the music of J. S. Bach and developed a healthy professional friendship with Haydn. Mozart wrote twenty-five works for the stage, varying use of both German and Italian operatic style in such masterpieces as *The Marriage of Figaro* (1786), *Don Giovanni* (1787), *Così fan Tutte* (1790), and *The Magic Flute* (1791). His works frequently develop the theme that servants may be wiser and more astute than their masters, perhaps reflecting Mozart's view of real life. He rebelled continually against authority and had a difficult time keeping steady employment as a composer because of his quarrels with superiors. This led to severe financial difficulties that aggravated his failing health.

Mozart and musicians of his time received commissions from patrons to compose music for an event or celebration, making quick composition necessary to please the employer. In 1788 alone, Mozart wrote his last three symphonies, a piano concerto, and numerous chamber pieces. A mysterious patron commissioned Mozart in the last years of his life to write a Requiem—a musical setting of the Mass for the Dead. Mozart was unable to finish the Requiem before he died at age thirty-five, seemingly from an acute kidney inflammation. Rumors of his cause of death soon spread, some implying that Italian composer Antonio Salieri poisoned Mozart out of professional jealousy. The tale gave rise to the successful play and movie, *Amadeus*. Nearly two centuries after his death, musicians, scholars, and the general public continue to recognize the musical genius of Mozart.

Wolfgang Amadeus Mozart, age 7, at the keyboard with his sister Maria Anna and father Leopold.

Lithograph by A. Schieferdecker. Courtesy of the New York Public Library.

Photo by James Heffernan. Courtesy of the Metropolitan Opera Association.

Don Giovanni has tragic as well as comic moments. At its conclusion, for example, the wicked Don is spirited away to Hell for his
numerous sins.

INSTRUMENTAL TIMBRES

Instruments, like voices, can be differentiated by two general characteristics, range and sound quality. A third identifying trait, peculiar to
instruments, is the method by which the sound is produced. If the
vibrating source is strings, the instruments are called *chordophones*; if
wind, *aerophones*; if a membrane, such as a drum head, *membranophones*. A fourth class of instruments, called *idiophones*, produce sound
from the material of which they are made, that is, they are self-
vibrators. Some are beaten, others scraped, shaken, plucked, stamped,
or rubbed. Finally, instruments that produce or amplify sound electronically are called *electrophones*.

Chordophones

Sound is produced on a chordophone when strings are plucked, bowed, or even hit. *Chordophones* may vary in size and shape as well as in number of strings. The simplest chordophone may have one string while a complex one, like a harp, may have as many as forty-seven strings. Guitars, mandolins, balalaikas, lutes, ukuleles, violins, and sitars are all chordophones. So, too, are kotos, chengs, and samisens.

Viols. Listen to William Byrd's (1543–1623) *Fantasy in 4 Parts (listening selections)* for treble, tenor, and two bass viols.

Selection no. 44

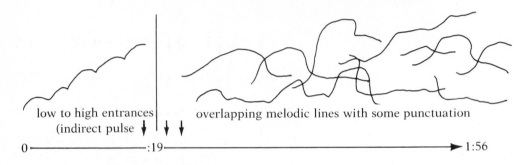

low to high entrances (indirect pulse

overlapping melodic lines with some punctuation

0 ————————:19———————————————————► 1:56

CONSORT This family *(consort)* of chordophones, called *viols,* was popular in the sixteenth and seventeenth centuries. Although viols are a forerunner of the modern violin family, they differ in several ways. Since there is less tension on their strings, their timbre is less brilliant and softer. The resulting thin and reedy tone makes them particularly suitable for compositions in which several melodies proceed at once.

FRET   Viols have six strings that pass from the main body of the instrument across a long neck, somewhat similar to a guitar, where they are then attached to tuning pegs. The neck has divisions called *frets* partitioning its length, again much like a guitar. When the performer moves his or her finger down the string (toward the main body of the instrument), the string is made shorter and each pitch produced is higher. The fret gives a precise location for raising each pitch sequentially.

All viols, treble, tenor, and bass, are played in a vertical position, resting between the performer's legs. The violin family gradually replaced the viols in the Baroque era, as composers began to prefer instruments capable of wider dynamic levels and heightened brilliance.

String Family. Violin, viola, cello, and string bass are all chordophones, known collectively as the *string family.* Although they differ in size, they all have a similar shape. All have four strings that pass over a bridge on the body of the instrument. The body is a resonating chamber that amplifies and enhances the sound. All are played most typically with a bow, but, unlike the viol, the violin and viola are played while held under the performer's chin. Only the cello and bass rest on the floor. Since there are no frets on the fingerboard, the players locate the correct point for a desired pitch by both touch and keen listening. To learn this skill takes many years of practice.

The *violin*, the soprano of the string family, has the highest range. Although the *viola, cello,* and *bass* are equivalent to alto, tenor, and bass, respectively, there is more overlap in the string family than with human voices because each instrument has such a wide range. In addition, each instrument has its own characteristic sound. The violin is brilliant while the viola has a darker, rich quality. The cello, like a tenor voice, also has a bright quality while the bass is low and dark.

All members of the string family may be played with or without the bow and are capable of numerous effects. When the bow is drawn across the strings near the bridge, harsh high overtones are produced, an effect called *sul ponticello.* The wood of the bow can be drawn or hit against the string, a technique called *col legno.* When two strings are sounded together, it is called a *double stop*; multiple stops using three or all four strings are also possible. A special device called a *mute* is placed over the bridge to restrict some overtones, producing a "glassy" effect. The performer can also pluck the strings, a technique called *pizzicato.* This may be done with either the right or left hand.

VIOLIN
VIOLA
CELLO
BASS

SUL PONTICELLO
COL LEGNO
DOUBLE STOP
MUTE

PIZZICATO

Photo by Tim Fuller.

The violin is most frequently played with a bow. The neck of the instrument does not have frets, so the performer not only must place his/her fingers in the correct position, but must listen and adjust each pitch slightly to be in tune.

Listen to Menuetto: Allegro ma non troppo: Trio from Haydn's Quartet in d minor, op. 76, no. 2 *(Quinten) (listening selections)* (nick-named the *Quinten* because Haydn uses the interval of a fifth in the first-movement melody). Haydn did much to establish the string quartet as a musical genre or category. He standardized the four-movement scheme, using a three-part or ternary form, ABA, in this case, in the third movement. The A section of this movement is similar to a round, with the cello and viola imitating the violins. The B section with its steady beat has a peasant-dance flavor, and is followed by a brief repetition of the A section.

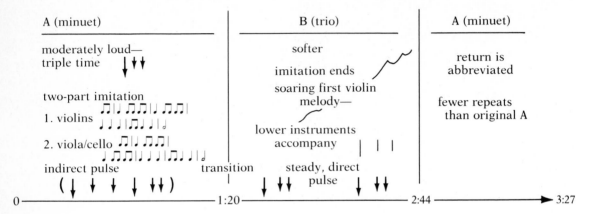

Concert Harp and Guitar.   The following chordophones are some-times used in the symphony orchestra but are not part of what is usually thought of as the string family. The *concert harp* is a string instrument with forty-six or forty-seven strings, characteristically with seven pedals at the base that are used to alter the pitches of the strings. Since each pedal both raises and lowers the pitch of a specific set of strings (e.g., all C strings), such a harp is said to have a *double action*.

The harp may be plucked or strummed by the performer's hands. A common technique is the *glissando*, a cascade of pitches produced by strumming all the strings in rapid succession.

The *guitar* is also a popular chordophone, occasionally used in the orchestra, but more commonly employed to accompany singing or to play solo pieces. Acoustic guitars, in both folk and classical styles, are those in which the body amplifies or resonates the sound. The guitar usually is fretted and has six strings, enabling it to encompass a wide range of pitches as well as harmonies.

Aerophones

Aerophones are wind instruments, producing sound when the column of air inside them is set into vibration by the action of someone

Modern concert harp
with 47 strings. It
stands 74″ high and
its longest string
is 62″.

Courtesy of Lyon and Healy.

Classical (Spanish)
guitar.

Courtesy of Yamaha International Corporation.

Franz Joseph Haydn (1732–1809) was born in Austria and as a young child was educated by his uncle. He began his musical career as a boy soprano in Vienna's St. Stephen's Cathedral, but was dismissed when his voice began to change during puberty. Turning to keyboard music composition and tutoring, Haydn observed the Classical music practice and techniques heard around him, and largely taught himself composition, theory, and counterpoint.

In 1761 Haydn was appointed as court musician to the Esterházy family, a royal clan that generously supported the arts. His patrons, Prince Paul Anton Esterházy and Prince Nikolaus Esterházy, required Haydn to provide daily chamber concerts, weekly operas, and orchestral works. The palace at Esterház offered Haydn access to resident musicians, instruments, and a library that fostered his musical productivity. While in the family's service Haydn composed most of his 83 string quartets, 80 of his 104 symphonies, numerous keyboard works, and nearly 20 operas. His contract demanded each commissioned work be performed without delay, and stipulated that he present himself in formal dress—including white stockings and powdered wig. Haydn was not allowed to publish his compositions until years after establishing his fame in Europe. When Prince Nikolaus died in 1790, Haydn moved to Vienna and under an arrangement with an

Franz Joseph Hadyn.

Photo by Fritz Heuschkel. Courtesy of the New York Public Library.

English impresario ventured to London to compose twelve symphonies.

Haydn, sometimes described as the "father of the symphony," standardized the Classical form of composition. His freedom to experiment and innovate while at the Esterházy palace allowed him to refine and perfect the technique that influenced both Mozart and Beethoven.

blowing. Any instrument that operates on this principle is an aerophone, whether trumpet, recorder, clarinet, or shakuhachi. Some aerophones will sound when a player buzzes into a metal cup-shaped mouthpiece. The vibration of the player's compressed lips pushes air through the body of the instrument, which, in turn, amplifies the sound. These are called *brass* instruments. Sound on a *woodwind* instrument is produced in one of three ways: the player blows across a hole, as with a flute; **SINGLE REED** against a single piece of wood cane, a *single reed*, as with a clarinet; **DOUBLE REED** or through two pieces of cane, a *double reed*, as with an oboe. All aerophones, whether brass or woodwind, thus require special placement of the performer's lips, teeth, and tongue in relationship to a **EMBOUCHURE** mouthpiece. This is called the *embouchure*, and the embouchure differs for each instrument, whether cornet, flute, clarinet, or bassoon.

Brass cup-shaped mouthpieces. The larger ones are used for the lower-sounding brass instruments.

Courtesy of Yamaha International Corporation.

Recorder.   Listen to *English Te Deum* (anonymous, c. 1300) *(listening selections)*. The composition is for two tenor recorders and chime bells in *descant* (higher countermelody). The recorder, an aerophone especially popular in the late Middle Ages and Renaissance, has a beak-shaped mouthpiece and a simple fingering mechanism, one thumb hole on the back and seven finger holes in front. It is played in vertical position. The resulting tone is soft and flute-like, suitable for chamber music or solos.

Selection no. 46
DESCANT

B-flat clarinet, a single-reed instrument (top); oboe, a double-reed instrument (bottom).

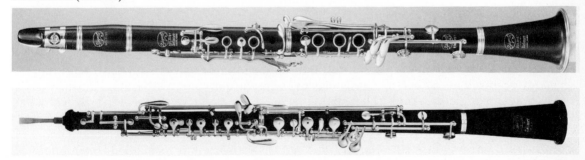

Courtesy of The Selmer Company.

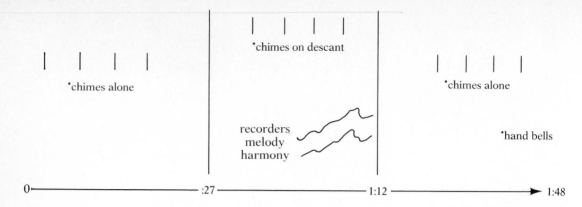

During the Renaissance recorders were used in consorts, much like the family of viols heard earlier. A consort of recorders includes descant (soprano), treble (alto), tenor, and bass. All recorders have similar patterns of fingering and each requires minute adjustment of the embouchure and breath support by the player to produce the best sound.

BROKEN CONSORT   This listening example is called a *broken consort*, since it includes instruments of different families. Broken consorts were preferred during the Middle Ages, whereas the Renaissance favored consorts of a single family.

Brass.   Brass instruments all use cup-shaped mouthpieces attached to a length of tubing that has been bent into the shape and configuration specific to each particular member of the instrumental family. The point at which the air emerges from the instrument is known as the **BELL**   *bell.* The main instruments of the brass family are the trumpet, French horn, trombone, and tuba, all of them with fairly wide ranges. The **TRUMPET**   *trumpet,* the highest and most brilliant, is used in the symphony orchestra to pierce through the layers of string sound. All brass instruments can produce a variety of pitches without the use of keys, through

No identifiable composer can be cited for many surviving compositions of earlier times. Sometimes the identity of the author is lost or the author simply remained anonymous. Medieval philosophy held that God was important above all, and service to the church was more important than earthly recognition. As a result, many composers, artists, sculptors, and architects did not sign their works. Only with the dawning of humanistic philosophy and the advent of printing and publishing during the Renaissance did individual artists begin to receive more recognition, a tendency that has prevailed throughout the last four hundred years.

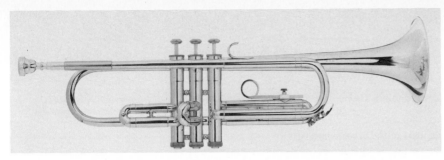

B-flat trumpet.

Courtesy of The Selmer Company.

the manipulation of lip pressure and alterations of air velocity. The trumpet additionally has three keys, or *valves*, working on a piston action, which are brought into play to achieve additional pitches. When it is depressed, each valve adds length to the tubing through which the vibrating column of air must pass. This generally lowers a pitch (or a series of pitches). Valves may be used singly or in combinations.

The bore (inner diameter) of the trumpet is cylindrical almost throughout its length, except where it flares at the bell. A *French horn* (or simply *horn*) has a conical bore, which means it widens slightly as it travels the length of the instrument.

FRENCH
HORN
BORE

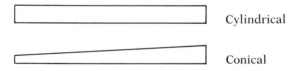

Cylindrical

Conical

This is an important distinction among brass instruments, since the shape of the bore affects timbre. Cylindrical instruments tend to have

Courtesy of The Selmer Company.

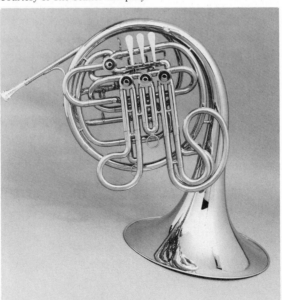

French horn (Double horn in F/B-flat) by Bach.

Trombone (top) and
three-valve tuba
(bottom).

Courtesy of The Selmer Company.

brilliance, while conical instruments are more blending. The French
horn has three rotary *valves* that perform the same pitch-altering
function as those on the trumpet. The range of the French horn is
especially wide, which allows it to serve both alto and soprano functions in the brass family.

TROMBONE   The *trombone* is a tenor brass instrument, brilliant in the upper
pitches, somber and dark in the lower. Its cylindrical bore gives its tone
sufficient edge to penetrate the many layers of string sound in the
orchestra. Since the typical trombone does not have valves, the slide
mechanism incorporated in its design enables the performer to change
pitches.

It is important to know that several different pitches can be
produced on a brass instrument with a single valve combination or a
single slide position. Which pitch is actually played depends on the

support and velocity of the performer's breathing as well as her/his skill on the instrument. Since the trombonist can adjust the position of the slide anywhere, it is easier to play small pitch intervals on this instrument than on other brass.

The tuba is the bass brass instrument. Some tubas have piston valves, like the trumpet, others have rotary valves like the French horn. The tuba frequently provides a steady beat or accompaniment but is also capable of solo work as well.

TUBA

Some orchestras include a variety of other instruments to augment the main core of brass. Trumpets, for example, are manufactured in varying sizes. The D trumpet is smaller than the standard B♭ model and is thus able to play higher. The *piccolo trumpet*, even smaller, is used to play extremely high musical passages.

PICCOLO TRUMPET

Cornets, more typically found in bands, are similar to trumpets but have a conical bore.

CORNET

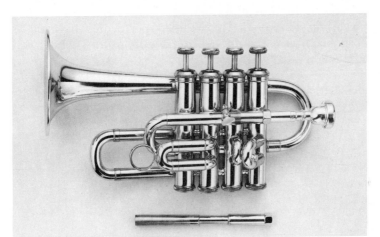

Four-valve Piccolo trumpet (with lead pipe to change from B-flat to A) by Bach.

Courtesy of The Selmer Company.

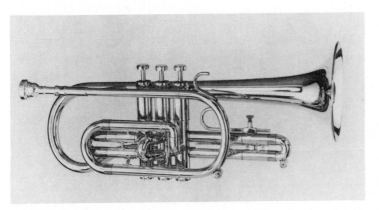

Cornet.

Courtesy of The Getzen Co., Inc.

Valve trombone.

Courtesy of The Selmer Company.

Trombones, too, are manufactured in different sizes, including alto, tenor, and bass, and thus vary in range and timbre. Some trombones are equipped with valves instead of a slide. Tubas are also made in different sizes and configurations, including the *sousaphone*, designed for marching bands. Other brass instruments include the *bugle*, which has no valves, and the *mellophone*, similar to the French horn but with piston valves.

SOUSAPHONE
BUGLE
MELLOPHONE

Selection no. 47
EUPHONIUM

Listen to Giovanni Gabrieli's *Canzon Septimi Toni no. 2* (1597) *(listening selections)*. This work is performed by four trumpets, two French horns, a trombone, and a *euphonium*, which is a small tuba, also called a baritone.

Mellophone (marching model) (left) and baritone (euphonium) upright bell model (right).

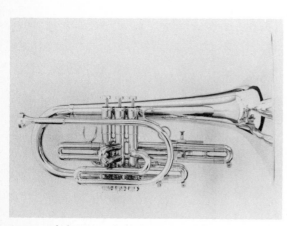

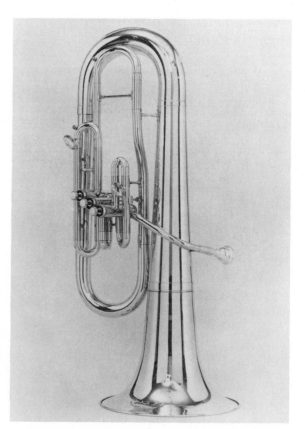

Courtesy of The Getzen Co., Inc.

The directorship of music at St. Mark's Cathedral was one of the most prestigious positions to be held in Europe during the Renaissance and Baroque periods. Because Venice supported and took much pride in its architecture, art, and music, the directorship was a coveted but exhausting position that involved composing, conducting, and performing. Among St. Mark's choirmasters were Giovanni Gabrieli (1557–1612), his uncle, Andrea Gabrieli (c. 1510–1586), Adrian Willaert (c. 1490–1562), and Gioseffo Zarlino (c. 1517–1590).

St. Mark's Cathedral, Venice, Italy, built between 1042 and 1085.

The style of *Canzon* is representative of the late Renaissance, especially of the Italian city of Venice. St. Mark's, the great cathedral of Venice, has balconies that are opposite one another. Gabrieli placed both vocal and brass choirs in these balconies and wrote music that took advantage of the architecture. Music in which two groups call and respond, as in this Canzon, is called *antiphonal*. Gabrieli's instrumental music is based on points of imitation, that is, one idea is echoed back and forth between groups, with contrast occurring through changes of dynamics and meter. This particular composition is unified by the return of the opening idea near the end (2:12).

ANTIPHONAL

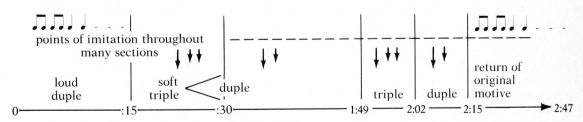

Woodwinds. Woodwind instruments seem like a diverse group but all share some common features. In general, all woodwinds are composed of a narrow tube through which the performer blows. Each has

Flute (French model)

Courtesy of Gemeinhardt.

several holes, with and without keys, along its column. The more holes that are covered, generally the lower the pitch that is produced. In contrast to brass instruments, where several pitches are possible with each valve or slide combination, woodwind instruments can usually produce only one or two pitches for each fingering.

FLUTE   The most common woodwind instruments are flute, oboe, clarinet, and bassoon. The *flute* is the highest. With a sound pattern similar to a sine wave, that is, free of overtones, the flute produces the clearest, purest tone of any instrument. Sound is produced by blowing across a
BLOW HOLE   small opening or *blow hole* in conjunction with manipulating the keys to change pitches. The flute is one of the few woodwinds held in hori-
TRANSVERSE   zontal or *transverse* position, the others being played in the vertical, forward position.

OBOE   The *oboe* is a double-reed instrument, which means the mouthpiece is made of two pieces of woodcane through which the performer expels air to cause vibrations. Its sound is complex and rich, full of overtones. It functions as either soprano or alto part in the woodwind family.

CLARINET   The *clarinet* is a single-reed instrument, with a single piece of shaved woodcane attached to a hard mouthpiece. It looks similar to the oboe but differs in timbre. Although penetrating in its top notes, it is mellow at the lower end of its tonal spectrum. The clarinet has a wide range and is one of the most versatile and popular of the woodwinds.

BASSOON   The *bassoon*, also double reed, is considerably larger than the oboe. Its added length requires the tubing to double back at the bottom of the instrument. Although the nature of its sound frequently casts it in a comic role, it is also quite capable of playing lyric and sensitive melodies. Within the woodwind family, the bassoon serves both as tenor and bass.

Bassoon.

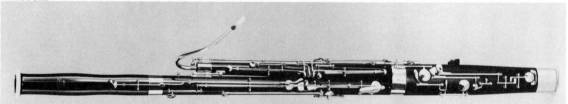

Courtesy of The Selmer Company.

Piccolo (top) being played by performer in marching band (bottom).

Like brass instruments, woodwinds are manufactured in varying sizes. The *piccolo*, a half-size flute, is used to play the highest part in most ensembles. Clarinets are made in varying sizes, too, including the small E♭ sopranino as well as lower alto and bass models. A tenor oboe is known as an *English horn*.

The *contrabassoon* is used to extend the range of woodwinds into the lowest pitches and thus requires several turns of the tubing in order to keep the fingering mechanism within the compass of the human hand. (Review Handel's "Hornpipe," which contrasts wood-winds with strings; see page 5.)

The *saxophone*, a popular single-reed instrument, fingers like other woodwind instruments, but because it is made of metal it seems like a hybrid blend of brass and woodwind instruments. Invented in the nineteenth century, it is manufactured in many sizes. Although alto and tenor saxes are heard in bands and jazz ensembles, they are less

PICCOLO

ENGLISH HORN

SAXOPHONE

English horn.

Courtesy of King Musical Instruments, Inc.

E-flat alto saxophone
(left) and B-flat
soprano saxophone
(right).

Courtesy of The Selmer Company.

frequently encountered in orchestral music. There is also the soprano
sax, which looks like a metal clarinet, as well as baritone and bass
models. All saxophones use an identical fingering system, which allows
the performer to transfer from one instrument to another with only
slight adjustments to embouchure and finger placement. In fact, all
woodwind instruments share analogous finger and music-reading systems to some extent. It is not uncommon to find a woodwind specialist
who can perform equally well on several of these instruments.

Selection no. 48   Listen to "One O'Clock Jump" performed by Count Basie and His
Orchestra *(listening selections).* Jazz musicians use the same instruments as do composers of symphonic music, with the exception of
double reeds and upper strings (although both of the latter have
appeared in jazz arrangements). This work features the saxophone
section of the Count Basie orchestra. The beat of "One O'Clock Jump"
is grouped in ♩. The repeating rhythm pattern heard under the main
RIFF   melody is called a *riff (ostinato).* Count Basie's arrangement is an
OSTINATO   example of Swing, a style of jazz popular in the 1930s. Since the
ensemble is larger than earlier jazz groups, arrangements, with the
exception of solos, were notated (written out) rather than improvised.

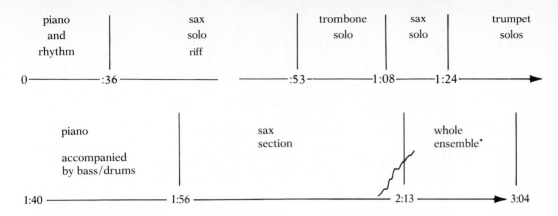

piano		sax		trombone	sax	trumpet
and		solo		solo	solo	solos
rhythm		riff				

0————————:36—————————————:53———————1:08————1:24—————————→

piano		sax		whole
		section		ensemble*
accompanied				
by bass/drums				

1:40 ————————————— 1:56 ————————————————— 2:13 ————————— 3:04

*Piano, 3 trumpets, 3 trombones, 1 alto, 2 tenor, 1 baritone sax, guitar, bass, drums.

Membranophones

The third category of instruments, which produce sound when their head or *membrane* is struck, is popularly referred to as the drum family. Although drum heads were originally made from animal hide, plastic is commonly used now. Membranophones appear in many cultures of the world, from our own bass and snare drums to the Indian tabla and the Moorish darubuka.

Within the orchestra, this class of instruments is part of the percussion section and includes *bass drum*, a double-headed membranophone, and *snare drum*, double-headed but struck on only one side, with wire "snares" placed against the opposite head to rattle

BASS DRUM
SNARE DRUM

Bass drum (left) and snare drums (right).

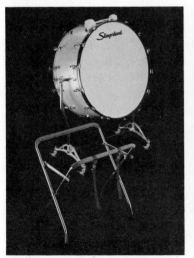

Courtesy of Slingerland Drum Co.

Timpani (top);
(bottom) conga
drums (left) and
timbales (right).

Courtesy of Slingerland Drum Co.

when the drum is struck. Snare and bass drums are called percussion

INDEFINITE PITCH instruments of *indefinite* pitch because the tone they produce is not
sustained long enough to be perceived as a distinct note.

TIMPANUM   The *timpanum*, which has a single head stretched over a kettle-
DEFINITE PITCH shaped body, is a drum with *definite* pitch. The alternate name, *ket-*
KETTLEDRUM *tledrum*, is an appropriate reference to its appearance. A mechanism
within the body or around the circumference of the rim is used to
raise or lower the pitch. Modern kettledrums have a pedal that, when
depressed, tightens the drum head and raises the pitch. Conversely,
when the pedal is released, the pitch is lowered. *Timpani* is the plural
designation for kettledrums, while timpanum means one. Some compositions may call for four or five timps, since a single timpanum can
produce only those pitches within the interval of a fifth. Each kettle
therefore has a head and body of different size, which enables the
percussionist to play numerous pitches over the entire set.

BONGO   Other membranophones include the *bongo drums, congas*, and
CONGA *timbales*, which are similar to one another in that they have a single
TIMBALES head covering a wooden shell. Bongos and congas are usually played
with the bare hand, while timbales are struck with a pair of thin sticks.
MALLET Most membranophones are struck with some type of *mallet*, stick, or
brush, each producing a different kind of sound and therefore allowing

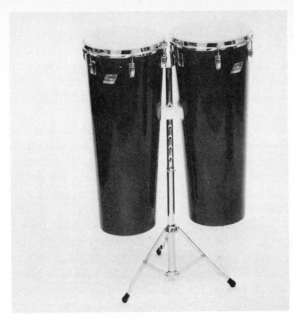

Bongo drums.

Courtesy of The Selmer Company.

the percussionist to vary the basic timbre of his or her instrument according to the implement used for striking.

Listen to *Talking Drum with Accompaniment (listening selections).* *Kalungus* are African "talking drums," a special type of membranophone shaped like an hourglass, held under the performer's arm, and often played with a curved stick. The tension of the head, and therefore the pitch, is modified by squeezing the lacing on the drum shell. Since many languages in West Africa are tonal, with the pitch of the word determining its meaning, and since vocal inflections can be imitated on the kalungu, it is called the talking drum. "Talking," of course, is a relative term, and typically these drums can communicate standard phrases and expressions only. The term *kalungu* is generic; each tribal group uses its own local appellation for the instrument.

Selection no. 49
KALUNGU

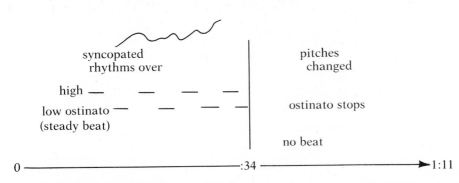

Idiophones

The fourth classification of instruments is the most diverse. Sound is produced from the instrument's own basic material when it is struck, scraped, rubbed, stamped, or shaken. Idiophones are thus self-vibrators. For this reason, *idiophones* (idio- meaning self-produced) vary greatly in appearance, size, shape, and timbre. Examples include *cymbals, castanets, tubular chimes, wood blocks, gongs,* and *temple blocks,* all of which are in the orchestral percussion family. Others include the *tambourine, triangle, guiro,* a wooden instrument scraped with a stick along its notched back, *maracas,* a fancy type of rattle, and *claves,* a pair of wooden sticks that are struck together. Idiophones used in the orchestra are normally made of wood or metal, but some from other cultures are made of stone.

GLOCKENSPIEL
CELESTA

Like membranophones, idiophones may have definite or indefinite pitch. Among those of definite pitch are the *tubular chimes* and the *glockenspiel* (orchestral bells), both of which are played with mallets (or padded hammers). The *celesta* is a glockenspiel with a keyboard and looks like a diminutive piano. The mechanism strikes the metal bar in the enclosed case when a key is depressed, allowing the performer to play melodies that would be impossible with two mallets.

Some idiophones of definite pitch are made of wood. The *xylophone* is such an instrument, as is the *marimba,* which has a separate tubular resonator for each wooden bar or key. The timbre of the xylophone is brittle, that of the marimba, mellow.

The percussion section of an orchestra typically includes many membranophones and idiophones, requiring several performers to play them. Unlike the one person/one instrument rule prevalent in other sections of the orchestra, each percussionist may be responsible for playing several instruments.

Selection no. 50

Listen to Edgard Varèse's *Ionisation (listening selections).* Varèse had a penchant for using brass, woodwinds, and especially percussion in, at least for his time, unusual ways. *Ionisation,* written in 1931, is "organized sound" using percussion instruments only. The work is performed by thirteen percussionists, each of whom is responsible for playing two or three instruments:

NOMENCLATURE OF INSTRUMENTS FOR THE THIRTEEN PERFORMERS

1. Crash, cymbals, bass drum (very deep)
2. Gong, tam-tam (high), tam-tam (low)
3. Two bongos, side-drum, two bass drums (medium size and large) laid flat
4. Tambour militaire, side-drum
5. Siren (high), string-drum
6. Siren (low), slapstick, guiro
7. Chinese blocks (high, middle register, and low), claves, triangle

Courtesy of Slingerland Drum Co.

Orchestral bells (glockenspiel) (left), xylophone (top right), and marimba (bottom right).

8. Snare-drum (with snares relaxed), maracas (high and low)

9. Tarole, snare-drum, suspended cymbal

10. Cymbals, sleigh bells, and later tubular chimes

11. Güiro, castagnettes, and later celesta

12. Tambourine, anvila (high and low), and later grand tam-tam (very deep)

13. Slapstick, triangle, sleigh-bells, and later piano

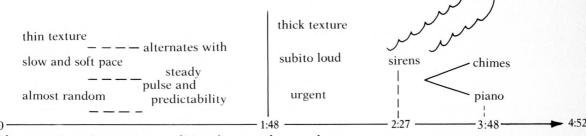

The score is written using traditional note values and meters.

29. EDGARD VARÈSE (1883-1965), *Ionisation* (1931)

Edgard Varèse as a young composer.

Courtesy of the New York Public Library.

Edgard Varèse (1883–1965) was born in Paris, lived in Berlin during his early years as a composer, then settled in New York City in 1915. Introducing new ways to organize and perform music, he profoundly influenced the direction of twentieth-century composition. He was trained as an engineer but became a composer, bringing with him fresh, scientific focus to the field of music. Varèse explored new sound resources in his music, varying combinations of timbre and expanding the traditional sounds a single instrument could produce. He considered tone quality more important than melody and harmony, and the arrangement of the notes in a chord more important than traditional form. Through his use of rhythm and quality of tone, his works generate their own design. Instead of developing a musical theme, as is done in conventional forms of composition, Varèse used contrasting blocks of sound to determine the course of his work. The sounds themselves, coherent and of varying quality, became most important.

Varèse was one of the earliest composers to embrace electronic composition after World War II, especially in *Déserts* (1949–1954), which combines tape sounds with live performance of wind instruments, and in *Poème Électronique* (1957–1958), which was created entirely on magnetic tape and commissioned for the Brussels World's Fair. Although his music was poorly received when initially performed, Varèse lived to see the recognition of his work as masterful and instrumental to the development of modern music.

Although *Ionisation* is not program music, it conveys the flavor of urban civilization, of technology and machines, largely through the use of idiophones and membranophones.

Keyboard Instruments

Some instruments are hybrids that do not fit clearly into other categories. The *piano* is such an instrument. Although it is a chor- PIANO dophone, it is typically found in the percussion section of the orchestra, not with the string family, since its strings are hit by felt hammers inside the instrument, actuated by the keyboard. Pianos usually have eighty-eight keys. For the higher pitches, one hammer will hit two or three strings when the key is struck. Only on the lowest pitches is a single string set into vibration by the action of the key. The *harpsichord* HARPSICHORD

Grand piano (top)
and electronic organ
(bottom).

Courtesy of Kimball International.

is a special chordophone, too, in which the strings are plucked, rather than struck, as described in Chapter Three.

Organs, beyond being keyboard instruments, almost defy classification. Electronic organs generate sound through electronic impulses, but pipe organs are a type of aerophone. When a key is depressed, air is released into a pipe, causing the vibrations that produce sound. For each special timbre on an organ, one pipe is needed for each key. This special set of pipes (timbre) is called a *rank* and an organ may have several ranks. If the organ has sixty-one keys and twenty ranks, this results in 1220 (61 × 20) pipes, since each pipe usually makes only one sound. Each rank is actuated by a *stop*, a device that lets air from the reservoir flow into that particular set of pipes when a key is depressed. "Pulling out all the stops" literally means to play using all the pipes.

ORGAN

RANK

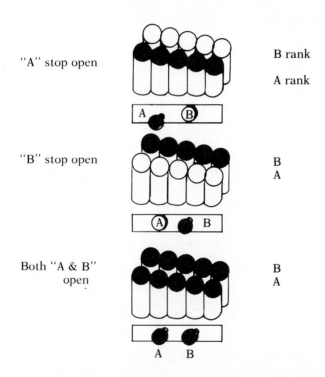

Listen to J. S. Bach's *Schübler Chorale* no. 1 S. 645 *(listening selections)*. Written by Bach in 1746, this composition is almost like a symphonic piece for the organ. An example of a type of work called a chorale prelude, it is based on a *chorale*, a hymn tune sung by the entire congregation in Protestant churches. In the seventeenth and eighteenth centuries, to prepare the worshippers and remind them of what they were to sing, the organist typically improvised a *chorale*

Selection no. 51

CHORALE

CHORALE
PRELUDE

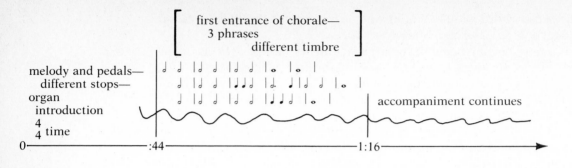

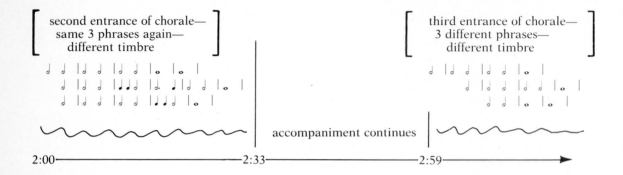

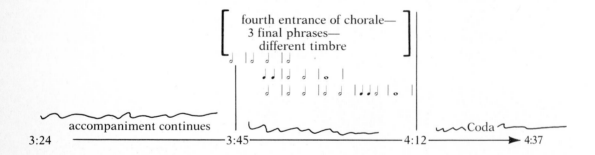

fourth entrance of chorale—
3 final phrases—
different timbre

accompaniment continues

3:24   3:45   4:12   Coda   4:37

prelude, weaving in fragments of the chorale melody to follow. These improvisations were later written down. In this example, the chorale tune is clearly distinguished from the other melodies on the organ by the use of contrasting timbres, each timbre produced on a different set of pipes or rank.

In Bach's time, organs usually had two keyboards, a set of pedals, as well as between twelve and thirty-five stops. This enabled the organist to play each line with clear and distinct timbres, as in this chorale prelude.

Top, left to right: electric bass and electric guitar; bottom, left to right: amplibass marimba and digital synthesizer.

Courtesy of Yamaha International Corporation.

Electrophones

Electrophones are the newest class of instruments. In reality, there are few purely electronic instruments. Electronic organs produce sound by the action of oscillators, each of which is programmed to produce a given sound. These sounds can be combined, as on a pipe organ. The **SYNTHESIZER** *synthesizer* is also an electrophone that both produces and modifies sound. It enables composers either to create new timbres or to try to duplicate those of acoustic instruments. Finally, many conventional acoustic instruments may be connected to contact-mikes to produce innovative timbres electronically. Listen to John McLaughlin's "Open Country **Selection no. 52** Joy," played by the Mahavishnu Orchestra *(listening selections)*. Jazz musicians have incorporated electronic sounds since the early 1950s. **FUSION JAZZ** This particular composition is an example of *fusion jazz,* a type that draws on other styles of music for inspiration (in this case, country-western) and uses it for improvisation. Fusion music, which has been popular since the 1970s, has included sources derived from rock and even Eastern-based music, like Indian ragas.

The instruments here are guitar, bass, percussion, violin, electronic keyboard, and Moog (synthesizer), an interesting blend of acoustic and electronic sounds.

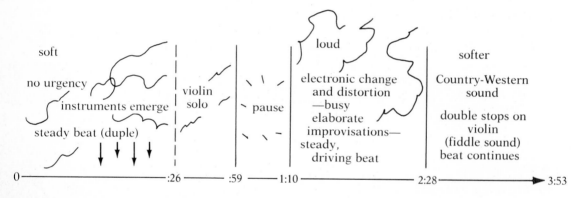

Symphony orchestra, arranged as shown on p. 137.

Photo by Tim Fuller.

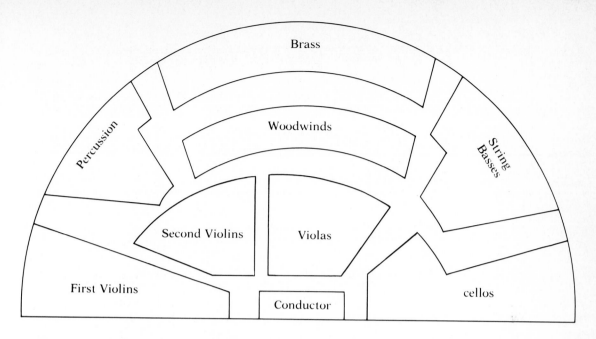

Placement of Instruments in the Orchestra

Although conductors may differ slightly in their placement of the strings, woodwinds, brass, and percussion in the orchestra on stage, the string family is generally close to the conductor, on either side and in back of the podium, while woodwinds are usually placed midstage, with the brass and percussion at the back. This traditional arrangement undoubtedly helps achieve optimal blending of the timbres for both performers and audience.

SCORE ORDER AND TRANSPOSITION

The arrangement of instrument parts in a written score for orchestra is fairly standardized. The piccolo part is the highest and appears at the top of the written score. The remainder of the woodwind family follows, high to low, including flute, oboe, clarinet, and bassoon. The next area is brass, arranged high to low, followed by the percussion section and the string family, which is on the bottom of each page. If there is a solo instrument, its part is printed between the percussion and string section.

SCORE ORDER

Instrumental parts on the full score (p. 138) are identical to the lines performers read. Instruments are typically pitched in a given key or fundamental by tradition. Some instruments are pitched to sound an F, E♭, B♭, or A as their fundamental, most natural pitch. The fundamen-

tal key, however, has traditionally been *written* in C, a key without sharps and flats, since this is the easiest to read. When a B♭ trumpet plays C, it sounds a concert (actual) B♭. When the E♭ alto sax plays a written C, it sounds concert E♭. Instruments such as these are called *transposing* and include:

Clarinet (B♭ or A, sometimes E♭)
Trumpet (B♭ or D)
French horn (F or B♭)
Saxophone (B♭ or E♭)
Tuba (B♭ or E♭)

Many instruments are non-transposing, that is, when they play their C, it also sounds a concert C. This includes the string family, flute, oboe, bassoon, trombone, harp, and all keyboard instruments. Although transpositions are given in the full score, they do not affect the listener. Other than the occasional notation on a program that a piece is for the D trumpet or the clarinet in A, the average listener cannot tell whether the instrument is transposing or non-transposing.

NON-TRANSPOSING

Listen to Dies Irae and Tuba Mirum from Verdi's *Requiem (listening selections)*. This masterpiece brings together the timbres found in orchestra and chorus. A *requiem* is a Mass for the Dead. Verdi composed this particular piece to honor Allesandro Manzoni, an Italian patriot and writer whom he deeply admired. The sections usually found in a Mass are substituted in the requiem with texts concerning death and salvation.

Selection no. 53

REQUIEM

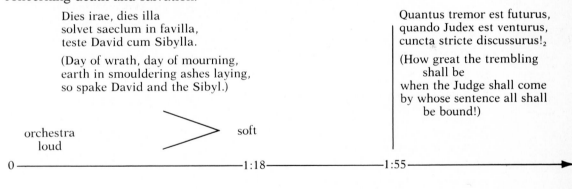

Dies irae, dies illa
solvet saeclum in favilla,
teste David cum Sibylla.

(Day of wrath, day of mourning,
earth in smouldering ashes laying,
so spake David and the Sibyl.)

Quantus tremor est futurus,
quando Judex est venturus,
cuncta stricte discussurus!₂

(How great the trembling
    shall be
when the Judge shall come
by whose sentence all shall
    be bound!)

orchestra
loud   soft

0 ——————————————1:18———————1:55———————————→

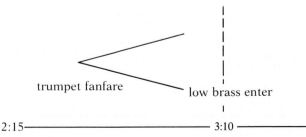

Tuba mirum spargens sonum,
per sepulchra regionum,
coget omnes ante thronum.₃

(The trumpet, sending its
    wondrous sound
through the tombs in every land,
shall bring all before the throne.)

trumpet fanfare   low brass enter

2:15———————————————— 3:10 ———————— 3:28 ——————————→ 4:36

TIMBRE AND STYLE PERIODS

The instruments available and the ways in which composers have used them have varied widely in the past 500 years. A brief outline of timbre in historical periods may help clarify these changes.

Period	Timbre	Examples
Medieval (before 1450)	Contrasting, bright sounds	English—*Te Deum*
Renaissance	Vocal timbres predominate. A cappella (unaccompanied) is the sound ideal for Catholic church music. Instruments are used for accompaniment, especially viols, recorders and organs. The sound ideal is a blend—one family or consort of instruments. Broken consorts are less common.	des Prez—*Sanctus* Byrd—*Fantasy* Gabrieli—*Canzon Septimi Toni no. 2*
Baroque	Both instrumental and vocal timbres are used. Contrast and brilliance are preferred. The modern violin family appears. Oboes, bassoons, trumpets, and harpsichord continuo are prevalent.	Quantz—Trio in C (Larghetto) Handel—"O Thou That Tellest" Bach—*Schübler Chorale*
Classical	The modern symphony evolves. Families of blended instruments are preferred, with strings and woodwinds most important, brass and percussion less important. The piano develops. A blended, homogeneous sound is favored.	Rossini—"Ecco Ridente" Mozart—"Madamina, il catalogo" Queen of the Night's Aria Haydn—Minuet/Trio Quartet in D, op. 76, no. 2
Romantic	The orchestra becomes larger and richer—more brilliant, providing much contrast. Special instruments such as the English horn and contrabassoon are used. Brass, especially trumpet and horn, become important because of the development of the valve mechanism, which gives them solo capability. Solo instruments become important in a virtuoso capacity, especially the violin and piano.	Schubert—*Who is Sylvia?* Puccini—"Un Bel Di" Bizet—*Habanera* Verdi—Dies Irae, Tuba Mirum
Impressionism	All instruments are available but transparency and clarity seem preferred ideals. Composers write subtle effects. Emphasis is on woodwind color and delicacy. The piano is important as a solo instrument.	
Twentieth Century	All timbres are used with more experimentation and exploration of their sound resources. Electronic instruments and the synthesizer become important after 1950. Tape manipulation of traditional timbres is common, as are percussive effects of all instruments.	Varèse—*Ionisation* McLaughlin—"Open Country Joy"

See also selections in Chapter 3, page 81.

Giuseppe Verdi (1813–1901) was renowned in his lifetime for opera composition. Born in Roncole, he studied in Milan where his earliest operas later premiered in the famous opera house, La Scala. Verdi eventually composed twenty-six operas, many of which remain masterworks of the repertoire, including *Rigoletto* (1851), *Il Trovatore* (1853), *La Traviata* (1853), *Un Ballo in Maschera* (1859), *Aida* (1871), *Otello* (1887), and *Falstaff* (1893).

The death of Italian poet Allesandro Manzoni

Giuseppe Verdi.

Lithograph by C. Debleis. Courtesy of the New York Public Library.

prompted Verdi to compose the *Requiem*. It was first performed in 1874 in the Church of San Marcos of Milan, using four soloists, an orchestra of nearly 100, and 120 chorus members. The work is gigantic in scope and uses particularly rich vocal and orchestral timbres to convey its fateful message. Although Verdi's fame rests on his operas, the *Requiem* also shows the underlying penchant for drama that characterized all of his musical works. When he died, the entire country mourned him and, not surprisingly, his *Requiem* was performed.

SUMMARY

Understanding of timbre is basic in learning music appreciation. Vocal timbres are designated as soprano, alto, tenor, and bass, with specialty voice-types occurring in each of these, such as the coloratura soprano or lyric tenor. Like color in the visual world, aural color or timbre provides a multitude of sounds to set moods and express feelings in music. All instrumental timbres can be classified as chordophone, aerophone, membranophone, idiophone, or electrophone. There are composite timbres provided by large groups, including the symphony orchestra and choirs. Chamber music is designated by the number of performers, such as duet, trio, quartet, and larger ensembles. The timbres of the symphony orchestra are grouped into four families: strings, woodwinds, brass, and percussion.

STUDY GUIDELINES

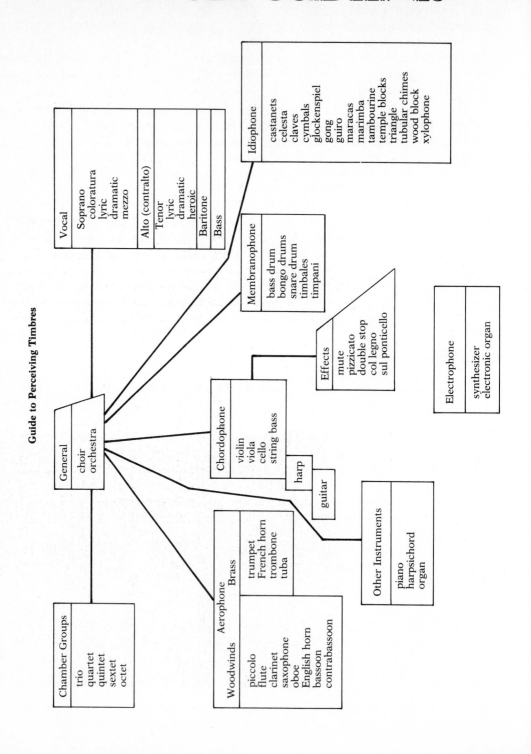

Guide to Perceiving Timbres

General
choir
orchestra

Vocal

Soprano
coloratura
lyric
dramatic
mezzo

Alto (contralto)

Tenor
lyric
dramatic
heroic

Baritone

Bass

Idiophone
castanets
celesta
claves
cymbals
glockenspiel
gong
guiro
maracas
marimba
tambourine
temple blocks
triangle
tubular chimes
wood block
xylophone

Membranophone
bass drum
bongo drums
snare drum
timbales
timpani

Effects
mute
pizzicato
double stop
col legno
sul ponticello

Chordophone
violin
viola
cello
string bass

harp

guitar

Electrophone
synthesizer
electronic organ

Other Instruments
piano
harpsichord
organ

Aerophone

Brass
trumpet
French horn
trombone
tuba

Woodwinds
piccolo
flute
clarinet
saxophone
oboe
English horn
bassoon
contrabassoon

Chamber Groups
trio
quartet
quintet
sextet
octet

KEY TERMS AND CONCEPTS

A cappella
Aerophone
  Brass family
    French horn
    Trombone
    Trumpet
    Tuba
  Woodwind family
    Bassoon
    Clarinet
    Flute
    Oboe
    Saxophone
Aria
Broken consort
Chamber groups
  Octet
  Quartet
  Quintet
  Sextet
  Trio
Choir
Chordophone
  String family
    Cello
    String bass
    Viola
    Violin
Concert harp
Consort
Definite pitch
Electrophone
  Synthesizer
Embouchure
Euphonium (baritone)
Guitar
Harpsichord

Idiophone
  Celesta
  Cymbals
  Gong
  Marimba
  Xylophone
Indefinite pitch
Membranophone
  Bass drum
  Snare drum
  Timpani
Organ
Overtones (partial vibrations)
Piano
Rank
Recitative
Recorder
Requiem
Sankyoku
Score order
Sine wave
Symphony orchestra
Timbre
Trio sonata
Viol
Vocal timbre
  Alto (contralto)
  Baritone
  Bass
  Soprano
    coloratura
    dramatic
    lyric
    mezzo
  Tenor
    dramatic
    heroic (heldentenor)
    lyric

EXERCISES

1. Listen to a classical music radio station for one hour.
    a. Name each composition you hear.
    b. Categorize it as orchestra, chamber group, or choir.

    c. If you hear a chamber group, try to identify specifically the number of players and type of group.

    d. Identify by name predominant solo timbres you hear in the foreground.

        (Use page 142 as a guide for listening)

2. Listen to a recording of an act from an opera *without* reading about it first. Try to determine the voice types and the role you think each is playing. After thirty minutes, check your impressions against what you find written on the record jacket. Listen again.

3. Classify the voices of ten friends as soprano, alto, tenor, or bass according to their speaking voices. Check with each to see if they know their vocal type.

4. List ten singers, pop, rock, jazz, opera, etc., and listen to a recording of each, classifying each by voice type. Which has the greatest range? Which has the widest emotional expression? Why?

5. Find a picture book of instruments of the world. Classify them as chordophone, aerophone, membranophone, idiophone, or electrophone. If you find aerophones, try to determine which way air is set into vibration. If you find membranophones or idiophones, try to classify them as instruments of definite or indefinite pitch.

6. Listen to a classical record with many short selections. On the first hearing, identify by name the predominant timbres in the foreground for each selection. On a second hearing, concentrate on the timbres in the background, again identifying them, when possible, by name. What do you notice? What effect does the timbre have on the feeling and mood of the music? (Use page 142 as a guide.)

	First hearing (Foreground)	Second hearing (Background)
Selection One		
Selection Two		
Selection Three		

7. List timbres you would consider happy. List timbres you would consider sad. What other adjectives can be used to describe timbres? Find recordings that prove your point.

8. Choose a favorite piece of art music and listen to it several times until you have completed the chart. (See pages 62, 83, and 142 for help.)

   Name of work _____

┌──── Timbre ────┐		Dynamics	┌──────── Rhythm ────────┐				
Foreground	Background		Tempo	Beat/ no-beat	Direct/ Indirect beat	Deviations from the beat	Accent groups (meter)

CHAPTER REVIEW

Match items in the two columns. Each blank has only one correct answer. Answers in Appendix.

1. _____ embouchure
2. _____ coloratura soprano
3. _____ lyric soprano
4. _____ mezzo soprano
5. _____ string quartet
6. _____ brass quartet
7. _____ pizzicato
8. _____ score order
9. _____ consort
10. _____ rank
11. _____ antiphonal
12. _____ aria
13. _____ recitative
14. _____ euphonium
15. _____ electrophone
16. _____ partial vibration
17. _____ octet
18. _____ quintet
19. _____ sine wave

A. Carmen
B. plucked
C. call-response
D. woodwinds, brass, percussion, strings
E. family of like instruments
F. position of mouth, teeth, and tongue
G. five players
H. small tuba (baritone)
I. two violins, viola, cello
J. sings floridly in high register
K. overtone
L. two trumpets, French horn, trombone
M. synthesizer
N. Madame Butterfly
O. eight players
P. sound wave without overtones
Q. set of organ pipes
R. emphasizes music more than words
S. emphasizes words more than music

FOR FURTHER LISTENING

Brass
French Horn

Mozart	Concerto in D major for Horn and Orchestra, K. 412
Tchaikovsky	Symphony no. 5 in e minor (second movement)

Trombone

Hindemith	Sonata for Trombone and Piano

Trumpet
Bach	*Brandenburg Concerto* no. 2 in F major (piccolo trumpet)
Hindemith	Sonata for Trumpet and Piano

Tuba
Berlioz	*Symphonie Fantastique* (Fifth movement, Dies Irae)
Moussorgsky	*Pictures at an Exhibition:* "The Ox Cart" (In Ravel's orchestral transcription)

Harpsichord
Falla	Concerto for Harpsichord and Orchestra
Martin	Concerto for Harpsichord and Small Orchestra
Scarlatti, D.	Harpsichord Sonatas*

Organ
Bach	Orgelbüchlein
Franck	Chorale no. 3 in a minor

Percussion
Antheil	*Ballet Mécanique*
Chávez	Toccata for Percussion
Milhaud	Concerto for Percussion and Small Orchestra
Roussel	Concerto for Eight Percussion Instruments

Piano
Beethoven	Sonata no. 12 in A$^\flat$ major Sonata no. 23 in f minor
Chopin	Etudes Polonaises Sonata no. 2 in b$^\flat$ minor, op. 35
Debussy	*Children's Corner* Suite

Strings
Cello
Bach	Suite no. 5 in c minor for unaccompanied cello
Barber	Concerto for Cello and Orchestra
Bloch	*Schelomo*

*Also recorded on piano.

Fauré	*Elégie* for Cello and Orchestra
Haydn	Cello Concerto in C major
Saint-Saëns	*Carnival of the Animals:* "The Swan"
Shostakovitch	Sonata for Cello and Piano
Tchaikovsky	*Variations on a Rococo Theme*

String Bass

Dragonetti	Concerto for Double Bass with Piano
Koussevitsky	Double Bass Concerto
Saint-Saëns	*Carnival of the Animals:* "The Elephant"

Viola

Bartók	Concerto for Viola and Orchestra
Bloch	*Jewish Pieces* for Viola and Piano

Violin

Bach	Partitas for solo violin
Bartók	Sonata for Unaccompanied Violin
Beethoven	Violin Concerto in D major
Berg	Violin Concerto
Brahms	Violin Concerto in D major
Mendelssohn	Concerto in e minor for Violin and Orchestra

Harp

Fauré	*Impromptu* for Harp Solo
Ravel	*Introduction and Allegro* for Harp and Strings

Voices: *Combined*

Bach	Cantata no. 140, *Wachet auf, ruft uns die Stimme*
Beethoven	Symphony no. 9 in d minor (fourth movement)
Brahms	*Ein deutsches Requiem*
Fauré	*Requiem*
Handel	*Messiah* (choruses)
Verdi	*Requiem*

Voices: *Solo*
Alto *(contralto)*

Handel	*Messiah:* "Then shall the eyes of the blind" "He shall feed His flock"
Ponchielli	*La Gioconda:* "Voce di donna"
Wagner	*Das Rheingold:* "Weiche Wotan"

Baritone
Bizet	*Carmen:* "Toréador en garde"
Gounod	*Faust:* "Avant de quitter ces lieux"
Handel	*Semele:* "Where e'er you walk"
Rossini	*The Barber of Seville:* "Largo al factotum"

Bass
Gounod	*Faust:* "Mephisto's Serenade"; "Le Veau d'or"
Mozart	*The Magic Flute:* "O Isis und Osiris"
	The Marriage of Figaro: "La vendetta"
Verdi	*Requiem:* Confutatis

Soprano: Coloratura
Delibes	Lakmé: "Bell Song"
Donizetti	*Lucia di Lammermoor:* Mad Scene
Rossini	*The Barber of Seville:* "Una voce poco fa"
Verdi	*Rigoletto:* "Caro nome"

Dramatic
Handel	*Messiah:* "I know that my Redeemer liveth"
Verdi	*Aida:* "O patria mia"
Wagner	*Tannhauser:* "Dich teure Halle"

Lyric
Bizet	*Carmen:* "Je dis que rien"
Puccini	*La Bohème:* "Mi chiamano Mimi"; "Quando m'en vo'"

Mezzo
Bizet	*Carmen:* Séguidille
Offenbach	*Tales of Hoffmann:* Barcarolle
Saint-Saëns	*Samson and Dalila:* "Mon coeur s'ouvre à ta voix"

Tenor: Dramatic
Leoncavallo	*I Pagliacci:* "Vesti la giubba"
Puccini	*Tosca:* "E lucevan le stelle"
Verdi	*Rigoletto:* "La donna è mobile"
Wagner	*Lohengrin:* "In fernem Land"

Lyric
Bizet	*Carmen:* "La fleur que tu m'avais jetée"
Puccini	*La Bohème:* "Che gelida manina"

Woodwinds
Bassoon

Hindemith	Sonata for Bassoon and Piano
Mozart	Concerto in B$^\flat$ major for bassoon and orchestra, K. 191

Clarinet

Berg	*Four Pieces* for Clarinet and Piano
Hindemith	Sonata for Clarinet and Piano
Mozart	Concerto in A major for Clarinet and Orchestra, K. 662

Contrabassoon

Ravel	*Ma Mère l'Oye:* "Beauty and the Beast"

English Horn

Copland	*Quiet City*
Sibelius	*The Swan of Tuonela*

Flute

Bach	Sonata in a minor for unaccompanied flute
Handel	Sonata in F major for Flute and Continuo, op. 1, no. 11
Hindemith	Sonata for Flute and Piano Sonata for Two Flutes
Martinù	Sonata for Flute and Piano
Milhaud	Sonatine for Flute and Piano

Oboe

Britten	*Phantasy* for Oboe and String Trio
Handel	Sonata in B$^\flat$ major for flute, oboe, and continuo

Piccolo

Ippolitov-Ivanov	*Caucasian Sketches:* "March of the Sardar"

Saxophone

Dubussy	*Rhapsodie* for Saxophone and Orchestra
Ibert	*Concertino da Camera* for Saxophone

Instruments of Other Cultures
China
> *China: Shantung Folk Music,* Nonesuch Records H-72051
> *China's Instrumental Heritage,* Lyrichord Discs LL 92
> *Chinese Folk Opera,* Bruno Hi-Fi Records BR-50157

Japan
> *Gagaku: The Imperial Court Music of Japan,* Lyrichord Discs LL126
> *The Koto Music of Japan,* Nonesuch Records HS 72005

Indian
> *Classical Indian Music,* Odeon Records
> *Folk Music of India,* Folkway Records #4409

Indonesia
> *Music of Indonesia,* Folkways Records FE 4537

In general
> UNESCO Collection (Musical Anthology), Barenrieter-Musicaphon

CHAPTER FIVE

PITCH AND MELODY

◆

PITCH
MELODY

FREQUENCY

CPS
HERTZ

AUDIBLE
FREQUENCY
SPECTRUM

All sound has four properties, three of which already have been discussed: rhythm, dynamics, and timbre. This chapter will examine the fourth property of sound: *pitch*, the relative highness or lowness of a tone, as well as *melody*, the rhythmic combination of several pitches into a musical unit.

Pitch is a function of *frequency*, which refers to the speed with which a sound source vibrates. Faster vibrations create higher sounds, while slower vibrations produce lower ones. The speed of vibration is measured in *cycles per second* (cps), also called *hertz*.

The range of pitch that we are able to hear is quite wide, from 16 hertz to approximately 16,000. This is called the *audible frequency spectrum*. Some animals, such as cats and bats, can hear even higher, as much as 40,000 cps.

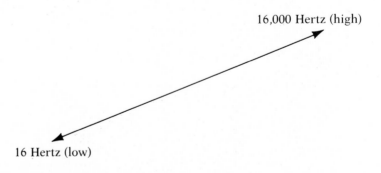

16,000 Hertz (high)

16 Hertz (low)

The audible frequency spectrum is wider than any one instrument can play. The lowest note on the piano, for example, is about 27 hertz, while the highest is only approximately 4,100. The highest instrument in the orchestra, the piccolo, can produce a pitch slightly over 8,000 hertz. Notes higher than this are perceived as overtones, higher (partial) and fainter vibrations that accompany the main tone production by a musical instrument. The audible frequency spectrum is the primary sound source used by the composer to write a melody, which is defined as successive pitches of varying duration combined to create meaningful unity.

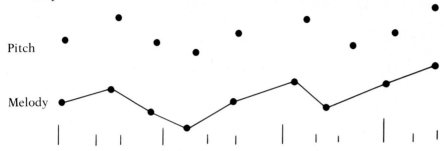

Pitch is thus the raw ingredient, melody one of its products. An understanding of how pitch is determined and used will help the listener develop appreciation for melody and its effect in music.

University of Arizona Museum of Art, gift of Edward J. Gallagher.

Line in the visual arts is somewhat like melody in music. *Construction #74*, Jose de Rivera, American, chrome.

Instruments of other cultures may reflect a different division of the audible frequency spectrum. Ch'in from China (Ming Dynasty).

Photo by K.H. Han. Northern Illinois University.

PITCH ORGANIZATION AND OCTAVES

The Division of the Audible Frequency Spectrum

The audible frequency spectrum is usually divided into specific pitches. Although the same audible frequency spectrum is available for the use of each culture of the world, few have divided it alike. In India it is divided into intervals smaller than are found in Western music, while other cultures, such as in Bali (Indonesia) employ wider intervals than we do. Some countries use only five distinct pitches, others have even fewer, but some specify a great many more, as many as 22. Similarly, each culture calls its pitches by a different system of names. We label ours by letters—a, b, c, d, e, f, and g—or by the solfège system of do, re, mi, fa, so, la, ti, do. The Chinese, who use five pitches, label theirs kung, shang, chiao, chih, and yü.

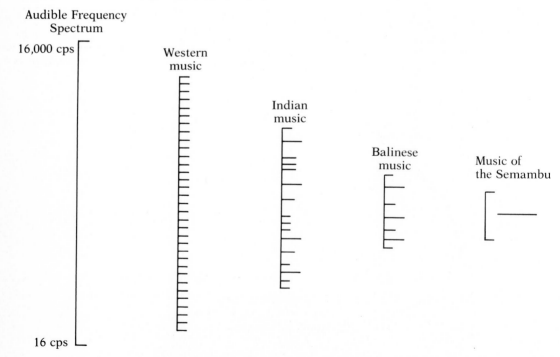

Solmization has been common in the Western world to indicate pitches, the so-called do-re-mi's. Originally the scale was indicated as:

ut re mi fa sol la

The tones were derived from the medieval Hymn to St. John the Baptist and each of the above syllables of the text began on the next note of the scale, as depicted in the adjoining column.

labii reatum,
   Sanctum Joannes.
   Solve polluti
   famuli tuorum,
   Mira gestorum
   Resonare fibris
Ut queant laxis

In India the scale (raga) is designated by:

Ni (Nishada)
Dha (Dhaivata)
Pa (Panchama)
Ma (Madhyama)
Ga (Gandhara)
Re (Risabha)
Sa (Sadja)

In Bali it is:

Ding
Dang
Dung
Dèng
Dong

These words describe the sound each pitch makes when played on a metal xylophone.

The Octave

Many Western cultures use the *octave* as a basic measurement of pitch. Acoustically an octave can be defined as the tone that vibrates at twice the frequency of the home tone, duplicating the original tone, but in a higher register. The word "octave" may also be used to refer to the *distance* between two notes of the same pitch, character, and letter name but with exactly double the frequency. Therefore we can say that an octave is a pitch that vibrates twice as fast as another pitch but has the same name. For example, all C's on the piano can be considered octaves or multiples of octaves. This can best be demonstrated acoustically. If a string sounds a pitch which is called C, it will sound C an octave higher if it is divided in half. If either half is, in turn, divided into half, another C, an octave higher yet, is produced. If the original string vibrated at 16 hertz, each half will vibrate an octave higher, 32 hertz. If halved again, the higher octave vibrates at 64 hertz.

16			C				
32		C			C		
64	C		C		C		C
128	C	C	C	C	C	C	C	C

If the entire audible frequency spectrum were divided similarly, there would be ten resulting octaves.

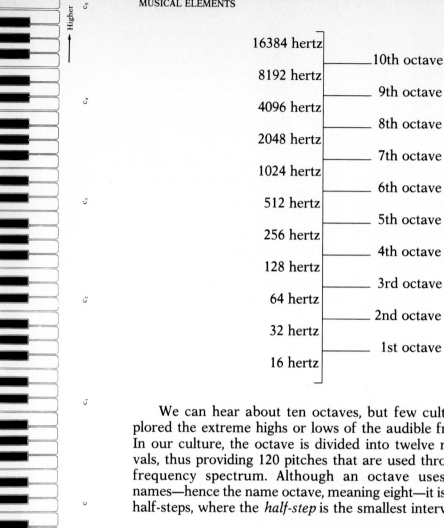

16384 hertz
        10th octave
8192 hertz
        9th octave
4096 hertz
        8th octave
2048 hertz
        7th octave
1024 hertz
        6th octave
512 hertz
        5th octave
256 hertz
        4th octave
128 hertz
        3rd octave
64 hertz
        2nd octave
32 hertz
        1st octave
16 hertz

We can hear about ten octaves, but few cultures have ever explored the extreme highs or lows of the audible frequency spectrum. In our culture, the octave is divided into twelve roughly equal intervals, thus providing 120 pitches that are used throughout the audible frequency spectrum. Although an octave uses only eight letter names—hence the name octave, meaning eight—it is divided into twelve half-steps, where the *half-step* is the smallest interval between pitches.

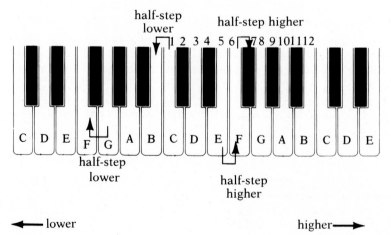

Through much of the history of Western musical composition the half-step could be defined as the closest pitch above or below any given pitch. Recent borrowings from other musical cultures have reduced this interval in some instances to the quarter tone or even the microtone.   HALF-STEP

However, the interval in most common usage in the West remains the half-step. Its denotation of pitches can best be demonstrated on a piano keyboard.

Note that c_1 designates middle C, an exact pitch on the piano.

The distance separating pitches of the same letter name is an octave; c_2 is an octave higher than c_1. The keys between octaves all have specific names. White keys are identified by consecutive letters, A–G. Black keys, the names of which are derived from the adjacent white key, occur between all of the white keys except B–C and E–F. Our Western tuning system divides the octave into twelve tones, yet our notational system contains only seven letter names. Thus additional

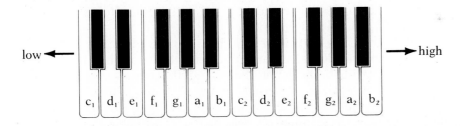

Subscripts are used with pitch letters to designate an exact octave. On the piano, c_1 denotes an exact pitch—middle C. The entire piano keyboard is a repetition of the pattern given in the text, but the bottom pitch is AAA, not c_1. There is an octave between any two pitches of the same letter name, for example, GG and G, c and c_1, and $b\flat_3$ and $b\flat_4$. Although an octave uses eight pitch names, it contains, as seen above, twelve half-steps. The entire piano keyboard is slightly more than seven octaves with each octave having an identical arrangement of white and black keys. The lowest pitch on the piano is AAA, the highest is c_5. See keyboard on page 156.

symbols are needed to identify some pitches. These symbols, deviations from a key signature often called *accidentals*, modify a pitch by raising or lowering it one half-step. When a pitch is a half-step higher (higher = to the right), it is called a sharp (♯). If a half-step lower (lower = to the left) it is called a flat (♭). The black key between C-D is called c sharp (♯) as well as d flat (♭), between d-e, it is called d♯ or e♭.

MELODY

Pitch is a property of sound that can be explored scientifically, especially in the discussion of frequency and octave divisions, but in music, isolated pitches are not as important as the horizontal combination of several into meaningful units called melody. Melody is thus the organization of pitches of varying duration into a framework that provides a sense of line or completeness, much like a sentence. Although melodies can often be hummed or sung, this is not the criterion for judging something as a melody. Any succession of pitches, however fragmentary to the listener, constitutes a melody.

Selection no. 54   Listen to the Prelude from Arnold Schoenberg's *Suite* for piano, op. 25 *(listening selections)*. This prelude is comprised of continuous sweeps of pitches that make it seem fragmentary. Melody in the traditional sense is difficult to perceive on first hearing since each unit is short and not particularly "singable." Nonetheless, these units are considered melodies since they consist of several pitches combined within an organized framework.

Schoenberg was not interested in writing traditional melodies as composers of the eighteenth and nineteenth centuries had done. In his music, as in much music of the twentieth century, short melodic gestures have replaced the logical and predictable melodies of earlier eras. Although many listeners would say there is no melody in Schoenberg's Prelude, with numerous hearings one can begin to discern the logical pattern within the sweep of pitches. By definition, any arrangement of successive pitches into units makes a melody, regardless of whether or not it is singable.

Contour
The characteristic direction of pitches in a melody is called its *contour*. All identifiable melodies have a contour, a specific curve or profile that results from the upward or downward motion of pitches. Typical contours include:

Arnold Schoenberg.
Courtesy of the New York Public Library.

Arnold Schoenberg (1874–1951) was an Austrian-born composer who greatly influenced the development of modern compositional techniques. Although he received traditional musical training as a youth, playing the violin and studying the music of Classic and Romantic masters, Schoenberg later introduced a revolutionary method of musical organization. At age sixteen he began formal training in music theory and composition under Alexander von Zemlinsky, a Viennese composer. Schoenberg's earliest compositions were Romantic with traditional melodies. Gradually he evolved a new style of composition, called *twelve-tone* writing. Pitches in the twelve-tone system, although arranged in traditional melodic units, can sound bewildering because all twelve tones of the chromatic scale are used. *Prelude* is typical of twelve-tone musical composition. Melody seems to be absent and the harmony seems particularly harsh, but the pitch relationships are the untraditional element.

During the period before World War II, Schoenberg moved to the United States where he taught at U.S.C. and U.C.L.A. His musical ideas became very important in the 1950s. Among his works are *Verklärte Nacht, Pierrot Lunaire, Gurre-Lieder,* and *A Survivor from Warsaw.* Schoenberg's music, although rigidly organized and mathematically logical, perplexes listeners who expect a traditional melody.

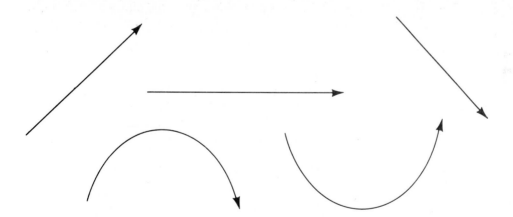

The pitches in a melody can move up or down, remain at the same level, or combine these actions. The contour inherent to a melody is a means by which a composer can help the listener distinguish among several that may occur in a composition. Any melody that appears often enough in a composition to assume prominence is called a *theme,*   THEME which functions much like the main character in a novel, play, or movie. A theme is easily recognizable in a composition because it is stated near the beginning and, since it may return throughout the work, provides a source of unity.

Listen to Bedřich Smetana's *The Moldau (supplemental listening).* In this *symphonic poem,* a one-movement program piece for orchestra, the Czech composer describes the course of the river Moldau from its source, high in the mountains, to the city of Prague. The composition has many changes in mood reflecting events occurring along the bank of the river. Each melody used thus has a distinctive contour that helps the listener identify what is happening.

SYMPHONIC POEM

First a brook trickles, representing the origin of the river. No distinctive melody is used here, but as the brook joins other streams the river theme (1:09) emerges. It has a distinctive contour that is easily remembered and returns periodically throughout the composition. Then a peasant wedding celebration is heard (3:48), as well as water nymphs reveling (5:38) in the water. The original river melody then returns (7:51), growing in volume as the river advances. When the river passes over rapids (8:30), turbulence is felt in the music. A penultimate, majestic statement of the river melody is heard (9:43), then a new, final theme (10:10), followed by a dramatic ending.

The preface to the work contains this program analysis:

> Two springs pour forth in the shade of the Bohemian Forest, one warm and gushing, the other cold and peaceful. Their waves, gayly flowing over rocky beds, join and glisten in the rays of the morning sun. The forest brook, hastening on, becomes the river Vltava (Moldau). Coursing through Bohemia's valleys, it grows into a mighty stream. Through thick woods it flows, as the gay sounds of the hunt and the notes of the hunter's horn are heard ever nearer. It flows through grassgrown pastures and lowlands where a wedding feast is being celebrated with song and dance. At night wood and water nymphs revel in its sparkling waves. Reflected on its surface are fortresses and castles—witnesses of bygone days of knightly splendor and the vanished glory of fighting times. At the St. John Rapids the stream races ahead, winding through the cataracts, hewing out a path with its foaming waves through the rocky chasm into the broad river bed—finally, flowing on in majestic peace toward Prague and welcomed by time-honored Vysehrad. Then it vanishes far beyond the poet's gaze.

The Moldau is one of six symphonic works, collectively entitled *Má Vlast* (My Fatherland), that Smetana composed in 1874. *The Moldau*

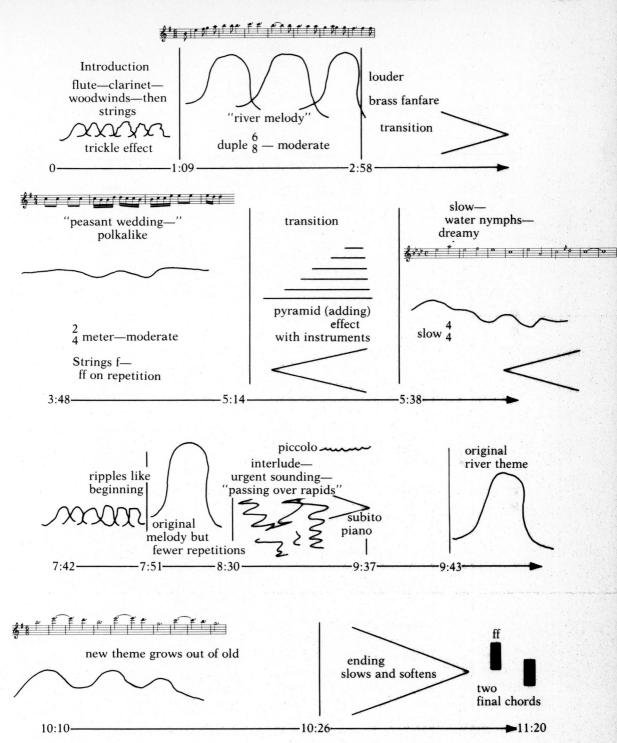

Bedřich Smetana (1824–1884) was a forerunner of many great nationalistic composers of the nineteenth century including his Bohemian countryman, Antonin Dvořák. Though his first compositions met only moderate critical response, in 1866 his opera *The Bartered Bride* was proclaimed a masterpiece and later performed around the world. The opera's overture, often used as a symphonic work, has folk-like qualities characteristic of much of Smetana's

Bedrich Smetana.
Courtesy of the New York Public Library.

music. In spite of losing his hearing from a syphilitic infection, Smetana composed the symphonic masterwork, *Má Vlast*. Returning to opera composition, Smetana tried to duplicate the success of *The Bartered Bride,* but response to later operatic works never met his expectations. He suffered several mental breakdowns and eventually died in an insane asylum. It is interesting that, as in the case of Beethoven, some of Smetana's greatest music was written after he had lost his hearing.

(Vltava) is the second and best known of the six. It is tragic that the symphonic cycle was composed shortly after the composer went suddenly and completely deaf. It thus took him five years to compose the works, and he was never able to hear any of them. *Má Vlast* is probably Smetana's greatest contribution to the field of Romantic instrumental music.

Melodic Progression

Melodies may be made up of a smooth progression of pitches lying close together, like the "river melody" of *The Moldau,* or of a jagged sweep of pitches like the melody of Schoenberg's Prelude. When adjacent pitches are used in a stepwise progression to create a smooth, CONJUNCT   flowing line, the melody is said to be *conjunct.*

conjunct melody

When, on the other hand, the melody progresses in a jagged line characterized by skips and even leaps, it is said to be *disjunct*.

disjunct melody

Composers may differentiate themes by making one conjunct, another disjunct. Both types of progression, of course, can be combined into the same melody.

Listen to Allegro vivace, the first movement of Felix Mendelssohn's Symphony no. 4 in A major, op. 90 *(Italian) (supplemental listening)*. There are three themes, each slightly differentiated by contour and progression.

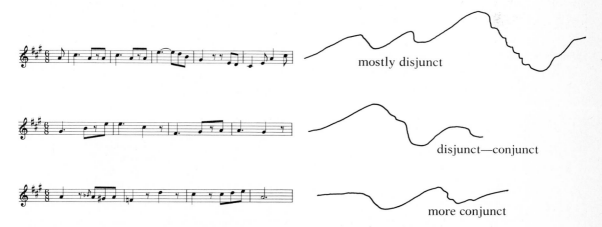

mostly disjunct

disjunct—conjunct

more conjunct

This movement is in ternary form in which the first section, A, is repeated (AABA). Each of the first two A sections has a small ending (or codetta) of its own, while the coda of the final A section blends the several preceding melodies in summation.

Mendelssohn, inspired to write the symphony after a trip to Italy in 1830, scored it for flutes, oboes, clarinets, bassoons, horns, trumpets, timpani, and strings. He found Italy a happy and sunny country, which undoubtedly accounts for this movement's exuberance, but it contains little else that is Italian. Although Mendelssohn completed the work in 1832 and conducted a performance of it in 1833, it was not published during his lifetime since he always considered it slightly less than perfect and wanted to polish certain sections before allowing publication.

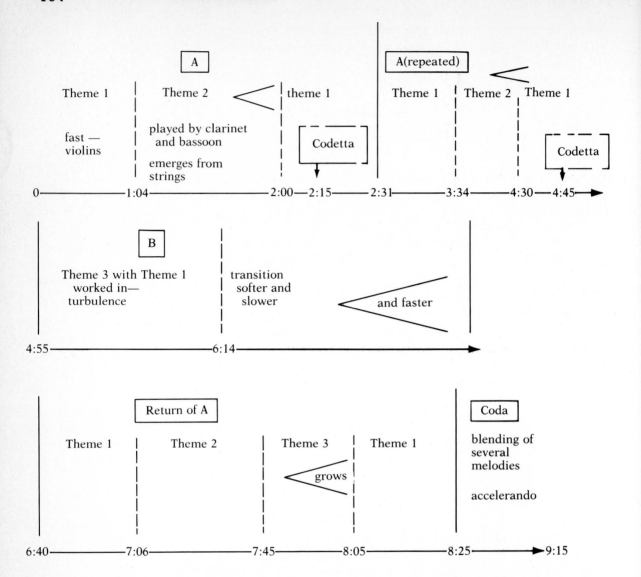

Intervals

The difference between two pitches is called an *interval.* Intervals may be measured both numerically and qualitatively.

Numerical.   The numerical value of an interval between pitches can be found by counting pitch names between the two pitches, including those at the beginning and ending. For example, the distance between c_1 and c_2 is an octave because it includes 8 letters: *C* D E F G A B *C.* The THIRD   distance between C and E is a third because it includes three pitch names, C, D, and E. The numerical value is ascertained by counting the

Felix Mendelssohn (1809–1847) was born in Hamburg to a wealthy Jewish family. He studied piano and violin as a child and was exposed to a rich cultural environment. The family wealth permitted him to travel throughout Europe and to Scotland, where he began the *Hebrides Overture* and later the *Scotch* Symphony. As an adult, Mendelssohn led the lower-Rhine music festival in Düsseldorf, conducted the prestigious Gewandhaus Orchestra in Leipzig, and in Berlin served as Royal Music Director. He composed symphonies, concertos, overtures, incidental music, and an oratorio, his works combining the exuberance and pathos of the nineteenth century with the logic characteristic of the eighteenth century. He did much to revive and popularize the music of J. S. Bach, whose compositions had become obscure following his death in 1750. As a member of a Berlin choral society, Mendelssohn came across Bach's *St. Mathew Passion* and convinced the director to have it performed, recognizing early the mastery of Bach's music. Although Mendelssohn died at age thirty-eight,

Felix Mendelssohn.
Courtesy of the New York Public Library.

he left an extensive legacy of music, including the popular "Wedding March" from his incidental music for *A Midsummer Night's Dream.*

number of half-steps between the two pitches. As we have learned, an octave has eight letter names, including the same beginning and ending pitches, and twelve half-steps.

Qualitative. Intervals may also be identified with a qualitative classification that refers to their special sound quality. Some intervals—seconds, thirds, sixths, and sevenths—have two common forms, *major* and *minor.* The larger form is called a major interval, the smaller form, a minor interval. A major interval is always one half-step larger than its corresponding minor interval. For example, the interval between C and E is called a major third because it includes three letter names and four half-steps. The distance between C and E♭ is called a minor third because it is smaller than the major interval by one half-step. Remember that the flat symbol (♭) placed next to a letter lowers the pitch by one half-step.

MAJOR
MINOR

Perfect, Augmented, and Diminished. Other qualitative terms used to describe intervals include perfect, diminished, and augmented. The intervals of a fourth, fifth, and octave are called *perfect* intervals because they have only one form, rather than a larger and a smaller form, as is true of seconds, thirds, sixths, and sevenths. These intervals have a pure, open, and hollow sound when the two pitches are sounded together. When a perfect interval is made larger or smaller by a half-step, it does not become a major or minor, but is rather *diminished* (made smaller) or *augmented* (made larger). Minor intervals may also be made diminished by reducing the distance between the two pitches by one half-step. For example, the minor seventh C to B♭ becomes a diminished seventh when we add an additional flat (♭) symbol, thus C to B♭♭. Major or perfect intervals can be made augmented by adding an additional half-step or sharp. For example, the fourth C to F will become an augmented fourth (also called diminished fifth or "tritone") by adding a sharp or one half-step, C to F♯. For our purposes, it is enough to hear the difference between major and minor intervals, a quality that will become important later in our discussion of harmony.

Range

NARROW
WIDE

Range refers to the distance from the lowest to highest pitch in a melody. We usually speak of ranges as being *narrow* or *wide*. Folk songs often have a range of an octave or less, and are said to have narrow ranges. Designating a range as wide means that the distance between the lowest and highest tone is in excess of an octave. "The Star-Spangled Banner," for example, has a wider range than does "America."

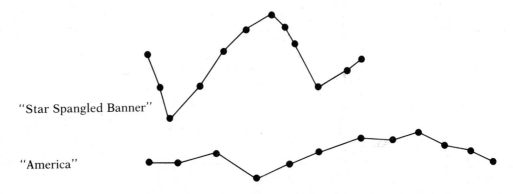

"Star Spangled Banner"

"America"

Selection no. 55

Listen to the Australian Cloud Chant (from Northeast Arnhem Land) *(listening selections)*. In this example the range of the singer is very narrow, involving only a few pitches.

Singer

Clapping sticks   / / / / / / / / / / / / / / / / / /

Didjeridu

0 ————————————————————————➤ 2:50

Perfect is a designation used to indicate the *quality* of an interval. An octave c to c_1 is correctly called a perfect octave. Other perfect intervals include the distance of five half-steps, such as C to F, which is called a perfect fourth, and the distance of seven half-steps, such as C to G, which is called a perfect fifth.

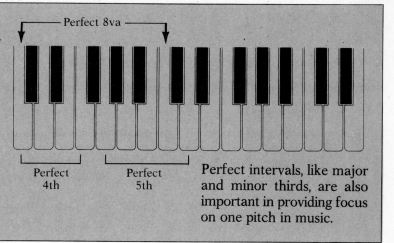

Perfect 8va

Perfect 4th

Perfect 5th

Perfect intervals, like major and minor thirds, are also important in providing focus on one pitch in music.

This selection comes from Australia's Arnhem Land (Northeastern area) but is typical of aboriginal music from many parts of the world. The performer half-speaks and half-sings, while the accompaniment is provided by clapping sticks (wooden idiophones) and the *didjeridu*, an aerophone made from the hollowed-out limb of a tree.

DIDJERIDU

Didjeridu, an Australian aerophone (about 48″ long).

The player either hoots through the long tube or provides a continuous droning note, as here, by buzzing his lips. He breathes in continuously through his nose, stores the air in his cheeks, and thus keeps the pitch going without pause. The range of the didjeridu is the narrowest possible, only one pitch, determined by the size of the tree limb. The words to this song, with translation, are roughly:

bulong-or   dauwudon   narong   dang-um
cloud   (wind) blowing   along   that

ngalin   bugu   wema-linggan
we   very   sorry here (stop)

jurong-ain   nining-oin   djinagoi
we people   belonging   (that) country

ngali   jurong-o   djaruna   bailma
we   people   song   song

laiang-ani   burung-gali   wata
"song"   "song"   wind

narung-an   ngaling-go   bulbulwa
comes up   own   five clouds

morogan-ba   njinan   narong
flower   "set"   along

ngoili   gapul
on   water.—A.P. Elkin

Henry Purcell (c. 1659–1695) was a great English composer who as a youth served as both choirboy and instrument repairer at the Chapel Royal. As an adult, he played organ at Westminster Abbey and wrote music for church service, including numerous anthems, odes, and cantatas. He composed theater music, including incidental music to *The Fairy Queen* and *King Arthur*, as well as the opera *Dido and Aeneas*. Purcell was widely acclaimed as a composer in his day and was buried beside other national celebrities in Westminster Abbey.

Westminster Abbey, London, England, founded in 1065 by Edward the Confessor, has been the scene of 38 coronations and also a place of employment for Henry Purcell.

Listen to Henry Purcell's "Thy Hand, Belinda" from the opera *Dido and Aeneas* (1689) *(listening selections)*, an example of melody with a wide range. The aria is being sung by Dido to her servant, Belinda. Dido has just been abandoned by her lover, Aeneas, so the mood is one of great sorrow. In comparison with the Australian aboriginal music, wider ranges are observed in both the voice and instrumental parts:

Selection no. 56

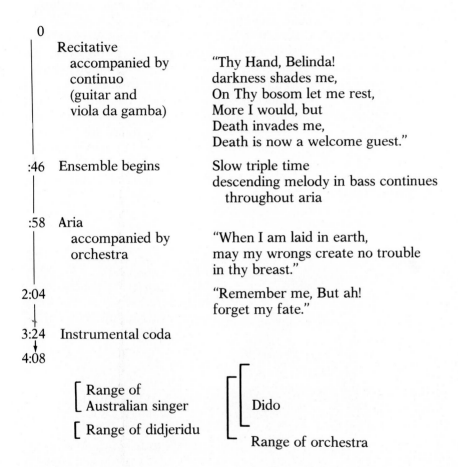

0

Recitative
accompanied by
continuo
(guitar and
viola da gamba)

"Thy Hand, Belinda!
darkness shades me,
On Thy bosom let me rest,
More I would, but
Death invades me,
Death is now a welcome guest."

:46   Ensemble begins

Slow triple time
descending melody in bass continues
   throughout aria

:58   Aria
accompanied by
orchestra

"When I am laid in earth,
may my wrongs create no trouble
in thy breast."

2:04

"Remember me, But ah!
forget my fate."

3:24   Instrumental coda

4:08

⌈ Range of
⌊ Australian singer

⌈ Range of didjeridu

⌈⌈
  ⌊ Dido
⌊
Range of orchestra

Articulation

Articulation refers to the way pitches are played or attacked in a melody. If the pitches are connected smoothly, the effect is called *legato*. Legato articulation is often marked by a slur, a long curving arc over a segment of the melody that indicates that the pitches should be smoothly connected. Legato is achieved on string instruments by

LEGATO

long, smooth motions of the bow, on wind instruments with soft tonguing techniques, and by the singer with the smooth expulsion of a single breath.

STACCATO

Staccato, the opposite of legato, means a detached way of playing in which tiny breaks are inserted between pitches. Staccato articulation is often marked by small dots placed underneath the notes to be played in a detached manner. Staccato is achieved in various ways. Short strokes of the bow may be used on a string instrument, wind players will tongue each tone more distinctly, while singers will interrupt the flow of air to make each pitch crisply distinct.

Selection no. 57

Listen to "Samuel Goldenberg and Schmuyle," from Modest Mussorgsky's *Pictures at an Exhibition (listening selections).* This work, one of Mussorgsky's most famous, was inspired by a posthumous exhibition of the paintings of Victor Hartmann, a close friend of the composer. Mussorgsky wrote a short movement for each painting or sketch in the exhibition, unifying the entire suite with a recurrent walking theme or promenade. Pictures that Mussorgsky included are "The Old Castle," "Catacombs," "The Great Gate of Kiev," and of course "Samuel Goldenberg and Schmuyle," a sketch of two Polish Jews. Mussorgsky had always been fond of the picture, and Hartmann had in fact made a gift of it to him.

Modest Mussorgsky (1839–1881) appears as an anomaly in the musical world of the nineteenth century. Born to a wealthy Russian family in 1839, he had many advantages as a youngster, including lessons on the piano. As a young man, he trained for a position in the army, paying for the privilege to command troops. The abolition of serfdom in 1861, however, liquidated his family's land and money. He became a clerk in the Ministry of Transport for the rest of his life, which was undoubtedly shortened by his abject liv-

Modest Mussorgsky.
Courtesy of the New York Public Library.

ing and alcoholism. He became bitter and found his only relief in music. Mussorgsky was intent on composing and joined with

"The Russian Five," a group of composers devoted to advancing the cause of nationalism in Russian music. Because he was not trained in the art of composing and orchestration, Mussorgsky's musical works sometimes contain harmonic crudities and undue dissonance. Nonetheless, he has become an influence on many contemporary composers because of his dramatic and moving works that include *Pictures at an Exhibition, A Night on Bald Mountain,* and the great Russian folk opera, *Boris Godunov.*

In this movement the two businessmen, one rich and powerful, one poor and obsequious, talk and then argue together. The low, legato sounds describe the rich man, Samuel Goldenberg, the high, staccato melody is Schmuyle. The musical sketch is direct, revealing a marked contrast between the two men by difference in melody and articulation.

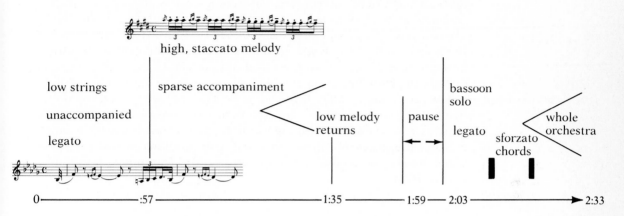

MELODIC STRUCTURE

Motive, Phrase, and Cadence

Language has meaning to us because words are organized into phrases, sentences, and paragraphs, each unit clearly delineated by punctuation points. Melodies are also organized into units, with points of punctuation, somewhat similar to spoken language.

While pitches are the smallest unit of music, *motives* are the MOTIVE smallest unit of musical *meaning*. A motive is defined as a rhythmic grouping of notes combined to form a fragment that, in turn, becomes the building block of a larger structure, such as a melody.

Oh, beau - ti - ful for spa-cious skies, for am - ber waves of grain.

Motive = ♩ | ♩. ♪ ♩   Contour =

The motive, in this case an uneven pattern (♩ ♩ ♩. ♪ ♩) with a descending ⌐ contour, is heard twice in the first line of

PHRASE   "America, the Beautiful." The entire line of melody is called a *phrase*. A phrase in music is analogous to a phrase in spoken language, that distance set off by the span of a breath or a natural pause in thought. Vocal phrases are often the normal span of one's breath, at least in simple hymns and folk songs, although phrases can be of any length. Trained instrumentalists and singers can sustain much longer phrases than the unskilled performer. The ending of a phrase is called a **CADENCE**   *cadence*, a point of rest or repose where a breath is usually taken. There is such a cadence at the end of the first phrase of "America, the Beautiful," where the word "grain" is held slightly longer than others in the phrase. Cadences that occur in the middle of a composition, and convey the impression of only a brief pause with more music still to **INCOMPLETE**   follow, are called *incomplete cadences*. The following diagram shows **CADENCE**   the four-phrase structure of "America, the Beautiful," including its motives and cadences. Although in this example each phrase is equal to four measures of music, in other compositions phrases may be either shorter or longer, and frequently vary in length within the same composition.

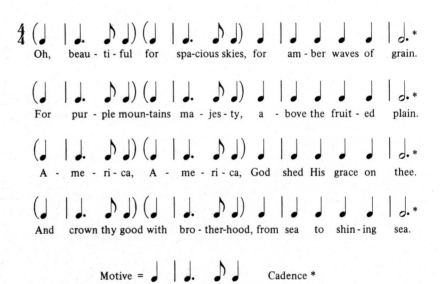

There is only one cadence in this example that sounds final or conclusive, that is, like the end of something. This is the one that occurs on the word "sea." Since it sounds like, and is, the termination **COMPLETE**   of the song, it is called a *complete cadence*. However, as will be shown, **CADENCE**   complete cadences are not restricted to the ends of compositions, but can also appear in their midst.

Period

Another song is analyzed below. Here there are four phrases, with incomplete cadences at the ends of phrases 1 and 3 and complete cadences at the ends of phrases 2 and 4.

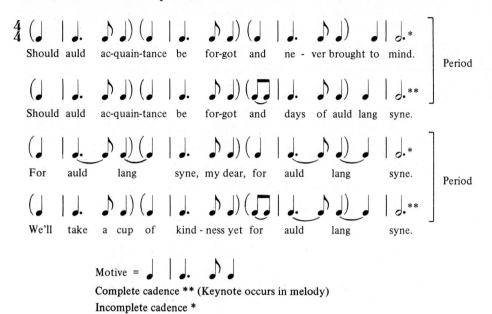

In considering the relationship between phrases 1 and 2, as well as between 3 and 4, it can be observed that one phrase is like a question, the next like an answer. This pairing of phrases is called a *period* and it consists of an *antecendent* phrase, which has an incomplete cadence, followed by a *consequent*, which has a complete cadence. Periods or phrase pairs can be complete songs in themselves or may be used, as here, to build larger sections and compositions.

ANTECEDENT
CONSEQUENT

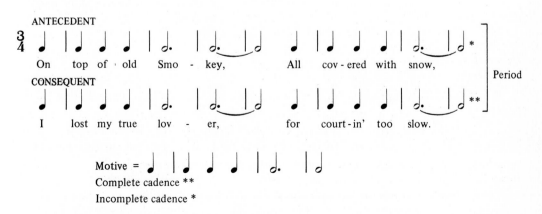

Listen to Trepak (Russian Dance) from Piotr Ilyich Tchaikovsky's *Nutcracker Suite,* op. 71a *(listening selections).* Trepak consists entirely of two periods.

Selection no. 58

Follow this graph as you listen. The overall form is AABA.

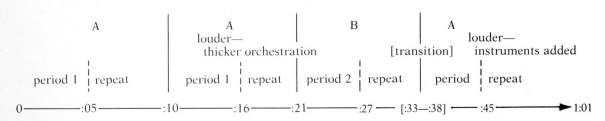

Tchaikovsky was commissioned to write *The Nutcracker* by the St. Petersburg Opera in 1891. The story of the ballet is derived from E.T.A. Hoffmann's *The Nutcracker and the Mouse King,* in which a young girl falls asleep on Christmas Eve and dreams that a nutcracker is transformed into a prince who battles an army of mice. The prince spirits her away to Jam mountain, where the Sugarplum Fairy rules. Here they are entertained by dances, including the Dance of the Sugarplum Fairy, Arabian and Chinese dances, Waltz of the Flowers, and this example, Trepak, a Russian dance. These dances have been

Piotr Ilyich Tchaikovsky (1840–1893) was a great Russian composer born, like Mussorgsky, to a well-to-do family. Because Tchaikovsky's life was haunted by tragedy, much of his music is brooding and ominous. He studied law as a young man, but in his early twenties decided to become a composer and entered the St. Petersburg Conservatory. He thereafter devoted his life to music. Tchaikovsky was supported in his work by a mysterious patron, Madame von Meck, whom he never met. Their only contact for several years was through letters.

Tchaikovsky was well known as a composer during his lifetime through his six symphonies, suites, concertos, and tone poems, including the Overture-Fantasy, *Romeo and Juliet*, the 1812 *Overture*, and the famous Piano Concerto no. 1. When he toured the United States in 1891, he was surprised how well Americans knew his compositions. Tchaikovsky's music, which was largely European derived rather than Russian nationalistic, was the accepted sound in Russia and very popular. In spite of his success, Tchaikovsky suffered from depression and many hidden fears throughout his life. At the peak of his career, Madame von Meck abruptly stopped her funding and correspondence with Tchaikovsky. Deeply hurt, he continued to compose. Tchaikovsky wrote his last symphony, the *Pathétique*, just prior to his death at age fifty-three. Melancholy and passionate, it is regarded as a final testament of Tchaikovsky's life, embodying his

Piotr Ilyich Tchaikovsky.
Courtesy of the New York Public Library.

pain and philosophy of fatalism. After conducting the premiere of *Pathétique* in St. Petersburg, Tchaikovsky ignored warnings against drinking the city's water in light of a raging cholera epidemic. He soon developed symptoms of the dreaded disease and died, giving rise to widespread rumors he had committed suicide.

extracted from the complete composition and are frequently performed in concerts as the *Nutcracker Suite*, which Tchaikovsky arranged in 1891. The music of *The Nutcracker* is considered an unusually joyous and brilliant exception to Tchaikovsky's usually more sombre musical output.

MELODIC FOCUS

Tonic

In many melodies, one pitch generally stands out as being more important than any of the others, because it frequently begins and ends the composition, is the basis for the scale and harmony, and may even appear more frequently than the other pitches. This pitch may occur at complete cadences and may even terminate the composition. The pitch that provides such a focus in each melody is called the tonic. For example, when a composition is said to be in the key of C, C is the tonic.

Scales

The other pitches are related to the tonic in a *scale*, a series of pitches arranged in ascending (and descending) order above (or below) the tonic.

$$c_2$$
$$b_1 \text{ (tonic)}$$
$$a_1$$
$$g_1$$
$$f_1$$
$$e_1$$
$$d_1$$
$$c_1$$
$$\text{(tonic)}$$

The tonic both begins and ends the scale and is the only pitch used twice. The scale is normally bound by an octave, c_1 to c_2, in this case.

MAJOR   The two scales most commonly used by composers are the *major*
MINOR   and *minor*, both of which are termed *diatonic*, that is, using five
DIATONIC   whole-steps (W) and two half-steps (H). A *whole-step* is two half-steps
WHOLE-STEP in the same direction, such as from C to D or E to F♯. The difference
between major and minor is where the half-steps and whole-steps fall.

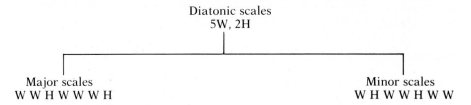

Diatonic scales
5W, 2H

Major scales
W W H W W W H

Minor scales
W H W W H W W

The C major scale, for example, begins on C, and uses these pitches, as seen on the keyboard:

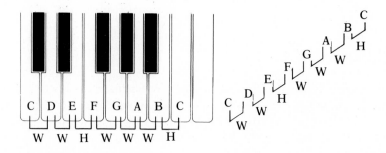

C D E F G A B C
W W H W W W H

A c minor scale contains these pitches:

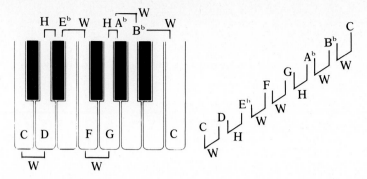

Although these examples show c as the tonic, a scale may be built with any pitch as tonic, as long as the half- and whole-step relationships are observed.

D major is:

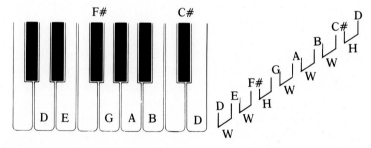

while d minor is:

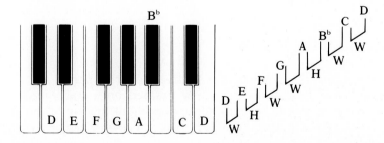

The composer really has twelve pitches from which to choose the tonic for a scale, but in order to maintain the half- and whole-step pattern, sharps (♯) and flats (♭) are necessary. A variety of scales on a variety of pitches thus provides a wealth of melodic material for the composer. In reality, the composer probably begins with a melody in his or her mind, and only considers what scale and tonic it is in when setting it down on paper with musical notation.

Among scales, major and minor are the most common, although contemporary composers use many others, some borrowed from the Middle Ages.

    The *modes,* also diatonic scales, are rooted in medieval music. The mode at the top of the adjacent column, which also has five whole-steps and two half-steps, is called the Dorian.

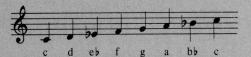

There are also non-diatonic scales such as the *whole-tone* scale, which uses only whole-steps between adjacent pitches.

A *chromatic* scale has only half-steps.

RAGA
MICROTONE
QUARTER TONE

    Scales of other cultures often contain intervals smaller than the half-step. This is true of Indian scales, *ragas,* which have *microtones,* that is, gradations of pitch smaller than a half-step. Western composers have experimented with *quarter tones* (one-half of a half-step) in recent time, particularly involving instruments, such as the violin or trombone, that are able inherently to play these smaller intervals. Synthesizers also have the capability of playing infinitely variable intervals, thus opening new tonal possibilities for the adventurous composer.

NOTATION OF PITCH

Pitch notation, like rhythm, has evolved over a period of several hundred years. Pitches are presently notated on a staff similarly to points on a graph, with higher ones appearing at the top of the graph, lower ones at the bottom. Furthermore, successive pitches are read left to right.

Clef

Clefs are reference points used to locate exact pitches on the staff, and there are two that are most commonly used. The *G clef* identifies g_1 through the curve of its tail, which carries the line on the staff designated as g_1. The staff on which the G clef is placed is identified as the *treble staff*.

TREBLE STAFF

The *F clef* identifies f (below c_1) by enclosing with two dots the line on which f appears. This staff is known as the *bass staff*.

BASS STAFF

Staff

Lines as well as spaces between the lines are used to represent pitch in sequence. The following shows the pitches above and below g_1 and f, respectively.

Traditionally, five lines and four spaces have been used to designate pitches. This is called a *staff*.

When ϕ and 9 are placed on their respective staffs, the following pitches can be designated:

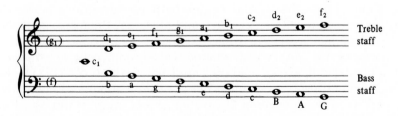

When the treble staff and bass staff are placed together, the b, c_1, and d_1 that separate them are positioned in the spaces between with the addition of a *ledger line* for c_1. The two staffs together are called the *grand staff*.

LEDGER LINE
GRAND STAFF

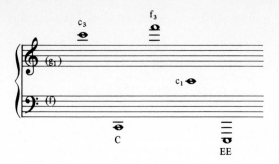

A ledger line is a short line drawn to indicate the position of a pitch above or below the treble and bass staff. It is a kind of abbreviation of a complete staff line. The entire audible frequency spectrum can be represented on the grand staff in this manner.

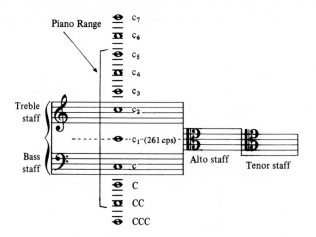

Where Instruments Read

The piano, harpsichord, and organ read on the grand staff. High instruments, such as flute, clarinet, and oboe, use the treble staff while lower instruments, such as tuba, trombone, string bass, and bassoon, use the bass staff. Other instruments whose range is between the two staffs, near middle c (c_1), read on a staff where the *C clef* (|B) is used. This clef identifies c_1 as the line between the two curved elements of the clef, as in the preceding illustration. Viola music is almost always in the alto staff. Cello, trombone, and bassoon occasionally use the tenor staff.

Instruments that play extremely high or low may give out a sound that is actually an octave higher or lower than the note read on the staff. The piccolo, for example, reads c_2 but actually sounds an octave higher, c_3. The symbols *8va* (play an octave above from where written)

8VA

Concert Grand Piano
by Steinway & Sons,
New York, 1903.

Smithsonian Institution Photo #33722-C.

and *8va basso* (play an octave below from where written) are used to   8VA BASSO
indicate that a given pitch or series of pitches will sound an octave
higher or lower than notated. These notational conventions allow the
composer to keep the pitches generally on the staff rather than use
ledger lines.

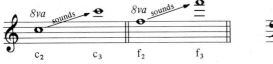

The position of a melody on a staff shows its contour. "Joy to the
World," which begins with a descending contour,   CONTOUR

assumes the same profile when the melody is notated.

Accidentals, Key Signatures, and Articulation

When an occasional sharp or flat is needed, it is notated by placing a ♯(sharp) or ♭(flat) in *front* of the given pitch.

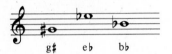

ACCIDENTAL   This temporary addition of the sharp or flat, called an *accidental*, is cancelled by the next bar line.

In other cases, sharps or flats are placed at the beginning of a composition and at each new line of music. This notation is called the *key signature* and indicates that all notes with that pitch name will be played as sharps or flats throughout the composition.

KEY

SIGNATURE

The exception is when a *natural sign* (♮), another example of an accidental, is used to cancel out the sharp or flat for a particular measure. As with the other accidentals, a natural, too, is cancelled by the next bar line.

Sharps or flats placed at the beginning of a composition also establish the tonal center, the pitch that is most important in the composition and that serves as its basic organizing structure.

Articulations such as legato and staccato, described earlier in the chapter, are notated as:

Quarter tones are also notated in a variety of ways, including:

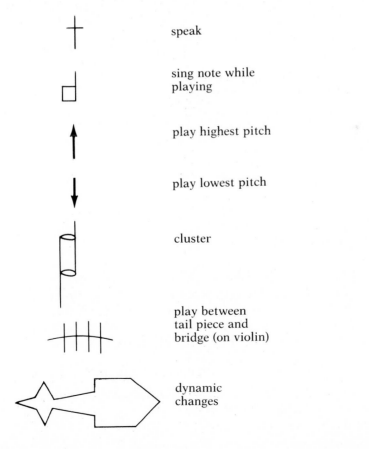

| ¼ up from f♯ | ¼ up from b♭ | ¼ up from e | ¼ up from g | ¾ up from g | ¼ down from e | ¾ down from e |

Finally, composers may also invent new symbols to designate pitch when the traditional system does not provide a way to notate a sound they want.

speak

sing note while playing

play highest pitch

play lowest pitch

cluster

play between tail piece and bridge (on violin)

dynamic changes

MELODY AND STYLE PERIODS

The use of melody has changed throughout the historical periods in music, as summarized in this chart.

Period	Melody	Examples
Medieval	Narrow range.	
Renaissance	Range is somewhat wide and with conjunct progression. Phrases and cadences tend to overlap.	
Baroque	Range is wide and melodies are both conjunct and disjunct, depending on whether played or sung. Major and minor tonality develops. Phrases tend to be long.	Purcell—"Thy Hand, Belinda"
Classic	Ranges are moderate. Phrases are short with clearly delineated cadences. Major and minor sounds prevail. Melodies are contrasted by articulation.	
Romantic	Ranges are wide; melodies, dramatic and emotional.	Mendelssohn—Allegro vivace Smetana—*The Moldau* Moussorgsky—"Samuel Goldenberg and Schmuyle" Tchaikovsky—"Trepak"
Impressionism	Melodies are fragmentary and motivic. Melody, as a whole, is de-emphasized.	
Twentieth Century	All possibilities of the past are used. Melody is not as important as in earlier times. A few composers have experimented with quarter- and microtones.	Schoenberg—Prelude, op. 25

See also selections in Chapter 3, p. 81; Chapter 4, p. 140.

SUMMARY

Melody can be defined as the perception of successive pitches as a cohesive unit. Pitch by itself is determined by frequency of vibration: the higher the frequency, the higher the pitch. Although we can discern an audible frequency of ten octaves, 16 to 16,000 hertz, most of the music systems of the world use a narrower range and a variety of intervals. In the West, the octave is divided into twelve equal half-steps.

Melodies are identifiable by both their contour (direction) and progression (conjunct and disjunct), but are also characterized by range, whether narrow or wide, as well as by articulation, which includes legato and staccato.

A motive, the building block of melodies, is the smallest unit of musical meaning. Melodies are organized into breathable units called phrases, each of which ends with a musical punctuation or cadence. Phrases may be paired into antecendent and consequent, called a period. In addition, melodies usually have a tonic, a main pitch that establishes the tonality.

Tonality is determined by the scale upon which the melody is built, the most common being the major and minor diatonic scales. Some composers and cultures have incorporated smaller intervals, such as quartertones and microtones, in their scales.

Melodies are notated on a staff consisting of lines and spaces. Clefs, particularly the G and F clefs, provide a reference pitch within the treble and bass staffs, respectively. When the two staffs are placed together, the result is called a grand staff. Each instrument or voice reads on some portion of the grand staff according to its range.

STUDY GUIDELINES

Guide to Perceiving Melody

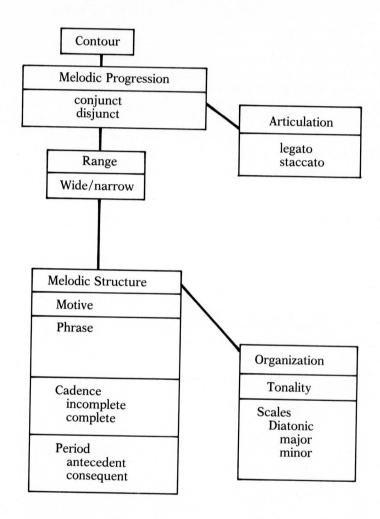

KEY TERMS AND CONCEPTS

Accidental
Audible frequency spectrum
Bass staff

Clef
   F clef (bass 𝄢)
   G clef (treble 𝄞)

Contour
Cycles per second (cps or Hertz)
Diatonic
8va
Flat ♭
Frequency
Grand staff
Half-step
Interval
Key Signature
Ledger line
Melodic articulation
   Legato
   Staccato
Melodic progression
   Conjunct (stepwise)
   Disjunct (skipwise)
Melodic structure
   Cadence
      Complete
      Incomplete
   Motive

Period (paired phrases)
   Antecedent
   Consequent
Phrase
Tonality
Tonic
Melody
Microtone
Natural sign ♮
Octave
Pitch
Quarter tone
Range
Scale
   Major
   Minor
Sharp ♯
Staff
Theme
Treble staff
Whole-step

EXERCISES

1. Draw the contour of the first phrase of the following tunes:

   a. Twinkle, twinkle, little star, how I wonder what you are.
   b. Oh, when the saints, go marchin' in, oh, when the saints go marchin' in.
   c. Way down upon the Swanee River, far, far away.
   d. From the halls of Montezuma, to the shores of Tripoli.
   e. Silent Night, Holy Night, All is calm, all is bright.

2. Using the five tunes listed under number 1, answer the following questions:

   What kind of cadence ends each phrase? How can you tell?
   Which of the phrases is basically conjunct? Disjunct?
   Major? Minor? Would you say the range is wide or narrow?

3. Choose a favorite vocal popular song from a record, listen several times, and discuss the following, using page 186 as a guide.

Name of Composition	Contour (draw)	Phrase (structure)	Melodic Progression (conjunct/ disjunct)	Range (wide/ narrow)	Melodic Articulation (legato, staccato)	Tonality (major/ minor)

4. Listen to the main melody in each of the following and draw the predominant contour in the area provided. Provide information on other areas through repeated hearings, using pages 62, 83, 142, and 186 as guides.

Selection	Contour	Melodic Progression (conjunct, disjunct)	Range	Melodic Articulation (legato, staccato)	Tonality
Grieg—*In the Hall of the Mountain King* (Selection no. 18)					
Handel—"For Unto Us A Child Is Born" (Selection no. 28)					
Stravinsky—"Gavotte with Two Variations" (Selection no. 9)					
Schubert—*Gretchen am Spinnrade* (Selection no. 19)					

5. Place the following notes on the grand staff:

c_1 a_1 $d\flat_2$ e   B   CC f_3 A

CHAPTER REVIEW

Match items in the two columns. Answers in Appendix.

1. _____ antecedent
2. _____ cadence
3. _____ disjunct
4. _____ 𝄢
5. _____ contour
6. _____ consequent
7. _____ codetta
8. _____ audible frequency
    spectrum
9. _____ theme
10. _____ conjunct
11. _____ 𝄞
12. _____ motive
13. _____ staccato
14. _____ octave
15. _____ tonic
16. _____ legato
17. _____ half-step
18. _____ range

A. 16—16000 Hertz
B. phrase ending
C. detached
D. smooth and connected
E. stepwise melodic movement
F. distance from lowest to
    highest pitches
G. G clef
H. small coda
I. melodic direction
J. question phrase
K. small musical idea
L. answer phrase
M. F clef
N. very important melody
O. melody with jumps and skips
P. c_1 and c_2
Q. most important pitch in a
    melody
R. C to C♯

FOR FURTHER LISTENING

Conjunct-Disjunct
Brahms

Symphony no. 3 in F major
First movement, opening theme (disjunct)
Fourth movement, opening theme (conjunct)

Debussy	*Prélude a l'Après-midi d'un Faune*
	First theme (conjunct)
Webern	Concerto for Nine Instruments (disjunct)

Contour (Opening Theme)

Brahms	Symphony no. 1 in c minor: First movement
Copland	*Music for the Theater:* Fourth movement

Range

Wide

Schumann	*Kinderscenen:* no. 7, "Träumerei"
Stravinsky	*Petrouchka:* "Russian Dance"

Narrow

Sibelius	*Finlandia:* Principal theme

Scale

Structure
(Phrase)

Bach	Cantata no. 140: Final chorale (AAB)
Chopin	Prelude no. 20 in c minor, op. 28 (ABB)
Saint-Saëns	*Carnival of the Animals:* "Turtles" (phrases $aa_1bb_1{=}AB$)
Schubert	*Du bist die Ruh'* (AA_1BB_1 each verse)

Diatonic

Mozart	Sonata in A major, K. 331: First movement theme
Ravel	*Pavane pour une Infante Défunte*

Non-Western

African Music
Folkways Records FW 8852

Chinese Folk and Art Songs
Spoken Arts Records #205

Music of Indonesia
Folkways Records FE 4537

The Ragas of India
Folkways Records FL 8368

CHAPTER SIX

HARMONY

❖

Harmony can be defined as two or more different pitches being sounded at the same time. For example, c and g create harmony when they are sounded together; c, d♭, d, and d♯ also create harmony when sounded simultaneously. C and c do not create harmony, however, since they are octaves—the same pitch eight notes apart. Only two or more *different* pitches will create harmony.

Music without the added dimension of harmony would sound incomplete to Western listeners. Since most European-based music contains harmony, its sound seems normal to us. By contrast, the music of India is almost devoid of harmonic contrasts. The concept of harmony includes the term *chord*, which is the simultaneous sounding of at least three pitches. The broader term *harmony* refers both to the use of chords as building blocks and to movement from one chord to another.

CHORD

Listen to "Lao Sên Sao Tien" (Old Monk Sweeping the Buddhist Temple) *(listening selections).* The instrument in this selection is a Chinese mouth-organ called the *sheng*, one of the few Chinese instruments that plays harmony. The sheng is made of a combination of gourd and bamboo. The gourd provides an air reservoir, somewhat like a pipe organ, with several bamboo tubes extending from it, each with a brass reed. There is a finger hole on the back of each bamboo pipe. In performance, the player cups the gourd in the hands and sucks air in through the mouthpiece. When the hole of a pipe is covered with a finger, air is drawn through the reed, thereby producing sound. Many Chinese wind instruments, including the sheng, have changed little since ancient times.

Selection no. 59
SHENG

Sheng, Chinese mouth organ. The gourd in this example has been replaced with a metal air reservoir.

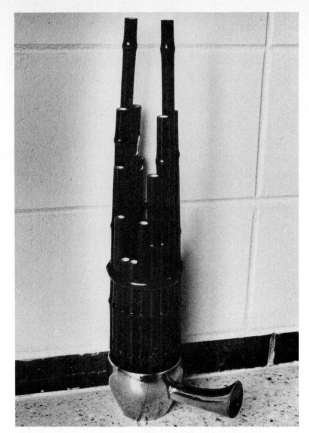

Photo by K.H. Han. Northern Illinois University.

Music of the sheng moves in chord-like fashion, as heard here—each melody note is supported by a chord, resulting in harmony. The melody in this example is repeated several times with little variation.

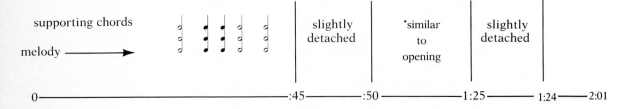

supporting chords

melody ⟶

| | slightly detached | •similar to opening | slightly detached | |

0 ————————————————————:45———:50————————1:25———— 1:24————2:01

In the typical fashion of Chinese music, this composition is programmatic, depicting the regular motion of a monk sweeping the temple courtyard with his broom. The melody is a fourteenth-century folk song from Shantung (North China).

Depth in sculpture is somewhat like the dimension harmony provides in music. *Makutu (Opus 505),* Barbara Hepworth, English, 1969, bronze.

University of Arizona Museum of Art, gift of Edward J. Gallagher, Jr.

CHORDS

The Triad

The most common type of chord is the *triad,* the basis for almost all harmony in the Western world. A triad is a chord composed of three different pitches, each separated by the interval of a third. One note serves as the *root,* an important scale tone upon which the triad is built. For example, a triad on c uses c, e, and g as its three pitches (left below). In this case e is the *third* (a third above c) and g is the *fifth* (a fifth above c). If the root of the triad is the lowest-sounding tone, it is said to be in *root position* (right below).

ROOT

THIRD
FIFTH
ROOT
POSITION

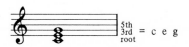

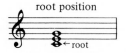

INVERSION

Selection no. 60

When a pitch other than the root is the lowest-sounding tone of the triad, the form is called an *inversion*.

Listen to F. J. Morton's "Dead Man Blues" performed by the Red Hot Peppers featuring Jelly Roll Morton on piano (1926) *(listening selections)*. This composition uses triadic harmony, that is, most chords are triads. The selection opens with an allusion to Chopin's Funeral March, followed by improvisation on the clarinet, trumpet, and trombone. The style is called *New Orleans* jazz, developed around World War I. There is little emphasis on solos in New Orleans jazz; the interest is more in collective improvisation, as in the first and last chorus. The harmony throughout is primarily triadic.

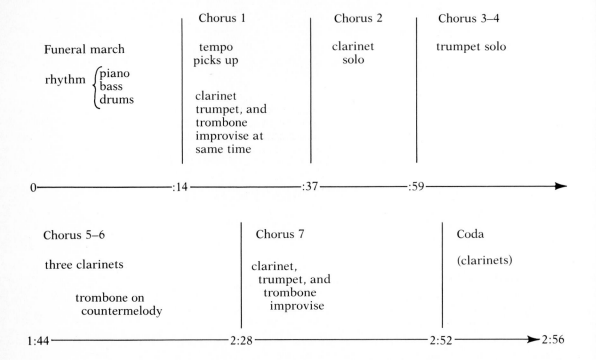

	Chorus 1	Chorus 2	Chorus 3–4
Funeral march	tempo picks up	clarinet solo	trumpet solo
rhythm {piano, bass, drums}	clarinet trumpet, and trombone improvise at same time		

0 ———————— :14 ———————— :37 ———————— :59 ————————▶

Chorus 5–6	Chorus 7	Coda
three clarinets	clarinet, trumpet, and trombone improvise	(clarinets)
trombone on countermelody		

1:44 ———————— 2:28 ———————— 2:52 ————▶ 2:56

Extended Chords

SEVENTH

Several chords other than triads can be used by composers. The *seventh* chord (7th) has an additional pitch added to the basic triad, giving it four different pitches. The chord is called a seventh because an interval of a 7th is formed between the root and the added pitch. When

"Jelly Roll" Morton (1885–1941) once claimed to have invented jazz. Whether this is true or not is open to conjecture; nonetheless, he certainly was present when it first occurred. Morton as a youth studied the piano in New Orleans, and in 1904 became an itinerant musician living in New York, Chicago, St. Louis, and Los Angeles. He made his earliest recordings in 1923 and later worked with his band the Red Hot Peppers, recording in 1926 "Dead Man Blues." Jelly Roll, whose real name was Ferdinand Joseph, synthesized the New Orleans Dixieland style of jazz, using collective improvisation and individual solos in his ensemble. Because he wrote some of his music in traditional notation, many consider him one of the first true jazz composers.

additional pitches are added to a triad, as with the seventh, the result is called an *extended* chord. Other extended chords are *ninths, elevenths,* and *thirteenths,* named in each case for the interval formed between the root and added pitch.

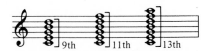

As with triads, extended chords are used in both root position and inversion. Extended chords tend to provide more tension than triads because they use more than three pitches, a topic that will be discussed below in the section on consonance and dissonance.

TENSION

Quartal/Clusters
Triads and extensions are not the only means for constructing chords. Composers also use fourths instead of thirds to build chords, in which case the harmony is called *quartal* (built on 4ths) as opposed to *tertian* (built on 3rds).

QUARTAL
TERTIAN

Chords may also be constructed entirely of seconds, which results in what is called a *cluster.*

CLUSTER

These chords taken together provide a rich source of harmonic material for composers. In certain historical periods, chords and harmony have been used in a predictable manner. In general, certain classes of chords have been favored by composers of a set era. Rarely would one find all types of chords used in the same composition. During the Classic Period, for example, tertian harmony predominated. Extended chords were employed more freely during the Romantic Period, and as a result the music seems a bit more tense than that of the Classic Period. In the present century, tension is much more common. The seventh chords of the eighteenth century, often surprising in the context of tertian harmony, sound quite normal and relaxed in the twentieth century amid harmony that may be predominantly quartal. Composers in this century are relatively free to use any means of creating harmony, whether traditional or unorthodox.

Selection no. 61   Listen to Béla Bartók's "Maruntel" from *Rumanian Folk Dances* *(listening selections)*. "Maruntel" is the fifth dance in a suite by the Hungarian composer. Since chord extension, quartal, and cluster harmonies are used, the harmony is tense.

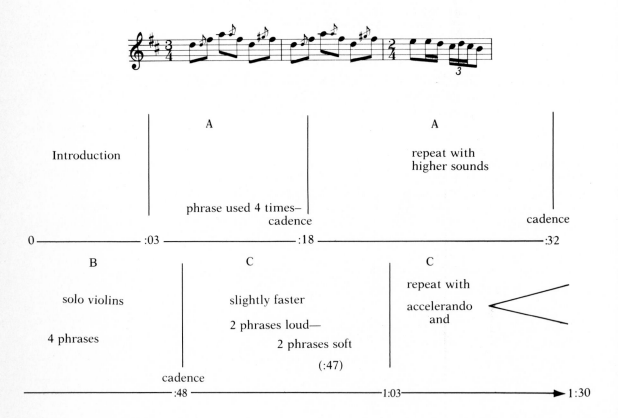

Béla Bartók (1881–1945) was a renowned Hungarian composer who even at a young age showed a great deal of interest in the music of his country. Because his father died with Bartók was eight years old, his mother became an itinerant school teacher, which allowed the youth to travel and collect music from many regions of Hungary.

As a man Bartók attended the Royal Hungarian Music Academy in Budapest, where he met Zoltán Kodály, a fellow countryman who was also interested in preserving the folk music of Hungary. Together, they spent eight years collecting and classifying thousands of folk melodies of their homeland.

Bartók ultimately became a professor at the Budapest Conservatory but fled to the United States before World War II. He received an honorary degree from Columbia University in 1940 and continued to compose. Among his more important works are six string quartets; a piano pedagogy work, *Mikrokosmos; Music for Strings, Percussion, and Celesta;* and several concertos, including the popular Concerto for Orchestra. Throughout his life Bartók experienced financial difficulties in spite of his regard as a composer. After his death, ironically,

Bela Bartok.

Photo by C. Leirens. Courtesy of the New York Public Library.

performances of his compositions increased dramatically.

CONSONANCE AND DISSONANCE

Relative Nature

Consonance and *dissonance* represent stability and instability in harmony, respectively. A chord is considered *consonant* if it feels stable, that is, if it has a feeling of having arrived at a comfortably centered resting point. Conversely, a chord is *dissonant* if it has tension, which means it sounds as if it seeks fulfillment or resolution. The same descriptions may hold for a series of chords or a particular passage of music. Certain compositions are generally more dissonant than others. The concept may be clarified by thinking of consonance and dissonance as a continuum with consonance on the right, dissonance on the left. A chord (or an entire composition) at X is the most dissonant, while one at Z is most consonant. Thus a chord at Y can be considered

CONSONANT

DISSONANT

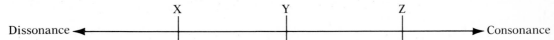

Dissonance ← | X | Y | Z → Consonance

dissonant when compared to Z, but consonant when compared to X. Distinctions between consonance and dissonance are also affected by the timbre of the composition, its intensity and context, and, most important, by the number of pitches used and intervals within a chord.

Intervals and Number of Pitches

Some intervals are considered more consonant than others. Fifths, thirds, and sixths are perceived as being consonant, while seconds, fourths, and sevenths are considered dissonant. If a chord is constructed of several consonant and *one* consonant interval, it will probably be perceived as a dissonant chord. A chord with *many* dissonant intervals, of course, will be perceived as even more dissonant.

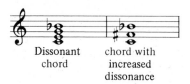

Dissonant   chord with
chord   increased
           dissonance

The number of pitches used also has a bearing on a chord's dissonance. A chord with three different pitches is usually less dissonant than one with eight.

3 pitches   8 pitches

Intervals and pitches are not mutually exclusive; it is almost impossible to build a chord with four or more pitches without including at least one dissonant interval. It is thus apparent why triads, with only two intervals, sound consonant, while extended chords, clusters, and quartal harmony generate more dissonance.

Augmented and diminished intervals are usually considered more dissonant than major, minor, or perfect intervals. An *augmented fourth*, which is a half-step wider than a perfect fourth, is quite dissonant:

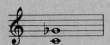

as is the *diminished fifth*, a half-step narrower than a

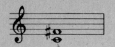

perfect fifth. On the keyboard, these two intervals result in the sounding of the same pitches, but the actual spelling of the interval on the staff determines whether it will be labeled a fourth or a fifth.

Other Factors

The *voicing* of the chord, that is, the manner in which the pitches are
arranged, is another factor influencing the perception of dissonance.
Dissonant intervals sound less dissonant when they are spaced over a
wide range (e.g., four octaves) than if placed within one or two octaves.

VOICING

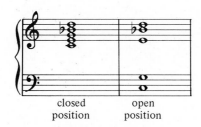

closed
position

open
position

The former arrangement is called *closed position,* whereas the latter
is *open position.* Close spacing of intervals tends to heighten their
dissonant qualities.

CLOSED AND
OPEN
POSITION

Finally, timbre and intensity also affect dissonance. A chord played
softly by six flutes will seem less dissonant than the same chord played
by six trumpets at a forte level.

TIMBRE
AND
INTENSITY

Historical Perspective

Perceptions of relative dissonance and consonance vary in different
eras, so these values are usually considered within historical context.
In the Renaissance, most vocal music was quite consonant, while in
the Romantic era dissonance was more pronounced. Some have
claimed that all music in the present century is dissonant, but composers of today still provide release or consonance in their music, even
though this "consonance" probably has more tension than music of
earlier periods, such as the eighteenth century. Consonance and dissonance thus provide degrees of tension and release in music of all
historical periods; in a sense, new norms and tolerance for consonance
and dissonance are established in each period.

◄——[20th Century][Romantic]————————————————————————[Renaissance]——►

Dissonance   Consonance

Listen to *Sit Gloria Domini* (parallel organum) *(listening selections). Organum* is a term used to describe the first harmony used in
Western music, especially in the period between the ninth and thirteenth centuries. Its effect is often open and hollow sounding. The
intervals of harmony in organum are almost always fourths and fifths,
which may seem dissonant to today's listeners.

Selection no. 62
ORGANUM

The *Sit Gloria Domini* is an example of *parallel organum* (ninth and tenth centuries). The melody or principal voice *(vox principalis)* is accompanied by a strictly parallel part, which moves on a note-for-note basis an interval of a fourth lower. This parallel part is called the *vox organalis* (voice of organum).

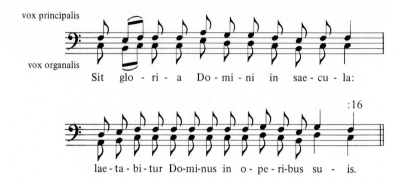

The development of organum in the vocal church music of the Middle Ages gradually led to harmonic innovations in music, resulting ultimately in the sounds that now characterize most Western music.

HARMONIC RHYTHM

Harmonic rhythm refers to the speed with which chords change. In some compositions one chord may serve as the harmonic framework for an entire measure, phrase, or even section. Such an effect is referred to as slow harmonic rhythm. Other compositions may use many chord changes, in which case they are said to have a fast harmonic rhythm.

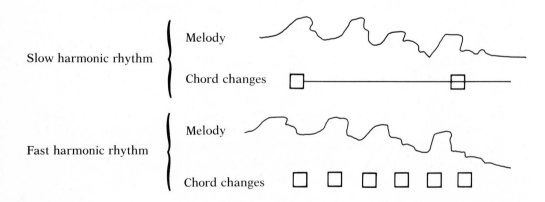

Harmonic rhythm has little to do with the tempo of a composition. A slow and stately Bach chorale may have chord changes on every beat or even between the beats; conversely, a fast Vivaldi concerto movement may utilize one chord for several measures. Composers in the Baroque period often wrote in a fast harmonic rhythm, with the result that their music, even in a slow tempo, seems busy. Music of the Classic period may sound less complicated because composers of that time favored a slower harmonic rhythm.

Listen to Verse VII (Chorale) from J.S. Bach's *Christ lag in Todesbanden* (Christ lay by death enshrouded) *(listening selections)*. There is a chord change on every beat of this chorale. The melody is sung by the sopranos, while harmony is provided by altos, tenors, and basses. The voice parts are also doubled by instruments. In a few places the harmony even changes between the beats, on ♫ (eighth) notes, which results in a fast harmonic rhythm.

Selection no. 63

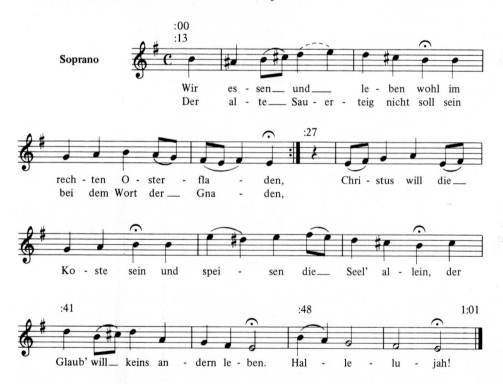

This *chorale* is from one of Bach's best-known cantatas, *Christ lag in Todesbanden*. A *cantata* is much like an oratorio, since it has arias, recitatives, duets, choruses, and an orchestral accompaniment. However, it is usually smaller in scope, lasting twenty to thirty minutes instead of several hours, and may be either sacred or secular.

CHORALE
CANTATA

Bach was Kapellmeister in Leipzig from 1723 until his death in 1750. Part of his job was providing music at two churches, St. Nicholas and St. Thomas. The necessity of both selecting and composing so much music led Bach to rework many of his compositions, including the cantatas.

Church cantatas in the Lutheran service frequently end with performers and congregation singing the chorale (hymn tune) upon which the entire cantata is based. This is true of *Christ lag in Todesbanden*, which was composed for Easter day in 1724. The entire work consists of a set of seven variations on the chorale melody, with the seventh and final version the simplest and most direct, as heard here.

VERSE VII—CHORALE

Wir essen und leben wohl im rechten
Oster fladen; der alte sauerteig nicht
soll sein bei dem Wort der Gnaden; Christus
will die Koste sein und speisen die
Sell'allein, der Glaub' will keins andern
leben. Hallelujah!

With loving hearts we keep today the
feast of God hath us given. Before His
Word slinks hence away the old and evil
leaven. Christ himself the feast hath
spread, by Him the hungry soul is fed with
living Bread down come from heaven.
Alleluia!

TEXTURE

Texture is defined as the relationship of melody to harmony. Although a melody may be performed without accompaniment, it is much more typical to have a harmonic background. Harmony may come as the result of chords being played with the melody. Harmony is also created when compatible melodies are played together.

Monophony

Monophony, or *monophonic* texture, is a single unaccompanied melodic line, with no contrasting harmonic tonalities. An unaccompanied folk song is a good example, whether sung by one singer or by several in unison.

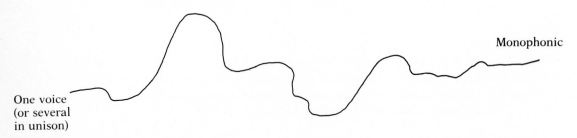

One voice
(or several
in unison)

Monophonic

Photo by Tim Fuller.

A solo dancer is much like a monophonic texture, one line of activity without background.

Similarly, a clarinet, oboe, trumpet, and piano, all playing the identical melody in unison, are playing monophony, despite the presence of several different instruments with contrasting sound qualities. Various instruments may even play the same melody at different octaves (C, c, c_1, etc.) but the texture is still monophonic.

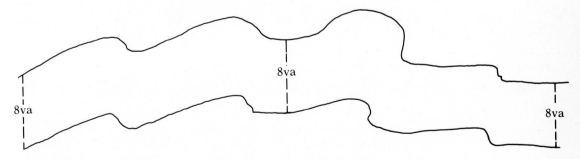

Although monophony is common in the short folksong form, it may also occur momentarily in a longer composition of art music to provide variety. But lengthy compositions with a solely monophonic texture are more typical of non-Western music or of medieval examples of Western music.

Selection no. 64　　　　　Listen to Adam de la Hale's "Bergeronette" *(listening selections).* This monophonic example from the Middle Ages is pure melody without accompaniment.

Secular musicians of the Middle Ages commonly performed and composed pieces like "Bergeronette." Little is known of the musicians; some were itinerant students called *jongleurs* or *goliards* who were exclusively performers. Others actually wrote the music and were called *trouvères, troubadours,* and *minnesingers.*

Adam de la Hale (c. 1230–1288), a trouvère, wrote *Le Jeu de Robin et de Marion,* a pastoral play with incidental music, for the French court at Naples. Folk songs like "Bergeronette" were included. Undoubtedly the secular music of the Middle Ages was not always performed monophonically, since there are examples that use instrumental accompaniment.

TRANSLATION

ROBIN: Sweet shepherdess, give me your garland.
MARION: Robin, would you wish me to put it on your head as a token of love?
ROBIN: Yes, you shall be my love and have my girdle, my purse and my clasp. Sweet shepherdess, give me your garland.
MARION: Willingly, my sweet love.

Heterophony
A second type of texture is called *heterophonic,* a form similar to monophony, but not common in Western music. In heterophony, two or more versions of the same or a similar melody are heard at the same time.

Melody 1
Melody 2

One melody may occasionally be more elaborate than the others, but all melodies are typically in unison at cadences. This texture is most characteristic of music from Indonesia, Japan, and China.

Listen to *Golden Rain Hudjan Mas (listening selections).* The orchestra is called a *gamelan* and is indigenous to the islands of Indonesia, particularly Java and Bali. This particular selection is from Bali, where the predominant sound is provided by various forms of an instrument called the *gangsa,* an idiophone whose metal keys are played with mallets. Some have five keys or bars, while others have as many as nine.

Selection no. 65
GAMELAN

GANGSA

Top, Balinese
Gamelan Angklung,
made by I. Made
Gableran of Blahbatu
Village, Bali, 1978;
center, Jegogan, a
metallophone similar
to the gangsa; bottom,
Gong Ageng.

Photos by K.H. Han. Northern Illinois University.

Everyone in the gamelan plays the same melody or a slightly varied version of it at the same time, with heterophony the result. Drums are used to heighten the tension and keep the beat, while the gong provides punctuation at the ends of important phrases and sections.

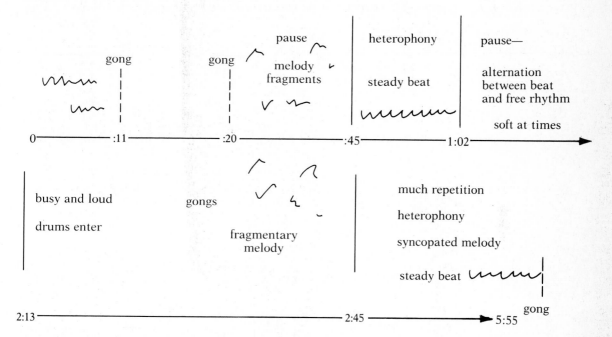

Homophony

In *homophony*, the most common texture in Western music, one melody is sung or played by one instrument (or by several in unison) with harmonic accompaniment.

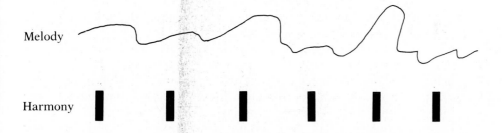

In a symphonic work, a melody in the winds accompanied by strings is homophonic. Church hymns and chorales are usually homophonic, too. Even the individual pianist playing a melody in the right hand and an accompaniment with the left is creating homophony.

ARPEGGIO

OSTINATO

There are several ways to provide accompaniment for a melody. Simple triads in root position or inversion may be used. Chords may be *arpeggiated*, that is, the pitches played successively, one after another, instead of simultaneously. A repeated chordal pattern called an *ostinato* (like a boogie-woogie bass) may be called into play. In most cases, such an accompaniment reinforces the beat and meter.

Triads   Arpeggio   Ostinato
(broken chord)

As long as there is *one* principal melody with harmonic accompaniment, the texture is considered homophonic.

Selection no. 66

Listen to the first movement Allegro of Mozart's Horn Concerto no. 3 in E♭, K. 447 *(listening selections.)*. This movement is homophonic for almost its entire length. The form is ternary and two themes are used.

CADENZA

The themes are tossed back and forth between horn and orchestra in the A section. The B section is then short and dramatic, with the return of A occurring at 3:40. Finally, there is a *cadenza*, a brilliant passage for an instrumental soloist, in this case the horn (5:38), near the end. This provides the only notable change from the homophonic texture.

SOLO CONCERTO

Solo concertos, especially popular during the Classic period, are written for such instruments as piano, violin, and horn. Since concerto means "to compete" together, there is a healthy duality and interchange between soloist and orchestra, a musical struggle to maintain balance. The only indication in the listening selection that the horn has the upper hand is in the cadenza, in which the soloist is expected to improvise (or play someone else's improvisation) and display his or her technical superiority. Solo concertos are almost always written in three movements. Whereas second movements tend to be slow and lyrical, and third movements fast and playful, the moderate tempo here is typical of many first movements.

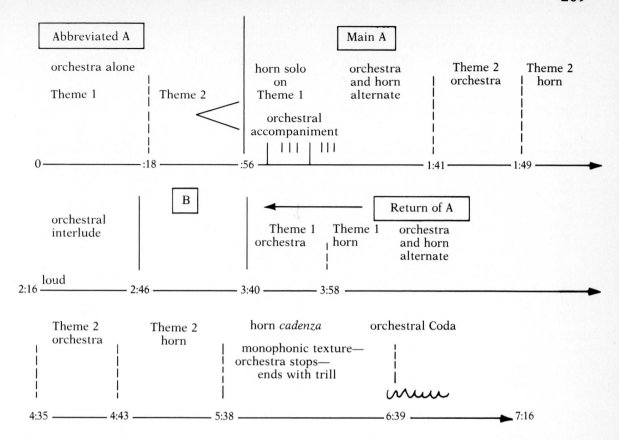

Polyphony

The fourth type of texture is called *polyphonic*. Polyphony is defined as several melodies that sound simultaneously and thus generate their own harmony.

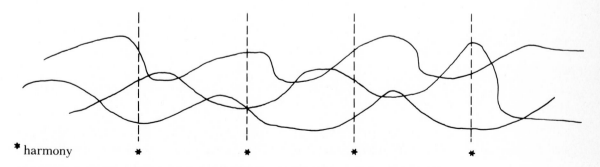

* harmony

A minimum of two voices or melodies is necessary to create polyphony, but some composers have written as much as eight-voice *counterpoint*,   COUNTERPOINT

Solo concertos were attractive to Mozart because of their inherent struggle, evidenced in his works for piano, violin, flute, oboe, bassoon, and harp as well as the horn. Four horn concertos were written between 1782–1787 for the performer Ignaz Leitgeb, a friend of the family. Mozart loved to tease and torment his friend by providing ludicrous musical directions in the score. Horn Concerto no. 3 in E♭, however, is the only one of the four free of these directions. Many critics and musicians consider it Mozart's finest and most significant horn concerto.

Because the French horn of Mozart's time did not have valves, the performer coaxed all pitches from the instrument by varying lip pressure, as with a bugle, and manipulating with a hand the air passing through the bell. Even on a contemporary instrument equipped with rotary valves, consummate technical mastery is essential to perform this concerto.

French horn with rotary valves.

Courtesy of Yamaha International Corporation.

a term used to describe the note-against-note nature of polyphony. Three- and four-voice polyphony are probably the most common.

Polyphony can also be created when a melody is sung as a round. Although this is the use of *one* melody, it differs from heterophony in that each part occurs at a different *time,* rather than overlapping with variations.

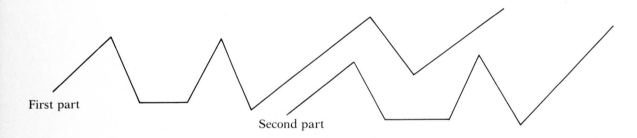

First part

Second part

Selection no. 67   Listen to the Sanctus from Palestrina's Mass *Aeterna Christi Munera (listening selections).* This is polyphony written for four voices. The order of entrances is soprano (1), alto (2), tenor (3), and bass (4). Then the four independent but complementary voices interweave polyphonically throughout.

(Original note-values halved)

(Sung a tone lower)

REMAINDER OF TEXT

Pleni sunt coeli et terra gloria tua.
Hosanna in excelsis.

COMPLETE TRANSLATION

Holy, holy, holy, Lord God of hosts.
Heaven and earth are full of Thy glory.
Hosanna in the highest.

Prior to the nineteenth century, one type of texture dominated in each period. But Western composers during the last two centuries have taken the opportunity to use all types of texture except heterophony within a single composition.

Several dancers doing similar movements are much like a polyphonic texture. *Rehearsal,* Liz Whitney Quisgard, American, 1955, oil on masonite.

University of Arizona Museum of Art, gift of Edward Joseph Gallagher, Jr.

Selection no. 57

Listen again to "Samuel Goldenburg and Schmuyle" from Mussorgsky's *Pictures at an Exhibition (listening selections).* This selection, already examined, provides a good example of three of the four textures discussed.

Palestrina (c. 1525–c. 1594) is the name of a small town near Rome where Giovanni Pierluigi was born. He has always been known by his place of birth, simply Palestrina, rather than by his given name.

Because Palestrina was musically trained in Rome, he spent his adult professional life serving its churches: St. Peter's, St. John Lateran, and St. Mary Major's. He was employed at St. Peter's from 1571 until his death, supervising the musical revisions of the liturgy mandated by the Council of Trent, the church

Palestrina.

Reproduction of etching by F. Bottcher from a portrait preserved in the Vatican Library. Courtesy of the New York Public Library.

council called to meet many of the criticisms raised by the Protestant Reformation. Palestrina's characteristic vocal style is four- or five-part polyphony, with each voice part imitating the others. This was considered the ideal sound for a cappella singing of Catholic church music in the Renaissance. The coverage of vocal lines results in triadic harmony, with very little dissonance. Palestrina wrote approximately 100 masses, aiming for technical smoothness and beauty, rather than for impact or originality.

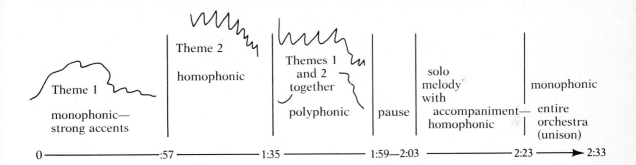

Theme 1
monophonic—
strong accents

Theme 2
homophonic

Themes 1
and 2
together
polyphonic

pause

solo
melody
with
accompaniment—
homophonic

monophonic

entire
orchestra
(unison)

0 ———————— :57 ——————— 1:35 ——————— 1:59—2:03 ————————— 2:23 ——→ 2:33

NOTATION OF HARMONY

Harmony is most frequently notated as a vertical combination of pitches on a staff.

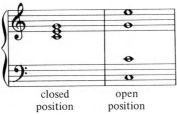

closed   open
position   position

LETTER SYMBOLS

Musicians also use a variety of abbreviations as harmonic indicators. These abbreviations include the use of letter symbols above a melody, with each letter representing a given chord.

TABLATURE

Tablature is another type of abbreviation, which shows a performer's finger position. A guitar tablature shows the placement of the performer's fingers on the strings of the instrument. Tablatures are also used for showing lute, ukulele, and banjo harmonies.

x = leave that string out of the chord

Abbreviations for harmony are not strictly contemporary inventions; they were used in earlier periods as well. During the Baroque period, for example, keyboard performers were required to provide harmony and embellishments when they played in an instrumental ensemble as part of the continuo. They used an abbreviation for harmony, called *figured bass*, in which the bass line is provided for the performer, certain designations being then both notated and assumed.

FIGURED BASS

A bass pitch without a number denotes a triad in root position on that note. A $_6$ under a pitch means a triad in inversion, as does $^6_4$. There are numerous designations for notes to be left unharmonized or for those representing seventh chords. In addition, the keyboard performer was expected to play chordal pitches in any octave while keeping the bass line relatively intact. Ornamentation could be added freely. The balanced *realization* of this multitude of options and instructions was left to the skill of the performer, so although the bass line would be the same at every performance, the actual placement of chord times and harmonies could be different, even when executed by the same artist.

REALIZATION

Since harmony is now notated on staff, even for works that originally used the figured-bass abbreviation, the realization of a figured bass is not required of most keyboard performers of today.

HARMONY AND STYLE PERIODS

More than any other element, harmony helps differentiate among style periods in music. The following chart summarizes harmonic use.

Period	Harmony	Examples
Medieval	These textures are used: Early—monophonic Middle—organum, primitive polyphony in 4ths and 5ths Late—polyphonic	*Sit Gloria Domini* Adam de la Hale—"Bergeronette"
Renaissance	Texture is polyphonic, and the basis of harmony is the triad.	Palestrina—Sanctus (Mass *Aeterna Christus Munera*)
Baroque	There is a contrast between homophonic and polyphonic textures. Harmony is triadic and a fast harmonic rhythm is common.	Bach—*Christ lag in Todesbanden*
Classic	Homophonic textures predominate and harmony is triadic. Slow harmonic rhythms prevail.	Mozart—Allegro (Horn Concerto no. 3 in E♭, K. 447)
Romantic	All textures except heterophonic are used but homophony is the most important. Extended chords—7ths, 9ths—are common, providing more dissonance. Composers often treat harmony quite individually.	Mussorgsky—"Samuel Goldenburg and Schmuyle" (*Pictures at an Exhibition*)
Impressionism	Texture is largely homophonic. Extended chords and open spacing are common. Many chord inversions are used, as are clusters and quartal harmony.	
Twentieth Century	All textures are used, with polyphonic texture becoming very important. Much dissonance occurs. Clusters and quartal harmonies as well as quarter tones are used in harmonies.	Bartok—*Rumanian Folk Dances* "Dead Man Blues"

See also selections in Chapter 3, p. 81; Chapter 4, p. 140; Chapter 5, p. 184.

SUMMARY

Harmony is the vertical sonority that occurs in music, particularly in the movement from chord to chord. It provides an added dimension that is expected in music of the Western world.

Chords are integral to harmony and may be classified as dissonant or consonant, depending upon the pitches used. Dissonance and consonance, analogous to tension and release, are not absolutes, however, and what was considered dissonant in one period may no longer be so considered. Consonance and dissonance may be used to describe chords, sections of a composition, or an entire work.

Triads are chords that consist of three pitches separated from one another by the interval of a third. Triads, like all chords, are used in both closed and open position as well as in root position and inversion. Other chord types are sevenths, ninths, elevenths, and thirteenths, as well as quartal harmony and tone clusters.

Melody alone or the interplay of melody with its harmony creates four textures in music: monophonic, heterophonic, homophonic, and polyphonic. The last two are the most commonly used in Western music.

Harmony is usually notated on a staff, but musicians may also use abbreviations such as chord symbols and tablatures. In the past, a figured-bass was used to indicate harmony and chord structures.

STUDY GUIDELINES

Guide To Perceiving Harmony

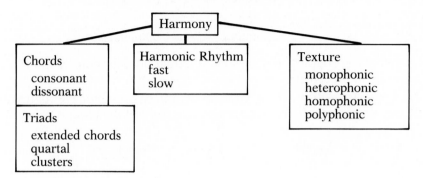

KEY TERMS AND CONCEPTS

Arpeggio (arpeggiated)
Chord
Cluster
Consonance
Counterpoint
Dissonance
Extended chords
  Elevenths
  Ninths
  Sevenths
  Thirteenths
Figured Bass
Harmonic Rhythm
Harmony
Organum
Ostinato

Quartal harmony
Root position
Tablature
Tertian harmony
Texture
  Heterophonic
  Homophonic
  Monophonic
  Polyphonic
Triad
  Fifth
  Root
  Third
Voicing
  Closed position
  Open position

EXERCISES

1. Listen to a short composition (5–10 minutes) and plot the change
   between consonance and dissonance on the following chart:

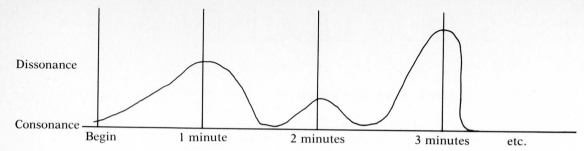

What is creating the dissonant effect in this composition? The consonant effect?

2. Listen to the following compositions and check which type of texture predominates. If the texture changes, record the change as well.

Selection	Monophonic	Heterophonic	Homophonic	Polyphonic
Handel— "For Unto Us" (Selection no. 28)				
"Rainy Day Blues" (Selection no. 3)				

3. Compare the harmonic rhythm (speed of chord changes) in each of the following compositions as well as the texture.

Selection	Harmonic Rhythm (Slow—medium—fast)	Texture (Mono-, hetero-, homo-, polyphonic)
Mozart—Allegro (Horn) Concerto no. 3 (Selection no. 66)		
Bach—Toccata in d minor (Selection no. 5)		
Dowland—Orlando Sleepeth (Selection no. 11)		
"Lost Your Head Blues" (Selection no. 8)		

4. Listen to the following compositions several times and fill in detail relative to each area. (See the pages specifically listed for help.)

Selection	Rhythm page 62	Dynamics page 83	Timbre page 142	Melody and Pitch page 186	Harmony page 217
1. J. S. Bach—Brandenburg Concerto no. 4, First movement (supplemental)					
2. Beethoven—Symphony no. 7 in A major, Third movement (supplemental)					
3. Murat Music of North Borneo (Selection no. 1)					
4. Copland—"Dance" from *Music for the Theatre* (Selection no. 93)					

CHAPTER REVIEW

Match items in the two columns. Answers in Appendix.

1. _____ root position
2. _____ triad
3. _____ extended chord
4. _____ cluster
5. _____ monophonic
6. _____ homophonic
7. _____ arpeggio
8. _____ heterophonic
9. _____ polyphonic
10. _____ consonance
11. _____ dissonance

A. root is lowest pitch
B. chord built of seconds
C. two or more versions of the same melody played simultaneously
D. feeling of release
E. two or more different melodies
F. sevenths, ninths, etc.
G. melody and accompaniment
H. tension
I. broken chord
J. three tones separated by thirds
K. pure melody

FOR FURTHER LISTENING

Consonance
    Palestrina   *Missa Brevis:* Kyrie

Dissonance
Bartók	Quartet no. 5
Webern	Concerto for Nine Instruments

Harmonic Rhythm
Beethoven	Sonata no. 18 in E♭ major: Third movement (fast)
Wagner	*Das Rheingold:* Prelude to Act I (slow)

Texture

Heterophonic

Japanese Koto Music with Shamisen and Shakuhachi
Lyrichord Discs LLST 7131
Javanese Court Gamelan
Nonesuch Records H-72044

Homophonic
Chopin	Nocturne in E♭ major, op. 9, no. 2
	Prelude in e minor, op. 28, no. 4
Handel	"Largo" (from *Xerxes*)
Tchaikovsky	*Nutcracker Suite:* "Waltz of the Flowers"

Monophonic
Bach	Partita in d minor (no. 2) for unaccompanied violin: "Gigue"
Stravinsky	*Petrouchka:* "Charlatan's Solo"

Polyphonic
Bach	*The Art of Fugue*
	Mass in b minor: Dona nobis pacem; Kyrie
	Two-Part Inventions
Handel	*Messiah:* "And With His Stripes"

Variable Texture
Bach	Toccata and Fugue in d minor
Debussy	*La Mer*

TONALITY

◆

MAJOR TONALITY	ATONALITY
MINOR TONALITY	NOTATION OF TONALITY
MODULATION	TONALITY AND STYLE PERIODS
BITONALITY AND	SUMMARY
POLYTONALITY	STUDY GUIDELINES

Tonality in music is defined as a feeling of pitch center, that is, the preference of one pitch over others. We thus speak of a composition as being in C major or f minor, in reference to the pitch that serves as its musical focus. As seen earlier, this important note is called the *tonic,*   TONIC
and provides the basis for the melody as well as the harmony. Tonality is therefore an element that combines both melody and harmony.

MAJOR TONALITY

One of the most common tonalities is *major.* A major scale, in this case, provides the melodic framework that, in conjunction with harmony, establishes the tonality of a composition. For example, if a musical composition is in C major, the pitches in the melody, arranged in ascending order within one octave, form a major scale with C as the starting pitch. C is thus the tonic pitch.

Primary Chords: I, IV, V₇

Harmony is determined from this scale by the three chords most often associated with it: a triad on the first pitch, the *tonic;* a triad on the fourth pitch of the scale, the *subdominant;* and a triad on the fifth   SUBDOMINANT
pitch, the *dominant.*   DOMINANT

221

Most simple songs in C major can be accompanied by these three chords. The dominant triad, however, is almost always used with the added fourth note, a 7th above the root, and is therefore called a **DOMINANT 7TH** *dominant 7th* chord.

These three chords, designated by Roman numerals—Tonic = I, Subdominant = IV, Dominant 7th = V_7—provide the basic harmony in any major key. A musical composition usually begins and almost always ends with the I chord. Progression from V_7 to I is typical at complete cadences, while other important punctuation points use either the I, IV, and V_7 chords. Because of their importance in establishing tonality, these three chords are called *primary chords*.

Secondary Chords

Composers may use triads and extended chords on other scale tones that are called *secondary* chords, designated as ii *(supertonic)*, iii *(mediant)*, vi *(submediant)*,, and vii *(leading tone triad)*. (It is common practice in designating triads to use C or I to refer to a major triad, c or i for minor.)

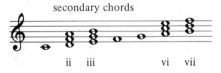

secondary chords

Selection no. 3   Listen to "Rainy Day Blues" *(listening selections)*. Lightnin' Hop-
12-BAR BLUES kins is singing a *12-bar blues*, accompanied on the guitar with I, IV, V_7 chords. Blues, as seen earlier, are constructed on a rhymed couplet with the first line repeated. There is typically a standard chord progression for each line of poetry in most renditions of the blues.

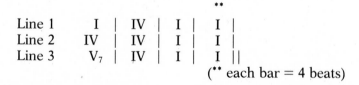

Listen to the chord progressions and how they are repeated for each new verse of the blues. Even the guitar improvisation in Verse 4 uses the same harmonies.

> **Blues** is a musical style that combines elements found in spirituals and field hollers (work songs) with fundamental chords learned in church. Evolving after the Civil War, blues is also a state of mind, reflecting the singer's despair and melancholy but without total pessimism. Country singers like Lightnin' Hopkins and urban blues singers like Bessie Smith have used the twelve-bar format of this style. Early instrumental jazz, especially New Orleans style, also adapted the form. Blues primary I, IV, and V_7 chords decisively established harmony and provided a framework for the birth of rock'n'roll in the 1950s.

Introduction—guitar ostinato on I

Verse 1

               I   IV
"Lord, I'm just sitting down here thinking what am
                                            I   I
           I going to do on this rainy day.
               IV   IV
Yes, I'm just sitting down here thinking what am
                                        I
           I going to do on this rainy day.
               V_7 IV
Well, it don't look like the clouds ever are going
                                  I   I
           let the sun shine another day.

Verse 2

                      I   IV
Yeah, you know if it keeps on raining Old Lightnin' can't
                     I   I
         make no time.
      IV   IV
Yes, you know if it keeps on raining Old Lightnin' can't
                     I   I
         make no time,
        V_7 IV
Yes, you know I can't help but worry and bother, oh Lord,
                          I   I
        about that little girl of mine.

Carl Sandburg, Don
Freeman, American, c.
1940, oil on canvas.

University of Arizona Museum of Art, gift of C. Leonard Pfeiffer.

MINOR TONALITY

The minor scale, which uses i, iv, and v chords, establishes tonality in
minor keys. One note of the minor scale is frequently altered to make
a V (major) instead of a v (minor chord), that is, the seventh pitch of
the scale is raised one-half step, thus providing a dominant 7th chord.

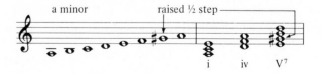

As with major keys, i, iv, and V$_7$ are used at key cadences and punctuations to establish the tonic.

Listen to Verse VI of Bach's *Christ lag in Todesbanden (listening selections)*. This movement of the cantata is its sixth verse, demonstrating minor tonality throughout. The basis of the harmony is triadic, as in the Lightnin' Hopkins selection, but in this case minor chords are used.

Selection no. 68

VERSE VI—SOPRANO AND TENOR DUET

So feiern wir das hohe Fest, mit Herzensfreud' und Wonne; das uns der Herre scheinen lässt, Er ist selber die Sonne; der durch seiner Gnaden Glanz erleuchtet uns're Herzen ganz, der Sönden Nacht ist verschwunden. Hallelujah.

So let us keep the Easter feast with joy and jubilation! The rising Sun from out the east now bringeth us salvation. In His ever glorious grace behold we now His radiant face: sin-laden night is departed. Alleluia!

Hearing the difference between major and minor chords and tonalities is basic to music appreciation, but there is no quick way to acquire the skill. The title of a composition often tells the listener whether to expect major or minor (Prelude in e minor, Waltz in A major, etc.). Unfortunately, this is useful only in very short compositions with a constant tonality. In longer compositions, the tonality usually changes several times.

Cues for hearing major and minor come from scales and triads themselves. The major scale has a wider interval between the tonic and the third pitch, consisting of four half-steps:

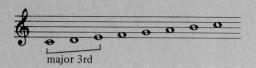

major 3rd

The distance between the tonic and third pitch is smaller in a minor scale—three half-steps—and sounds different:

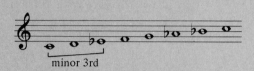

minor 3rd

Hearing the difference between major and minor thirds is also important for differentiating between major and minor triads, since the same interval is heard between root and third:

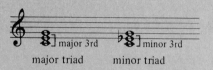

major 3rd   minor 3rd

major triad   minor triad

MODULATION

A musical composition of any length seldom remains in one tonality throughout. Typically, it will *modulate*—that is, change tonics—once, twice, or several times. A symphony in C major may begin and end in C major, but will probably modulate to other keys in between. Modulation is therefore a means whereby composers can achieve harmonic variety.

Selection no. 69 Listen to Louis Armstrong's performance of Harold Arlen's "I Gotta Right to Sing the Blues" *(listening selections)*, an example with two modulations. The song begins in one key, modulates for the singer (:04), and then modulates back to the original key at the conclusion of the vocal solo (1:13). This version of "I Gotta Right to Sing the Blues" thus begins and ends in the same key.

Louis (Satchmo) Armstrong recorded "I Gotta Right to Sing the Blues" in Chicago in 1933. The instruments are trumpet, trombone,

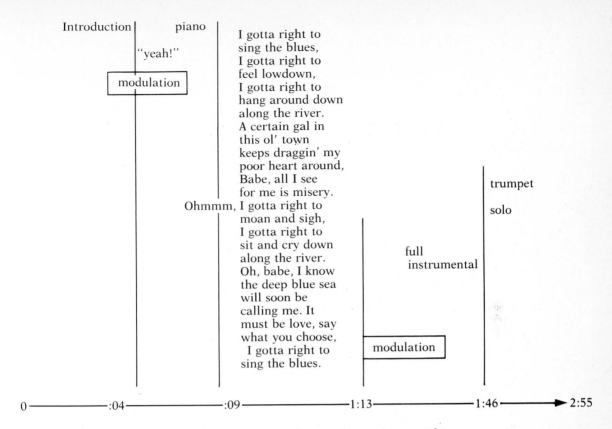

clarinet, alto and tenor saxophones, piano, guitar, bass, drums. This particular style is usually called Chicago jazz.

CHICAGO JAZZ

Louis Armstrong.
Courtesy of the New York Public Library.

Louis Armstrong (1900–1971), a famous black American jazz trumpeter, was the son of an illiterate factory worker. He grew up near Storyville, the red-light district of New Orleans, where he was arrested at age thirteen for firing a gun at a New Year's Eve party. Sent to a reform school, he learned to play the cornet. After his release, his first break came in 1919 as a jazzer in Kid Ory's Band. In 1922 he joined "King" Oliver's Creole Jazz Band in Chicago and later formed his own groups, including the Hot Five. He rapidly won admirers worldwide for his style of improvisation, and set an endurance record hitting high C on the trumpet 280 times in succession. Throughout his career, his fame as a jazz stylist never faltered.

Instrumental jazz began around the turn of the century in the New Orleans red-light district called Storyville. When this area was closed down after World War I, many jazz musicians emigrated to Chicago. Chicago-style jazz uses seven or eight performers, a group larger than that found in New Orleans jazz. Except for the solo improvisations that became very important in this style of jazz, parts are notated. The saxophone, an instrument that was not used in the earlier style, was

SCAT SINGING

incorporated, and, *scat singing*, nonsense syllables sung in improvisation, is also typical. In addition, popular songs of the period are the basis of Chicago-style jazz, rather than the 12-bar blues progressions on which the New Orleans style was predicated.

Relative Keys

Modulations often occur from major to minor tonalities, or vice versa. For every major tonality there is a relative minor that has the same key signature (same number of sharps or flats) but a different tonic. A common modulation is from a minor key to its *relative major*, or from a major key to its *relative minor*. The relative minor of C major is a minor; conversely, the relative major of a minor is C major. In major, the relative minor scale begins on the sixth pitch (cdefg*a*bc), whereas in minor, the relative major begins on the third pitch (ab*c*defga). Modulation from a major to its relative minor or vice versa is common and convenient in music, since neither the key signature nor pitches used are changed, only the tonic.

Parallel Keys

Selection no. 21

Listen to the Allegretto Grazioso, the third movement of Dvořák's Symphony no. 8 in G major *(listening selections)*. Several modulations occur in this movement, especially between g minor and G major, which are *parallel keys* (major and minor scales with the *same* tonic).

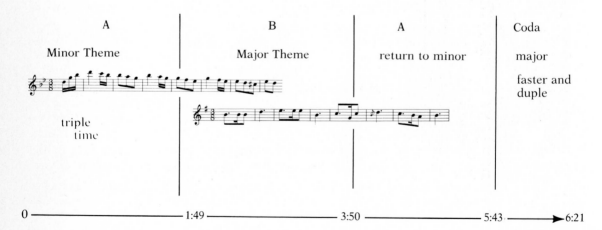

Some theorists call a change from major to minor with the same tonic a change of mode. Each key change here serves to define the section and form of the movement.

Circle of Fifths

Keys are often arranged in a circle of fifths to show the relationship between major and minor as well as to provide a sequence of the logical progression of key signatures as sharps or flats are added. C major, the key of no sharps and flats, is shared with its relative minor, a. Any key to the right is progressively a fifth higher and has one additional sharp. Any key to the left is progressively a fifth lower and has one additional flat. At six sharps or six flats, the circle is complete, since g♭ = f♯ (at least on the keyboard).

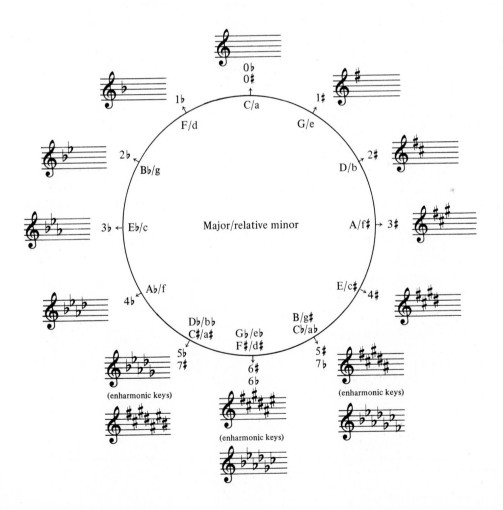

ENHARMONIC   Pitches and keys that sound the same but are notated differently are called *enharmonic*. B♭ and A♯ are enharmonic, as are C♯ and D♭. Since there are twelve notes in each octave, it is possible to have twelve major keys in our tonal system, each with a relative minor.

The circle of fifths is a theoretical construct that enables musicians, especially composers, to see the availability of keys and the relationships among these, especially in terms of the key signatures.

BITONALITY AND POLYTONALITY

Some twentieth-century composers have written compositions in which two or more tonalities are used simultaneously. Unlike modulation, in which one key is changed successively to another, *bitonality* means that two keys are heard simultaneously. Although this might seem to be a confusing musical state, bitonality and *polytonality* (literally, many keys simultaneously) can provide excitement in music.

Selection no. 25   Listen to Charles Ives's *Putnam's Camp (listening selections)*. Bitonality and polytonality occur throughout most of this movement.

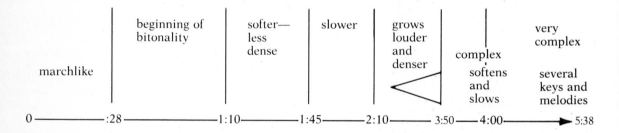

Since Ives's father was a bandmaster who made Charles practice piano scales in two different keys simultaneously, it is not surprising that the composer adopted bitonality as a norm.

ATONALITY

Atonality is the absence of a tonal center in music in which the composer studiously avoids "favoring" one pitch over others. In other words, there is no tonic note.

Twelve-Tone Music

DODECAPHONY   Austrian composer Arnold Schoenberg formulated a system of atonal writing called *twelve-tone* music or *dodecaphony*. The twelve tones of the octave are arranged by the composer in what is called a *tone row*, and each is assigned a position by number. Intervals used in tonal music (thirds and sixths) are typically avoided in favor of seconds and sevenths, but a composer can arrange the twelve pitches in any order he or she likes.

TONE ROW

Manipulation of the Tone Row

A melody written with these pitches, one through twelve, in sequence is the original *tone row*. The row may then be played backwards (12 to 1) in a version called *retrograde*. Other manipulations are *inversion* (upside down) as well as *retrograde-inversion* (backwards and upside down). These four basic manipulations may also be transposed to any new location.

RETROGRADE
INVERSION

Although purists of twelve-tone writing insist that the sequence of pitches in the tone row be observed in all manipulations, many composers use these devices more freely, allowing repetitions and deviations as they feel necessary to create a musical composition.

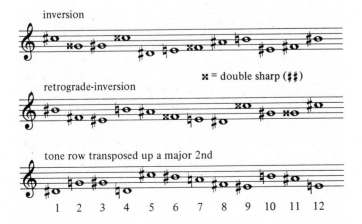

Harmony is often provided by combining two or more row manipulations in polyphony or by combining tones of the row into chords.

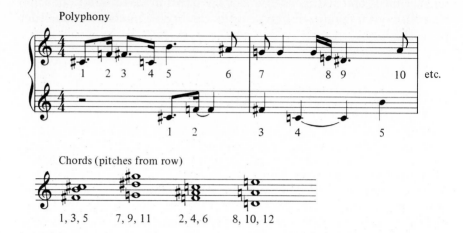

Polyphony

Chords (pitches from row)

1, 3, 5   7, 9, 11   2, 4, 6   8, 10, 12

Twelve-tone writing may seem somewhat mathematical, but the same criticism may be applied to major or minor scales. In the hands of a masterful composer, it can be an expressive system. Although dissonant when compared to major and minor tonalities, the twelve-tone system has been used extensively in the present century. Tension and release, pattern and design are inherent in the twelve-tone form, although they are not usually as obvious as in music of earlier periods.

Listen to the Prelude of Schoenberg's *Suite* for piano, op. 25 *(listening selections)*. Schoenberg's tone row for this work is:

Selection no. 54

1   2   3   4   5   6   7   8   9   10   11   12

The opening part for the right hand is:

1 2 3   4   5   6   7 8   9   10 11 12

At the beginning the left hand plays a transposed version simultaneously against this original tone row. Retrograde, inversion, retrograde-inversion, and additional transpositions then follow.

The suite is the first composition that Schoenberg wrote completely in twelve-tone technique. In his earlier works, such as *Pierrot Lunaire* and *Die glückliche Hand,* he had searched for a new system.

Only after a six-year hiatus from composing did he arrive in 1923 at the twelve-tone principles that revolutionized contemporary composition. The *Suite* for piano, opus 25, followed in 1924, as did his Third Quartet (1926) and Variations for Orchestra, all written using tone rows.

NOTATION OF TONALITY

Tonality is usually notated with a key signature placed on the staff at the beginning of each composition and on each subsequent line, showing pitches are sharp or flat throughout.

Key of F major — (all b's played flat)

Key of A♭ major — (all b's, e's, a's and d's played flat)

Key of D major — (all f's and c's played sharp)

Key of E major — (all f's, c's, g's and d's played sharp)

Each major and relative minor has its own key signature, as shown on the circle of fifths. Key signatures are written on both staffs (for the piano)

Key of D major

or on the staff from which an instrument reads. Although a modulation within the composition may necessitate a new key signature at some midpoint, accidentals may also be used to indicate a change of tonality.

D major   (modulation)   F major

Bitonal compositions may use two key signatures or employ accidentals, but atonal works typically use accidentals throughout, rather than key signatures.

TONALITY AND STYLE PERIODS

Tonality has been structured differently in each historical style period, as this chart summarizes.

Period	Tonality	Examples
Medieval and Renaissance	Medieval scales called modes are used.	
Baroque	Major and minor tonality begin to replace the modes. Modulation is often to relative keys.	Bach—*Christ lag in Todesbanden*
Classic	Tonality that is clearly major and minor is favored. Modulation is both to relative and parallel keys.	
Romantic	Major and minor tonality prevails. Composers use distant and sudden modulations.	Dvořák—Allegretto grazioso (Eighth Symphony)
Impressionism	Major, minor, and modal scales are used, as well as the whole-tone scale.	
Twentieth Century	All types of tonality are used, with some emphasis on bitonality and atonality.	Ives—*Putnam's Camp* Schoenberg—*Suite for piano, op. 25*

See also selections in Chapter 3, p. 81; Chapter 4, p. 141; Chapter 5, p. 184; Chapter 6, p. 215.

SUMMARY

Tonality is the feeling of pitch center in a musical composition, the preference for a tonic, which becomes the focus for both melody and harmony. In major and minor keys, the triad on this pitch is called the tonic (I). Other primary triads are the subdominant (IV) and the dominant (V), most frequently used as a seventh (V₇). Secondary chords, supertonic (ii), mediant (iii), submediant (vi), and leading tone triad (vii), when used, provide harmonic variety.

Modulation, a change of key, is another means whereby a composer can achieve harmonic variety. Modulations may be to closely related keys, such as the relative major or minor, as well as to the dominant or subdominant key, but some composers modulate freely to almost any tonality.

Bitonality is the use of two tonalities simultaneously, while polytonality is the use of many. Atonality is the absence of a tonic and thus negates any tonal feelings. Twelve-tone composition, in which a tone row of twelve pitches is manipulated by retrograde, inversion, and retrograde-inversion, as well as transposition, is one way of achieving atonality.

STUDY GUIDELINES

Guide to Perceiving Tonality

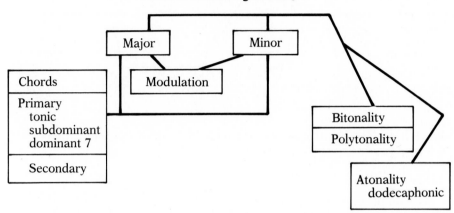

KEY TERMS AND CONCEPTS

Atonality
Bitonality
Enharmonic
Modulation
Parallel key
Polytonality
Primary chord
   Dominant seventh (V$_7$)
   Subdominant (IV)
   Tonic (I)

Relative key
Secondary chord
Tonality
Tonic
Twelve-tone music (Dodecaphony)
Tone row

EXERCISES

1. The following compositions have a modulation from major to minor and from minor to major. Keep a timing for each and tell at which point (time) the modulation occurs.

a. Mozart—Rondo-Allegro, *Serenade* in G, K. 525 (Selection no. 72)
b   Chopin—Etude no. 12 in c minor, op. 10 (Selection no. 4)
c   Haydn—Menuetto (Allegro ma non troppo): Trio (Selection no. 45)

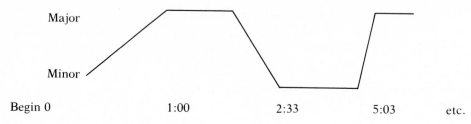

Major

Minor

Begin 0   1:00   2:33   5:03   etc.

2. What is the relative major or minor of each of the following?

C major   a minor
F major   d minor
G major   e minor
D major   g minor
E major   b minor
B♭ major   c minor
E♭ major

CHAPTER REVIEW

Match items in the two columns. Answers in Appendix.

1. _____ tonality
2. _____ V₇
3. _____ I
4. _____ IV
5. _____ 12-bar blues
6. _____ G major and g minor
7. _____ bitonality
8. _____ atonality
9. _____ G♯ and A♭
10. _____ modulation
11. _____ C major and a minor
12. _____ tone row

A. parallel keys
B. uses twelve different pitches
C. tonic triad
D. two tonalities at once
E. enharmonic keys
F. absence of tonality
G. preference for one tone
H. relative keys
I. subdominant triad
J. change of tonality
K. dominant seventh chord
L. rhymed couplet, first line repeated, using primary chords

FOR FURTHER LISTENING

Atonality
Ruggles	*Men and Mountains*
Webern	Symphony for Small Orchestra, op. 21

Extended chords
Ravel	*La Valse*
Stravinsky	*Le Sacre du Printemps* (The Rite of Spring)

Modulation
Beethoven	Sonata no. 20 in G major: Second movement (G major to D major to G major, modulation to dominant)
Chopin	Sonata no. 2 in b♭ minor, op. 35, 3rd movement (b♭ minor to D♭ major to b♭ minor) (modulation to relative major and back)

Polytonality
Ives	*Psalm 67*
Milhaud	*Suite Provencale* (begins in B♭ and F major simultaneously)
Stravinsky	*Petrouchka:* "Chez Petrouchka," Second theme (C and F♯ major)

Triadic Harmony
Brahms	Symphony no. 1 in c minor: Fourth movement

SECTION III
MUSICAL FORMS

◆

All of the elements discussed in Section II lead to perception of music at a micro-level, in which the details are isolated one from another. In Section III they are brought back together at a macro-level. The word "form" is used to describe the overall design of music, and this design depends upon the interrelationship of the basic elements—rhythm, melody, harmony, and tonality—as well as the expressive elements—timbre and dynamics. Form is explored in Section III, first in single-movement designs, then in compositions in which there are several movements, and finally in genres that do not clearly or consistently fall into either of these categories.

FORM IN SINGLE MOVEMENTS

❖

FORM	SONATA-ALLEGRO FORM
STROPHIC FORM	MUSICAL EXTENSIONS
PROCESSIVE FORM; THEME	IN FORM
AND VARIATIONS	FORM AND STYLE PERIODS
RETURN FORM	SUMMARY
ADDITIVE FORM	STUDY GUIDELINES

FORM

Form is design in music, dependent upon *unity* and *variety* in the use of musical ideas. A musical idea is a collection of notes taken together to make an entity. Therefore, the most minimal musical idea may be a motive, or, more commonly, a melody or a theme. A musical idea, in a larger sense, also may be a chord progression or several phrases joined by a common motive. Although form refers to the design both of single movements and of compositions consisting of several movements, only single-movement forms will be discussed in this chapter. UNITY
VARIETY

Composers throughout history have evolved forms that provide unity and variety in music, but these have never been inflexible molds into which musical ideas are merely to be poured. Rather, form has developed from musical practice, particularly in instrumental music where words have not imposed a point of unity as they can in vocal music.

The form of a single movement usually fits into one of four basic designs. If the repetitions of the large sections of a composition occur without musical change, then that piece is said to be in *strophic* form. Strophic form is represented by AAA and, although common in vocal STROPHIC

PROCESSIVE

RETURN

ADDITIVE

music, rarely occurs in instrumental works. A second design is called *processive* form, which means repetition with variation. It is represented by $AA_1A_2A_3\ldots$. A third design involves repetition with contrast, in which a new musical idea occurs between repetitions of the principal idea. This is called *return* form. Its simplest arrangement is ABA, while ABABA and AABA are slightly more complex configurations. Composers may introduce additional ideas, in such dispositions as ABACA, ABACADA, or ABACABA, so long as the first musical idea "returns" at the end of the movement. A fourth design in music, with no repetition, is called *additive* form, represented as ABCD.... Each category will be discussed in more detail.

Strophic

Processive

Return

Additive

Return form in painting. *Symmetrical Composition in Yellow, Orange, and Brown,* Howard Conant, American, 1974, acrylic on poster board.

Photo by Western Ways. University of Arizona Museum of Art, gift of Edward J. Gallagher, Jr.

STROPHIC FORM

Strophic form is used primarily in vocal music, where a short musical structure, typically four to eight phrases in length, is repeated for each verse of a song. Lyrics are not generally considered as a structural element in form, so the repetition of the music is the identifying factor.

A	A	A	A. . . . .
Verse 1	Verse 2	Verse 3	Verse 4

Each repetition of A is generally the same length. Protestant hymn tunes used for congregational singing are usually strophic, as is most folk and popular music. Strophic form is limited in its expressive possibilities, since it is difficult to sustain interest in a composition that repeats the same music for six or more verses, even when the lyrics change. When strophic form is used in art music it is usually in a short composition such as a lied or chanson. The composer often employs it when the poetry to be set is arranged in stanzas or regular strophes.

Listen to Franz Schubert's "Who Is Sylvia?" (1826) *(listening selections).* Shakespeare's lines from *Two Gentlemen of Verona* are ar-

Selection no. 42

ranged in three strophes or stanzas, so it is not surprising that Schubert composed this lied in strophic form. Each musical verse has an identical phrase structure and accompaniment. Variety can be provided in performance by changes in musical dynamics that correspond to the lyrical differences in each repetition.

PROCESSIVE FORM: THEME AND VARIATIONS

Processive form is represented as A $A_1A_2A_3$.... Each section, as with strophic, is usually of comparable length.

ORNAMENTS

To provide variation among sections, composers frequently alter the melody. That is, the melody may be more elaborate in A_1 than in A through the addition of ornaments or other melodic modifications. The harmony and the rhythm can also change, as well as the timbre and dynamics. Changes, of course, may occur simultaneously in several elements. Although it is common for variations to become more complex as the composition unfolds, this is not always true. Many composers will include variations that are less complex than the original theme, almost like an outline version.

Selection no. 70

Listen to music of "Ahorohani" (work song) from the Black Caribs of Honduras *(listening selections)*, an example of processive form. Vocal improvisations occur over a steady beat and the repeated melodic ostinato. As the piece develops these improvisations become bolder and more elaborate, with several soloists taking turns singing.

The text alludes to the proverbial lazy man who will not help his woman build a new house. Since she has no male relatives to help her, she must build it herself, and the music helps alleviate the task.

The words are:

Marudunbadiwa	luma
No show we will	to him
(We will not show him)	
Maredutunu	Mabunaditimuna
Not good with me	Not build—he like house
(He's not good to me)	(He doesn't like to build a house)
Mati	Mayoritetima
No brother No uncle I have	
(I have no brother nor uncle)	
Lun labunu	muna
To build	house

Maredutunu   eieri   luma
Not good with me man   for that
(I won't be good for that man).

—Doris Stone

The Black Caribs, representing a mixture of Indian, African, and Anglo cultures, inhabit the southern West Indies and the northern coast of South America. Their music has pronounced rhythmic vitality, with vocal improvisations similar to those found in jazz.

The only specific term used to describe a processive movement is *theme and variations.* Composers begin with either a well-known melody or a newly composed one and write variations on it, three or four being common. Jazz performers use a popular song on which to build their improvisations. Composers such as Bach and Mozart were also masters of improvisation, and many compositions from their time are the result of the subsequent notation of an improvisation.

THEME AND VARIATIONS

Sectional Variation

Theme and variations may be considered either sectional or continuous. In a *sectional* variation, each individual variation maintains the identical phrase and harmonic structure as the original theme. If a theme has four phrases, each variation will have the same.

Theme	Variation 1	Variation 2 ...
Phrase 1	Phrase 1	Phrase 1
Phrase 2	Phrase 2	Phrase 2
Phrase 3	Phrase 3	Phrase 3
Phrase 4	Phrase 4	Phrase 4

Processive form, much like a visual theme and variations, can be observed in a painting. *Composition of Women,* Marcello Boccacci, Italian, 1957, oil on board.

University of Arizona Museum of Art, gift of Edward J. Gallagher, Jr.

Listen to "Gavotta con due Variazioni" from Stravinsky's *Pulcinella* Suite *(listening selections)*. This is an example of a sectional variation, with each variation following the phrase structure of the original theme. Cadences delineate each section.

Selection no. 9

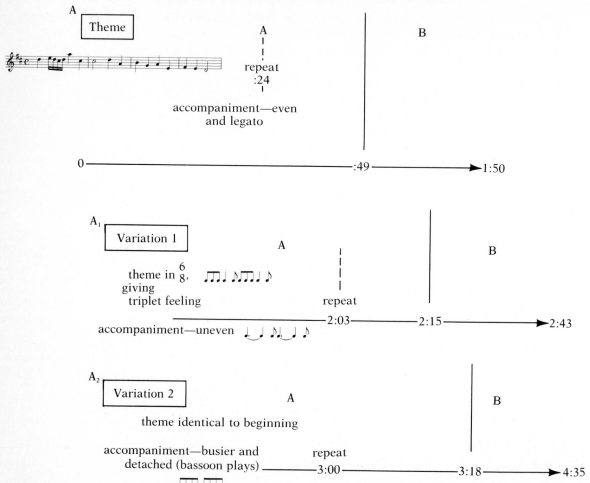

Continuous Variations

Continuous variations are just what the term suggests. They run together without a complete cadence and thus differ in both length and structure. Two types of continuous variations are the *passacaglia* and *chaconne*.

GROUND BASS   ***Passacaglia.***   The passacaglia has a melody in the bass, a *ground bass*, often eight measures long, over which melodic decorations are added. The ground bass is usually repeated without pause, while with each repetition the musical events occurring above the bass line are varied every eight bars. Although the bass melody can be transferred momentarily to the treble, it usually returns to the bass.

The term "passacaglia" comes from the Spanish word *pasacalle*, meaning to "pass along the street," in reference to dances and songs performed in the street. In Bach's time the term referred to a slow, minor variation on a ground bass in triple time. Undoubtedly performers of the time, much like today's jazz performers, created passacaglias by improvising on a ground bass, and later wrote the variations in musical notation.

Listen to J. S. Bach's Passacaglia in c minor *(listening selections)*.   Selection no. 71
This passacaglia begins with a statement of the melody in the pedals of the harpsichord. The minor theme is in ¾ meter.

Theme

Melodeon by Carhart, Needham & Co., New York, 1864. This instrument has two manuals linked by a coupler, suction bellows, and a range of five octaves. The melodeon is an early name for the American organ, or harmonium.

Smithsonian Institution Photo #56346.

Twenty variations follow. The theme remains in the bass for half of these and then moves to the upper keyboard. There is almost no pause between variations.

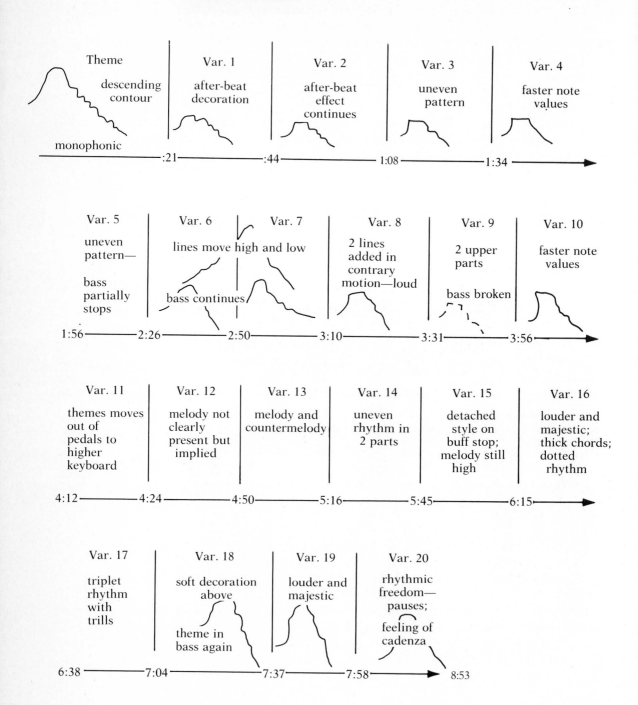

Since tonality is c minor throughout, variety is created by rhythmic change as well as use of stops on the harpsichord. Although the manuscript is prefaced with "Cembalo e pedale," which means harpsichord and pedal, the work is most frequently heard on organ. Even orchestral transcriptions have been made. This particular example is performed on a pedal harpsichord.

Chaconne. A chaconne is similar to a passacaglia except that a chord progression, rather than a ground bass, is used as the theme.

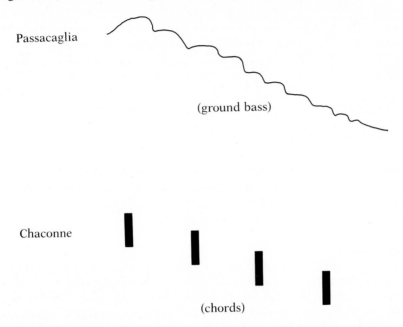

Listen to Allegro energico e passionato; Più allegro, the fourth movement of Brahms's Symphony no. 4 in e minor *(supplemental listening)*. Brahms made extensive use of variation form, as evidenced in his *Variations on a Theme by Paganini* and *Variations on a Theme by Handel.* His style is Romantic, since he added to the basic variational structure the emotion, timbres, and harmony associated with the late nineteenth century.

The Fourth Symphony in e minor, his last symphony (and also the last he heard performed in public before his death in 1897), was first performed in 1885. Despite his historical placement within the Romantic period, Brahms preferred the logic of Classical design and form in most of his works, including this Fourth Symphony. The fourth and final movement is a chaconne, the theme for which was borrowed from a Bach cantata, #150, *Nach dir, Herr.* Brahms's ability to provide variety within the unity of the eight-measure theme is quite masterful. The theme is stated using this harmonic progression:

Thirty variations plus a coda then follow. Although these are not as easy to follow as sectional variations or the variations in Bach's passacaglia, the spirit of the original theme is kept throughout the entire movement. The larger tempo groupings—fast (variations 1–9), slow (10–15), fast (16–30)—provide an overall ternary division within the movement. (See page 251.)

RETURN FORM

Return form is quite common in Western music, since the return to an original idea at the end of a movement provides closure and summary, as well as symmetry.

Simple Return

Ternary. The most basic return is *ternary*, ABA, in which sections are usually delineated by a complete cadence. Since the repetition of A is identical with its first appearance, composers have developed a shorthand for indicating the return of A without notating it again completely. This is called *da capo*, meaning "from the beginning," with the instruction "D.C. al Fine" at the conclusion of the B section telling performers to repeat the A section to "Fine," the finish.

DA CAPO

OVERALL FORM

Fast	Slow	Fast
theme and nine variations	Variations 10 through 15	variations 16 through 30 plus coda

0 ———————— 2:50 ———————— 6:20 ——————▶ 10:45

SPECIFIC FORM

Theme	Var. 1	Var. 2	Var. 3	Var. 4
brass	off-beat— soft— pizzicato	woodwinds— off-beat accent in accompaniment	strongly detached woodwinds-brass	legato strings

0 ———— :13 ———— :28 ———— :43 ———— :56 ——————▶

Var. 5	Var. 6	Var. 7	Var. 8	Var. 9	Var. 10
strings with woodwinds added	strings on wandering melody	uneven (dotted) string melody	busy melody even— softer	triplet string melody ritards	slow— call-response

1:14 ———— 1:30 ———— 1:49 ———— 2:08 ———— 2:27 ———— 2:50 ——————▶

————— SLOWER —————

Var. 11	Var. 12	Var. 13	Var. 14	Var. 15	Var. 16
tempo picks up a little	flute solo slow and rubato	major clarinet and oboe	brass in homophony soft and hymnlike	louder brass with woodwinds strings	return to original theme in fast tempo and full orchestra

3:12 ———— 3:28 ———— 4:15 ———— 4:58 ———— 5:36 ———— 6:20 ——————▶

Var. 17	Var. 18	Var. 19	Var. 20	Var. 21	Var. 22	Var. 23
tremolo strings with surges in woodwinds	brass	detached— call/response with brass/ woodwinds	fanfarelike— triplets	detached with	soft and detached	loud string counter melody

6:33 ———— 6:45 ———— 6:57 ———— 7:10 ———— 7:22 ———— 7:35 ———— 7:45 ——————▶

Var. 24	Var. 25	Var. 26	Var. 27	Var. 28	Var. 29	Var. 30	Coda
brass loud— answered by strings/ woodwinds	tremolo strings and brass answer	horns rit.	woodwinds and	strings	woodwinds and strings pizzicato	strings loud— sharp accents	like beginning but draws on ideas from many variations

7:59 ———— 8:11 ———— 8:25 ———— 8:39 ———— 8:53 ———— 9:07 ———— 9:21 ———— 9:42 ——————▶ 10:45

Selection no. 12

Listen to Chopin's Mazurka no. 24 in C, op., 33, no. 3 (1838) *(listening selections)*. Only two of the three sections of this mazurka are written out. The return of A is notated with a D.C. al Fine.

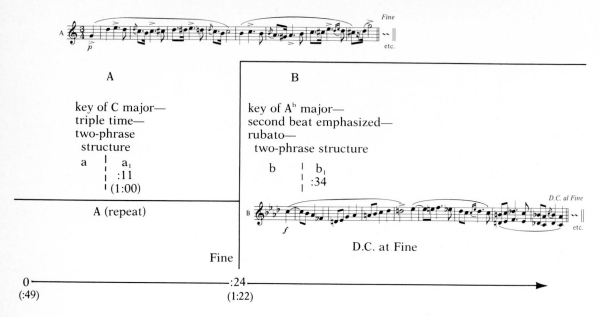

Ternary form is also used with the initial A repeated, AABA. In this case the first A is usually enclosed by double bars (and dots) to indicate the repeat before D.C. al Fine is observed, the double dots being an instruction to repeat all material encompassed between them.

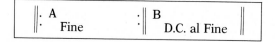

Repetition of the final A (e.g., ABAA) would not be appropriate. Composers (and performers) prefer to repeat initial sections only, since this helps establish musical ideas and themes. The repeat at the end serves as a reiteration and reinforcement of the themes expressed earlier.

Another use of ternary form is with the third section slightly varied.

A	B	A_1

A_1 may either be more elaborate or a slightly abbreviated version of the original statement.

Rounded Binary. *Rounded binary* (two-part form) is similar to ternary,but the return is extremely short only alluding to the opening material, that is, reminding the listener of the opening material without presenting the entire A section again.

A	B(a)

Rondo. *Rondo,* a special return form, is often used as the final movement of a larger composition. ABA may be a rondo, as may ABABA, ABACA or ABACABA. Sections between the A's are called *episodes* and may involve change in tonality but A sections, which are frequently abbreviated as the movement progresses, normally maintain the original tonality. Rondos are typically fast and playful in character, so the term not only connotes a return form but a particular spirit and tempo as well.

EPISODE

Listen to Rondo-Allegro from Mozart's Serenade in G, K. 525, *Eine kleine Nachtmusik* (A Little Night Music) *(listening selections).* Mozart's rondo (1787) has two major thematic concepts. Although these alternate, A always returns.

Selection no. 72

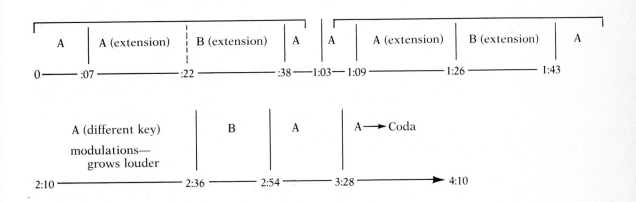

Although *Eine kleine Nachtmusik* was composed for string quartet, it is usually performed by a larger string ensemble. There are four movements, and this rondo is the finale.

Compound Return

Each main section of a compound structure contains a subsidiary form (or design) within it. In compound ternary form, as opposed to simple ABA, the structure could be:

Main Sections	A	B	A
Subsections or	(aba)	(cdc)	(aba)
	(aababa)	(cdcd)	(aba)

Each main section is comprised of two or three parts, with possible repeats. However, if an initial main section contains repeats, its recurrence probably will not. Note in the second possible version of the above example that although the initial statement of A involves repeats of both the a and b subsections, in the return of A the subsections follow a simple aba return pattern.

Minuet and Trio.   *Minuet and trio* is a compound ternary form. Since the minuet is repeated, there are three main sections:

A	B	A
Minuet (aababa)	Trio (ccdcdc)	Minuet (aba)

Each large section is typically in two or three parts, with repeats.

Selection no. 45 Listen to Menuetto (Allegro ma non troppo): Trio from Haydn's Quartet in d minor, op. 76, no. 2 *(Quinten) (listening selections)*. The six opus 76 quartets were a set written in 1797, late in Haydn's life and showing his maturity as a Classical composer. Op. 76, no. 3, in C major *(Emperor)*, is best known because Haydn used his own Austrian national anthem as the theme for four variations in the slow second movement. This theme, perhaps best known with the words starting "Deutschland, Deutschland über alles," has also been used as a Protestant hymn.

The listening example is the third movement of the string quartet #2. It is in compound ternary since each large section (A B A) has its own form. Both A and B sections are rounded binary, with the initial subsection returning briefly after the introduction of new material (b or d, respectively).

A	B	A
a a b(a) b(a)	c c d(c) d(c)	a b(a)

(written)

‖: a :‖‖: b(a) :‖	‖: c :‖‖: d(c) :‖
0 :23	1:20 1:47
(:11) ‖ (:49)	(1:33) ‖ (2:07) D.C.

‖ a ‖ b(a) ‖ Fine
2:44 ————— 2:56 ————— 3:27

Haydn has clearly differentiated each section. A is minor and polyphonic, since the two violins are imitated by the viola and cello. B is in major, with the first violin playing the melody. Here the texture is homophonic. The repetitions are notated by double bars and dots as well as use of a D.C. at the end of B. Repeats are not observed in the final A.

A   MENUETTO
Allegretto, ma non troppo

Scherzo and Trio. A *scherzo and trio* is similar to a minuet and trio. A scherzo, however, which literally means a musical joke, is often more vigorous and playful than the minuet. Beethoven is the composer whose works provided the most extensive development of this form. He often constructed it as a compound rondo. Listen to the Presto (Scherzo) from Beethoven's Symphony no. 7 in A major, op. 92 *(supplemental listening).*

A	B	A	B	A
(Scherzo)	(Trio)	(Scherzo)	(Trio)	(Scherzo)

ADDITIVE FORM

In additive form, new material appears without any repetition of previously stated musical ideas (for example, ABCD). Compositions of this century are frequently organized in this manner, especially some electronic and avant-garde works. Nineteenth-century composers of lieder also used additive form. Such a setting of an art song is called *through-composed* (durchkomponiert). Composers used this form when changes in events or emotions in the story being told made repetition of the music impractical, or when the poetry was not clearly set into strophes.

THROUGH-COMPOSED

Listen to Franz Schubert's *Erlkönig* (The Erlking) *(listening selections).* Schubert, who wrote this lied when he was eighteen, based it on Goethe's ballad describing a father riding on horseback at night with his sick son. The boy has visions of the king of elves, a symbol of death, pursuing them. When they arrive home, the boy is dead. He has succumbed to the Erlking.

Selection no. 73

One singer must portray four roles in this work: narrator, father, son, and Erlking. Schubert has delineated each part by range and dynamics. The melody continually changes as the drama unfolds, providing a typical example of through-composed (additive) form. Although the piano provides some unity with its galloping rhythm, the entire composition finds unification in the narrative related by the singer.

Schubert's love of German poetry helps to explain his imposing production of art songs. Although he wrote 142 in 1815, the year that *The Erlking* was composed, he received little recognition then or during his lifetime. Fame came forty years after he died, when his "Unfinished" and "Great C major" symphonies were published.

Fast

etc.

	(:21)	
Narrator:	Wer reitet so spät durch Nacht und Wind?	Who rides so late through night and wind?
	Es ist der Vater mit seinem Kind;	It is a father with his child;
	Er hat den Knaben wohl in dem Arm,	He has the boy there in his arms.
	Es fasst ihn sicher, et halt ihn warm.	He clasps him safely, and holds him warm.
	(:46 interlude)	
Father:	Mein Sohn, was birgst du so bang dein Gesicht? (low)	My son, why do you hide your face so fearfully?
Son:	Siehst, Vater, du den Erlkönig night? (high)	Father, do you not see the Erlking?
	Den Erlkönig mit Kron und Schweif?	The Erlking with his crown and train?
Father:	Mein Sohn, es ist ein Nebelstreif.	My son, it is a streak of mist.
	(1:22)	
Erl King:	"Du liebes Kind, komm, geh mit mir! (coaxing voice)	"Sweet child, come away with me!
	Gar schöne Spiele spiel ich mit dir;	Such lovely games I will play with you;
	Manch bunte Blumen sind an dem Strand.	There are many pretty flowers on the river bank;
	Meine Mutter hat manch gülden Gewand."	My mother has many a golden robe." . . .
	(1:44)	
Son:	Mein Vater, mein Vater, und hörest du nicht.	My father, my father, do you not hear

	Was Erlkönig mir leise verspricht?	What the Erlking is softly promising me?
Father:	Sei ruhig, bleibe ruhig, mein Kind; In dürren Blättern säuselt der Wind. (2:04)	Be calm, stay calm, my child; It is the wind rustling in the dry leaves.
Erl King:	"Willst, feiner Knabe, du mit mir gehn? Meine Töchter sollen dich warten schön; Meine Töchter führen den nächtlichen Reihn; Und wiegen und tanzen und singen dich ein." (2:21)	"My handsome boy, will you come with me? My daughters will take good care of you, My daughters, they lead the nightly dance And will rock and dance and sing you to sleep."
Son:	Mein Vater, mein Vater, und siehst du nicht dort Erlkönigs Töchter am düstern Ort?	My father, my father, do you not see The Erlking's daughter in yonder dark?
Father:	Mein Sohn, mein Sohn, ich seh es genau, Es scheinen die alten Weiden so grau. (2:48)	My son, my son, I see it plainly. It is the old grey willow gleaming.
Erl King:	"Ich liebe dich, mich reizt deine schöne Gestalt, Und bist du nicht willig, so brauch ich Gewalt."	"I love you, your beauteous form attracts me; And if you are unwilling, I will use force."
Son:	"Mein Vater, mein Vater, jetzt fasst er mich an! Erlkönig hat mir ein Leids getan!" (3:12)	My father, my father, now he takes hold of me, The Erlking has hurt me!
Narrator:	Dem Vater grauset's, er reitet geschwind. Er hält in Armen das ächzende Kind. (pause) Erreicht den Hof mit Müh und Not; In seinen Armen das Kind war tot. (3:54)	The father shudders, he rides apace. Holding the moaning child in his arms; He reaches the homestead with desperate effort; In his arms the child was dead.

English translation by Gerard Mackworth-Young. From *200 Songs in Three Volumes*. Volume 1, Schubert. New York: International Music Co., 1961.

SONATA-ALLEGRO FORM

Sonata-allegro, an exception to the framework of the four basic designs, is a compound form with three sections called, respectively: (1) *exposition*, (2) *development*, and (3) *recapitulation*.

Exposition.   In the exposition, two themes are introduced (or exposed). The key relationship between the two themes is important. When the first theme is in major, the second is often in the dominant major key (a fifth higher).

Exposition	Theme 1	Major
	Theme 2	Dominant Major

However, if the first theme is minor, theme 2 typically modulates to the relative major (a third higher).

Exposition	Theme 1	Minor
	Theme 2	Relative major

In either case, there is almost always a modulation to a new key for the introduction of the second theme in the exposition. These two ideas, like two characters in a novel, provide musical material for the rest of the movement.

Development.   In the second main section, the two themes are developed, hence the name, development. Composers have not been as predictable here as they have been in the exposition. Both themes may become the basis for musical manipulation, which can include modulation, change of dynamics and timbre, and treatment of both themes polyphonically. The development usually involves suspense and surprise, and may be either brief or quite long. Some composers have chosen to develop one of them only or even to introduce new musical ideas in the development.

Recapitulation.   At the conclusion of the development, the third section, recapitulation, presents both themes again. This time, however, both are in the key in which the first theme was stated in the exposition. If originally major, both are now in the same major; if originally minor, both are now in the same minor. The entire movement thus begins and ends in the same key.

Exposition	Development	Recapitulation
Theme 1 major Theme 2 dominant major	polyphonic treatment; modulation; change of intensity; change of timbre	Theme 1 major Theme 2 major
	or	
Theme 1 minor Theme 2 relative major		Theme 1 minor Theme 2 minor

Listen to Allegro vivace assai, the first movement to Mozart's Quartet no. 14 in G major, K. 387 *(listening selections)*. Mozart wrote this quartet in 1782, and three years later dedicated it, along with five other quartets, to his friend and mentor, Haydn. In this movement, theme 1 is in G major

Selection no. 74

while theme 2 is in D major, the dominant major. Only in the recapitulation does it appear in G major.

In this recording the exposition is repeated, an option open to performers. Hearing the first section repeated emphasizes the main themes for the listener, somewhat like rereading the opening chapter in a novel to clarify delineation of the main characters. The development uses theme 1 only, tossing it to various instruments and modulating freely to several keys.

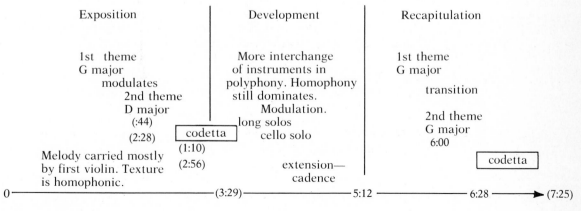

Repeat   1:43

Solo singer and
orchestra. Zubin
Mehta conducts the
New York
Philharmonic, with
contralto Maureen
Forrester as soloist.

Photo© Federico Diaz.
Courtesy the New York Philharmonic.

MUSICAL EXTENSIONS IN FORM

INTRODUCTION
TRANSITION
EPISODE

CODA
CODETTA

All musical forms, whether simple or compound, may have extensions added before, between, or after main musical ideas. These are known by various terms. An *introduction* opens a work before the first A is heard, while *transitions* or *episodes* are placed as bridges between main musical ideas, providing interest and building suspense for the listener, especially if they delay the return of a musical idea. An extension at the end is called a *coda*. A coda (also called a *codetta* if it is very short) concludes a section or an entire movement, often by alluding to musical ideas used earlier. It serves in some ways as a musical summary.

| introduction | A | B | transition | A | coda |

All extensions help provide a smooth flow and continuity before and between the main musical ideas of a composition.

Selection no. 37

Listen to "O Thou that Tellest Good Tidings to Zion," an aria from Handel's *Messiah (listening selections)*. It is convenient that composers provide soloists accompanied by orchestra or piano with transitions and interludes to catch their breath and composure. Such passages are apparent in this aria, which also includes an introduction and a coda.

| Theme introduced | Voice
orchestra answers phrases of contralto | orchestral interlude | Voice
call-response | orchestral interlude | Voice
call-response |

0 —————— :33 —————— 1:37 ———— 1:50 ———— 3:03 ———— 3:16 ——► 4:58

"O THOU THAT TELLEST GOOD TIDINGS TO ZION"

Isaiah xl: 9

thou   that tell-est good   ti - dings to Zi - on,

etc.

FORM AND STYLE PERIODS

Period	Form	Examples
Medieval and Renaissance	Variation forms are most important, with some use of return form.	
Baroque	Sectional and continuous variations—passacaglia and chaconne—and binary form are common.	Bach—Passacaglia in C minor Handel—"O Thou That Tellest Good Tidings to Zion"
Classic	Return form is most common, including ABA, rondo, minuet and trio, and sonata-allegro form. Variations are usually of the sectional type.	Mozart—Allegro vivace assai (Movt. 1, Quartet in G) Mozart—Rondo-Allegro (*Serenade* in G) Haydn—Minuet and Trio (Quartet in D minor) Scarlatti—Sonata in C, L. 454
Romantic	Classic forms prevail but form is bent to follow emotion of the composer. Art song is strophic, return, and through-composed.	Schubert—"Who Is Sylvia?" Schubert—Erlkönig Brahms—Allegro energico . . . Fourth movement of Symphony in e minor Chopin—Mazurka no. 24 in C major, op. 33, no. 3
Impressionism	Form is not important but return form is still used.	
Twentieth Century	All types of forms are used. Additive is especially important.	Stravinsky—"Gavotte with Two Variations"

See also selections in Chapter 3, p. 81; Chapter 4, p. 140; Chapter 5, p. 184; Chapter 6, p. 215; Chapter 7, p. 234.

SUMMARY

There are four basic designs defining form in music. Strophic, overall unity, is most common in vocal music. Processive form, the basis of theme and variations, is repetition with change. Theme and variations are either sectional or continuous. Return form, repetition with contrast, includes simple ternary form, rounded binary, rondo, and compound ternary forms, such as minuet and trio or scherzo and trio. Additive forms are continuously variable, without repetition of musical ideas and include through-composed compositions. A special musical form is the sonata-allegro, which has three sections: exposition, development, and recapitulation. Two themes with special key relationships are the source of organization in the sonata-allegro. All forms may include extensions such as an introduction, transition, and coda.

STUDY GUIDELINES

Guide to Perceiving Form

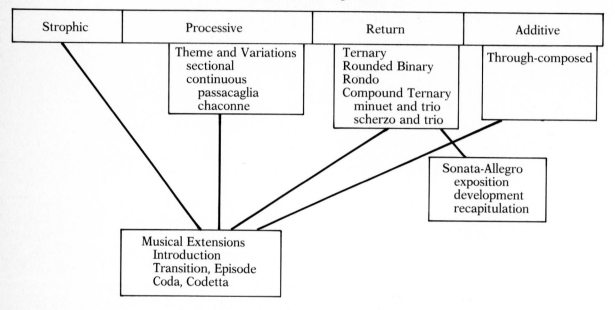

KEY TERMS AND CONCEPTS

Additive Form
  Through-composed
    (durchkomponiert)
Compound Return
  Minuet and Trio
  Scherzo and Trio
Form
Musical Extensions
  Coda
  Introduction
  Transition
Processive Form

Theme and Variations
  Continuous
    Chaconne
    Passacaglia
  Sectional
Return Form
  Rondo
  Ternary ABA
    Da capo (D.C. al Fine)
Sonata-allegro
  Development
  Exposition
  Recapitulation
Strophic Form

EXERCISES

1. Attend a live concert and try to identify each movement as strophic, processive, return, or additive.
2. Try to find examples of the strophic, processive, return, and additive designs in painting, sculpture, architecture, poetry, or commercial art.
3. Choose some selections on records and listen for form several times, trying to identify:

    a. the overall design category (strophic, processive, return, or additive)
    b. the exact ordering of musical ideas (ABA, $AA_1A_2A_3$)
    c. the placement of musical extensions before, between, and after the main musical ideas.

    (Use page 268 as a guide)

CHAPTER REVIEW

Match items in the two columns. Answers in Appendix.

1.	_____ strophic	A.	final section of sonata-allegro form
2.	_____ processive	B.	AAA
3.	_____ exposition	C.	variations on a ground bass
4.	_____ coda	D.	ABA
5.	_____ return	E.	lieder arranged in groups
6.	_____ additive	F.	A $A_1A_2A_3$
7.	_____ simple binary	G.	middle section of sonata-allegro form
8.	_____ passacaglia	H.	AB
9.	_____ through-composed	I.	opening section of sonata-allegro form
10.	_____ song cycle	J.	variations on a chord progression
11.	_____ chaconne	K.	Durchkomponiert
12.	_____ development	L.	introductions, transitions, interludes
13.	_____ recapitulation	M.	musical ending
14.	_____ musical extensions	N.	ABCDE

FOR FURTHER LISTENING

Binary Form

Bach   *Partita* no. 5 in G major: Allemande; Courante; Sarabande; Passepied; Gigue (AA_1 form in each)

Mozart   Quintet in A major, K. 581: Second movement (ABAB)

Chaconne

Bach   *Partita* no. 2 in d minor for unaccompanied violin: Chaconne

Purcell   *Chaconne* in g minor (*Great*)

Compound Ternary

Beethoven   Symphony no. 5 in c minor: Third movement (ABA)

Mozart   Concerto in A major for Piano and Orchestra, K. 488, Second movement (ABA)

Passacaglia

Bach   Mass in b minor: Crucifixus

Bizet   *L'Arlésienne* Suite no. 2: "Carillon"

Rondo

Beethoven   Concerto no. 3 in c minor for Piano and Orchestra: Third movement (ABACABA)

Sonata no. 8 in c minor: Second movement (ABACA); Third movement (ABACABA)

Debussy   "Minstrels" from *Preludes*, Book I, no. 12 (ABACA)

Mendelssohn   *Rondo Capriccioso* (piano)

Ravel   *Pavane pour une Infante Défunte* (ABACA)

Sonata-allegro form

Beethoven   Symphony no. 1 in C major: First movement

Brahms   Symphony no. 1 in c minor: First movement

Haydn   Symphony no. 97 in C major: First movement

Mendelssohn   *A Midsummer Night's Dream:* Overture

Mozart   *Eine kleine Nachtmusik,* K. 525: First movement

Ternary
Chopin	Prelude no. 15 in D♭ major (ABA₁)
Mendelssohn	*Elijah:* "Lift thine eyes" (ABA₁)
Saint-Saëns	*Carnival of the Animals* "The Elephant" (ABA) "The Swan" (ABA)

Theme and Variations
Beethoven	Symphony no. 3 in E♭ major: Fourth movement
Brahms	*Variations on a Theme by Haydn,* op. 56a
Britten	*The Young Person's Guide to the Orchestra*
Mozart	Sonata in A major, K. 331: First movement
Paganini	*Caprice,* no. 24
Ravel	*Bolero*

FORM IN MULTIMOVEMENT COMPOSITIONS

❖

INSTRUMENTAL COMPOSI-
TIONS—SONATA FORM

VOCAL COMPOSITIONS—
THEATRICAL FORMS

MULTIMOVEMENT FORMS AND
STYLE PERIODS

SUMMARY

STUDY GUIDELINES

Single movements, while sometimes heard alone, are generally grouped by the composer into a larger composition. A multimovement composition thus has unity, furnished by its timbre and tonality, and variety, provided by changes in tempo and musical material between movements. Some compositions use new material in each movement, while in others, ideas from one movement appear cyclically in later sections. All instrumental categories can share the same thematic material among movements. A *cyclic symphony*, which became common in the nineteenth century, uses the same theme in two or more movements. Most compositions are performed with only a slight pause between movements, although some run the movements together in a single unified sweep. There are numerous multimovement compositions to be discussed both in instrumental and vocal music.

INSTRUMENTAL COMPOSITIONS—SONATA FORM

SONATA   The *sonata* is one of the most common forms in instrumental music. The term, derived from the Italian word "suonare," meaning "to sound," is a general one, indicating an instrumental (not a vocal) genre.

Sonatas are also referred to by more specific names. A sonata for orchestra is a *symphony,* while one for two violins, viola, and cello is a *string quartet.* A sonata for a solo instrument (or a group of soloists) with orchestral accompaniment is a *concerto.* One written for a solo instrument with piano accompaniment is simply a *sonata* (i.e., flute sonata, violin sonata). A *piano sonata,* of course, utilizes only one instrument, since the piano provides its own accompaniment. A *sonatina* is a scaled-down sonata, often written for teaching purposes.

SYMPHONY
STRING
QUARTET
CONCERTO

SONATINA

Symphony

Since the various types of sonata developed simultaneously, during the eighteenth century, all of the configurations share certain traits in common. No two of them are identical in construction, but various points of overlap are unmistakable. For example, symphonies and string quartets are usually in four movements with each movement providing contrast in tempo with the preceding one. Typically:

First movement	Moderately fast (Allegro)
Second movement	Slow (Andante)
Third movement	Moderately fast (Allegro)
Fourth movement	Fast (Presto)

The entire composition is usually united by key relationship, that is, the tonic key is the tonality in movements one, three, and four, while the subdominant is preferred for the second movement. This does not mean modulation will not occur within the other movements, only that movements one, three,and four begin and end in the home tonality. Thus a symphony in D major has an overall tonality focused on D.

The form of each movement is also somewhat standardized. Composers have frequently used this scheme:

First movement	Sonata-allegro form
Second movement	Ternary (ABA), theme and variations, or sonata-allegro form
Third movement	Compound ternary (either minuet and trio or scherzo and trio)
Fourth movement	Rondo or sonata-allegro form

Listen to the Presto (Scherzo) from Beethoven's Symphony no. 7 in A major, op. 92 *(supplemental listening).* Beethoven's 7th symphony, composed in 1812, is in four movements:

1.	Poco sostenuto: Vivace	A major
2.	Allegretto	a minor
3.	Presto: Presto meno assai	F major
4.	Finale: Allegro con brio	A major

Unless one counts the long introduction (poco sostenuto) of movement one, there is no slow movement in this symphony. Since each movement has a striking rhythmic quality, the symphony has been labeled the "Apotheosis of the Dance" (Wagner) as well as "Ronde des Paysans" (Dance of the Peasants) (Berlioz). In this third movement, Beethoven used minuet and trio form but enhanced it with new playfulness, justifying use of the term "scherzo," a musical joke. Because the trio and scherzo are both repeated, the resulting form is ABABA, instead of ABA.

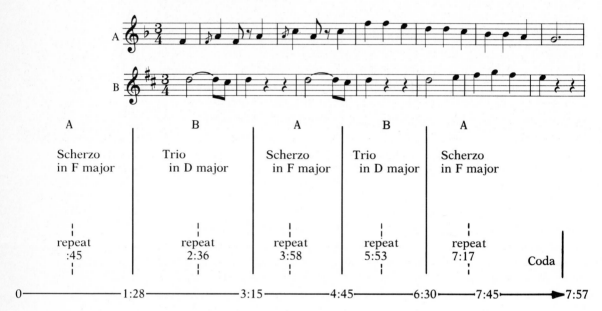

Solo Sonata/String Quartet

Because solo sonatas and concertos are usually written in three movements, they do not generally include a minuet movement. This is an important distinction. In addition, solo sonatas and string quartets are often smaller in scale and therefore typically shorter than symphonies and concertos.

Concerto

Solo Concerto.   Concertos are written either for one soloist or for a small group of soloists. The former type is called a *solo concerto* and has been a popular form since the last half of the eighteenth century. The piano and violin are favorite solo instruments for this type of concerto, where there is typically a great deal of musical interplay between soloist and orchestra. Themes are introduced in one part, then

Photo © 1986 Steve J. Sherman. Courtesy the New York Philharmonic.

DOUBLE
EXPOSITION

imitated in another. At times the soloist may carry the melody while
the orchestra accompanies; at other times the roles are reversed.

Although the movements of a solo concerto follow the norms cited
above, with the exclusion of the minuet movement, the first movement
is somewhat modified. Ordinarily, performers have the option of
whether or not to repeat an exposition, but concertos usually have a
double exposition, in which case both expositions *must* be performed.
First the orchestra presents the themes without modulation. In the
second exposition, in which the soloist begins, the key relationship
between themes then follows the traditional norm whereby, if the first
theme is major, the second is in dominant major, or if the first is minor,
the second is relative major. The development section allows interchange between soloist and orchestra. After the recapitulation, in
which both themes reappear in the original key of the first theme, the
soloist plays a *cadenza* that draws on the previously stated musical
ideas. In earlier times, they were improvised differently for each
rendition, but nowadays performers play cadenzas that have been
written out. Cadenzas have been supplied by the original composer of
the work, by other composers of later generations, or by influential
performers whose contributions seem particularly apt.

CADENZA

Although cadenzas generally occur near the end of the first movement, some composers have included them in the second or third
movement as well. Solo concertos, written to be performed with
orchestral accompaniment, are occasionally performed in recital with
a pianist playing a reduction of the orchestral score as accompaniment.

Concerto Grosso.   A concerto written for several soloists is called a *concerto grosso*. A small group of soloists called the *concertino* alternates with the orchestra, which is called the *ripieno* or *tutti*. The concerto grosso does not necessarily follow the same formal scheme as a solo concerto. Candezas may or may not be included, and sometimes only one theme is stated in the first movement. Variety is still provided by the alternation of thematic statements by concertino and ripieno. The concerto grosso was especially popular during the seventeenth and the first half of the eighteenth centuries, but twentieth-century composers have also utilized the format.

Listen to the Allegro of the first movement of Bach's *Brandenburg Concerto no. 4 in G major, BWV 1049 (supplemental listening)*. The concertino consists of one violin and two flutes. The flutes function as a single unit (except where marked by an asterisk), playing in thirds and sixths with each other while the violin answers and weaves a countermelody around them.

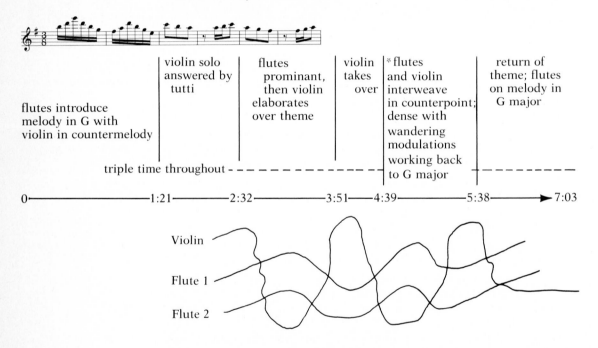

The majority of the work in this movement falls on the soloists, especially the violin. At times the tutti is silent and accompaniment is left to the ever-present continuo. Elsewhere the tutti reinforces the harmony. Although there are modulations, the tonality of G major opens and closes the movement. Since one theme is used repeatedly in various keys and contexts, this movement is considered

MONOTHEMATIC   *monothematic.*

The six Brandenburg concertos were written by J. S. Bach while he was court music director at Cöthen from 1717 to 1723. Employed by Prince Leopold, a nobleman who understood music and was enthusiastic about its performance, Bach had many excellent performers at his disposal and produced a vast repertoire of orchestral works. Employment by the Prince also offered many social advantages because he permitted Bach and the other musicians to travel with him. While vacationing at a spa, the Margrave of Brandenburg, Christian Ludwig, heard Bach's music and subsequently commissioned these six concertos in 1719. Bach dedicated and sent the works to him some two years later. Because the Margrave collected musical scores like some people buy museum pieces, it is not known whether he actually heard the works performed or merely stored them away. All of the Margrave's collectibles were sold at his death and each concerto sold for the equivalent of about ten cents. Only in 1850 were they finally published. The six compositions represent the artistic peak of the Baroque concerto.

Sonata—Special Types

Two special types of sonata were also popular in the Baroque era.

Sonata da Chiesa.   The *sonata da chiesa* (church sonata) is in four movements, its mood reserved and stately. Typically written for a small group of instruments, the movements alternate tempos, slow-fast-slow-fast.

Sonata da Camera.   In contrast to the sonata da chiesa, the *sonata da camera* (chamber sonata), written for solo instruments as well as chamber and larger groups, is based on dance rhythms. The dance-derived rhythms serve to distinguish the two types of sonata, but in addition, the sonata da camera, more popularly known as a *suite* or *partita*, consists of four principal dances or movements, with optional dances placed between the Sarabande and Gigue.

Prelude or Overture
Principal Dances:
    Allemande   Moderate quadruple time
    Courante   Fast triple time
    Sarabande   Slow triple time
      Optional Dances:
        Air
        Bourrée
        Gavotte
        Minuet
        Passepied
  Gigue   Fast compound quadruple time

In addition, a Baroque suite often began with an introductory movement, such as a short prelude or overture, in free form. Since composers added other dances between the Sarabande and Gigue, as seen in the above diagram, the four-movement scheme was the bare minimum. Much as a twentieth-century composer might base a movement on a tango rhythm, Baroque composers based their suites on rhythms of dances that had once been popular. It should be clear, however, that these suites were purely for listening, not social dancing.

It was common for each dance in the suite of the Baroque period to be binary. The form by letters was either AB or AA$_1$, but more important was the typical modulation to the dominant at the close of section 1 and back to the tonic at the close of section 2.

section 1	section 2
A	B (or A$_1$)
tonic .... dominant	dominant .... tonic

Selection no. 14   Listen to Domenico Scarlatti's Sonata in C, L. 454 (K. 309) *(listening selections)*. Scarlatti is credited with over 600 solo harpsichord sonatas, most written in one-movement binary form. Thematic material in the A sections (C major) reappears at the beginning of the B section (G major, the dominant key), with the original tonality returning at the conclusion (C major). Although this scheme was standard, modulation may also occur from minor to relative major, then back to minor. These changes of tonality are also important in the sonata-allegro form, which many believe evolved from the binary form.

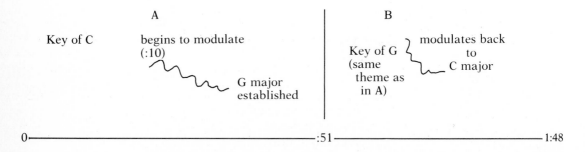

Listen to the Bourrée and Hornpipe from Handel's *Water Music (supplemental listening)*. Written for orchestra, *Water Music* contains twenty movements, including airs, allegros, and andantes. Because there are so many movements, the complete work is rarely performed. Rather, five or six movements are selected by the conductor to form a shorter suite. The Bourrée and Hornpipe, movements nine and ten

Domenico Scarlatti (1685–1757) was a contemporary of both Bach and Handel. During his professional career, which began in Italy, he lived in Portugal and Spain, serving the royal families as teacher and composer. His sonatas are etude-like, each dealing with some aspect of keyboard technique, whether arpeggios, rapid figurations, repeated notes, scales, or trills. Because sonatas are short, they are often per-

Domenico Scarlatti.
Drawing by Joseph Muller. Courtesy of the New York Public Library.

formed in groups to provide contrast for the listener.

Scarlatti's music tends to be thinner in texture and less complex than the work of many Baroque composers. It also has clear cadences, concise motives, and short phrases, showing a departure from the complexity of the Baroque period and pointing the way to the simplicity and clarity characteristic of the Classic period.

of the original twenty, are almost always included in such a reduced suite. Both movements use two ideas each, A and B, but repetitions, orchestration, and dynamics help provide variety *within* a single movement, while tempo and meter are used to provide contrast between movements.

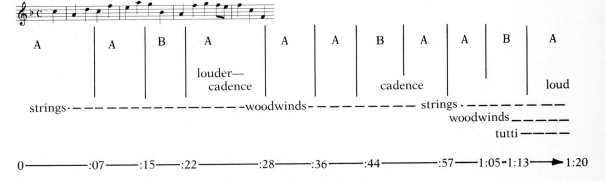

Each section here has two phrases, an antecedent and a consequent, which, it may be recalled, is a period, consisting of a questioning phrase and an answering phrase. The overall division is:

Strings dominate (4 sections)   AABA
Woodwinds dominate (4 sections)   AABA
Strings/woodwinds (3 sections)   ABA

When a composition is built of many movements, it is possible for each individual movement to have greater internal unity than a segment of a piece with fewer divisions, since it does not have to stand alone. This larger view of form thus results in this division:

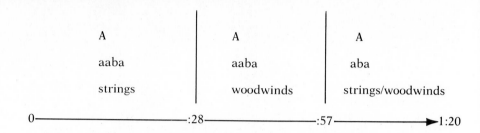

The Hornpipe provides contrast in theme and meter:

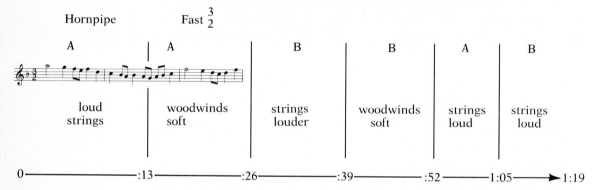

Modern Suite.   Although the suite as a form declined in popularity in Classic and early Romantic periods, it has been revitalized in this century. The modern suite is an instrumental composition with several movements, the form no longer prescribed and key relationships quite varied. Although the relationship to dance no longer necessarily exists, some famous suites of this century have been derived from ballet scores.

Selection no. 75   Listen to the Finale from Stravinsky's *Firebird* Suite *(listening selections)*. The complete *Firebird* was commissioned by Diaghilev in 1909 for a ballet based on a famous Russian folk tale. The ballet itself was introduced in 1910. Stravinsky subsequently arranged it as an orchestral suite in 1912, and made further revisions in both 1919 and 1945.

In the story, Prince Ivan Tsarevich captures the miraculous Firebird, who promises to give him a magic feather if she is released. The bird is freed and the magic feather subsequently granted. The power of the feather gives the Prince strength to defeat a diabolical ogre, Katschei. The Finale accompanies the gradual awakening of the

Princess and the growing love between the couple. It is based on this theme:

VOCAL COMPOSITIONS—THEATRICAL FORMS

As with instrumental compositions, there are numerous types of vocal compositions, three of which developed in the Baroque period. These are *opera, oratorio,* and *cantata,* all of which use solo voices accompanied by orchestra. In addition, each is primarily theatrical.

Opera

Opera, which is sung drama, originated in Florence, Italy, in around 1600, as a result of various concerted attempts to revive Greek drama. Characters in opera sing to one another or to themselves, or address the audience directly. Sometimes, this singing is for dramatic emphasis, at others purely for the beauty of the music.

Aria and Recitative. A solo song in opera, when the action stops and the emphasis is upon musical considerations, is called an *aria.* In contrast, declamation and conversation occur in a *recitative,* delivered quickly and used to advance the plot between the arias. Although arias are generally lyrical and display the vocal technique of the singers, the purpose of recitative is largely dramatic. Words, phrases, and sections of an aria may be repeated for poetic effect but this seldom happens in recitative. In addition, the melodies of arias are usually ornate as well as wide in range, whereas in recitative only a few pitches may be used.

The earliest operas consisted totally of recitative, but the composer Monteverdi (1567–1643) provided sections with greater musical emphasis by repeating phrases and words, thus relieving the monotony of pure ongoing recitative. By the middle of the seventeenth century, composers had evolved a practice of alternating recitative with arias, thereby generating both musical and dramatic interest. This tradition lasted for one hundred and fifty years until the late Romantic era, when composers began to use a continuous singing style rather than separating the drama clearly into recitative and aria.

A scene from Puccini's *Madama Butterfly*. Puccini's operas *Madama Butterfly* and *Girl of the Golden West* were based on successful plays by the American playwright and theatrical manager David Belasco.

Photo by James Heffernan. Courtesy of the Metropolitan Opera Association.

ENTR'ACTE

Libretto.   An opera is a cooperative musical and dramatic event. It begins with a story, a plot whose historical period, dramatic events, and distinctive characters influence the kind of music to be composed to bring it to life. The stories of operas are seldom original conceptions but rather are generally derived from previously written sources, such as novels and plays, or the Bible, folklore, and mythology. Whatever the source, the *librettist* is the person who adapts the story and creates a *libretto*, the text of opera, which delineates characters and establishes situations for musical treatment. The composer, in collaboration with the librettist, then sets the libretto to music, using some situations for arias, others for recitative. The orchestra sets the mood with an overture and entr'actes (musical introductions to subsequent acts), accompanies the singing, and provides continuity within and between scenes and acts. A chorus may be used if appropriate, and many operas include ballet as well. Opera is a unique dramatic genre in that several persons can sing separate strands of concerted numbers simultaneously, each delivering a message to the audience.

Unlike spoken drama, opera demands that the singer-actors be inexorably tied to the temporal requirements of the music. There is no room for missed cues and altered lines since stage action and orchestral activity are largely dependent upon musical directions, and each action and movement must conform to the time provided for it by the musical score.

Production. Production of an opera is again a cooperative as well as expansive project, requiring several specialized participants. The *stage director* is responsible for establishing the movements of the singers, while the *musical director,* who may conduct the orchestra as well, oversees the singing and musical interpretation. There are also individuals responsible for sets, costumes, props, and lighting, and perhaps a choreographer. All work as a team to bring the written work of composer and librettist to fruition.

STAGE
DIRECTOR

MUSICAL
DIRECTOR

For the viewer, opera is a special type of musical presentation, full of aural and visual spectacle. Some operas are quite long, lasting four or more hours and utilizing a large cast, while others are chamber works lasting less than an hour, with only a few singers. In reality, an opera is *about* singing and is generally not as dramatically viable as a play. Plots are typically condensed and the libretto may even be in a language foreign to the listener. Nonetheless, the musical presentation in itself can frequently be a satisfying experience.

A scene from Rossini's *The Barber of Seville* in which (left to right) Rosina (Marilyn Horne), Count Almaviva (Rockwell Blake), Figaro (Pablo Elvira), and Dr. Bartolo (Enzo Dara) each present their respective points of view concerning developments in the plot.

Photo by James Heffernan. Courtesy of the Metropolitan Opera Association.

Photo by Louis Melancon. Courtesy of the Metropolitan Opera Association.

Grandiose stage design and spectacle in opera are illustrated by this scene from Wagner's *Lohengrin* in a production conceived by Wieland Wagner, grandson of the composer.

Oratorio

In that there are solo singers and a chorus, an *oratorio* resembles an opera. Other techniques similar to the operatic form are division of the narrative into acts and use of aria and recitative in alternation. However, although the narrative unifies the libretto, the oratorio is not staged, so there are no sets, costumes, or props, nor do singers act out their roles. Rather, an oratorio is somewhat akin to a concert version of an opera, and is therefore less inherently dramatic. In addition, the chorus is usually more important than in opera. The subject matter, frequently drawn from the Old Testament, gives it a quasi- religious flavor, but the oratorio differs from the Mass in that the text is not liturgical. Most oratorios are written for concert hall.

Cantata

The *cantata,* a third vocal genre that also developed during the Baroque period, uses operatic convention but, as with oratorio, is unstaged. The word "cantata," from the Italian *cantare,* simply means "to sing." The earliest cantatas, generally secular *(cantata da camera),* were written as entertainment for nobles. The religious cantata *(cantata da chiesa)* was developed later, becoming particularly important in the Lutheran church service.

A cantata is distinguished from an oratorio by being smaller in scope and also more lyric than dramatic. Although both involve aria and recitative, use of the chorus is not as common in a cantata.

MULTIMOVEMENT FORMS AND STYLE PERIODS

Period	Form	Examples
Medieval/ Renaissance	Paired, binary dances Suites	
Baroque	Suite Cantata Oratorio Opera Concerto grosso	Handel—*Water Music* Bach—*Brandenburg Concerto* no. 4 in G major
Classic	Sonata Symphony String quartet Solo sonata Solo concerto Opera	
Romantic	Symphony (often program) Solo concerto Solo sonata Opera/music drama Cyclic works	Beethoven— Symphony no. 7 in A major, op. 92
Impressionism	Suite Opera	
Twentieth Century	All multimovement forms, especially suites (ballet) Opera Solo and grosso concertos String quartet	Stravinsky—*Firebird Suite*

See also selections in Chapter 3, p. 81; Chapter 4, p. 140; Chapter 5, p. 184; Chapter 6, p. 215; Chapter 7, p. 234; Chapter 8, p. 266.

SUMMARY

A sonata is an instrumental composition in several movements. The symphony and string quartet are sonatas in four movements, whereas a concerto, a work for solo instrument and orchestra, is usually in three movements, with a solo cadenza at the end of the first movement. A concerto grosso combines a large (ripieno) and a small (concertino) musical group. Both solo concertos and concerto grossos are in three movements. The Baroque sonata includes the sonata da chiesa as well as the secular sonata da camera or suite, whose movements are stylized dances. A cyclic sonata is one in which a musical idea or theme is used in several of the movements.

Large vocal compositions with several movements include opera, oratorio, and cantata, all of which use the elements of recitative, aria, and orchestral accompaniment. Although opera is staged, oratorio and cantata are performed as concert pieces.

STUDY GUIDELINES

Guide to Perceiving Multimovement Forms

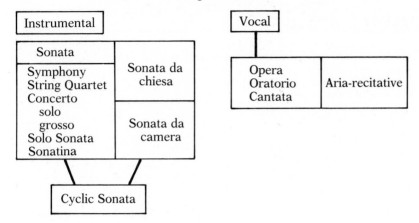

KEY TERMS AND CONCEPTS

Cantata
Concertino
Cyclic Sonata
Double Exposition
Monothematic
Opera
  Aria
  Librettist
  Libretto
  Musical director
  Recitative
  Stage director

Oratorio
Ripieno
Sonata
  Concerto
   Grosso
   Solo
  Da camera (Suite)
  Da chiesa
  Sonatina
Solo Sonata
String Quartet
Symphony

EXERCISES

1. Attend a live performance of a symphony, chamber group, or a solo instrumentalist. What multimovement forms did you hear and how do they compare with the prototypes discussed in this chapter? (Substitute a radio or television recital if you are not able to attend a live performance.)

2. Attend an opera, oratorio, or cantata performance. How many elements discussed in this chapter did you notice? How are unity and variety provided in a long vocal work? (Substitute a radio or television performance if needed.)

CHAPTER REVIEW

Place the terms below in one of these two general categories:

    A. Instrumental Compositions
    B. Vocal Compositions

Answers in Appendix.

1. _____ oratorio
2. _____ string quartet
3. _____ concerto grosso
4. _____ recitative
5. _____ cantata
6. _____ concertino

7. _____ suite
8. _____ opera
9. _____ symphony
10. _____ aria
11. _____ sonata
12. _____ libretto

FOR FURTHER LISTENING

Cantata (Church)
    Bach   Cantata no. 140, *Wachet auf, ruft uns die Stimme*

Concerto

Grosso
    Bach   Brandenburg Concertos (nos. 1 through 6)
    Vivaldi   Concerto Grossos

Solo
    Bach   Concerto no. 2 in E major for Violin and Orchestra

    Bartók   Concerto for Violin and Orchestra
    Beethoven Concerto in D major for Violin and Orchestra
    Berg   Concerto for Violin and Orchestra
    Brahms   Concerto in D major for Violin and Orchestra Concertos for Piano and Orchestra (nos. 1 and 2)

Grieg	Concerto in a minor for Piano and Orchestra
Khachaturian	Concerto for Violin and Orchestra
Liszt	Concerto no. 1 in E♭ major for Piano and Orchestra
Mendelssohn	Concerto in e minor for Violin and Orchestra
Rachmaninoff	Concerto no. 2 in c minor for Piano and Orchestra
Saint-Saëns	Concerto in g minor for Piano and Orchestra
Schumann	Concerto in a minor for Piano and Orchestra
Tchaikovsky	Concerto in D major for Violin and Orchestra

Opera

Berg	*Wozzeck*
Bizet	*Carmen*
Donizetti	*Lucia di Lammermoor*
Gounod	*Faust*
Humperdinck	*Hansel and Gretel*
Leoncavallo	*I Pagliacci*
Mascagni	*Cavalleria Rusticana*
Menotti	*Amahl and the Night Visitors*
Monteverdi	*L'Incoronazione di Poppea*
Mozart	*Don Giovanni*
	The Magic Flute
Offenbach	*The Tales of Hoffmann*
Puccini	*Madame Butterfly*
Verdi	*Aida*
	Otello
	La Traviata
Wagner	*Die Meistersinger*
	Tannhäuser

Operetta, Comic and Folk Opera

Friml	*Rose Marie*
	The Vagabond King
Gershwin	*Porgy and Bess*
Gilbert and Sullivan	*The Gondoliers*
	H.M.S. Pinafore
	Mikado
Herbert	*Naughty Marietta*
	Sweethearts
Menotti	*The Old Maid and the Thief*
	The Telephone

Romberg	*The Student Prince*
Rossini	*The Barber of Seville*
Smetana	*The Bartered Bride*

Oratorio

Elgar	*The Dream of Gerontius*
Handel	*Judas Maccabaeus*
	Messiah
Haydn	*The Creation*
Mendelssohn	*Elijah*
	St. Paul

Sonata

Baroque

Bach	Sonata no. 3 in E major (violin and harpsichord)
Corelli	Sonata in g minor, op. 5, no. 5
Handel	Sonata in F major for Flute and Continuo, op. 1, no. 11
Vivaldi	Sonata in A major (violin and piano)

Post-Baroque

| Beethoven | Sonata no. 2 in A major (piano) |
| Chopin | Sonata no. 2 in b♭ minor, op. 35 (piano) |

Sonatina

| Clementi | Sonatinas, op. 36 (piano) |
| Ravel | *Sonatine* (piano) |

String Quartet

Bartók	Six string quartets
Beethoven	Sixteen string quartets
Bloch	Quartet no. 2
Brahms	Quartet no. 2 in a minor
Haydn	Sixty-eight string quartets
Mozart	Quartet no. 14 in G major, K. 387
Schoenberg	Quartet no. 4
Schubert	Quartet no. 14 in d minor
Schumann	Quartet in A major
Stravinsky	Three Pieces for String Quartet

Suite

Baroque
Bach	*English* and *French* Suites
	Partita no. 2 in d minor for Unaccompanied Violin
Corelli	Sonata in e minor, op. 5, no. 2
Handel	Suite no. 5 in E major (harpsichord)

Nineteenth-Twentieth Century Suites
Bizet	*L'Arlésienne* Suite no. 2
Copland	*Music for the Theater*
Debussy	*Children's Corner Suite*
	Suite Bergamasque
Ravel	*Le Tombeau de Couperin*
Thomson	Suite from *The Plow that Broke the Plains*

Symphony
Beethoven	Nine symphonies
Berlioz	*Symphonie Fantastique*
Brahms	Four symphonies
Dvorák	Nine symphonies
Franck	Symphony in d minor
Haydn	(c.) One hundred symphonies
Mozart	(c.) Fifty symphonies
Prokofiev	Classical Symphony in D major
Schumann	Symphony no. 3 in E♭ major
Tchaikovsky	Six symphonies

CHAPTER TEN

ADDITIONAL GENRES

❖

KEYBOARD GENRES
SOLO VOCAL GENRES
CHORAL GENRES
ORCHESTRAL GENRES

ADDITIONAL GENRES AND
   STYLE PERIODS
SUMMARY
STUDY GUIDELINES

Many compositions, whether consisting of one movement or several, differ from those described in Chapters Eight and Nine and therefore do not lend themselves as readily to generalization. These diverse types will be discussed in this chapter in four categories: keyboard genres; solo vocal genres; choral genres; and orchestral genres.

KEYBOARD GENRES

There are many compositions written for piano, organ, harpsichord, or clavichord, without orchestral or other instrumental participation. All of these instruments can play both melody and accompaniment. This is undoubtedly the reason why keyboard instruments have been popular with composers and performers for some four hundred years, and why so many special types of music have been written specifically for them.

Toccata
Prominent in the keyboard genre is the *toccata* (from the Italian *toccare*, "to touch"), a piece written to display the manual dexterity of the performer. Typically, a toccata is free in form, that is, additive,

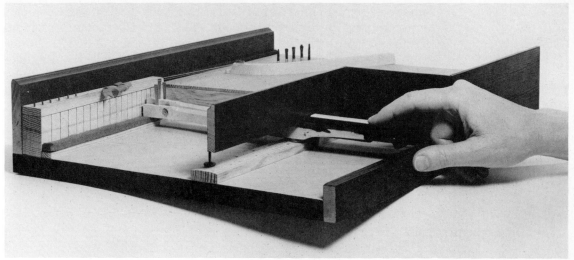

Smithsonian Institution Photo #74282.

Model of the clavichord action. The middle tangent at the end of the key that is being depressed is striking its pair of strings.

containing a flavor of improvisation through the use of scale passages, chordal sections, and arpeggios that a performer might use if the piece were being created impromptu. It is usually in one movement, whether performed alone or as a movement of a longer composition. Contemporary composers now use the term to describe a composition that follows the stylistic guidelines of the early toccatas, whether for keyboard or some type of instrumental ensemble. Whether or not for keyboards, toccatas are typically "showy."

Prelude

A *prelude* is, by definition, a composition that "precedes" something, whether ceremony, symphony,or another musical movement. In practice, however, this distinction does not always occur. Although a piano prelude (or a set of preludes) may occur early in a recital, the choice is really left to the discretion of the performer. A specialized prelude, the *chorale prelude,* is an organ composition that precedes a church service. Such works probably originated as improvisations by individual church organists during the sixteenth century, later to be more formally organized into written compositions in the seventeenth and eighteenth centuries.

CHORALE PRELUDE

Listen to J. S. Bach's *Schübler Chorale* no. 1, S. 645 *(listening selections).* Bach used an already existing chorale as the basis for many of his organ works. Some settings, as in his *Orgelbüchlein* (Little Organ Book), are simple, with melody appearing in the highest part supported by a homophonic texture. In contrast, other chorale settings, as in this listening example, are polyphonic, with the chorale tune appearing

Selection no. 51

phrase-by-phrase, interwoven with other melodies through complex counterpoint. This example is one of the six Schübler chorale preludes (BWV 645–650) arranged by Bach between 1746 and 1749. The chorale melody is by Philipp Nicolai (1556–1608) and is called a Schübler chorale because it is the first of a group of six published by Schübler starting in 1746. It is a virtuoso work, suitable not only for worship but for concert as well.

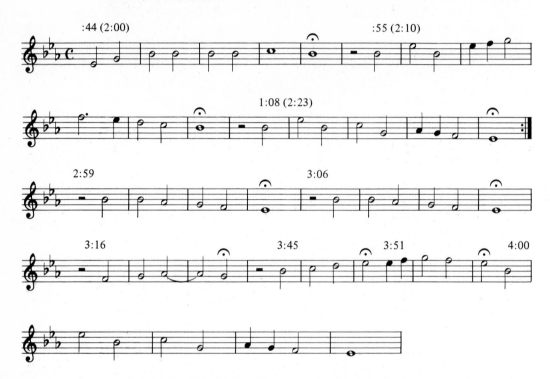

Composers during the Romantic period wrote short piano works with one theme, which they called preludes. It is now typical for the descriptive term "prelude" to be applied to any composition that is short and monothematic.

Etude

An *etude* (literally, study) is a composition written to help students master a technical problem on a particular instrument. Etudes have been written for every type of solo instrument. It is not uncommon for an etude to transcend its educational purposes and become a popular concert or recital selection. Chopin's piano etudes are a notable example of this phenomenon. Each etude singles out a technical problem for a pianist, such as rapid scales in the left or right hand, chromatic (half-step) passages, octaves, trills, and arpeggios.

Chamber organ by John Snetzler, London, 1761. This instrument has only one manual but was capable of playing several stops. There is a swell shutter in the lid of the case.

Smithsonian Institution Photo #71423.

Listen to Chopin's Etude no. 12 in c minor, op. 10 *(listening selections).* This etude develops left-hand technique for the pianist, particularly the ability to accompany with complicated chromatic patterns while playing a simple melody in the right. According to the directions given to the performer:

Selection no. 4

> The principal aim of this study for the Left Hand is to teach the student to economize his strength. The player who husbands it for the climaxes, and carefully observes (simply from a technical standpoint) the accents and the numerous crescendos and decrescendos, will discover that the piece by no means demands such enormous powers of endurance as would appear needful at first glance. (Friedheim revision of the etudes, G. Schirmer, 1916, Vol. 33, p. 5).

Chopin wrote twenty-seven etudes; the opus 10 etudes, comprising twelve of the total and published in 1833, were dedicated to fellow pianist Franz Liszt, another composer whose piano etudes represented a significant proportion of his compositional output.

Fugue

SUBJECT   A fugue is a polyphonic composition that uses one theme, the *subject,* as the musical idea. Fugues were originally written solely for keyboard instruments, but today are composed for combinations as varied as a string quartet, the sections of a vocal choir, or various instruments or sections of a symphony orchestra. A fugue may be written in two, three, four, or even more voices (parts), in a form that can be likened to a round. There is, in reality, little that governs how a fugue is constructed. Typically, the subject is presented initially in one part and then introduced gradually in each subsequent part until all voices have entered.

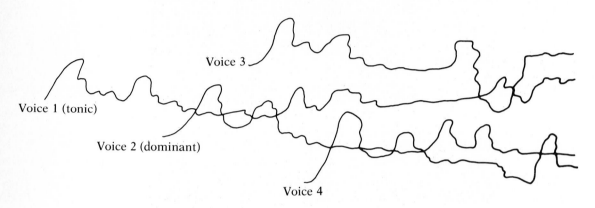

EXPOSITION   This is called the fugal *exposition.* Although it begins monophonically, it becomes polyphonic when the second voice enters. After the initial exposition in all the voices, there follows a section in which the subject

EPISODE   is not heard, called an *episode.* Each subsequent section in which the subject is heard is called an exposition. Fugues normally develop through an alternation of episodes and expositions. Only the initial exposition, however, is structured in the way shown in the diagram. After that statement, composers treat it quite freely, with the subject usually appearing in varying keys. The fugue often ends with a final presentation of the subject in the tonic key. In addition to serving as the organizing principle of an entire composition, fugal techniques are also used by composers in a section or part of a larger movement.

Selection no. 76   Listen to Bach's Fugue in c minor (BVW 582) *(listening selections).* This fugue is linked by Bach with the Passacaglia in c minor *(listening*

Selection no. 71   *selections),* since it uses the same theme for its subject. (The fugue is

usually performed after the passacaglia.) Because the subject is familiar from having first been heard in the passacaglia, Bach does not present it monophonically in the fugue. Rather, he simultaneously adds a new melody in the second voice. This is called a *countersubject.*

The subject is presented again in a third voice (:11) and then a fourth (:26). These two ideas, subject and countersubject, are then used throughout the work in alternation.

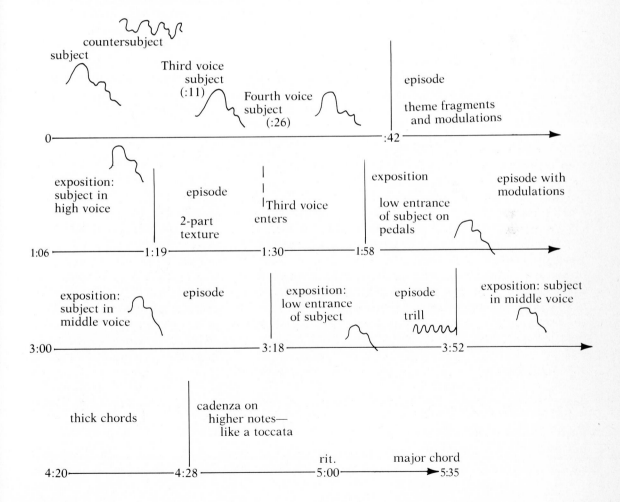

DOUBLE FUGUE

BI-THEMATIC

In this piece Bach has written a *double fugue* (in four voices), that is, one that uses two themes, subject and countersubject, throughout. Although the fugues most normally encountered are monothematic, this one is *bi-thematic,* as are all double fugues.

Bach is considered the supreme master of fugal writing. His subjects are short and rhythmically significant, thus being easy to hear and recognize in a contrapuntal texture. Bach was personally challenged by the mathematical logic of this form of composition. In *Die Kunst der Fuge* (The Art of Fugue), his last work (1749), published after his death in 1750, he demonstrated almost all the possibilities for fugal composition by writing fifteen fugues on the same subject.

Character Piece

Character pieces, short works for piano, were generally written during the nineteenth century. The range of possibilities within the classification is vast, but it is common for a character piece to be programmatic. Composers have often used titles to suggest the program, such as Schumann's "Dreaming" or "By the Fireside" (from *Scenes of Childhood,* op. 15).

CHARACTER CYCLE

Since each brief character piece usually displays a single mood or feeling, composers have often grouped several together into a *character cycle.* Performers may also group related character pieces when planning a recital, in order to form a broader panorama. A character cycle, such as Schumann's *Scenes of Childhood,* is normally performed without applause interrupting its various movements or pieces, much

Opus numbers give a rough chronology to a composer's work, reflecting date of publication more than date of actual composition. Although Beethoven was the first composer consistently to catalog his works by opus number, the practice can be traced to the early seventeenth century.

Not all composers, however, use opus numbers. Cataloguers and musicologists have worked out numbering systems for composers such as J. S. Bach, whose works are extensive but not numbered. BWV is a catalog numbering system compiled by Wolfgang Schmieder in 1950 for J. S. Bach's compositions. The initials BWV stand for Bach-Werke-Verzeichnis (Bach-Work-Catalog), and are sometimes substituted by S for Schmieder. Not a chronological listing, the numbers in the BWV system refer to a range of select genres: 1–250 to choral music; 250–500 to chorales, arias, and sacred songs; 525–770 to organ works, etc.

Mozart's works were catalogued by L. von Köchel and thus bear a K. or K.V. (Kochel-Verzeichnis) number. For Domenico Scarlatti, it was Longo (L) and Kirkpatrick (K); for Haydn it was Hoboken (H); for Vivaldi, Ryom (R); and for Schubert, Deutsch (D).

as any multimovement composition. Some examples from among the diversity of possible character pieces are discussed below.

Nocturne. The *nocturne* is a character piece. Although John Field, an Irish composer, is credited with inventing the nocturne, it was Frederic Chopin who popularized the form. A nocturne is usually written with a melody in the right hand of the piano and the left-hand accompaniment in arpeggiated chords. The tempo is typically slow and languid, suggesting an evening mood. Chopin also wrote waltzes, mazurkas, and polonaises, all of which are classified as character pieces.

Waltz. The *waltz* is in triple time. Its tempo may be either slow or somewhat fast.

Mazurka. The *mazurka*, a Polish dance, is also in triple meter. As with the waltz, tempo may be slow or fast. Placement of the strong beat in the mazurka, which might be expected at the count of one, as in most examples of triple meter, is more often found here on the second or third beat of each measure.

Selection no. 12

Polonaise. A *polonaise*, a dance in triple meter, has a moderate tempo. Since it developed originally as a court dance, its character is often stately.

Ballade. Another character piece is the *ballade*, a piece of changing moods that uses two themes. Listen to the Brahms *Ballade* in g minor, op. 118 *(listening selections)*. This ballade contrasts a dramatic first theme in section A with a lyric one in the B section.

Selection no. 17

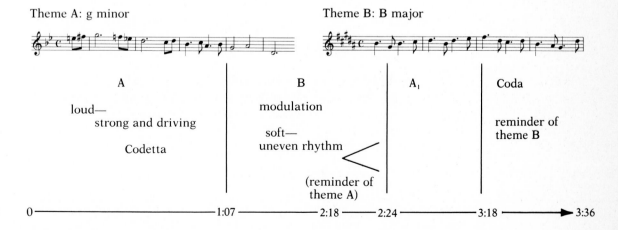

Johannes Brahms.
Courtesy of the New York Public Library.

Johannes Brahms (1833–1897) was born in Hamburg to an extremely poor family. His father recognized the child's musicality and scraped money together so Johannes could be given piano lessons at an early age. As a youth, Johannes gave music lessons to others, composed musical arrangements, and played in taverns to make his living. Eventually he was discovered and befriended by several significant persons in his lifetime, including Eduard Remenyi, a Hungarian violinist whom Brahms accompanied; Joseph Joachim, a violinist who was impressed with Brahms's pianistic and compositional abilities; and Franz Liszt, the celebrated Hungarian pianist/composer. The great German composer Robert Schumann and his wife, Clara, most significantly promoted his career and with him formed an intimate, lifelong friendship.

Nonetheless, success came slowly for Brahms. His first compositions were not well received, and Brahms out of necessity supplemented his income by performing and conducting. He was a self-critical composer who would not publish any work unless he considered it technically perfect. His first symphony was not released until he was forty-three.

Brahms wrote extensive piano works, including two concertos, three sonatas, numerous sets of variations, and thirty-five character pieces. The middle and low registers of his keyboard compositions are richly developed with cross-rhythms and lush melodies. Brahms produced masterpieces in every musical genre with the exception of opera. In addition to four symphonies, he composed overtures, including *Tragic Overture* and *Academic Festival Overture*, solo songs, lush choral works, chamber music, and a *German Requiem*, a large choral composition. His works ultimately gained a wide acceptance and when he died Brahms left a sizable estate in stark contrast to the poverty of his past.

SOLO VOCAL GENRES

ART SONG   There are fewer genres for solo voice than there are for keyboard composition. The most important is undoubtedly art song, a genre for solo voice and piano developed in the nineteenth century.

Lieder

Germany was the leading country of art song, where it is called *lied* (pl., lieder). It developed partially in response to the inspiration provided by the German writers who signaled the beginning of the Romantic era, including Goethe, Heine, and Morike, whose works many composers set to music. Lieder were written by many composers, including Schubert, Schumann, Brahms, and Hugo Wolf. Unlike operatic arias, which generally make broad, sweeping statements about emotion on a grand scale, lieder distill their emotional assertions to an intense, highly condensed exposition. Each word carries an abundance of meaning in lieder, and words and music are inexorably blended, making translation into another language difficult and frequently inappropriate. (Review *listing selections*). Selections no. 42, 73

Listen to Schubert's *Gretchen am Spinnrade (listening selections)* Selection no. 19
(see also pp. 44–45). Schubert composed this work in 1814 when he was seventeen years old, and it became one of the most important songs he composed during his short life. In this example, the voice has the melody throughout while harmony is provided by the piano. Accompaniment is in the form of arpeggios (broken chords), which provides the illusion of a spinning wheel turning.

Since the melody and harmony are repeated on the words "Meine Ruh ist hin, Mein Herz ist schwer," there is a feeling of "return" in the composition. The ending is almost identical to the beginning; such a return provides a sense of relief and fulfillment (see p. 302).

Song Cycles

Lieder may be grouped together by the composer when he or she wishes to present a story, convey a variety of contrasting moods, or even to honor a particular poet. These collections are known as *song cycles*, of which Schubert's *Winterreise* (1827) is one of the best known. Singers often group several lied together in recital, whether by the same composer or not, to form an appropriate set, but such program choices cannot be characterized as a unified song cycle.

Chanson

Although German composers dominated composition in the field of art song, French composers also have used the work of poets of their country, such as Verlaine and Baudelaire, in the composition of art songs. These are called *chanson*. Since the composer is attempting to portray the spirit of a particular poem, there is no set form for either lieder or chansons. Through-composed form is common, as are strophic and modified strophic, but even return form has been used, as in the preceding Schubert example.

main
theme
d minor

> Meine Ruh' ist hin,
> Mein Herz ist schwer;
> Ich finde, ich finde sie
> Nimmer und nimmermehr.

modulations

> Wo ich ihn nicht hab',
> Ist mir das Grab,
> Die ganze Welt ist mir vergällt.
>
> Mein armer Kopf ist mir verrückt,
> Mein armer Sinn ist mir zerstückt.

return
d minor

> Meine Ruh' ist hin,
> Mein Herz ist schwer;
> Ich finde, ich finde sie
> Nimmer und nimmermehr.

modulations

> Nach ihm nur schau' ich
> Zum Fenster hinaus,
> Nach ihm nur geh' ich
> Aus dem Haus.
>
> Sein hoher Gang, sein' edle Gestalt,
> Seines Mundes Lächeln,
> Seiner Augen Gewalt,
> Und seiner Rede Zauberfluss,
>
> Sein Händedruck, und ach, sein Kuss!

return
d minor

> Mein Ruh' ist hin,
> Mein Herz ist schwer;
> Ich finde, ich finde sie
> Nimmer und nimmermehr.

modulations

> Mein Busen drängt sich nach ihm hin.
> Ach, dürft ich fassen und halten ihn!
> Und küssen ihn so wie ich wollt',
> An seinen Küssen vergehen sollt',
> O könnt ich ihn küssen,
> So wie ich wollt',
> An seinen Küssen vergehen sollt'!
>   (last line repeated)

partial
return
d minor

> Meine Ruh' ist hin,
> Mein Herz ist schwer!

CHORAL GENRES

There are numerous other choral genres in addition to the opera, oratorio, and cantata discussed in Chapter Nine.

Mass

The *mass* is a form of choral work that originally was used solely in the liturgy of the Catholic church, but is now also written for non-liturgical purposes, such as public concert. The words are Latin and the text of each movement of the Ordinary is standard.

Kyrie
　　Kyrie eleison (Lord, have mercy)
　　Christi eleison (Christ, have mercy)
　　Kyrie eleison (Lord, have mercy)

Gloria
　　Gloria in excelsis Deo (Glory be to God on high)
　　Laudamus te (We praise Thee)
　　Gratias agimus tibi (We give Thee thanks)
　　Domine Deus (Lord God)
　　Qui tollis peccata mundi (Who takest away the sins of the world)
　　Qui sedes ad dexteram patris (Who sittest at the right hand of the Father)
　　Quoniam tu solus sanctus (For Thou only art holy)
　　Cum sancto spiritu (With the Holy Spirit)

Credo
　　Credo in unum Deum (I believe in one God)
　　Patrem omnipotentem (Father almighty)
　　Et in unum Dominum (And in one Lord)
　　Et incarnatus est (And was incarnate)
　　Crucifixus (Crucified)
　　Et resurrexit (And rose again)
　　Et in Spiritum Sanctum (And [I believe] in the Holy Spirit)
　　Confiteor unum baptisma (I confess one baptism)

Sanctus
　　Sanctus (Holy)
　　Hosanna in excelsis (Hosanna in the highest)
　　Benedictus qui venit (Blessed is He that cometh)

Agnus Dei
　　Agnus Dei (Lamb of God)
　　Dona nobis pacem (Give us peace)

Although solo singers, duets, and ensembles may sing some phrases or sections of each movement, a Mass, at least for concert purposes, consists largely of choral singing. Works of the Middle Ages and Renaissance are typically unaccompanied, but orchestral accompaniment may be included in works of later periods.

Selection no. 77

Listen to Guillaume de Machaut's setting of Agnus Dei I from *La Messe de Notre Dame (listening selections)*. This work is notable for two reasons: it is the first known setting of the Mass in four parts, and it is also the first known setting of the entire Ordinary of the Mass by one composer. The five movements are linked by an overall style as well as by the use of this motive:

The Mass is generally thought to have been written in 1364 to celebrate the coronation of Charles IV, King of France, although some authorities believe it was composed as early as 1337.

The medieval concept of consonance and dissonance is different from contemporary practices, particularly at cadences, and the harmony may thus seem hollow and even harsh. This four-part setting of

Guillame de Machaut (c. 1300–c. 1377) studied theology in his youth and took holy orders while still a young man. He became a canon—a clergyman in residence at a cathedral—at Verdun in 1330, Arras in 1332, and Rheims, the ecclesiastical center of France, in 1333. Rheims was an important cathedral in Northern France where the archbishops were responsible for crowning the king.

Machaut was also the notary and private secretary to King John of Bohemia. He traveled widely with the king, becoming intimate

Cathedral of Rheims, where Machaut was in residence, is an example of Gothic architecture built between 1225 and 1290.

with many of Europe's rulers. He was a composer and poet, rated by countrymen as highly as his contemporary, the Italian poet Petrarch. Machaut fulfilled all of his duties and functions in his free time from the cathedral at Rheims, composing more works than any other fourteenth-century composer. His compositions are, surprisingly, mostly secular, including ballades, virelais, and twenty-three motets. This historically important work, *La Messe de Notre Dame*, is one of the few sacred works written by the composer.

Paintings like this create the same feeling of religiosity as does a celebration of the Mass. *Assumption of the Virgin*, Borgognone, Italian, active 1481–1523 in Milan.

Courtesy of the New York Public Library.

the Mass opened up the sonority from the somewhat "closed" position found in medieval polyphony. Machaut based the Agnus Dei I on a Gregorian melody and achieved greater unity between the voices by using imitation. In actual practice, medieval masses may have been performed with instruments doubling (and even replacing) some of the vocal lines.

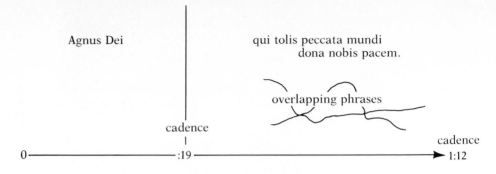

There is no standard way to designate a Mass. Palestrina's *Missa Papae Marcelli* was written to honor a Pope, while *Missa L'home arme* was named from the medieval tune that is used cyclically in each movement. Thirty masses were written based on this melody, including examples by Dufay, Obrecht, Ockeghem, and Josquin. A Mass may also simply be titled by its tonality, such as Bach's Mass in b minor.

A Missa Pro Defunctis (Requiem Mass) is a funeral Mass for the Dead *(listening selections)*. The usual Mass text is supplemented by words on death, and the joyful portions of the text are omitted.

Selection no. 53

Requiem aeternam dona eis,
    Domine,
et lux perpetua luceat eis.
To decet hymnus. Deus, in
    Sion,
et tibi reddetur votum in
    Jerusalem.
Exaudi orationem meam,
ad te omnis caro veniet.
Kyrie eleison, Christe
    eleison.

Eternal rest grant unto
    them, O Lord,
and let perpetual light
    shine upon them.
There shall be singing unto
    Thee in Sion,
and prayer shall go up to
    Thee in Jerusalem.
Hear my prayer,
unto Thee all flesh shall
    come.
Lord have mercy, Christ
    have mercy.

Dies irae, dies illa,
solvet saeclum in favilla,
teste David cum Sibylla.
Quantus tremor est futurus,
quando Judex est venturus,
cuncta stricte discussurus!

Day of wrath, day of
    mourning,
earth in smouldering ashes
    laying,
so spake David and the
    Sibyl.
How great the trembling
    shall be
when the Judge shall come
by whose sentence all shall
    be bound!

Motet

Another type of choral work is the *motet,* a composition written in polyphonic style that was an important vocal genre in the Middle Ages. A motet can be either sacred or secular and there is neither a set form nor text, although the language is usually Latin. Therefore, to a certain extent, each motet is unique.

The motet has a history dating back further than other choral genres, the word being used to describe a polyphonic composition probably as early as 1200. Throughout history the motet has remained choral and polyphonic, but it has sometimes been written for unaccompanied voices, later with instrumental accompaniment. It is usually a one-movement structure as compared to the five sections of the Ordinary of the Mass. Composers have often displayed their ability to write counterpoint in motets by providing imitation among the vocal lines, which also serves to unify the work.

Listen to John Dunstable's *Veni Sancte Spiritus (listening selections).* This motet is *isorhythmic,* which means it has a melody (or set

Selection no. 78
ISORHYTHMIC

Whereas the standard text of the Mass (Kyrie, Gloria, Credo, Sanctus, and Agnus Dei) is called the *Ordinary,* the text that changes according to the church year is called the *Proper.* In a concert version of the Mass, the Ordinary is used most often alone, without the accompanying seasonal Proper. When the Mass is celebrated in church, some parts are sung, others spoken depending on tradition and the wishes of the priest celebrating the service. When the entire text is sung, it is called a *Missa Solemnis* (High Mass), but is termed a *Missa Lecta* (Low Mass) when the text is spoken. The Missa Solemnis is usually celebrated on Sundays and special days, the Missa Lecta on ordinary days of the week.

Celebration of the Mass: left, "Come together in common . . . so that with undivided mind you may obey the bishop and the priests, and break one Bread which is the medicine of immortality and the antidote against death . . ."; above, procession leading to the Cathedral.

Courtesy of the Catholic Diocese of Tucson.

> ***John Dunstable*** (c. 1385–1453) was an important fifteenth-century English composer who wrote while in the service of French and British rulers. Sixty of his compositions are extant, including twelve motets. Dunstable contributed to fifteenth-century music his use of the declamatory motet, in which the musical rhythms of the composition are governed by the rhythm of spoken words. He is a somewhat pivotal composer between Middle Ages and Modern times, but because his music shows the English penchant for harmony in thirds and sixths, it is more "modern"-sounding than Machaut's historically earlier work.

COLOR
TALEA

of intervals) as well as a rhythmic pattern that persist throughout. The melody pattern *(color)* is played with the rhythm pattern *(talea)* using sometimes longer, sometimes shorter durations. Both color and talea are derived from a Gregorian melody, Veni sancte spiritus.

San-cti Spi-ri-tus ad-sit, no-bis gra-ti-a:

The translation (see page 309) is:

> Come, thou Holy Spirit, come!
> And from thy celestial home
> Shed a ray of light divine!
> Come, thou Father of the poor!
> Come, thou source of all our store!
> Come, within our bosoms shine!

Madrigal

A *madrigal*, the musical setting of a poem, is usually secular. The subject matter often deals with pastoral themes, love, or merriment. Most madrigals are written to an Italian or an English text, depending on the native tongue of the composer. They can be in three, four, or five voice parts and were intended for a small group of singers, with two or three persons on a part. Many make use of a repeated refrain or chorus.

A type of madrigal was popular in Italy as early as the fourteenth century, although the sixteenth century is considered the Golden Age of madrigal writing, especially in Italy. Madrigals of the time were written to be sung as courtly entertainment, rather than for public performance in concerts. In the late sixteenth century, largely through publications of a book called *Musica Transalpina* (an English translation of Italian madrigals), the form traveled to England. These English

madrigals are homophonic, since the melody is in the soprano line, not divided among the voices as in the Italian style. The form of English madrigals is usually clear and easy to discern.

Selection no. 33   Listen to Thomas Morley's "Now Is the Month of Maying" *(listening selections)*. The overall form of this madrigal is AB, repeated with the text changes, in this structure:

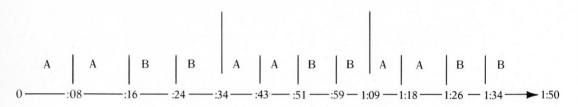

The AB alone is in binary form, but since the entire structure is repeated three times, the result is a large strophic form:

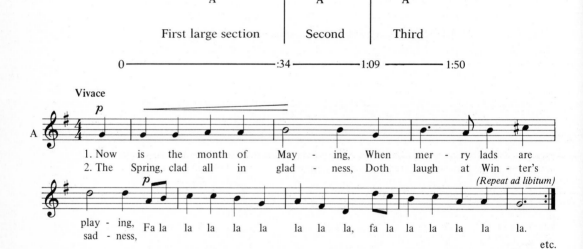

Thomas Morley (1557–1602) was an English composer who studied at Oxford University and ultimately served as organist at St. Paul's Cathedral in London. Under a patent granted to him by the English government, Morley controlled all music publishing, serving as editor, arranger, and printer of his own works and those of other composers. He edited a collection of twenty-five madrigals, *The Triumphs of Oriana*, a noteworthy collaborative work representing the music of twenty-three English composers. Many madrigals ended with the phrase, "Longlive fair Oriana," a tribute to Queen Elizabeth I, the reigning monarch of the period. A respected theorist, Morley wrote a treatise, *Plaine and Easie Introduction to Practical Musicke*, describing British musical practices and forms of that time.

Medieval scholars still study musical manuscripts in an effort to decipher what the earlier notation meant and how the music might have sounded.

Courtesy of the Catholic Diocese of Tucson.

ORCHESTRAL GENRES

Some orchestral genres have already been presented, leaving only the overture, tone poem, and program symphony to be discussed in this chapter.

Overture

An *overture* is a musical work that, like a prelude, precedes something, such as an opera, oratorio, or ballet. Some overtures have been merely a fanfare, used to attract attention to the subsequent performance. A FRENCH OVERTURE special type called the *French overture* was standardized by the composer Lully in the seventeenth century. It consists of two sections, a slow opening with dotted, uneven rhythm patterns, followed by a faster polyphonic section.

The second section typically ends with a slow coda. French overtures later were written with a third section, resulting from extension of this slow coda. The overall form was then ternary, with slow-fast-slow sectioning.

ITALIAN OVERTURE SINFONIA A second type of overture developed in the late seventeenth century that was fast-slow-fast. This is called an *Italian overture*, or *sinfonia*. Many believe that the popularity of French and Italian overtures led to the use of contrast in tempos between movements of instrumental works.

Listen to Handel's Overture to Suite no. 1 in F major *(Water Music)*, Maestoso-Allegro-Adagio e staccato *(supplemental listening)*. Handel's overture is French since it is in a slow-fast-slow pattern.

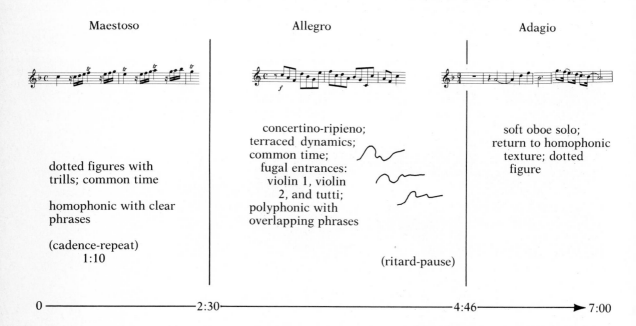

Maestoso   Allegro   Adagio

dotted figures with trills; common time

homophonic with clear phrases

(cadence-repeat)
1:10

concertino-ripieno;
terraced dynamics;
common time;
  fugal entrances:
  violin 1, violin
  2, and tutti;
polyphonic with
overlapping phrases

(ritard-pause)

soft oboe solo;
return to homophonic
texture; dotted
figure

0 ———————— 2:30 ———————————————— 4:46 ——————→ 7:00

Composers later began to write overtures that were not directly linked to a longer work, but were independent compositions intended CONCERT OVERTURE to serve as the opening selection at a concert of assorted works. These are called *concert overtures*.

Overtures of the Classic and Romantic periods, particularly in opera, often allude to themes to appear later in the complete work in arias or choruses. Richard Wagner was a master of presenting a catalog of operatic themes in his overtures. He called these themes *leitmotifs,* and his overtures are a capsule view of the complete opera.

Listen to the Prelude to Act III of Wagner's *Lohengrin (listening selections)*. Although Mozart was one of the first composers to use thematic material from the opera in the overture, the practice was brought to its greatest refinement by Wagner. Since it sets the scene for the wedding feast that leads into the well-known bridal march, the Prelude to Act III is really an overture for the last part of the opera. Wagner used three themes in the Prelude. The first two are similar to one another, with the third providing contrast through rhythmic variety and a softer dynamic level.

LEITMOTIF
Selection no. 10

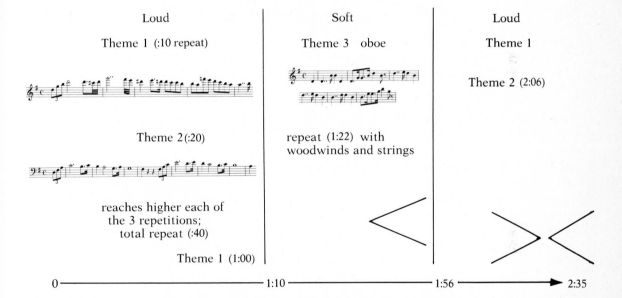

Tone Poem
The *tone poem,* a one-movement orchestral work inspired by an extra-musical idea, developed in the nineteenth century. It is also called a *symphonic poem,* and either tells a musical story or paints a musical picture. It is thus usually somewhat free in form and may incorporate a variety of moods and tempos.

Program Symphony
A *program symphony* is similar to a tone poem but consists of several movements, each of which describes or is inspired by a specific, non-

Richard Wagner (1813–1883) was a great German composer who developed a style of opera composition that transformed forever the concept of stage music. Although a student of writing and literature at the Thomasschule and the University of Leipzig, his greatest love was music. Wagner's first overture was written when he was sixteen, his first opera at twenty-one. He spent his early career as an opera conductor in Königsberg and Riga, all the while continuing to compose operas. Later serving as 2nd Court Chapel Master in Dresden, he completed both *Tannhäuser* and *Lohengrin.* Neither was successful or popular until Franz Liszt introduced *Lohengrin* in 1850.

Because of his revolutionary activities, Wagner was forced to live outside of Germany for years after the revolution of 1849. As an expatriate in Switzerland, he formalized his philosophy on opera, making it a

Richard Wagner.
Courtesy of the New York Public Library.

grand synthesis of music, text, acting, and staging—encompassed by the term *music-drama. Lohengrin* is a transitional work between traditional opera and this new style, in which Wagner wrote for a large orchestra, with expanded woodwind and brass sections. He also blurred distinctions between aria and recitative, making all singing continuous, bound to-

gether by the ever-present orchestra.

Tristan und Isolde (1859), *Die Meistersinger von Nürnberg* (1867), and all four works within the opera cycle, *Der Ring des Nibelungen,* were written in the new style. These works are elaborately staged presentations requiring enormous vocal and orchestral resources. Only the largest opera companies can mount such productions. Rich and lush harmonies and timbres characterize his music, with chords that change gradually and chromatically. Wagner's most avid critics of his day considered the music too dissonant and heavy to be enjoyable.

Wagner's patron, Ludwig II of Bavaria, built a special theatre for the composer in Bayreuth, still housing opera festivals of Wagner's works. His last music-drama was *Parsifal* (1882). He died while on holiday in Venice and his body was returned for interment at Bayreuth.

musical image or idea. Program symphonies have continued to be popular since their beginnings in the nineteenth century.

Listen to "Fete" from Debussy's *Three Nocturnes (supplemental listening).* Although Debussy conceived the three nocturnes as works for solos violin and orchestra, they eventually came to be thought of as a unified program symphony. The first two were performed as an orchestral work in 1900, the complete triptych in 1901. The term

Monet's painting of the west facade of Rouen Cathedral captured the movement of light and shadow across the building, a fleeting Impressionism much like the mood Debussy captured in his nocturnes. *Rouen Cathedral, West Facade*, Claude Monet, French, 1894, oil on canvas.

Courtesy of the National Gallery of Art, Washington, Chester Dale Collection.

"nocturne" in this case does not have the same connotation as when it is used to identify a Chopin nocturne, where it means a mood specifically evocative of evening. Rather, each movement in Debussy's work suggests an atmospheric setting of a different kind.

Movement one, "Nuages" (Clouds), portrays the passage of clouds across the sky; movement two, "Fetes" (Festivals), a restless atmospheric quality punctuated by flashes of light (provided by the brass section); and movement three, "Sirènes" (Sirens), a picture of the sea bathed in sunlight, incorporating women's voices in the orchestration.

Since Debussy was a master of suggestion, use of the term "Impressionism" to describe his music is justified. His purpose in "Fetes," by his own testimony, was to capture "the restless dancing rhythms of the atmosphere, interspersed with abrupt scintillations."

The themes of this work are:

ADDITIONAL GENRES AND STYLE PERIODS

The following genres developed in these specific periods, but have continued to be written in most subsequent eras.

Period	Genre	Examples
Medieval/Renaissance	Motet Mass Madrigal Toccata	Dunstable—*Veni Sancte Spiritus* Machaut—Agnus Dei I Morley—"Now Is the Month of Maying"
Baroque	Chorale Prelude Fugue Overture	Bach—*Schübler Chorale* no. 1, S. 645 Bach—Fugue in c minor, BMV 582 Handel—Overture to Suite no. 1 in F major
Classic (see selections on pages cited below)		
Romantic	Overture Etude Character pieces Tone poem Lieder, chanson Program Symphony	Wagner—Prelude to Act III of *Lohengrin* Chopin—Etude no. 12 in c minor, op. 10 Brahms—*Ballade* in g minor Schubert—*Gretchen am Spinnrade*
Impressionism		Debussy—"Fêtes" from *Three Nocturnes*
Twentieth Century (see selections on pages cited below)		

See also selections in Chapter 3, p. 81; Chapter 4, p. 140; Chapter 5, p. 184; Chapter 6, p. 215; Chapter 7, p. 234; Chapter 8, p. 266; Chapter 9, p. 285.

SUMMARY

This chapter has presented a variety of forms, techniques, and genres that do not fit clearly into the categories discussed in Chapters Eight and Nine. Keyboard compositions discussed are the toccata, a "touch" piece, and prelude, a composition that often precedes a longer work. The etude is a technical study, while a fugue is a polyphonic technique unified by a thematic subject. Character pieces include the nocturne, waltz, and ballade. When character pieces are arranged as an extended work, it is called a character cycle. All of these compositions for keyboard may be transcribed for other instruments from their keyboard original.

Art songs, a fusion of poetry and music, are written for solo voice and piano. These are called lieder when written in German, chanson if written in French. A song cycle is formed when several are grouped together thematically by the composer.

Choral genres include the Mass, the motet, a vocal composition written in an imitative polyphonic style, and the madrigal, a secular composition developed in Italy and England.

Additional orchestral genres include the overture, written to begin an opera, oratorio, or concert, as well as the tone poem, a one-movement programmatic work. A program symphony, which is similar, has several movements.

STUDY GUIDELINES

Guide to Perceiving Specialized Forms, Genres, and Techniques

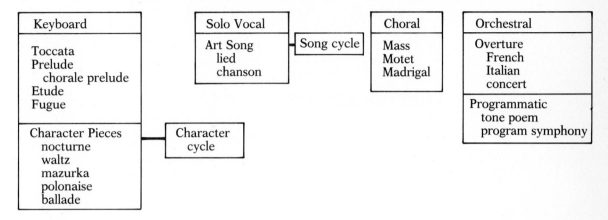

KEY TERMS AND CONCEPTS

Art Song
  Chanson
  Lied (lieder)
  Song Cycle
Character Cycle
Character Pieces
  Ballade
  Mazurka
  Nocturne
  Polonaise
  Waltz
Chorale Prelude
Etude
Fugue (fugal)
  Episode
  Exposition
  Subject

Madrigal
Mass
  Ordinary
Motet
Overture
  French
  Italian
Prelude
Program Symphony
Toccata
Tone Poem (Symphonic Poem)

EXERCISES

1. Attend a live concert or listen to one on radio or television. Which of the genres presented in this chapter did you hear? How do they compare with the prototypes discussed in this chapter?

2. What specific forms (strophic, processive, return, additive) were observed in movements of works heard in question 1? Can you describe the presentation of musical ideas by letters? (i.e., ABA, AA₁A, . . ., etc.)

CHAPTER REVIEW

Match items in the two columns. Answers in Appendix.

1. _____ isorhythm
2. _____ monothematic
3. _____ French overture
4. _____ waltz
5. _____ toccata
6. _____ song cycle
7. _____ subject
8. _____ etude
9. _____ mazurka
10. _____ tone poem
11. _____ Italian overture
12. _____ motet
13. _____ madrigal

A. fast-slow-fast
B. "touch" piece
C. one melodic unit used
D. musical study
E. uses talea and color
F. dance in triple time
G. slow-fast-slow
H. one-movement symphonic work
I. Polish dance in triple time
J. lieder linked by subject and/or poet
K. imitative vocal piece
L. fugal theme
M. secular vocal music popular in Italy and England during the Renaissance

FOR FURTHER LISTENING

Art Song

Brahms   "Dein blaues Auge"
                    "Wiegenlied"

Mussourgsky   "The Song of the Flea"

Schubert   "An die Musik"
                    "Du bist die Ruh'"
                    "Die Forelle"

Schumann	"Die beiden Grenadiere" "Ich grolle nicht"
Wolf	"Anakreons Grab"

Character Pieces
Brahms	Ballades, op. 10 Waltzes, op. 39 Romanze in F major, op. 118, no. 5
Chopin	Ballade No. 3 in A♭ major, op. 47 Impromptus, op. 29, 36, 51 Nocturnes, E♭ major, op. 9, no. 2 F♯ major, op. 15, no. 2 Waltzes, op. 64
Liszt	*Hungarian Rhapsody* no. 2 in c♯ minor *Mephisto* Waltz
Schubert	*Ländler* *Moments Musicaux*
Schumann	*Arabesques* *Fantasiestücke* *Papillons*

Chorale Prelude
Bach	*Ein' feste Burg ist unser Gott*

Etude
Chopin	Etude in C major, op. 10, no. 1 Etude in e minor, op. 25, no. 5 Etude in G♭ major, op. 25, no. 9
Liszt	*Etude de Concert* no. 3 in D major

Fugue
Bach	Fugue in b minor *The Well-Tempered Clavier*, Vols. I and II
Beethoven	*Der Grosse Fuge*
Brahms	*Variations and Fugue on a Theme by Handel*
Mozart	Fantasy and Fugue in C major, K. 394 Mass in c minor, K. 427: *Cum Sancto Spiritu*

Madrigal
	Triumphs of Oriana (a collection of English madrigals)

Mass
    Bach   Mass in b minor
    Palestrina   *Missa Papae Marcelli*

Motet
    Byrd   *Ergo Sum Panis Vivus*
    Des Prez   *Ave Maria*
    Victoria   *O Magnum Mysterium*

Overture
    Bach   Suite no. 3 in D major: Overture
    Beethoven   Overture to *Egmont*
                             Overture to *Leonore,* no. 3
    Berlioz   Overture: *The Roman Carnival*
    Brahms   *Academic Festival Overture*
                             Tragic Overture
    Handel   Overture: *Messiah*
    Lully   Overture: *Armide*
    Mendelssohn   Overture: *The Hebrides*
    Mozart   Overture to *The Magic Flute*
                             Overture to *The Marriage of Figaro*
    Rimsky-Korsakov   *Russian Easter Overture*
    Rossini   Overture to *William Tell*
    Schubert   Overture to *Rosamunde*
    Smetana   Overture to *The Bartered Bride*
    Tchaikovsky   *1812 Overture*
    Wagner   Overture to *The Flying Dutchman*
                             Prelude to *Die Meistersinger*
    Weber   Overture to *Der Freischütz*

Prelude
    Bach   *The Well-Tempered Clavier* (Vols. I and II)
    Chopin   Preludes, op. 28
    Debussy   Preludes
    Gershwin   Preludes

Program Symphony
    Beethoven   Symphony no. 6 in F major (*Pastorale*)
    Berlioz   *Symphonie Fantastique*
    Liszt   *A Faust Symphony*

Song Cycle

Fauré	*La Bonne Chanson*
Hindemith	*Das Marienleben*
Mahler	*Kindertotenlieder*
Moussorgsky	*Songs and Dances of Death*
Schubert	*Die Schöne Müllerin*
	Die Winterreise
Schumann	*Dichterliebe*

Toccata

Prokofiev	Toccata in d minor
Schumann	Toccata in C major, op. 7
Sweelinck	Toccata in a minor

Tone Poem

Dukas	*The Sorcerer's Apprentice*
Honegger	*Pacific 231*
Liszt	*Les Préludes*
Saint-Saëns	*Danse Macabre*
Sibelius	*The Swan of Tuonela*
Strauss, R.	*Till Eulenspiegel*

MUSICAL STYLES

❖

This final section, Chapters Eleven through Eighteen, selectively explores styles of music. Although there is undoubtedly more that unites music than separates it, the elements, as explored in Section II, and forms, as discussed in Section III, have not always been used in the same way, either historically or culturally. Section IV looks at some of music's attributes and places them within a historical or cultural perspective that will enable the reader to grasp more clearly the changing nature of the art forms alluded to in the first ten chapters. A broad sweep of music in historical context from medieval times to the present century, as well as a brief glimpse of jazz and non-Western styles, is presented in this section.

THE MIDDLE AGES: BEFORE 1450

❖

THE PERIOD 600–850	SUMMARY
THE PERIOD 850–1300	STUDY GUIDELINES
THE PERIOD 1300–1450	
(ARS NOVA)	

In music history, the period between A.D. 600 and A.D. 1450 is called the Middle Ages. From the decline of Rome in the early centuries A.D. to its fall in the fifth century, the Christian religion became the only stabilizing force in Western Europe. Thereafter, from 600 to 1450, the church largely dominated all aspects of life. Although the socio-economic system of this era was feudalism—a political hierarchy arranged for mutual protection—the church was the center of the arts. Examples of outstanding architecture in the period are Romanesque and Gothic cathedrals, while most sculpture and painting is found within or attached to the cathedrals. The music of the period, similarly, was used to complement the worship services conducted in such an environment.

Music did not remain unchanged during the Middle Ages. For this reason, musical development will be surveyed by dividing the era into three periods: A.D. 600–850; A.D. 850–1300; and A.D. 1300–1450.

THE PERIOD 600–850

Music for the church was not invented or composed in the year 600. It had existed earlier and was derived in part from the Jewish religious tradition as well as possibly from Greek, Near-Eastern, and Oriental

The Calling of the Apostles Peter and Andrew, Duccio di Buoninsegna, Italian, 1308/1311, tempera on wood.

Courtesy of the National Gallery of Art, Washington, Samuel H. Kress Collection.

music. Chants were much like folk music in the years before 600, composed by and around an individual, but passed on orally and therefore modified with the passage of time. Under Pope Gregory I (590–604), however, the liturgy of the Catholic church became standardized. Music for worship was codified and became known as *Gregorian chant.* Gregorian chant is the unifying body of music for all of the Middle Ages, extending even into the Renaissance.

Gregorian Chant: Characteristics and Text Setting

PLAINSONG   Gregorian chant, or *plainsong* as it is commonly called, was never composed purely for listening, but rather to accompany the celebration of church rituals, including the Mass. There are almost 3,000 extant melodies in the Gregorian repertory today.

The range of a Gregorian chant is usually narrow, an octave or less, and most chants are also conjunct. In addition, the text is Latin and the singing is performed with few dynamic changes. Texts of all Gregorian chants were retained in Latin, rather than the language of individual nations, until the 1960s, when changes in church ordinance permitted translation into local vernacular.

Listen to Kyrie Eleison and Agnus Dei *(listening selections)* (also see page 13). These two sections of the Ordinary of the Mass, Kyrie (first movement) and Agnus Dei (fifth and final movement), differ by nature of their text setting. In the Agnus Dei, each syllable of the text corresponds to one pitch in the melody, a type of text setting called *syllabic.*

Selection no. 7
KYRIE
AGNUS DEI

SYLLABIC

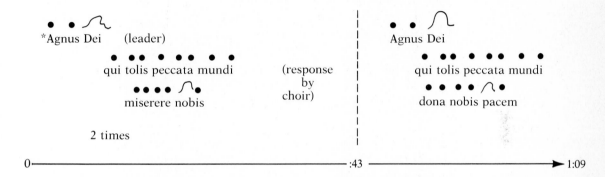

In the Kyrie, however, there are sometimes several pitches for one syllable of text, a style called *melismatic.*

MELISMATIC

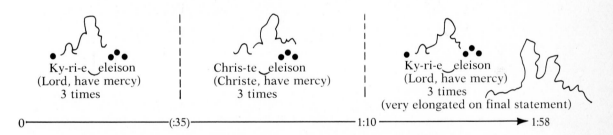

Some vocal compositions, in other forms as well as Gregorian chant, may combine sections in syllabic style with those in melismatic, thus providing variety within the melody itself. Contemporary popular music utilizes the same combination of styles, demonstrating the continuity of this compositional practice up to the present day.

Mode

Gregorian chant is monophonic and almost always sung by male voices. It has an ethereal quality because of its free, non-metric flow, with the melody typically rising and falling in an undulating motion.

This illuminated initial, from a fourteenth-century Latin Bible, shows Amos prophesying the fall of Samaria.

Courtesy of the Catholic Diocese of Tucson.

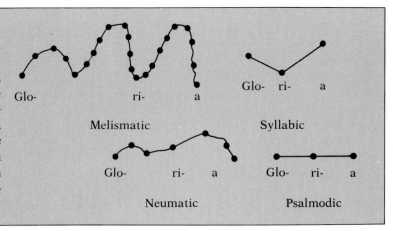

Settings that are melismatic and syllabic are common in all types of vocal music, including Gregorian chant, although some people recognize two other types of setting. In a *neumatic* setting, two or three pitches are used per syllable, while in *psalmodic* settings, one pitch is reiterated for several syllables.

The sound is neither major nor minor, although it bears characteristics of both, but rather modal. A *mode* is a diatonic scale used in the Middle Ages. There are eight such scales, classified as either *authentic* or *plagal.*

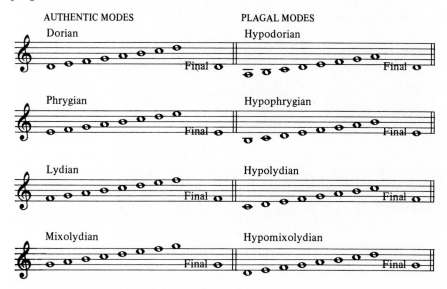

The contour of a melody written in an authentic mode typically rises from the final or tonic pitch and returns to this home pitch in an arched fashion. In contrast, a melody in a plagal mode ranges up and down around the final, typically beginning and ending at this tonic pitch. For every authentic mode there is a corresponding plagal mode, with each member of a pair sharing the same final or tonic pitch.

AUTHENTIC AND PLAGAL MODES

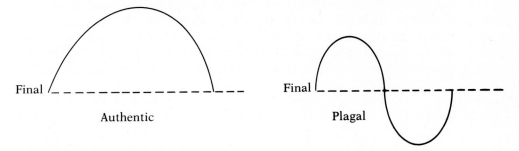

Gregorian melodies in authentic and plagal modes thus differ by their contour.

Although secular music existed in the Middle Ages, the church ultimately became the institution that preserved the art of the period, including its music, and therefore most of the extant music is religious.

Courtesy of the Catholic Diocese of Tucson.

Uses of Chant

Gregorian chant is used in both the Mass and the Canonical Hours. In addition to unison chanting, it is sometimes performed *responsorially* (leader and chorus) or *antiphonally* (two choirs in call-response).

Mass. Gregorian chant was used in the early Christian church to celebrate the *Mass*, one of the main sacraments. "Ite missa est," the phrase used to dismiss the congregation after the serving of the bread and wine, provides the derivation of the actual word "Mass." (Some Protestant sects call this service the Lord's Supper or Communion.) In the Catholic liturgy, there are sections of the Mass that are standard

ORDINARY   for most services. These are called the *Ordinary* of the Mass and
PROPER   include the Kyrie, Gloria, Credo, Sanctus, and Agnus Dei. The *Proper* of the Mass, by contrast, changes text to fit the church season. For example, since Lent, the forty days before Easter, is a penitential season, the text and music used in the Mass during this period in the church year reflect this solemnity. Since Eastertide itself is a joyous

occasion, the Proper of the Mass changes to reflect a spirit of celebration. The Proper, which thus changes from Sunday to Sunday, season to season, includes musically the Introit, Gradual, Alleluia (or Tract in penitential seasons), Offertory, and Communion. (The Gloria, which is part of the Ordinary, is omitted during the two penitential seasons, Advent and Lent.)

Canonical Hours. Gregorian chant is also used in the *Canonical Hours*, observed daily in many churches and monasteries. There are eight Hours (Offices). The earliest is *Matins* (before sunrise), followed by *Lauds* (sunrise), both of which used music. Prime (6:00 A.M.), *Terce* (9:00 A.M.), *Sext* (noon), and *Nones* (3:00 P.M.) are usually spoken, but *Vespers* (sunset) involves the use of music. *Compline*, which follows Vespers, is also spoken and completes the eight Canonical Hours.

In sections of the Mass or Canonical Offices in which the text is minimal (Kyrie, Agnus Dei, or Alleluia) or which are suitable for extended solos rather than group performance, melismatic settings are common. Conversely, in those sections in which the text is long (Credo) or in which the congregation participates, a syllabic setting is more typical.

Christianity grew popular during the Middle Ages because of its ability to absorb many of the practices and customs of other religions. Congregations, too large to meet in private homes, for the first time began to meet in churches. The earliest Christian church was called a basilica, a simple rectangular building with a long interior nave to seat the congregation. Although their exteriors were unadorned, the early churches were decorated beautifully inside with mosaics and frescoes. Visual representation in the churches was typically flat and two-dimensional, with

Madonna and Child with Angels, Niccolo di Ser Sozzo Tegliacci, Italian, c. 1360, tempera on wood.

University of Arizona Museum of Art, gift of Samuel H. Kress.

figures appearing to float against a blue or gold background without depth, much like Gregorian chant is sung without harmonic background. Sculptured figures were symbolically significant rather than realistic or representational, and appear abstract and somewhat mystical to worshippers of today.

THE PERIOD 850–1300

Changes in Chant

During this period, certain stylistic changes began to occur in Gregorian chant. Although some of these undoubtedly developed earlier, it was not until this time that scholarly treatises began to discuss the changes.

Trope. It had become common to add words to the standard Latin Gregorian texts. The usual places for the additions were before and between main sections, although some were even placed between two words of an authorized text. Such an insertion is called a *trope*. Some consist of a few words while others are lengthy poems. Troping is a creative extension of the Gregorian liturgy, used to amplify the existing

SEQUENCE words and music. (A *sequence* is a special trope added only to the Alleluia, a section that was typically melismatic.) The addition of words to pitches originally occurring as a melisma between two main syllables resulted in a syllabic style, and it is probable that tropes and sequences were used to simplify the singing of long, melismatic passages as well as to help explain the text. Since troping was especially common in the Ordinary of the Mass, the motivation may have been merely to provide variety.

Organum. The most important change in music in this period is the emergence of *organum*, a type of harmony. In its earliest appearance, organum is the simple addition of a second, dependent part that

TENOR-VOX
PRINCIPALIS duplicates the original chant (*tenor* or *vox principalis*) at the interval of a fourth (below) or fifth (above). This results in a primitive type of

DUPLUM-VOX
ORGANALIS polyphony in which the second part, termed the *duplum (vox organalis)*, parallels the main melody.

Vox principalis
(tenor)

Vox organalis
(duplum)

PARALLEL
ORGANUM

Selection no. 62

This is thus called *parallel organum*. (See page 200 for score.)

Listen to *Sit Gloria Domini (listening selections)*. This example comes from the medieval treatise *Musica Enchiriadis* (c. 850–900), a document that described musical practices of the time and showed the earliest examples of harmony.

Although vox principalis and vox organalis were often duplicated by higher voices:

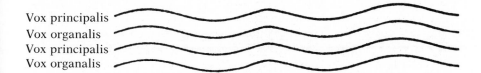

Vox principalis
Vox organalis
Vox principalis
Vox organalis

the texture remained two-part. Much speculation exists about why organum appeared and why it sounds as it does. Undoubtedly the human, creative impulse explains much change in music, but the use of intervals, fourths or fifths, is more difficult to assess. Since this is the natural range difference between bass and tenor voice, perhaps each voice part merely sang the main melody where it was more comfortable. It is possible that all early chant was sung antiphonally, with the answering chorus repeating the melody a fifth higher. If the result were then sung simultaneously, parallel organum would result. Experimentation and accident are common reasons why change occurs in all of the arts. In any event, the intervals of fourths and fifths create a resonance that can be especially striking in a building where sounds can reverberate freely, such as the medieval cathedral.

Organum soon underwent additional changes. The added part, the duplum, began to move more freely while a pitch in the tenor was sustained beneath. This is called *free organum.*

FREE ORGANUM

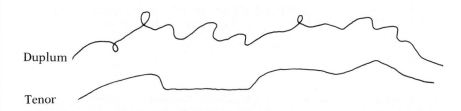

Duplum

Tenor

Listen to *Alleluia, Surrexit (listening selections).* The added part is now rhythmically freer. The setting is melismatic and the two parts move in *contrary motion*:

Selection no. 79

CONTRARY
MOTION

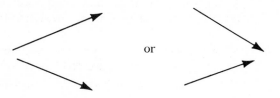

or

instead of the strict parallelism found in *Sit Gloria Domini.* Free
organum developed in the eleventh and twelfth centuries. The added
voice is now consistently above the plainsong, not either above or
below, as was true with parallel organum. Free organum allowed
melisma to occur in the added part over the tenor or original chant.

*The manuscript has F E.

TRANSLATION

Alleluia, Christ is risen, who created all things, and hath had compassion upon the human race.
Alleluia. The angel of the Lord came down from heaven, and approaching rolled away the stone and sat on it. Alleluia.

In the next development of organum, during the twelfth century, the duplum became even more melismatic and rhythmically free of the tenor. This is called *melismatic organum*. The tenor (invoking the original meaning of its word of derivation, *tenere,* to hold) maintains the Gregorian melody in long durations while the duplum moves in a highly ornamented, melismatic style. In order to sustain these extended tones, the tenor was at times undoubtedly performed on instruments.

MELISMATIC ORGANUM

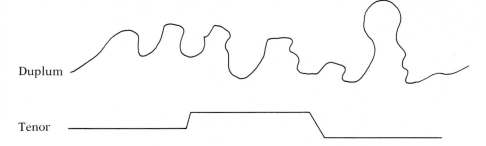

Duplum

Tenor

This style of writing was prevalent at the *School of Notre Dame* around 1200, particularly under the auspices of two composers, Leonin and Perotin. Leonin, who lived in the late twelfth century, compiled a book of organum for the Mass and the Offices. Perotin (c. 1160–1220) later revised this book, giving the duplum a consistent metric flow as well as adding a third *(triplum)* and even fourth *(quadruplum)* part to many of the organa. Listen to Perotin's *Benedicamus Domino* (organum triplum) *(supplemental listening)*—Text: Benedicamus Domino (Let us praise the Lord).

TRIPLUM
QUADRUPLUM
Selection no. 80

Medieval Consonance

The development of harmony in the Middle Ages changed the path of musical development in the Western world. With the appearance of organum, harmony became a viable musical element. The earliest harmony may sound strange to the modern listener because the intervals are not the same as those used as the basis of harmony in the eighteenth and nineteenth centuries. Whereas the contemporary ear is accustomed to hearing thirds and sixths, consonant intervals in the Middle Ages were unison, octave, fourth, and fifth.

Some of the most extraordinary works of art in Western history were produced between 1180 and 1220, including these two examples. Left, a parchment manuscript illustrating Christ bearing the cross (late twelfth-century France); rght, an enamel crucifix from Lower Saxony, currently part of East Germany. This nine-inch crucifix dates from the beginning of the thirteenth century.

Courtesy of the Catholic Diocese of Tucson.

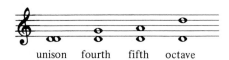

unison   fourth   fifth   octave

As a result, the music of the Middle Ages may sound hollow to many contemporary listeners.

Rhythmic Modes

The *rhythmic modes,* which also developed in this period, were used to indicate the duration of notes. Not to be confused with the pitch modes shown on page 331, these modes represented the repetition of certain patterns in triple meter. These are:

Original	Poetic Equivalents		Modern Equivalents
▇ ▪	/ ∪	1st mode (trochaic)	♩ ♪
▪ ▇	∪ /	2nd mode (iambic)	♪ ♩
▇ ▪ ▪	/ ∪ ∪	3rd mode (dactylic)	♩. ♪ ♩
▪ ▪ ▇	∪ ∪ /	4th mode (anapaestic)	♪ ♩ ♩.
▇ ▇	/ /	5th mode (spondaic)	♩. ♩.
▪ ▪	∪ ∪	6th mode (tribrachic)	♪ ♪

Two or three independent melodies in a composition could be performed together by citing the mode as well as the number of times it was to be repeated *(ordo)*. Ordo determines the length of each phrase.   ORDO

Mode 2, 4th ordo   ♩ ♩   ♩ ♩   ♩ ♩   ♩ ♩

The tenor part usually moved in the 3rd or 5th mode while duplum and triplum were set in the 1st, 2nd, or 6th. This system, known as *square notation*, was an appropriate solution for music writing of the period.   SQUARE NOTATION

Secular Music

The patterns that arise from the use of rhythmic modes also typify the secular music of the Middle Ages. Between the tenth and thirteenth centuries, an abundance of secular music was created and performed by itinerant musicians. Since it did not come under the official influence of the Church, not as much is known about it as has been passed on regarding religious compositions.

Secular Minstrels. Some secular minstrels, who earned their living as professional musicians, were engaged by medieval courts to entertain. They include the *jongleurs* in France, *Gaukler* in Germany, and *gleemen* in England. There were also student musicians called *goliards* who roamed the countryside. The entertainers sang songs of courtly love, satire, and current events. Secular music also developed among the *trouvères* (Northern France), *troubadours* (Southern France), and *Minnesingers* (Germany), whose social class was higher than other minstrels. They were usually noblemen who composed the music, but left the performance to the jongleurs. Since some of their music has been preserved, important names, such as Bernart de Ventadorn and Adam de la Hale, are known. Listen to Adam de la Hale's (c. 1240–c. 1288) "Bergeronette" *(listening selections* (see page 204 also).   Selection no. 64

Secular Songs. Secular songs were probably performed monophonically, somewhat like Gregorian chant, but there are distinct differences between secular and sacred types. Secular music is more flamboyant and adventuresome, wider in both vocal range and dynamic levels. Its rhythms usually follow one of the rhythmic modes and phrase structure tends to be clear and regular. The typical text setting is syllabic, with melismas occurring, if at all, near the end of the song, much like a small cadenza. The text, with the exception of the student-composed goliard songs, is not in Latin, but in the vernacular. Refrain forms are common, possibly to accommodate dance or group participation, and ballads of the period were often in strophic form. Although the Church tried to curtail the activities of secular musicians, some of their music has survived up to the present time.

Other Genres

Additional musical developments in the period between 850 and 1300 include motet and conductus, both of which date from the thirteenth century. Of the two, the motet proved the more enduring technique, and became increasingly important the last years of the Middle Ages.

Motet.   *Motets* developed from independent organa when new words, usually French, were added to the duplum. This additional part became known as the *motetus*, meaning voice above the tenor, and eventually the abbreviated term "motet" was used to designate the entire composition. Motets were popular in the thirteenth century. The upper voices are often set to French, while the tenor is Latin. Sometimes both secular and sacred texts were used in the same composition. In practice, instruments were often used on the slow-moving tenor line while the upper part became predominant.

Selection no. 81   Listen to *O Maria Maris Stella* (motet) *(supplemental listening)*. A solo tenor voice is hard on an upper part, accompanied by a fiddle and three tenor krummhorns. This anonymous motet was well known in the late 1200s.

O Maria maris stella,	O Mary, star of the sea,
plena gracie,	full of grace,
mater simul et puella,	at once mother and maid,
vas mundicie,	vessel of chastity,
templum nostri redemptoris,	temple of our Saviour,
sol iusticie,	sun of justice,
porta celi, spes reorum,	gateway of heaven, hope of the guilty,
thronus glorie,	throne of glory,
sublevatrix miserorum,	support of the distressed,
vena venie,	source of forgiveness,
audie servos te rogantes,	hear thy servants who cry to thee,
mater gracie,	mother of grace,
ut peccata sint ablata	that through thee today
per te hodie,	their sins may be washed away
qui te puro laudant corde	and they may praise thee with a pure heart
in veritate.	in truth.

Tenor:
VERITATEM

Composers of this period freely borrowed others' works, adding or deleting voices and texts as they wished. Composition was thus a communal effort, although the "collaborators" on a piece never actually worked together. One composer might use the tenor and duplum (motetus) of another composer's work, but add his own triplum. Since composers thought in terms of layers of sound—a horizontal approach to composing—rather than in vertical sonorities, beat by beat or chord by chord, harmony was almost incidental to the finished product. Just as the construction of a Gothic cathedral incorporated changing styles as several generations toiled to complete it, motets represent an organic approach to music building, growing by accretion, resulting in sonorities that, although not always consonant to modern ears, reflect medieval thinking and practice.

Churches, beginning in A.D. 1000, for two hundred years were constructed in what became known as the Romanesque style. The use of a round Roman arch characterizes this style. Such churches were constructed entirely of stone, with very thick walls to support the downward thrust of the towering groined vaults that curved to enclose the main body of the church. Large windows that would weaken the walls could not be used. The floor plan of the Romanesque cathedral was cruciform and similar to that of the earlier basilica, much like musical developments of this period incorporated and adapted the older Gregorian chant.

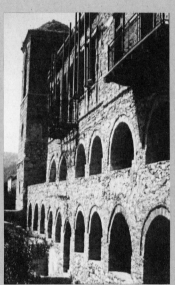

Photo by Daniel E. Arthur.

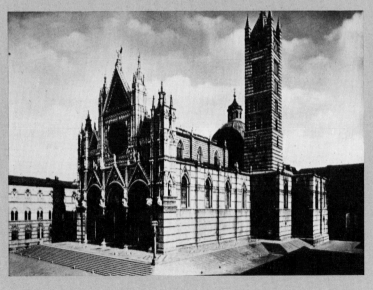

Left, a Romanesque Church: Siena—the cathedral and campanile; above, Roman arches in Northern Italy.

Conductus.   *Conductus* is another type of composition that developed in the period. A conductus is constructed on a freely composed tenor. Its duplum and triplum both use the same text and rhythm, thereby imparting to it a heightened sense of unity. It has a note-against-note style, in contrast to the sustained tenor of motets.

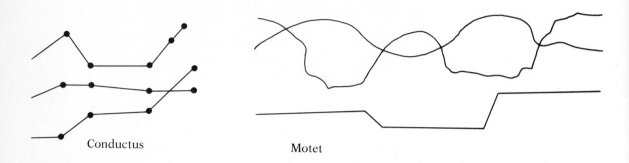

Conductus   Motet

Conducti are believed to have been derived from tropes chanted to "conduct" the priest into the church, which would account for the syllabic setting of the text. Conductus style thus refers to music that is chordal rather than being rhythmically diverse between parts.

Selection no. 82   Listen to *Vetus Abit Littera* (conductus) *(supplemental listening).*

Vetus abit littera	The ancient law is no more,
Ritus abit veterum	gone are the rites of old.
Dat virgo puerpera	A virgin has brought forth
Novum nobis puerum	and given us a new child,
Manus salutiferum	a healing gift,
Regem et presbyterum	a king and priest,
Qui complanans aspera	who makes the rough places plain,
Firmat pacis federa	strengthens the bonds of peace
Purgator est scelerum.	and cleanses us of our sins.
Felicis puerpere	The happy birth
Felix puerperium	from this blessed mother
Babylonis misere	recalls our exile
Revocat exilium	in the misery of Babylon.
Iam plebs ceca gencium	Already the blind heathen
Videns lucis radium	see a ray of light
Fracto mortis carcere	and the bonds of death broken,
Non adheret littere	and because of the Scripture
Propter evangelium.	do not follow the old law.
Funis pene rumpitur	Their bonds are nearly broken,
Nato rege glorie	for born is the king of glory;

Mortis torrens bibitur	the flow of death is swallowed up
Data lege gratie	and the law of mercy is bestowed on us.
Dies est leticie	It is a day of joy,
Lux iugis psallencium	a light is shed on the yoke of the singers;
Munus festi solvitur	a festival is celebrated.
Gaudeamus igitur	Therefore let us rejoice
Culpe data venia.	since forgiveness is granted for our sins.

THE PERIOD 1300–1450 (ARS NOVA)

The fourteenth century is often termed the *Ars Nova* in music history, a period during which the new ideas beginning to permeate the monolithic structure of the Church had a major influence on the nature of musical composition. Ideas that later were to develop into Renaissance philosophy had already manifested themselves in literature (Dante, Boccaccio, and Chaucer) and painting (Giotto).

Striving for Unity

Imitation.   Among the musical changes in the fourteenth century was increased use of imitation between voice parts, which provided greater musical unity. Harmony began more commonly to include thirds and sixths, and rhythm began to move in duple time *(tempus imperfectum)* rather than the triple time *(tempus perfectum)* that had dominated earlier music. In general, composers attempted to provide greater unity by incorporating rhythmic and melodic imitation between voice parts. The older practice of communal or augmentative composition gave way to the individual artist's writing an entire work on his own. As a result, this is the first period in which composers are identifiable. It was Philippe de Vitry (c. 1291–1361) who named the period *Ars Nova.* Other composers of note include Guillaume de Machaut (c. 1300–1377) of France and Francesco Landini (c. 1325–1397), working in Italy.

TEMPUS IMPERFECTUM
TEMPUS PERFECTUM

Isorhythm.   Although motets continued to be composed in this period, composers found newer ways to provide unity. The tenor, *cantus firmus* as it was now called, continued to be derived from Gregorian chant. Instead of repeating short patterns or ostinatos, however, longer melodies were brought into play. Both rhythm and melody were considered as units to be repeated. The rhythmic unit was called a *talea*, the intervals of the melody, the *color*. Repetition of talea and color in the tenor helped in achieving a degree of unity. Since the talea and color were also used in the duplum and triplum, the entire

CANTUS FIRMUS

TALEA
COLOR

Giotto (1266–1336), a Florentine painter, was one of the first artists of the late Middle Ages to portray figures more realistically than had been the medieval tradition. His madonnas are warmer and more compassionate, women rather than abstract symbols. Giotto also provided backgrounds in his paintings that conveyed perspective or depth, using an imaginary vanishing point to which all diagonal lines converged. Although by contemporary standards his efforts at realism do not match those of later painters, Giotto was a pivotal artist who signaled the beginning of the Renaissance at the end of the Middle Ages, much like the role assumed by Burgundian composers in music.

Courtesy of the Catholic Diocese of Tucson.

Courtesy of the National Gallery of Art, Washington, Samuel H. Kress Collection.

Above, *Ascension of Christ*, Giotto, Italian, c. 1266–c. 1337, detail of a fresco in Scrovegni Chapel, Padua, Italy; right, *Saint Anthony Distributing His Wealth to the Poor*, Sassetta and assistant, Sienese, c. 1440, tempera on wood.

composition was thus unified. A motet composed in this manner is called *isorhythmic*. Machaut is one of the first composers to set the entire Ordinary of the Mass using these principles, in *Messe de Notre Dame*. It has a four-part setting, typifying the practice that eventually became common in the Renaissance. Listen to Agnus Dei I from Machaut's *Messe de Notre Dame (listening selections)* (see pp. 304–306).

Selection no. 77

Madrigal. Composers of the *Ars Nova* also wrote secular music, a sign that the Church was beginning to lose influence. In Italy, the secular genres are the *madrigal* and *caccia.* The madrigal of the fourteenth century is not the same as the Renaissance genre of the same name. Although both are songs in the vernacular rather than Latin, the fourteenth-century madrigal was in two parts, an ornamented upper and a lower one in slower note-values.

Caccia. The *caccia* (plural, *cacce*) is a "chase" or "hunt" composition written in three parts. The lowest, which moves in slow note values, was usually performed by an instrument. The upper two are written like a round, thus exemplifying the "chasing" aspect of the music, since one part never quite catches the other. The text typically describes a fishing or hunting party or some other scene of heightened activity.

Listen to Giovanni de Firenze's "Con Brachi Assai" (With Plenty of Hounds) *(listening selections)*. The composer, Giovanni de Firenze (of Florence), also known as Giovanni da Cascia (of Cascia, a small village near Florence), lived in Verona during the fourteenth century. His only surviving works are three cacce, including "Con Brachi Assai," and sixteen madrigals.

Selection no. 83

In this example voice 2 imitates voice 1, with accompaniment provided by two viola da gambas (another name for the bass viol—gamba means "of the knees"). The caccia describes a hunting party on the Adda River near Milan.

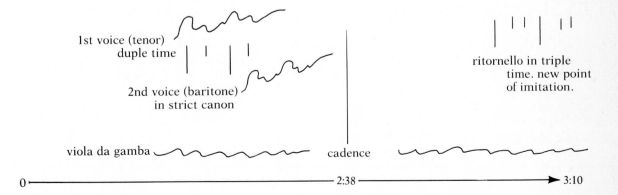

The text translation is:

0

> With hounds aplenty and hawks galore
> We hunted birds on Ad(d)a's shore;
> Some cried: "Go to't!" and others "O'er here!"
> "Varin!" "Come back, Picciolo!"
> Still others took the quail right on the wing,
> When a stormy downpour came.

1:16

> Never did greyhounds run through the land
> As did each hunter, to flee the storm;
> Some cried: "Give't here! Give me the cloak!"
> And thus: "Give me the hat!"—
> When I took cover, with my bird.
> Where a shepherdess struck me to the heart.

2:30   *Ritornello*

> She was alone there, so to myself I said:
> "Here's the rain! Here are Dido and Aeneas!"*

*In the ancient story of Aeneas, it was a rainstorm that carried his ship to Dido in Carthage.

Cacce were popular in Italy near the middle of the fourteenth century, as well as in France, where they were called *chace*, and Spain. Unlike the Italian cacce, French and Spanish examples are more like rounds, since they do not have the accompanying third voice heard here. In addition, the listening example has a second section in triple

Gothic art flourished in the thirteenth and fourteenth centuries. Development of the pointed arch enabled builders of the Gothic cathedral to achieve greater height than was possible with the Romanesque style, because the downward thrust of the ceiling could be supported by a series of flying buttresses. Because they no longer carried the entire weight of the ceiling vault, the walls became thinner and incorporated

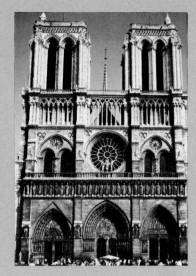

A Gothic church: Notre Dame á Paris, built between 1163 and 1250.

Photo by Daniel E. Arthur.

large stained glass windows. As the composers of the late Middle Ages were able to achieve greater unity in composition by the use of imitation and isorhythmic technique, contemporary architects designed a Gothic cathedral to achieve integrity in stone.

meter (2:3) known as *ritornello,* an element not generally found in cacce.

Medieval Instruments

Music of the late Middle Ages was performed both vocally and instrumentally, depending upon the availability of musicians and instruments. Among the instruments used were the *sackbut,* a forerunner of the trombone, the *shawm,* a double-reed instrument, and the *recorder,* a small aerophone.

SACKBUT
SHAWM
RECORDER

Alto recorder.

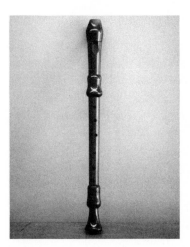

PORTATIVE
ORGAN

Portative organs, small, portable models that the performer played with one hand while pumping the bellows with the other, were common. The clavichord and harpsichord existed during this period, too. It is probable that contrasting instrumental and vocal timbres were preferred in polyphonic compositions so that each melodic line would stand out clearly. Listen to "Ay Schonsolato Ed Amoroso" *(listening selections).*

Selection no. 84

Musical Notation

The developments in notation in the late Middle Ages were remarkable, partly as a result of the need to write down and preserve the complex compositions that were being written. Although the French and Italians used somewhat different systems, in general each note could be divided perfectly (into triples) or imperfectly (into duples). The following scheme is a generalized but typical arrangement.

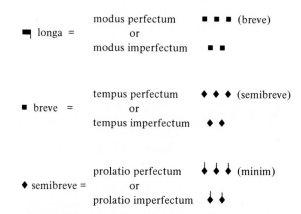

A perfect (triple) division was indicated by black notes, an imperfect (duple) by red. Pitches were notated on staffs, as earlier, with the use of three clefs:

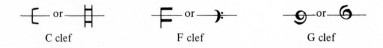

This notational arrangement was further refined during the Renaissance and in time evolved into the scheme still used in music.

SUMMARY

The period of the Middle Ages is generally bound by the years 600–1450. Gregorian chant is the unifying source for music in the entire period. Although it was first seen as monophonic song used for the Mass and Canonical Hours, tropes and sequences were added to augment the official words. Organum became the addition of a second part in parallel harmony, which eventually evolved into free and melismatic styles. The rhythmic modes were used to integrate the added voices of organa in early stages. Secular musicians of the period, including troubadours and minnesingers, wrote songs that follow the rhythmic modes. Toward the end of the Middle Ages the motet and conductus also developed. Tenors (canti firmi) are usually based on Gregorian chant.

In the *Ars Nova*, the final years of the Middle Ages, motets were further refined by isorhythmic principles, thus providing unity through repetition of talea and color. Secular forms included the madrigal and caccia. Although choral music predominates, instruments were used to double or replace voices in many polyphonic compositions. Notational developments include the use of black notes for perfect time, red for imperfect.

STUDY GUIDELINES

KEY TERMS AND CONCEPTS

Antiphonal
Ars Nova
Caccia (Cacce)
Canonical Hours
Cantus Firmus
Conductus
Final
Gregorian chant (plainsong)
Isorhythm
Madrigal
Mass
  Ordinary
    Agnus Dei
    Credo
    Gloria
    Kyrie
    Sanctus
  Proper
Mode
  Authentic
  Plagal
Motet

Motetus
Ordo
Organum
  Free
  Melismatic
  Parallel
Portative organ
Recorder
Responsorial
Rhythmic Mode
Sackbut
School of Notre Dame
Secular Musicians
  Minnesinger
  Trouvère, troubadour
Shawm
Text Setting
  Melismatic
  Syllabic
Triplum
Trope

CHAPTER REVIEW

Match items in the two columns. Answers in Appendix.

1. _____ Ordinary of Mass	A.	one syllable, one pitch
2. _____ Proper of Mass	B.	Matins, Vespers
3. _____ melismatic	C.	1300–1450
4. _____ tropes and sequences	D.	chordal style
5. _____ Canonical hours	E.	music of the "chase"
6. _____ early Middle Ages	F.	850–1300
7. _____ isorhythm	G.	medieval aerophone
8. _____ late Middle Ages	H.	Kyrie, Gloria, Credo,
9. _____ trouvères, troubadours		Sanctus, Agnus Dei
10. _____ syllabic	I.	600–850

11. _____ caccia
12. _____ period when organum first appeared
13. _____ responsorial
14. _____ Gregorian chant
15. _____ recorder
16. _____ conductus

J. textual interpolations
K. uses color (melody) and talea (rhythm)
L. changes according to day of church year
M. secular musicians
N. one syllable, several pitches
O. leader sings, chorus answers
P. plainsong

CHRONOLOGY OF MUSIC BEFORE 1450

Early Middle Ages: 600–850
    Pope Gregory   540–604

Middle Middle Ages: 850–1300
    Troubadours   1150
    Perotin   c. 1170
    Leonin   c. 1175
    Trouvères and Minnesingers   c. 1200
    Adam de la Hale   1237–1287

Late Middle Ages: 1300–1450
    Philippe de Vitry   c. 1291–1361
    Guillaume de Machaut   1300–1377
    Francesco Landini   c. 1325–1397
    Giovanni da Florentia (Firenze)   fourteenth century
    Vincenzo da Rimini   fl. c. 1350–1375
    Herman, Monk of Salzburg   1365–1396

FOR FURTHER LISTENING

From *Masterpieces of Music Before 1750*, ed. Carl Parrish and John F. Ohl (New York: Norton, 1951)
    Alleluia: *Vidimus Stellam* no. 2
    Antiphon: *Laus Deo Patri* no. 1
    Conductus: *De castitatis thalamo* no. 11
    Motet: *En non Diu!* no. 10
    Psalm: *Laudate Pueri* no. 1
    Sequence: *Victimae Paschali* no. 3

CHAPTER TWELVE

THE RENAISSANCE: 1450-1600

◆

THE BURGUNDIAN SCHOOL	MUSIC THEORY AND NOTATION
THE FLEMISH SCHOOL	SUMMARY
THE SIXTEENTH CENTURY	STUDY GUIDELINES

HUMANISM

The term "Renaissance" literally means a rebirth. During the late fifteenth and sixteenth centuries, many philosophers looked back to the ancient Greek and Roman world as the time when true culture existed. They regarded the years of the Middle Ages as a dark and mystical period, devoid of culture and innovation because of the power of the monolithic church structure. With the rediscovery of classical learning and thought, a rebirth thus occurred. In addition, the prevailing thought that humankind was important in achieving its own destiny, a philosophy called *humanism*, grew during this period, and was reflected in both science and art.

Music shared in the interdependent growth of all of the creative arts during the Renaissance. Religious music, particularly vocal, continued to be important, but developed qualities that make it seem quite balanced and graceful. Secular music also grew in importance and variety during the Renaissance, as did independent instrumental music.

In a way, the Renaissance is the beginning of modern times, and it is not surprising that music of the period still appeals to listeners. Although one does not hear this music often in public concerts, choirs, chamber groups, and even soloists occasionally perform compositions

Humanism and beauty become important in Renaissance art. *Venus Lamenting the Death of Adonis,* Tintoretto, 1518–1594, oil on canvas.

University of Arizona Museum of Art, gift of Samuel H. Kress.

from this period. Since the invention of movable type in the fifteenth century made possible the printing of music in the early sixteenth, numerous compositions of the Renaissance have been preserved and are available in authentic editions for performers. The turn from medieval music was not sudden, but occurred gradually in the French kingdom of Burgundy.

THE BURGUNDIAN SCHOOL

The kingdom of Burgundy included the territories of Northeastern France, Holland, and Belgium. Its capital was Dijon. The peak period of artistic development here was during the last half of the fourteenth and the first half of the fifteenth centuries when, under the rulers Philip the Good (1419–67) and Charles the Bold (1467–77), the arts, especially music, flourished. Composers were employed to provide courtly entertainment as well as sacred chapel music. Since the resources at Dijon were excellent, many composers were drawn from Northern Europe, England, and Italy to the court of the Burgundian rulers.

Among these composers was Gilles Binchois (c. 1400–1460), who served at the Burgundian court for the last thirty years of his life. Guillaume Dufay (c. 1400–1474), who was well-traveled and served at the Papal chapel in Rome and Florence, is associated with the Burgundian style, but the exact dates of his residency in Burgundy are not known. It is possible he never actually spent time at the court, but his ideas spread as influences on those in residence in Burgundy, without the need of his presence there.

Style

The Burgundian style includes the use of thirds and sixths, harmonically and melodically, thus creating a triadic sound. Although polyphony continued to be written in three parts, most of the interest shifts to the top melody. Since we are accustomed to hearing the melody in the uppermost part, this is obviously a concept that has passed on to modern times. Although triple time is common, duple is interspersed in longer works to provide variety. Two of the most typically Burgundian devices are *fauxbourdon* and the *7-6-1 cadence.* Fauxbourdon, meaning "false bass," is the use of triads in inversion below the top melody.

FAUXBOURDON

7-6-1 CADENCE

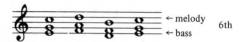

The bass thus parallels the melody at an interval of a sixth. Since the melody is in the top, the bass is no longer the true melody or cantus firmus, thus making the term "false bass" or fauxbourdon appropriate. The resulting chord is an inverted triad.

The second identifying characteristic of the Burgundian period is the 7-6-1 movement of the melody at cadences. Instead of the leading tone (7) resolving immediately to the 1 (or 8), it is delayed by movement downward to 6 before the final is heard.

Vocal compositions of the Burgundian court were no longer polytextual as they often had been in the Middle Ages but were unified by one text in the same language. Although older compositional techniques survived, including the use of isorhythm and conductus, the

trend is toward what would become the modern sound, with compositions integrated musically and textually.

Genres

Chanson.   One of the most important genres from the Burgundian
period is the *chanson,* a secular work with lyrics concerning love.
Written in three parts, most chansons were probably performed with
a solo voice on the top melody and instruments on the two lower parts.
Listen to Dufay's "Pour l'amour de Ma Doulce Amye" *(listening selec-*
tions).
Selection no. 85

(Original a fourth lower)

TRANSLATION

For the love of my sweet friend I want to sing this roundelay,
and give it her with all my heart that she may be the happier for it.

Cantus Firmus Mass. Burgundian composers also wrote settings of
the Mass at this time, when it was still common to use a Gregorian
melody as the theme. Unlike earlier composers, however, the Burgundians tended to use the same melody in all movements of the Mass. A
Mass composed in this manner is called a *cantus firmus Mass.* Particularly in the late years of the Burgundian School (1450), the tenor
was no longer the lowest part. Rather, a bass line was added beneath,
which results in the four-part texture preferred throughout the Renaissance. The voicing of sound from low to high thus became wider than
it had been at any other previous time in music history.

Range [Gregorian Chant [Organum [Medieval Motet [Burgundian Mass [Renaissance 4-5–part Polyphony

Motet. Burgundian composers also wrote motets, many of which
were composed similarly to the chanson, with the upper melody most
important. Instruments, especially sackbuts, krummhorns, viols, and
portative organs, double the voice parts in Burgundian music.

Composers of the Burgundian court evolved a style that sounds
familiar because its texture, triadic harmony, and equality of voice
parts were all moving closer to the compositional modes that became

standard in the eighteenth century and continue in common usage today. The music thus provides a transition between the styles of the late Middle Ages and the early Renaissance.

THE FLEMISH SCHOOL

The Flemish School, which was international in both outlook and membership, followed the Burgundian. Centered in southern Belgium (Flanders) and northern France, composers of this era developed the next important historical style beginning in the last half of the fifteenth century and continuing to about 1550. Since Flemish composers commonly held musical posts in all parts of Europe, it cannot be considered purely a Northern European movement.

Style

In sacred music, the Flemish composers continued to write Masses and motets and, although their music is not markedly different from works written by the Burgundians, many innovations of the earlier school became firmly established and refined by composers of the Flemish period. In particular, vocal parts achieved greater equality, accomplished through the use of consistent imitation between voices, including the contrapuntal techniques of *augmentation, diminution,* and *inversion*. In augmentation, the basic duration of every note in a theme is increased by proportion. The reverse occurs in diminution, with each note value being decreased. Inversion means literally turning a theme upside down.

AUGMENTATION
DIMINUTION
INVERSION

RETROGRADE
CANCRIZANS

Two other contrapuntal devices used in the period are *retrograda-tion,* presenting the theme backwards, and *cancrizans,* a technique that combines inversion and retrograde.

(All of these contrapuntal techniques are similar to those still in use by contemporary composers of twelve-tone music.) The Flemish composers not only mastered these techniques but also used them in such a way as to heighten artistic expression. Some composers used one melody as the basis of an entire composition, apparently taking delight in constructing a work with only these contrapuntal techniques. The result for a listener today is that such compositions seem well organized and structured because of the concern for providing unity among voice parts, even if one has difficulty identifying the technique used.

In general, composers of the Flemish tradition favored four-part polyphony. The bass line gives the music a rich sonority. In addition, the Flemish masters used triads in root position as key structural points in the music. Although modality still prevails, the sound is modern compared to the use of fauxbourdon by the Burgundians. Flemish masters also learned to provide variety in Masses and motets FAMILIAR STYLE by contrasting a highly imitative section with one in *familiar* (homophonic) style. Duets and trios (by vocal sections) are interspersed between the portions of four-voiced texture. The preferred sound is A CAPPELLA unaccompanied choir singing *a cappella*—literally, in a reserved, chapel style, but a term that is often used to mean any vocal performance without instrumental accompaniment.

Genres

Instead of merely borrowing a melody to link the movements of a Mass together, as the Burgundians had done, the Flemish composers borrowed whole sections of previously composed works, whether sacred or secular. The result is called a *Parody Mass.* (The word PARODY MASS "parody" in this case refers to the reuse of previously composed elements for an ultimately serious purpose, not with the comic intent implied by the word today.) Motives, themes, progressions, and even textures from other compositions could be incorporated into the Mass in this manner. The parody Mass gradually replaced the older cantus firmus technique.

Since it does not depend on a prescribed text as does the Mass, the motet was considered a more progressive form during the period. Words and phrases were often repeated and sections more clearly delineated by meter and cadences.

Secular forms that appear among the Flemish include the chanson and polyphonic lied, a contrapuntal setting of a folk song.

POLYPHONIC LIED

Renaissance architecture often incorporated classical shapes—the triangle, square, rectangle, and circle—as points of unity. Symmetry and balance were important attributes, reflected in the many churches built during this period. Interest in secular architecture also increased, particularly in palaces built for the wealthy nobles of Milan, Venice, Florence, and other Italian city-states. Architectural design often included surrounding structures and landscapes. Builders of the day favored the use of classical Greek architecture, using Doric, Ionic, and Corinthian orders, but columns served only decoratively, a mere pilaster attached to the facade. As with ancient buildings, the dome again became a favored structure to provide a roof in large buildings. Renaissance architects were less concerned with the organic, utilitarian qualities of a building than they were with its form, balance, and

Classical structures, including columns, pediments, and domes arranged symmetrically, were incorporated into Renaissance architecture. Above, St. Peters (Rome); below, Farnese Palace (Rome).

unity. Leading architects of the period included Brunellesco (1377–1446), Bramante (1444–1514), Michelangelo (1475–1564), and Palladio (1508–1580).

Composers

Several composers are associated with this period, including Johannes Ockeghem (c. 1420–1496), who wrote a dozen Masses, several motets, and chansons. He was one of the first composers of this period to write the bottom vocal line as a true bass. Ockeghem's phrase structure is long and his cadences widely spaced. Jacob Obrecht (c. 1450–1505) wrote about twenty-five Masses using the older cantus firmus technique, but experimented by placing cantus firmus in voices other than the tenor. His phrase structure is clear and symmetrical, with obvious cadences. Additional Flemish composers of note include Henricus Isaac (c. 1450–1517) and Pierre de la Rue (c. 1460–1518).

The avowed master of the Flemish style is Josquin des Prez (c. 1440–1521). He was born in the province of Hainaut in Northern Europe (border region between Belgium and France) but served several Italian courts, including the Vatican, for many years. He returned to his homeland in his later years and eventually died there. Although Josquin's greatest innovations appear in the motet, he also composed many Masses, using the parody technique.

Selection no. 34   Listen to the Sanctus from Josquin's *L'homme armé* Mass *(listening selections).*

THE SIXTEENTH CENTURY

This century, in which the techniques of the Flemish masters were brought to a culmination, has rightly been called the Golden Age of Polyphony. Musical activity and innovation now became widely dispersed throughout Europe. In addition, with the advent of Protestantism, a new type of church music developed in which the congregation participated. Secular music, particularly the madrigal, became important in this century. Instrumental music developed as accompaniment to church compositions as well as for listening alone in the secular examples. Each category will be discussed separately.

Catholic Church Music

Style. The innovations of the Flemish masters were further expanded and refined by sixteenth-century composers. Most style periods in art begin with experimentation and end with synthesis, and this is equally true of the Renaissance. The Mass and motet continued to be the main vehicles for Catholic polyphony. Composers had fully mastered contrapuntal style by the second half of the sixteenth century, and produced music of great beauty and tranquillity. They often wrote for more than four vocal parts, five being most common, which results in a breadth of sonority even fuller than the four parts of the Flemish school. A cappella style continued as the sound ideal for sacred polyphony. Compositional rules evolved and were discussed in musical treatises of the period on how to write counterpoint, including the treatment of dissonances. The basis of consonance was clearly the triad. Although modality continued, major and minor tonality was coming into use.

Composers.   The master of sacred polyphony in the sixteenth century was the Italian composer Giovanni Pierluigi da Palestrina (c. 1525–1594), who spent his entire life in Italy, serving at St. Peter's in the Vatican for his last two decades. He wrote over 100 Masses and 450 Motets. His style is an adaptation of Flemish counterpoint, including the imitation between voices. Although Palestrina used Gregorian melodies in some of his Masses and motets, many are freely composed. His style, elegant in detail, is considered the epitome of High Renaissance religious choral music. The compositions of Palestrina always show a clear correlation between text and music, each new phrase of text being set to a new melody or motive so that both textual and musical meaning are clear.

The Council of Trent, a church group that met during the Counter-Reformation from 1545 to 1563 to examine alleged abuses in the Catholic church, considered eliminating all polyphony from the Catholic liturgy. Such settings, it was claimed, made the text impossible to comprehend. Palestrina's skill in writing music demonstrated how text and music could be balanced to serve both liturgical and musical purposes and the polyphonic church style was thus perpetuated. Listen, for example, to the Sanctus from Palestrina's *Missa Aeterna Christi Munera (listening selections)* (see pages 210–211).

Selection no. 67

Other important composers of this same period are the Flemish master Orlando di Lasso (c. 1532–1594), who composed many motets, the Spanish composer Victoria (c. 1549–1611), who spent some time in Italy with Palestrina, and the Englishman William Byrd (1543–1623), who wrote both Anglican and Catholic church music. In addition, the Venetian School was influential in the late Renaissance, providing the impetus that led to Baroque styles in both music and painting. Characteristic of Venetian composers like the Gabrielis (Andrea, 1510–1586, and Giovanni, 1557–1612) is the use of two antiphonal choirs. The Venetians

Courtesy of the New York Public Library.

William Byrd, composer of both Catholic and Protestant church music.

frequently used instruments in addition to voices, thereby creating a richer texture. Music written for two or more groups, vocal or instrumental, in antiphonal style is called *polychoral*, and its development provided a pivot point into the Baroque style. Listen to G. Gabrieli's *Canzon Septimi Toni no. 2 (listening selections)* (see pages 120–121), which uses two brass ensembles antiphonally.

POLYCHORAL

Selection no. 47

Reformation Music

The Reformation dates from 1517, the year of Martin Luther's Ninety-Five Theses. Although the abuses leading to it had been articulated earlier, the sixteenth century marks the official beginning of the Reformation, which ultimately split the church into Catholic and Protestant sects.

With the Reformation music, which grew from Luther's desire to simplify the liturgy for congregational participation, several distinctions can be observed. Protestant music is set in the vernacular—in Luther's case, German. For the congregation Luther used settings of the texts designed for unison performance, composed by himself or written for his use by others. Such a hymn tune is called a *chorale*, and the first ones were published in 1524. They are metric, with typically short and regular phrases. Since one stanza of music is repeated for each new verse, the form is strophic.

CHORALE

Some of the first Protestant hymns borrowed Gregorian and secular melodies, but new words were set in the vernacular. A vocal composition of this sort, using a pre-existing melody, is called a *contrafactum*. Some Protestant chorales were newly composed, too, and Luther wrote several himself. The chorale tunes were later harmonized into four parts during the Baroque period, when composers incor-

CONTRAFACTUM

High Renaissance painters, absorbing the techniques and practices of an earlier generations, found their most important representatives in Leonardo da Vinci (1452–1519), Michelangelo (1475–1564), and Raphael (1483–1520). Painters of this period began to represent persons and objects more realistically, evidencing the prevailing humanistic philosophy. Actual human models now were painted to resemble "beautiful" individuals of the time, often painted more beautifully and perfectly proportioned than possible for any one individual. Perspective was consummately mastered by Renaissance artists, much as contemporary composers mastered various types of contrapuntal writing.

porated the chorale into longer compositions for the choir, such as the cantata. A polyphonic treatment of the chorale, sung by a trained choir, was often followed by the congregation's singing the same tune in unison.

Realistic depth was achieved by Renaissance painters using mathematical perspective based on geometrical principles of an imaginery vanishing point. *The Raising of Lazurus,* Panel #10, Fernando Gallego, Spanish, 1440–1510, tempera on wood.

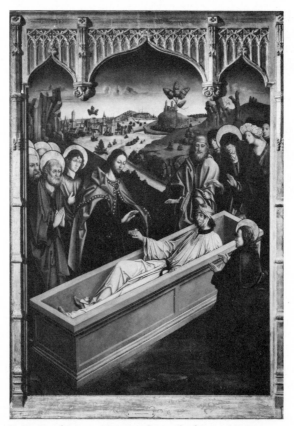

University of Arizona Museum of Art, gift of Samuel H. Kress.

Arrangement of foreground objects into symmetrical configurations against a pastoral background was common among Renaissance painters. *The Alba Madonna*, Raphael, Umbrian, c. 1510, oil on wood transferred to canvas.

Courtesy of the National Gallery of Art, Washington, Andrew W. Mellon Collection.

The practice of unaccompanied congregational singing in unison persisted until 1600. The *chorale motet*, which was developed at the end of the sixteenth century, is a vocal composition that treats the choral melody freely in a polyphonic setting, not unlike the earlier use of cantus firmus and parody techniques in the Mass. The chorale thus became an important unifying device for Protestant church music during the Baroque period. Listen to Praetorius's *Lobt Gott Ihr Christen Alle Gleich (listening selections)*, an example of a chorale performed by four sackbuts.

CHORALE MOTET

Selection no. 86

Secular Music—The Madrigal

Humanism, the spirit of the Renaissance, manifested itself in one respect by encouraging greater interest in secular ideas. Although music continued to serve liturgical purposes in the sixteenth century, secular music grew in importance. Since it is not bound by the traditions of sacred music, secular music often lends itself to experimentation, frequently resulting in a general stylistic change that may eventually have an impact on church music as well. Secular music during the Renaissance, of which the *madrigal* is the primary example, was noticeably different from church music. Besides using vernacular lyrics, a trait they shared with music of the Reformation, the madrigals incorporated spirited and lively rhythms that would have been out of place in any religious service of the time. Typical lyrics were either satirical or treatments of romantic or pastoral settings. Madrigals were most often freely composed and tend to be homophonic, particularly after 1500. Although polyphony occurs, it is clearly harmonically based.

Italy. Italy was the home of the sixteenth-century madrigal. The earliest composers are Adrian Willaert (c. 1490–c. 1562) and Jacques Arcadelt (c. 1505–c. 1568), and the mood of their works is not unlike sacred polyphony, quiet and meditative, with clear melody in the soprano voice accompanied by two or three additional parts. In the middle of the century, with composers like Lasso, five parts are typical and madrigals became more polyphonic. It was common to use tone painting (on a word such as "ascends" the melody rises, for example) in this period. The late madrigal, represented by the works of Don Carlo Gesualdo (c. 1560–1613), Luca Marenzio (1553–1599), and Claudio Monteverdi (1567–1643), became experimental, incorporating chromaticism (numerous sharps and flats and half-step changes) and solo voices.

England. The English madrigal, which developed after 1550, is derived from the Italian model. In 1588 a collection of Italian madrigals was translated into English *(Musica Transalpina)*, and English composers began to write their own. Thereafter, madrigals flourished throughout the Elizabethan era. English madrigals are clear in design, frequently in strophic form. Refrains are also common and the overall texture tends to be homophonic. English madrigals were performed by four to six people, one voice to a harmonic part. The playful quality is typical. Principal composers of English madrigals are Orlando Gibbons (1583–1625), John Wilbye (1574–1638), and Thomas Morley (c. 1557–1602). Listen to Morley's "Now Is the Month of Maying" *(listening selections)*, a madrigal in which each strophe is in two parts (A B), like a verse and refrain, repeated for three strophes. (See pages 80, 310.)

Selection no. 33

Instrumental Music

By 1500, instruments had become quite popular throughout Europe. Before this time instruments had been used merely to replace or double a voice part, so little idiomatic music had been written for them, that is, music that expressly fits the ability of a given instrument. Consequently, voice and instruments could be combined or substituted one for the other as the occasion demanded. In the sixteenth century, however, composers became aware of functions instruments could perform that voices could not: they could play melodies with wide ranges and skips; sustain long notes; execute rapid scales and arpeggios; and repeat notes and motives very rapidly. A body of independent instrumental music thus began to develop in the Renaissance.

Keyboard. Since they could play all the parts in an instrumental version of a vocal piece, keyboard instruments were especially popular. The organ of 1500 was much like present-day instruments, and the clavichord and harpsichord were also in existence at this time. Although the portative organ was no longer used, a small, portable reed organ, called a *regal,* was available during the sixteenth century. The *virginal,* a small harpsichord placed on the lap or on a tabletop, was also popular. The *spinet,* a term also used for the virginal or to describe a one-manual pentagonally shaped harpsichord, was an additional choice.

REGAL
VIRGINAL
SPINET

Listen to Salvatore's Toccata *(listening selections)* (see page 74), performed on a harpsichord, and Paumann's "Ellend du Hast" *(listening selections).* "Ellend du Hast" is played on the *clavichord,* which was developed in the late Middle Ages, possibly as early as the twelfth century. The instrument is two to five feet in length, the strings struck by a metal tangent activated by the key mechanism. Since the sound is small-scaled, only subtle changes of dynamics are possible. The clavichord was used more for the enjoyment of the performer than for communicating with an audience. It was also used frequently as a practice instrument for organists.

Selection no. 30
Selection no. 87
CLAVICHORD

Virginal by Andreas Ruckers, a four-octave instrument, C/E to c3.

Smithsonian Institution Photo #56309.

Sackbut, a forerunner
of the modern
trombone.

Aerophones.   Among the popular aerophones of the Renaissance are
the shawm, recorder, and sackbut, all of which were also used in the
Middle Ages. The *cornett*, a straight instrument of wood or ivory using
a cup-shaped mouthpiece, was also common, as was the *krummhorn*,
a double-reed instrument with a curved shaped and a pierced wind
cap covering the reed.

Chordophones.   The leading chordophone group of the Renaissance
was the *viol*. Unlike instruments of the violin family, which later
replaced them, viols have flat backs, sloping shoulders, and C holes on
front. They also have six strings (tuned A-d-g-b-e'-a') and use frets on
the fingerboard. All viols are played between the performer's legs,
never held under the chin. The principal sizes are treble, tenor, and
bass, the latter of which is also called *viola da gamba*.

Listen to Byrd's *Fantasy in 4 Parts (listening selections)* (see page
110), performed by a family of viols. The Renaissance sound ideal was
a timbre blended evenly from low to high. Thus, instruments were built

CORNETT
KRUMMHORN

VIOL

VIOLA DA GAMBA
Selection no. 44

in families, or *consorts*, in order to maintain continuity of timbre. We can speak of a consort of recorders, krummhorns, or viols. Although *broken* consorts were used, in which the instrumental family was incomplete, or included instruments from other families, a *whole* consort, a family of like instruments, like the viols in the Fantasy, was preferred.

WHOLE AND BROKEN CONSORTS

One of the most important solo instruments of the period was the *lute*, which had equal popularity as an accompaniment for singing. Lutes have a flat neck, are fretted, and are distinguished by a body shaped like a half-pear, with the pegbox at a right angle to the neck. The sixteenth-century lute had eleven strings arranged in six pitches *(courses)*, G-c-f-a-d,-g,. (The last pitch is the only one that is not doubled.) Lute technique includes polyphonic playing, rapid passages, and block chords. An elaborate type of notation, *tablature*, was used in the Renaissance to write compositions for lute by showing placement of the performer's fingers on the frets, thus avoiding the need to show pitches, keys, and accidentals on a staff. Although the Spanish used tablature for keyboard instruments too, its greatest application was to lute music. Listen to Dowland's "Orlando Sleepeth" performed on a lute *(listening selections)* (see page 33).

LUTE

COURSE

TABLATURE

Selection no. 11

Krummhorn (left), shown with cap removed in top right photo.

Tenor viol.

Genres. Form has always been a greater concern in instrumental than in vocal music, since a song can be integrated by its text. Instrumental music, in contrast, needs a clear design to maintain the interest of listeners. Composers in the Renaissance initially adapted vocal forms and genres for their instrumental compositions. The *canzona*, for example, is a lively instrumental version of a chanson, usually written in many sections contrasted by texture and theme. Imitation is common. A *ricercar* is similar, although with its vocal counterpart, a sacred work, the motet, a ricercar is usually slower and more dignified than a canzona.

CANZONA

RICERCAR

VARIATION FORM
DIVISIONS

PAIRED DANCES

Variation form was also popular, using a well-known tune as a theme. Variations during this time were commonly written as *divisions*, that is, with the number of notes in the melody increasing in each succeeding variation. This is particularly true for virginal and lute variations. Equally popular among instrumental forms were *paired dances*, a self-explanatory merger that combines first a slow and then a fast example of the species. Common groupings include the *pavane* (slow $\frac{4}{4}$) and *galliard* (fast $\frac{3}{4}$). Free, improvisatory compositions for solo instruments were also written in the Renaissance, including the fantasy, prelude, and toccata.

Artistic designs painted on harp, an example of Venetian art of the Renaissance.

Courtesy of the New York Public Library.

MUSIC THEORY AND NOTATION

Theorists

The Renaissance was a time when scholars began to classify and systematize information in all areas. In music, many theorists wrote treatises on polyphonic techniques. Tinctoris (1435–1511), a composer and theorist, described consonances and dissonances that were acceptable in practice, while Glareanus (1488–1563) described the new modes of major and minor that were evolving into musical practice. Mersenne (1588–1648) compiled a catalog of instruments that is still useful to music historians.

Notation

Musical notation in the period gradually changed to reflect the type of music being composed. In the late fifteenth and early sixteenth centuries, white notes gradually began to replace the use of black notes.

Breve　　　□

Semibreve　◇

Minim　　　◊̷

Modus, the division of the longa ⊟ , was no longer a consideration, but tempus and prolatio divisions were:

○　Tempus perfectum　　□ = ◇ ◇ ◇

C　Tempus imperfectum　□ = ◇ ◇

•　Prolatio major　　　◇ = ◊̷ ◊̷ ◊̷

(no dot) Prolatio minor　◇ = ◊̷ ◊̷

These could be combined in four ways:

⊙　Tempus perfectum prolatio major

□ = ◇ ◇ ◇

◇ = ◊̷ ◊̷ ◊̷　　$\dfrac{9}{8}$

☉　Tempus imperfectum prolatio major

□ = ◇ ◇

◇ = ◊̷ ◊̷ ◊̷　　$\dfrac{6}{8}$

○　Tempus perfectum prolatio minor

□ = ◇ ◇ ◇

◇ = ◊̷ ◊̷　　$\dfrac{3}{4}$

C　Tempus imperfectum prolatio minor

□ = ◇ ◇

◇ = ◊̷ ◊̷　　$\dfrac{2}{4}$

The triple (perfect) division of notes was generally abandoned in the late sixteenth century, and every duration was divided imperfectly, that is, into twos, as in our present notational system. Bar lines, however, were not used until the seventeenth century.

SUMMARY

The 150-year span of the Renaissance began with the Burgundian style of the fifteenth century. The contrapuntal techniques of the Burgundians were further refined between 1450 and 1550 by Flemish composers such as Josquin des Prez, who developed what became known as the Renaissance vocal style, a cappella and reserved. Flemish masters often used the parody technique in their Masses. In the sixteenth century, Renaissance Catholic church music was brought to culmination by Palestrina and Orlando di Lasso. Toward the end of the sixteenth century, the polychoral writing of the Gabrielis began to point to a new style that led ultimately to the Baroque era.

Protestant music of the sixteenth century used the chorale as its basis. Madrigals, a secular vocal genre, developed in both Italy and England.

Instrumental music also appeared independently during this period, particularly after 1500. The most common instruments used were the virginal, spinet, regal, cornett, and krummhorn. Instruments, such as viols, were built in consorts or families. The lute was a popular solo instrument. Favorite instrumental forms include canzona, ricercar, variations, and paired dances.

The basis of musical notation was white notes, using breves, semibreves, and minims. Although both duple and triple time were used, by the end of the sixteenth century most rhythmic durations were divided imperfectly, that is, into twos.

STUDY GUIDELINES

KEY TERMS AND CONCEPTS

A cappella
Burgundian School
Cantus Firmus Mass
Canzona
Catholic Church Music
Chanson
Consort
Contrafactum
Contrapuntal Techniques
Cornett
Fauxbourdon
Flemish School

Krummhorn
Lute
Madrigal
Paired Dances
   Pavane-Galliard
Parody Mass
Polychoral
7-6-1 cadence
Variations (Divisions)
Viol
Virginal

CHAPTER REVIEW

Match items in the two columns. Answers in Appendix.

1. _____ A cappella
2. _____ parody mass
3. _____ cantus firmus Mass
4. _____ lute
5. _____ paired dance
6. _____ whole consort
7. _____ chanson
8. _____ fauxbourdon
9. _____ virginal
10. _____ broken consort
11. _____ canzona
12. _____ variations
13. _____ madrigal

A. built on motives and textures of another work
B. solo Renaissance chordophone with 11 strings
C. a family of the same type of instruments
D. melody is in soprano and texture is in 3 voices
E. small keyboard instrument
F. a family of unlike instruments
G. divisions
H. instrumental version of a chanson
I. pavane-galliard
J. reserved, unaccompanied choral style
K. secular choral composition
L. false bass
M. built on a borrowed melody, either sacred or secular

CHRONOLOGY OF MUSIC OF THE RENAISSANCE (1450-1600)

John Dunstable	c. 1385–1453
Gilles Binchois	c. 1400–1460
Guillaume Dufay	c. 1400–1474
Johannes Ockeghem	c. 1420–1496
Johannes Tinctoris	c. 1435–1511
Josquin des Prez	c. 1440–1521
Jacob Obrecht	c. 1450–1505
Heinrich Issac	c. 1450–1517
Pierre de la Rue	c. 1460–1518
Martin Luther	1483–1546
Henricus Glareanus	1488–1563
Adrian Willaert	c. 1490–1562
Andrea Gabrieli	c. 1510–1586
Jacques Arcadelt	c. 1505–c. 1568
Giovanni Pierluigi de Palestrina	1525–1594
Orlando di Lasso	1532–1594
William Byrd	1543–1623
Tomás Luis de Victoria	c. 1549–1611
Luca Marenzio	1553–1599
Thomas Morley	c. 1557–1602
Giovanni Gabrieli	c. 1557–1612
Don Carlo Gesualdo	1560–1613
John Dowland	1562–1626
Claudio Monteverdi	1567–1643
Michael Praetorius	1571–1621
John Wilbye	1574–1638
Orlando Gibbons	1583–1625
Marin Mersenne	1588–1648
Giovanni Salvatore	fl. c. 1600

FOR FURTHER LISTENING

Byrd	*Ergo Sum Panis Vivus* (motet)
	The Carmen's Whistle (variations)
Dufay	*Se la Face ay Pale* (Mass)
Gibbons	*The Silver Swan* (madrigal)

Josquin Des Prez	*Absalon, fili mi* (motet)
	Adieu mes amours (chanson)
	Missa Pangua Lingua (Mass)
Lasso	*Matona, mia cara* (madrigal)
Marenzio	*S'io Parto, i'moro* (madrigal)
Obrecht	*Missa Fortuna Desperata* (Mass)
Ockeghem	*Missa Prolationum* (Mass)
Palestrina	*Missa Brevis* (Mass)
	Missa Sine Nomine (Mass)
	Stabat Mater (motet)
Victoria	*O Magnum Mysterium* (motet)

THE BAROQUE ERA : 1600-1750

❖

GENERAL CHARACTERISTICS   SUMMARY

VOCAL MUSIC   STUDY GUIDELINES

INSTRUMENTAL MUSIC

STILE ANTICO
STILE MODERNO

Musical styles do not change suddenly, so the shift from Renaissance to Baroque was gradual, beginning in the late sixteenth century and continuing throughout the early seventeenth. These changes, which first appeared in Italy, spread throughout Europe rather slowly. Although the year 1600 is a convenient watershed, in reality both Renaissance and Baroque styles existed side by side during the early seventeenth century. The former, referred to as *stile antico*, was evident in traditional religious music, while the latter, *stile moderno*, describes the developments in secular theatrical music.

GENERAL CHARACTERISTICS

AFFECTIONS

The Baroque style is different from the Renaissance in many ways. Baroque music tends to be theatrical, grandiose in scale, and dramatic in concept. It was common for composers in this period to consider feelings or *affections* as set categories, such as happiness, anger, terror, despair, or serenity. Although one feeling-state (affect) can be said to predominate in each movement or section of longer works, feelings change from one segment to the next, thus providing dramatic contrast. The tranquil, eternally peaceful mood of Renaissance sacred music was replaced with a more theatrical approach.

376

Baroque painters often heightened the dramatic impact of their canvases by letting space recede diagonally into the distance, thus drawing the viewer into the drama. *Christ at the Sea of Galilee,* Jacopo Tintoretto, Venetian, c. 1575/80, oil on canvas.

Courtesy of the National Gallery of Art, Washington, Samuel H. Kress Collection.

Concertato

Many of these changes were first observed in the Venetian school, where the polychoral style of competing choirs or instrumental ensembles developed in the late sixteenth century. This alternation of forces, called *concertato* style, is characteristic of Baroque music. The style can be heard in the alternation in various compositions between choruses, instrumental groups, two voice parts, two instruments, or even the two hands on a keyboard instrument.

Contrast is evident in other aspects of Baroque style. Unlike the equality of voices observed in the High Renaissance, soprano and bass lines dominate in Baroque music and the inner voices are relatively unimportant. The bass line, which is also called a *basso continuo*, is present in most Baroque music. Played generally by harpsichord and cello (or viola da gamba), it provides the harmonic foundation for the melody. The chordal role in the continuo was also provided by lute, guitar, or organ. The performers playing the continuo read from *figured bass,* a musical abbreviation that shows the bass line and uses numbered notations to indicate specific harmonic realizations. The harpsichordist or other chordal instrumentalist realized the implied harmonies as the composition was performed. The art of realizing a figured bass has been lost since the Baroque period, and editors now provide a complete score for continuo performers. Listen to the Allegro

BASSO CONTINUO

FIGURED BASS

Selection no. 31
from Vivaldi's Concerto in a minor for flute, two violins, and continuo (cello and harpsichord) *(listening selections)* (see pages 74–75).

Terraced Dynamics

Further contrasts in Baroque style may be heard in timbre and group sizes. The homogeneous blend of instruments of the same family, a whole consort, was the ideal sound in the Renaissance. Baroque composers preferred broken consorts, such as violin, oboe, and recorder, instruments whose timbres are different. It was common for a small group of instruments or vocalists *(concertino* or *soli)* to be contrasted in a composition with a much larger group *(ripieno* or *tutti)*. This is another aspect of concertato style, with the alternation of groups of different size providing a contrast in dynamics. This sudden change from loud to soft is called *terraced dynamics.*

CONCERTINO (SOLI)

RIPIENO (TUTTI)

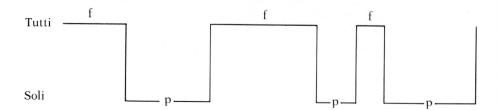

Although most evident in orchestral works, it can also be observed in solo performance on the organ or harpsichord. The sudden change between loud and soft occurs when the performer engages (or disengages) stops, resulting in more (or fewer) pipes or strings sounding. The resulting dynamics are terraced. Listen to the Allegro from Bach's *Brandenburg Concerto* no. 4 in G major, BWV 1049 *(supplemental listening)* (see page 276). This example shows the Baroque use of terraced dynamics through the contrast of the concertino (violin and two flutes) with the ripieno (entire string orchestra).

Rhythm

Another principle of Baroque music can be observed in its rhythm. Music of the period often has an inexorably steady beat, with few accelerandos or ritardandos. Since a strict beat and tempo govern each movement, contrast is provided between movements. A slow movement will often be followed by one in quicker tempo; in some compositions, a movement with a strict beat will be followed by music

SENZA BATTUTA

without any beat, referred to as *senza battuta.* This is most noticeable in vocal music that alternates aria and recitative. The aria is locked into a steady beat and tempo, whereas recitative is performed senza battuta, thus providing contrast. Similarly, a keyboard composition,

such as a fantasia, may be free in rhythm but will be followed by a
fugue with a steady beat. Listen to Bach's Toccata in d minor *(listening*   Selection no. 5
selections) (see page 10).

Texture

Polyphonic and homophonic textures were both used in the Baroque
period, providing contrast in texture within the same composition.
Composers began to think of the vertical movement of sonorities or
chords, rather than the linear polyphony typical of the Renaissance
and Middle Ages. Melodies were written to conform to chordal
progressions. The chords that were used are consonant to the modern
ear, since modality was in the process of being supplanted by major
and minor tonalities. This evolution began after 1600, and by 1700
modern tonality had generally replaced Renaissance modality. Theorists
of the day, such as Rameau, described these emerging concepts of
tonality and harmonic progression, so today we have a reasonably
clear idea of the progression of these changes. Listen to "For Unto Us
A Child Is Born" from Handel's *Messiah (listening selections)* (see pages   Selection no. 28
71–72). This example shows the use of both polyphonic and homophonic
textures alternating within the same composition.

Common Practice Theory

The theory of common practice, incorporating major and minor, exists
in music from the eighteenth through most of the nineteenth centuries,
while traditional music of the twentieth century often follows this
theory as well. In this period, the basis of harmony is the major or
minor scale, with triads constructed on each tonal degree.

MAJOR							MINOR						
I	ii	iii	IV	V(7)	vi	vii°	i	ii°	III	iv	V(7)	VI	vii°

Whether in major or minor, the *primary triads* constructed on the   PRIMARY TRIAD
first, fourth, and fifth degrees of the scale are the most important.
Although secondary triads may be used for contrast, primary triads
define the key and provide the basic harmony. Chord progressions
followed stereotyped patterns in the Baroque period, including progressions such as I-ii-V₇-I and IV-V₇-I. Modulation occurred between
closely related keys. Chords seem to change often, resulting in an
impression of fast harmonic rhythms. Polyphony is written to conform
to these established chord progressions, and even melodies are written
to outline triads, although this may be disguised by ornamentation.

Painting of the seventeenth century has many qualities associated with music of the Baroque period. It is often complex and dramatic and tends to have plasticity, seeming to spring from its two-dimensional frame. Painters achieved this energy by using striking contrasts of color and light, and arranging perspective or depth so that space seemed to recede diagonally into the distance, drawing the observer into the work. Baroque painters include Rubens (1577–1640), Rembrandt (1606–1669), and El Greco (1541–1614).

Madonna and Child with Saint Martina and Saint Agnes, El Greco (Domenikos Theotokopoulos), Spanish, 1597/99, oil on canvas.

Courtesy of the National Gallery of Art, Washington, Widener Collection.

Equal Temperament

A new concept in tuning called *equal temperament* developed in the Baroque period, allowing composers to modulate more freely. In equal temperament, the octave is the only interval in tune, all other intervals being a bit smaller or larger than they occur acoustically. Since twelve identical half-steps are used to divide the octave, sharps and flats become equal (i.e., c♯ = d♭) or enharmonic. The discrepancy that exists between distant tonalities (C major to F♯ major, for example) is thereby minimized. Equal temperament was proposed in the early sixteenth century but not widely adopted until the late Baroque. It facilitates modulation and proved advantageous to instrumental music, particularly keyboard genres. It is still the basis of tuning for composition and performance of Western music.

VOCAL MUSIC

Opera

The techniques and style that influenced all vocal music in the Baroque period first developed in Italy in the form that became known as opera. It is generally agreed that what we know today as opera began in the city of Florence around the year 1600. Scholars studying fragments of ancient Greek music had come to the conclusion that it had been *monodic*, that is, used one clear melody, performed with sparse accompaniment, that conveyed verbal and expressive meaning without being obscured by musical concerns. The composers among the group began to compose extended, narrative works in such a style. This was not the first modern attempt to combine music and drama; this had already been accomplished in Renaissance madrigal cycles. The music inspired by these studies, however, resulted in a new style of dramatic recitation, which came to be known as *recitative*. Recitative is sung speech in which the voice emphasizes the words more than melody. In opera of the Baroque period, it is accompanied by lute or harpsichord. In 1602 this new style of dramatic singing, called *monody*, was presented in a book called *Le Nuove Musiche* (The New Music), a series of songs written by Caccini.

MONODY

RECITATIVE

The chief traits of early Florentine opera were stories based on mythology, the dry style of singing called monody, and the sparse accompaniment provided by the basso continuo. Although these early operas have had little appeal for today's average operagoer, they have historical importance and have been the subject of several recent revivals as part of the reawakening of interest in early music.

Claudio Monteverdi (1567–1643) was the first composer to adapt the Florentine innovations, including plots derived from mythology, and create a viable musical entity. Since the uninterrupted recitative of the first opera was monotonous, Monteverdi included solo sections of a more musical nature in his *Orfeo* of 1607. These were a forerunner of the musical form that became known as *aria*. He also added dances and vocal ensembles, using several accompanying instruments (forty in all). If a solo song were strophic, Monteverdi would add vocal variations on each subsequent verse to provide variety. Although his solo songs are not arias in a modern sense, he began the delineation between aria and recitative that later became typical of operatic composition.

Opera is the single genre in music that has remained popular from the Baroque era to the present day, as evidenced by this 1936 painting of an audience at the Metropolitan Opera House in New York. *Monday Night at the Metropolitan,* Reginald Marsh, American, c. 1936, tempera and oil.

University of Arizona Museum of Art, gift of C. Leonard Pfeiffer.

During the seventeenth century, opera spread from Florence to other Italian cities—Rome, Venice, and Naples—as well as to other countries, and became more like opera as we know it today. Important differences remained, however. One of the major reasons why seventeenth-century opera is of more interest historically than in performance is that many of the leading heroic parts were written for *castrati*, neutered male singers with voices of a range and volume impossible to duplicate today. Although many of these operas have been revived in recent years, their vocal demands are so specialized that it is doubtful that they will sustain a major proportion of the performing repertory.

CASTRATI

Varying nationalistic styles developed as the operatic form was disseminated throughout Western Europe. *Opera seria* is the loftiest Italian style, using characters derived from mythology and often tragic in nature. *Opera buffa*, which developed from the comic interludes placed between acts of opera seria, is lighter. The characters are realistic and sometimes comic. Both types are completely sung, alternating recitative and aria. French *opéra comique* is not necessarily comic, but is lighter in effect since it typically uses spoken dialogue instead of recitative. English *ballad opera* is also light and has realistic characters, often of the criminal classes. Dialogue is spoken, as it is in *Singspiel*, a German folk opera form that evolved from the English style. These classifications apply during most of the late Baroque period and into the Classic. Opera in the nineteenth century, although remaining regionalistic in plot and language, took on more of an international flavor in terms of style, with most nations producing operas of similar character.

OPERA SERIA

OPERA BUFFA

OPÉRA COMIQUE

BALLAD OPERA

SINGSPIEL

Listen to the lament ("Thy Hand, Belinda") from Purcell's *Dido and Aeneas* (1689) *(listening selections)* (see page 169). Dating from the spread of the operatic form to England in the late seventeenth century, this selection illustrates the characteristic way arias were composed during this period, including the use of variation on a ground bass.

Selection no. 56

Oratorio

Early in the Baroque period, operatic techniques were adapted to other vocal genres. The *oratorio*, which is like an unstaged opera on a quasi-religious subject, developed in this way, becoming a substitute for opera during penitential church seasons such as Lent when stage productions were prohibited. Two types of oratorio, both retaining the religious orientation of subject matter, gradually emerged during the seventeenth century. The *oratorio latino* is in Latin, with choruses the most important component. *Oratorio vulgare*, however, is in the vernacular, with solo singing providing a stronger balance to the choral element. Early oratorios maintain a distinction between recitative and

ORATORIO LATINO
ORATORIO VULGARE

Baroque sculpture can best be characterized by one word—fluency. It seems to burst from its pedestal. Strong diagonal lines create movement and plasticity, and incorporate the space surrounding the statue as part of the sculptural group. The play of light and shadow on the surface, called *chiaroscuro* in art, results from the texture of the actual stone or bronze. The entire effect is often striking and dramatic. Among the Baroque sculptors were Puget (1622–1694) and Bernini (1598–1680), the latter also an architect who designed the colonnades enclosing St. Peter's piazza in Rome.

aria, the latter in strophic or variation form. George Frideric Handel (1685–1759) represents the mature Baroque oratorio style in *Israel in Egypt, Solomon,* and *Messiah,* where the distinction between oratorio vulgare and latino no longer applies. He assembled soloists, choruses, and orchestra, using the chorus as a unifying factor for the powerful solo and orchestral segments. Listen to "O Thou That Tellest Good Tidings" from Handel's *Messiah (listening selections)* (see pages 95–96, 262–265).

Selection no. 37

Exuberance and dynamic portrayal are characteristic of Baroque sculpture. *David*, Gian Lorenzo Bernini, Italian, 1623, marble.

Cantata

Cantatas are smaller in scale than oratorios. Although a cantata may use soloists and orchestra, its overall length is not as great as an oratorio. An oratorio may have thirty arias and/or choruses, whereas a cantata may have only three or four. Nonetheless, recitative still alternates with aria, and some narrative typically unifies the work. Like oratorios, cantatas are unstaged; some are religious in tone, intended for liturgical use, others are simply concert pieces and may utilize a secular theme.

Chorale Cantata. The adaptation of the cantata for the Lutheran church service was the *chorale cantata,* which typically ends with the congregation singing the chorale in unison. In this respect, it is like a set of variations that is concluded by presentation of the theme. Lutheran composers of cantatas include Heinrich Schutz (1585–1672), Dietrich Buxtehude (1637–1707), and J. S. Bach, whose contribution alone exceeds 200 works. Listen to Verse VI (Soprano-Tenor Duet) and VII (Chorale) of Bach's *Christ lag in Todesbanden (listening selections)* (see pages 201–202, 225).

Selection nos. 68, 63

Verse Anthem. Anglican church music of this period was also derived from operatic style. Many English composers, including John Blow (1649–1708) and Henry Purcell (c. 1659–1695), wrote *verse anthems* in which soloists sing in alternation with a full chorus, often with a concluding fugal section on "Hallelujah." Handel wrote compositions in this style, notably the English Anthems (1716–18) commissioned by the Duke of Chandos. By the end of the Baroque period, most church music was accompanied by instruments and a cappella style was rarely heard.

INTRUMENTAL MUSIC

During the Baroque period instrumental music became as important as vocal. For the first time in music history, instruments were extensively used for more than accompaniment. Sonatas, suites, and concertos, as well as keyboard works such as toccata, fantasy, and fugue, were composed and performed. In general, Baroque instrumental music was not standardized. Composers wrote for whatever instrumental combinations were available. Baroque music was written for an immediate purpose, rather than for posterity, and audiences preferred to hear new works, not compositions of earlier periods. Although this created an environment in which the composer continually had to produce, the reward was immediate performance of one's music.

Flute with tuning joints by Heinrich Grenser, Dresden, late eighteenth or early nineteenth century. This flute is nearly identical to the kind used by Baroque performers.

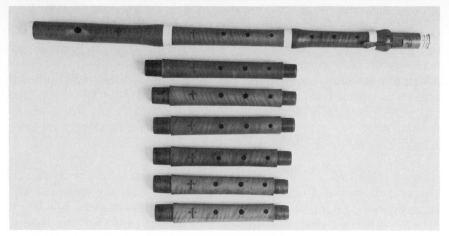

Smithsonian Institution Photo #79-11244.

Instruments

Many instruments in today's orchestra existed during Baroque times, at least in incipient form. Woodwinds in use at the time included the flute, oboe, and bassoon.

TRANSVERSE FLUTE

Woodwinds.   The transverse flute originally was used as a military instrument, but Lully, the French composer, introduced it into the orchestra in the mid-seventeenth century. Around 1650 its bore was changed from cylindrical to conical and one key was added, thereby making the tone suitable for solo work as well as orchestral, since the technical improvements made it a more maneuverable instrument. The Hotteterres, a family of flutists, are credited with making this change. Jean Hotteterre (1648–1732) also constructed his flutes in three sections, enabling a performer to lengthen or shorten them, depending on which section was inserted. This allowed the performer to tune the instrument more precisely. Listen to the Larghetto from Quantz's Trio in C major *(listening selections)* (see pages 92–93), which uses flute, recorder, and continuo.

Selection no. 35

Modern flutes. The flute was radically changed in mid-nineteenth century to become the instrument of today, made of metal instead of wood.

Courtesy of Yamaha International Corporation.

This nineteenth-century clarinet, with only five keys, all other holes being covered by the performer's fingers, is similar to the Baroque clarinet, an early adaption of the chalumeau.

OBOE

BASSOON

The oboe is a descendant of the shawm, an outdoor medieval instrument, but it was refined during the seventeenth century and became suitable for concert use. The bassoon developed in this same century from the *curtal*, a double-reed instrument of the Renaissance. Although flutes, oboes, and bassoons had fewer keys than their modern-day counterparts, they were essentially similar to the instruments we know today. This is not true of the clarinet. Its seventeenth-century forerunner, the *chalumeau*, was a single-reed instrument that played only in a low register. Around 1700, Johann Denner (1655–1707) added a speaker key to it, which enabled the chalumeau to sound an octave higher, increasing its range by the addition of the upper clarion register. During the later years of the Baroque period, additional modifications were incorporated and the modern clarinet was created. Since the clarinet absorbed the chalumeau, its lowest register is still referred to by that name. The term "clarionet" was first applied in 1732. The instrument was not used extensively, however, until the late Classic period (c. 1800). All woodwind instruments, of course, were further modified and improved in the nineteenth century.

CLARINET
CHALUMEAU

Brass. Brass instruments of the Baroque period include the trumpet, an instrument that had been used for outdoor celebrations such as military parades since the fourteenth century. These trumpets and the contemporaneous *French horn* had no valves, so they were able to play only pitches of the harmonic series. During the Baroque period, attempts to create a more versatile trumpet included use of a slide, like the trombone, as well as side-holes covered by keys.

TRUMPET
FRENCH HORN

An additional tube or *crook* that changed the harmonic series was often inserted in the trumpet or horn. This did not provide additional pitches, only an alteration in the basic overtone spectrum of the instrument. Thus, in the Baroque period, the trumpet and horn were limited to fanfares in low and middle registers. Melodies had to be in the high register where the overtones lie closer together. Valves were invented in 1813, and during the nineteenth century the trumpet and horn became viable orchestral instruments.

CROOK

Natural trumpet by Christian Wittman, Nuremburg, late eighteenth or early nineteenth century. Like Baroque instruments, this instrument was capable of playing only on natural overtones.

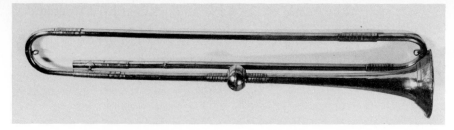

Smithsonian Institution Photo #55261.

TROMBONE

The trombone changed little during the Baroque period except to assume its present size and enlarge the bell. Like its medieval ancestor, the sackbut, its slide mechanism enabled the trombone to play all pitches. Composers, however, rarely used the instrument except for ceremonial or military music. Although it occasionally appeared in the opera orchestra, it did not become a regular orchestral participant until nearly 1850.

Keyboard.   Among keyboard instruments, the organ was prominent in the Baroque period, as were the harpsichord and clavichord. Such stringed keyboard instruments, as the latter two, are generically called *klaviers*. The pianoforte, a third type of klavier, was invented during

KLAVIER
PIANOFORTE

Orchestral horn with tuning crooks by M.A. Raoux, Paris, c. 1840. Crooks were used to change the natural harmonic series of horns (and trumpets) during both the Baroque and Classical periods. The valves at top are a later addition.

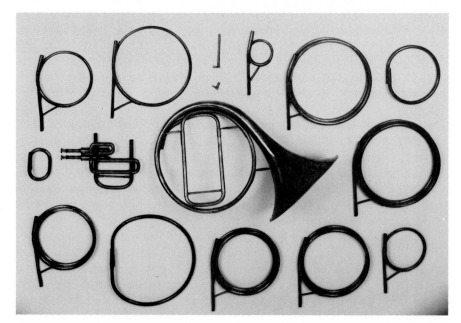

Smithsonian Institution Photo #75-6702.

this period. Bartolomeo Cristofori (1655–1731), who tried to create a harpsichord sensitive to touch, is credited with inventing the piano in 1709. Its invention generally passed unnoticed at the time and it was not until the Classic period that composers began to write specifically for the piano. Therefore the term "klavier," when used in the Baroque period, refers to the harpsichord and clavichord. Listen to Bach's Passacaglia in c minor (BWV 582) *(listening selections)* (see pages 247–249), performed on a pedal harpsichord.

Selection no. 71

Strings. Because of their brilliance and versatility, the violin family began to replace the viols in the early Baroque period. Cremona, the famed home of violin making, in Italy, is where the Amati, Guarneri, and Stradivari families developed the violin. Since this time, instruments of the violin family have really changed very little. Listen to *Gavotte en Rondeau* from Bach's Partita no. 3 in E major for Violin (S. 1006) *(listening selections)* (see page 40).

Selection no. 15

Compositions

The variety of instruments available gave Baroque composers a rich palette of timbre for their compositions. Most preferred to use sharply differentiated timbres, providing contrast between melodic lines or between melody and bass.

Keyboard. Among the compositions written for solo instruments, keyboard music is the most diverse in form. The *fantasia* and *prelude* are short compositions with a feeling of improvisation. *Toccatas* are keyboard pieces that demonstrate the performer's dexterity, while a *chorale prelude* is a composition that integrates a chorale tune. *Fugues*, which were popular in the period, were often written for the organ, and it is common for the performer to use a different registration on the organ for each statement of the subject, thus allowing entrances to be heard clearly. Listen to Bach's Fugue in c minor (BWV 582) *(listening selections)* (see pages 296–298). *Variation* forms, including passacaglia and chaconne, are common, as is the *suite* or *partita*, a multimovement form with at least four basic dances (movements): the allemande, courante, sarabande, and gigue.

Selection no. 76

Chamber Music. Chamber music of the period is always accompanied by the basso continuo. A favorite grouping is the *trio sonata*, a confusing term identifying a selection performed by four instruments: two solo instruments plus the continuo, comprised of harpsichord and cello (or viola da gamba). In a trio sonata, the two solo instruments play in imitative counterpoint while the continuo accompanies. Trio

TRIO SONATA

sonata is a term that also may be applied to larger ensembles in which there are two main melodies and accompaniment.

Other multimovement forms that developed are the *sonata da chiesa*, a four-movement work in a slow-fast-slow-fast arrangement, and the *sonata da camera*, or *suite*, which has contrasting dance movements, each of which is usually binary. Baroque composers were prolific in their production of chamber music and there is a wealth written for all performance levels, from amateur to virtuoso.

Orchestral. The orchestra of the Baroque era was dominated by strings. Woodwinds, when used, were in pairs, such as a pair of flutes, oboes, or bassoons. Except for festive ceremonial music, brass and percussion were seldom incorporated. Since the orchestra did not have a conductor in the modern sense, it was jointly directed by the CONCERT MASTER harpsichordist and the *concert master*, the leader of the violins, who gradually assumed more control in the late eighteenth century when the harpsichord was no longer used for continuo. Orchestras were not conducted by a leader with baton, however, until the nineteenth century.

Listen to the "Bourrée" from Handel's *Water Music (supplemental listening)* (pages 278–280). Orchestral music of the Baroque includes the SUITE   *suite*, of which the complete *Water Music* is an example, and the OVERTURE   *overture*. An overture was used as prelude to such longer works as operas and cantatas. Concertos were also popular during the period, CONCERTO GROSSO especially the *concerto grosso* type in which a small group of soloists (concertino) is contrasted with the entire orchestra (tutti). The concerto grosso is usually in three movements, fast, slow, fast. The *solo* SOLO CONCERTO *concerto*, especially those written for violin, became popular around 1700. Although the solo instrument is featured to a greater extent than in the concerto grosso, the three-movement structure was still utilized.

SUMMARY

Baroque music is characterized by its exuberance and energy. The music is technically involved, written for performers who are virtuosos on their instruments. Writing during this period became idiomatic, that is, an instrumental part no longer sounds as if it could easily be performed by the voice. Rather, composers were more explicit in designating the timbre they wanted in each composition.

Characteristics of Baroque music are the concertato style, affections, basso continuo performing from a figured bass, terraced dynamics, contrasting timbres, and a relentless beat (sometimes contrasted with sections in senza battuta). Tonality, based on primary triads, replaced modality, and the development of equal temperament facilitated modulation equally well to all major and minor keys.

Most vocal music was influenced by operatic conventions, including the contrast between aria and recitative. Opera began in Florence with a style of singing called monody, but sections of greater interest, that is, arias, were gradually incorporated, providing contrast to the recitative. Cantatas and oratorios were influenced by operatic style.

Instrumental music also developed and became equal in importance to vocal. Several improvements were made in woodwind instruments, and the viol was gradually replaced by the violin. Brass and percussion instruments, however, were relatively unimportant in the period. Among keyboard genres that developed are the toccata, fugue, and variation. The trio sonata was an important chamber form. The orchestra was dominated largely by strings; important genres for it include overture, suite, and concerto, both grosso and solo.

STUDY GUIDELINES

KEY TERMS AND CONCEPTS

Affections

Basso Continuo

Cantata

Chalumeau

Chorale cantata

Concertato Style

Concerto

  Grosso

  Solo

Crook

Equal Temperament

Klavier

Monody

Oratorio

Overture

Recitative

Ripieno (tutti)

Senza Battuta

Sonata

Stile antico

Stile moderno

Suite

Terraced dynamics

Trio Sonata

CHAPTER REVIEW

Define each of the following with one or two words. Answers in Appendix.

1. _____ _____ the I, IV, and V$_7$ chords
2. _____ _____ new style in the Baroque period
3. _____ tutti
4. _____ _____ musical shorthand
5. _____ solo melody with sparse accompaniment
6. _____ set of dances
7. _____ _____ division of keyboard octave into twelve half steps
8. _____ _____ dynamics in layers

CHRONOLOGY OF MUSIC OF THE BAROQUE (1600–1750)

Guilio Caccini	c. 1550–1618
Jacopo Peri	1561–1633
Ottavio Rinuccini	1562–1621
Claudio Monteverdi	1567–1643
Heinrich Schütz	1585–1672
Stefano Landi	c. 1590–1655
Florentine Camerata	1600

Pier Francesco Cavalli	1602–1676
Giacomo Carissimi	1605–1674
Marc' Antonio Cesti	1623–1669
Jean-Baptiste Lully	1632–1687
Dietrich Buxtehude	c. 1637–1707
Jean Hotteterre	1648–1732
John Blow	1649–1708
Johann Pachelbel	1653–1706
Arcangelo Corelli	1653–1713
Johann Denner	1655–1707
Bartolomeo Cristofori	1655–1731
Henry Purcell	c. 1659–1695
Alessandro Scarlatti	1660–1725
Antonio Vivaldi	1678–1741
Georg Philipp Telemann	1681–1767
Jean Philippe Rameau	1683–1764
Johann Sebastian Bach	1685–1750
Domenico Scarlatti	1685–1757
George Frideric Handel	1685–1759
Johann Joachim Quantz	1697–1773

FOR FURTHER LISTENING

Bach	Brandenburg Concertos Cantata no. 140, *Wachet auf, ruft uns die Stimme*
Corelli	Concerto Grosso no. 8 in g minor *Sonata da chiesa* in e minor, op. 3, no. 7 Trio Sonata in A major, op. 4, no. 3
Froberger	Suite in e minor
Handel	*Israel in Egypt* (oratorio) Rinaldo (opera) Sonata no. 4 in D major for violin and harpsichord Trio Sonata in B$^\flat$ major (flute, oboe, continuo) *Water Music* (suite)
Lully	*Alceste* (opera)
Monteverdi	*Incoronazione di Poppea* (opera)
Scarlatti, D.	Keyboard sonatas
Schütz	*The Christmas Story*
Telemann	Trio Sonatas
Vivaldi	*The Four Seasons*, op. 8

THE CLASSIC ERA: 1750-1825

◆

GENERAL CHARACTERISTICS	VOCAL MUSIC
ORCHESTRAL MUSIC	SUMMARY
CHAMBER MUSIC	STUDY GUIDELINES

The term "Classic" has been used to describe all art music, whether of the seventeenth, eighteenth, or nineteenth century. Although one may use the term in this manner to describe compositions of lasting interest and value, regardless of when they were created, in music history the Classic era is considered the period between 1750–1825. This is when certain stylistic traits evolved into common usage and were employed by a majority of composers. In this chapter, music of this period will be referred to as Classical, the period itself as the Classic period.

Classical traits in music in general include clear design and simplicity. The music is almost always absolute, not programmatic, and has a feeling of poise and reserve. Its appeal lies in an inherent order and objectivity.

Since the traits of one period gradually fade away as those of the next emerge, the Baroque era did not suddenly end and the Classic begin in 1750. A style change can take several decades to occur. Composers may practice both styles during such a transitional time, and only from the advantage of hindsight does a music historian declare a given date as a convenient watershed between the two.

ROCOCO   In reality, *rococo* art was transitional between the two periods in the early eighteenth century. The energy and heaviness of Baroque art ultimately produced a reaction in the opposite direction. Rococo art, specifically as manifested in the visual arts, is highly ornamented. In architecture, rooms were decorated with elaborate scrolls and shell work (*rocaille* means shell). Light and delicate colors were used in painting, especially by artists such as Watteau, Boucher, and Fragonard. Subjects were pastoral and pretty, emphasizing the sentimental and the rustic. Rococo art is charming, playful, and much less ponderous than the Baroque. This style in music, called *style galant,* resulted in musical compositions somewhat different from the Baroque. Opera plots became simpler, characters more commonplace: disrespectful servants, lovely maidens, gallant heroes. Simpler, almost folk-like melodies predominated. In instrumental music, the harpsichord was a favored instrument and the suite was a typical genre, especially those with a minuet movement. Trio sonatas continued to be popular. The rococo style is intimate and sentimental, thus providing a break from the monumental works of the late Baroque period and leading gradually into the distinctive practices associated with the Classic era.

STYLE GALANT

Paintings of the Rococo period depict trivial subjects that were treated sentimentally, not unlike the music of the same period. *The Swing,* J. H. Fragonard, 1732–1806, French.

Composers of style galant include the Frenchmen François Couperin (1688–1733) and Louis Nicolas Clérambault (1676–1749). In Germany the music of Georg Philipp Telemann (1681–1767) shows similar traits, as does that of the Italian Domenico Scarlatti (1685–1757). Listen to Scarlatti's Sonata in C major, L. 454 (K. 309) *(listening selections)* (pages 38–39, 278) for a representative example of style galant.

Selection no. 14

GENERAL CHARACTERISTICS

Melody/Phrase

Around the middle of the eighteenth century, composers began to incorporate and adapt rococo musical traits into the new style, known as Classicism. Classical music is clearly and logically organized in a manner that can be readily recognized by the listener. Melodies are short and consist of easily remembered motives. Phrase structure, too, is clear and regular, usually four measures in length, punctuated by a cadence. The phrase structure is typically a series of antecedent-consequents, grouped into periods, with the periods then providing points of unity and contrast as the composition unfolds and develops. This provides a logical ordering of musical events, motives, melodies, phrases, periods, and sections, to create a movement.

Selection no. 45

Listen to the Menuetto (Allegro ma non troppo): Trio from Haydn's Quartet in d minor, op. 76, no. 2 *(listening selections)* (see pages 12, 254–256). Most compositions have an inherent beat, and metric groupings are either in 2, 3, or 4. Here, of course, the meter is in 3's (triple).

Harmony

Harmony in the Classic period is not strikingly differently from that of the Baroque, since major and minor scales and chords are still its basis. Composers, however, preferred a slower harmonic rhythm during this era, with one triad often providing accompaniment for a large part of a phrase. In addition, composers increasingly thought homophonically. When they used polyphony, it followed the typical chord progressions of the period. Melodies were written and harmonized by triads (and seventh chords for the dominant). A favored accompanying figure is the *Alberti bass*, a broken chord accompaniment used extensively by Domenico Alberti in his keyboard works.

ALBERTI BASS

Alberti Bass

Above, the Greek Parthenon (Athens), an ancient Classic building; right, St.-Louis-des Invalides (Paris, by Jules Hardouin Mansart), completed 1735.

Classical architecture of the eighteenth century developed following a renewed interest in architecture of the ancient world, sparked by the excavation of two Roman cities that had been buried by lava since A.D. 79—Herculaneum in 1738, and Pompeii in 1763. J. J. Winckelmann's text, *History of Ancient Art,* was published in 1764 and promoted further the interest in finding "noble simplicity and quiet grandeur" in the arts, the new Classicism. In architecture, the interest led to the construction of such buildings as the Petit Trianon at Versailles and the Place de la Concorde in Paris, designed and completed in the decade following 1753 by Jacques-Anges Gabriel (1698–1782).

As in the Renaissance, architects favored classic orders and domes, designing buildings that emphasized form and symmetry. Architects of the period include Soufflot (1709–1780), Stuart (1713–1788), and Langhans (1733–1808), the latter modeling the Brandenburg Gates of Berlin after the Propylaea on the Acropolis in Athens.

Rules governing harmonic usage were articulated by theorists of the time, including Jean Philippe Rameau (1683–1764).

Dynamics

Classic restraint was especially noticeable in composers' treatment of dynamics. Rather than using terraced dynamics for dramatic contrast, crescendo and diminuendo were preferred for changes between loud and soft. Alternation between concertino and ripieno, typical of Baroque practice, was no longer the customary procedure.

Form

Perhaps the areas of form and timbre best characterize Classic practices. During the period between 1750 and 1825, formal schemes became standardized, as did the instrumentation of several performing groups.

Form has been defined as design in music. Classic composers achieved symmetry in single-movement forms by providing clear points of unity and variety. These are present in such schemes as ABA, the rondo types (ABABA, ABACA, and ABACABA), minuet, and trio, as well as sonata-allegro. Not only were sections clearly delineated, but standard key relationships developed for modulation. Favored key changes, which evolved from the binary dance-forms of the Baroque suite, are tonic to dominant, as well as minor to relative major. Listen to Allegro vivace assai from Mozart's Quartet no. 14 (K. 387) *(listening selections)* (see page 261), which provides a demonstration of the sonata-allegro form (described in Chapter Eight).

Selection no. 74

Theme and variations in the period are almost always sectional, in which the phrase structure and form of the theme is clearly retained in each variation.

Timbre

The preference for certain timbres resulted in standardized instrumental combinations during the Classic period, of which the symphony orchestra is the leading example. During the Baroque period, instrumentation was not rigidly set by a composer. Composers wrote for whatever instrumental combinations were available to them, thus reflecting the pragmatism of the time. Baroque composers in general preferred contrasting instrumental timbres, such as two violins with oboe and flute. Although the continuo (harpsichord and cello or viola da gamba) was always present to fill in harmony, even this practice began to change among Classical composers during the middle of the eighteenth century, when they began to think of instruments as families: strings, woodwinds, brass, and percussion, somewhat like the Renaissance concept of a whole consort.

The Symphony Orchestra. The symphony orchestra developed specifically in two geographical areas, first in Italy and then in Austria and Germany around 1745. G. B. Sammartini (1701–1775) of Milan developed the use of contrasting themes and tonalities within the sonata-allegro form. In Vienna, the composers Georg Matthias Monn (1717–1750) and Christoph Wagenseil (1715–1777) adopted his technique and finally, in the German city of Mannheim, Johann Stamitz (1717–1757) brought the pre-Classic symphony to the level it achieved at the advent of the Classic masters Mozart and Haydn, as well as

Michael Haydn (1737–1806) and Karl Ditters von Dittersdorf (1739–1799). The symphony orchestra of today is not substantially different in structure from the core orchestra as it developed in the middle of the eighteenth century.

Strings.   The string family, consisting of violin, viola, cello, and double bass, gradually replaced viols in the Baroque period. Although instruments of the violin family have only four strings, they are able to play with increased brilliance and tone. The structural changes introduced in violins by the villagers of Cremona (Amati, Stradivari, and Guarneri) and Brescia were gradually adopted throughout Europe. By 1750 these instruments were preferred over viols and thus became the core of the Classic orchestra, where they were divided into sections comprising first and second violins, violas, cellos, and double basses. With the establishment of lower strings as a vehicle for carrying the harmony, the continuo part was discarded.

Woodwinds.   Woodwinds are also participants in the Classic symphony, usually in pairs. Flutes, oboes, and bassoons are typical throughout the late Classic period, at which time a pair of clarinets was also added (Mozart, 1788). The woodwinds thus provide contrast to the homogeneity of the string sound. They were used to play second themes or to carry contrasting sections.

Brass.   Although brass instruments at this time were not equipped with valves, two French horns and two trumpets were used in the Classic symphony. These instruments could only play notes of the natural harmonic series:

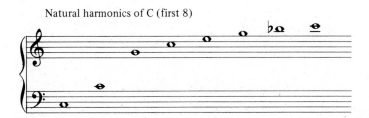

Natural harmonics of C (first 8)

therefore limiting them to the beginnings or endings of movements, where fanfare-like passages might be employed. They were not able to play melodies, nor could they modulate to a remote key. Thus, a symphony in D would call for two horns in D and two trumpets in D. Most innovations on brass instruments of the period, such as the slide, did not expand the instruments' capabilities. Brass instruments did use a *crook*, an added piece of pipe placed in the instrument's tubing to shorten or lengthen it, thus changing its basic harmonic series. A D   CROOK

Timpani, Germany, eighteenth century. These drums were tuned by a handle to tighten or loosen the screws around the rim.

Smithsonian Institution Photo #68800.

instrument, for example, could be fitted with a crook to lengthen it for use in a composition in C. Crooks were changed only between compositions, not during, and instruments using them were still limited to pitches of a set overtone series.

Percussion.   Percussion instruments were also relatively unimportant during the Classic period. Two timpani, tuned to tonic and dominant of the main tonality, were commonly used. Since there was no mechanism that could enable the percussionist to change the pitch of the heads quickly, as is possible with modern kettledrums, they were silent when compositions modulated to other keys.

Modern timpani have a pedal with a wire cord inside to adjust the tension and pitch of the heads.

Courtesy of The Selmer Company.

Left, piano by John Broadwood and Son, London, 1794; below, model of English grand piano action.

Smithsonian Institution Photos #56404 and 74285.

Piano. The Classic era saw the piano emerge as the most important keyboard instrument. Although invented in the early part of the eighteenth century, it was neither well-known nor taken seriously by composers until after 1750. Since their strings were thinner and the frame was wood, the earliest pianos were not as brilliant or as powerful as the more substantial instruments of today. Unlike its forerunner, the harpsichord, the piano was touch-sensitive and dynamic changes could thus be shaded by the player's touch. It became a favorite medium for solo sonatas and concertos during the period and has continued in its popularity to the present day.

ORCHESTRAL MUSIC

The Symphony

The *sonata* is the most important instrumental genre that continued to be refined in the Classic period. Sonatas were composed for large and small groupings as well as for solo instruments. Composers gradually evolved standard procedures for key relationships as well as number of movements.

SONATA

When sonatas were written during the Baroque period, the number of movements was variable. In the Classic period, three or four

Neo-Classic painters include David (1748–1825) and Ingres (1780–1867), both of whom considered the formal arrangement of a painting most important. They chose to portray subjects from ancient Greek and Roman mythology, emphasizing line, contour, and the symmetrical arrangement of figures and objects. They brought impeccable precision to their works, rendering objects with exactness to the most minute detail. David became the official painter to Napoleon and even followed him into exile.

Neo-Classic paintings of the late eighteenth century reflect the same concern for symmetry, balance, and restraint that may be heard in Classical music of the same period. *The Oath of the Horatii*, Jacques-Louis David, French, 1786, oil on canvas.

Courtesy of The Toledo Museum of Art, gift of Edward Drummond Libbey.

movements became standard. Multi-sectioned sinfonias, such as the Italian and French overture, were undoubtedly sources of inspiration for the Classical sonata. During the Classic period, a sonata written for symphony orchestra came to be called a *symphony*, and was almost always in four movements. The form is relatively unchanged to this day.

First Movement: Sonata-Allegro Form.   The first movement of a symphony is *sonata-allegro*, a form that has been discussed in Chapter Eight. This form has standard key relationships. The Exposition presents two themes, like two characters in a novel or drama. When theme one is major, theme two is in the dominant major, but if theme one is minor, theme two will be relative major. These contrasts of tonality help differentiate each theme. In addition, composers further contrasted their themes by making the first bold and dramatic, and the second lyric. The first, at least in orchestral sonatas, may be played by strings, the second by woodwinds. In the Development, the middle section of the sonata-allegro movement, these themes, singly or in combination, are brought into conflict by sudden modulation, polyphonic treatment, and changes of dynamics and timbre. In the Recapitulation, both themes reappear sequentially in the original tonality of the first theme, thus resolving the musical conflict of the middle section. Since tension and release are inherent, the sonata-al-legro form is a good example of Classical duality and symmetry.

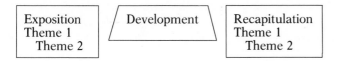

Composers liked this structure because it proved aesthetically satis-fying to them and to their audiences. Although the plan is somewhat formulaic, they found pleasure in using the formula creatively, such as in moving from one tonality to the next, adding a slow introduction, or appending transitional and ending material, such as interludes and codettas. Much as a novelist or playwright can provide new insight within a basic plot design, composers of the Classic period were continually able to bring freshness and surprise to an established form.

As the term "sonata-allegro" suggests, the opening movement of a symphony is moderately fast in tempo. The tonality at the opening is re-established at the conclusion of the movement, that is, a first movement that begins in C major will also end in C major, no matter the number of modulations that occur between.

Second Movement: ABA or Theme and Variations. The second movement of a symphony is nearly always slow. Although sonata-allegro (with new themes, of course) was sometimes used for this movement, composers generally preferred a less rigidly structured design, either *ABA* or sectional theme and variation. Classical composers favored the subdominant tonality in this movement. (That is, if the first movement is in C, the second is then in F.) As with the first movement, although modulations occur within, the subdominant tonality at least begins and concludes the movement.

COMPOUND TERNARY

Third Movement: Minuet and Trio. The third movement of a symphony is *compound ternary* form, *minuet* and *trio*, with repetition of the minuet providing the third section and overall symmetry.

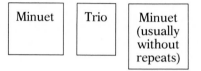

Although the minuet stays in one tonality, there is a modulation in the trio, with a return to the original key in the third section. Minuet themes generally do not occur in the trio, nor do themes from the trio appear in the surrounding sections. The tempo of this movement is usually moderate, although it can sometimes be fast, and the meter is consistently triple. Phrase structure and sectioning, as expected in a dance-derived musical form, are quite regular. It is interesting that the minuet is the only dance form of Baroque sonatas that was used by Classical composers.

Fourth Movement: Rondo. The final movement of a symphony is usually in *rondo* form, such as **ABABA**, **ABACA**, or **ABACABA**. Each A section is in the tonic tonality, while episodes, the contrasting B and C sections, modulate to closely related keys. Rondos are usually in allegro or presto tempo, thus providing a lively and playful conclusion to the four movements. Although composers sometimes used a sonata-allegro for the final movement, rondos are much more frequent.

Among the symphonists of the Classic period, the Viennese masters Mozart, Haydn, and Beethoven brought the genre to new heights. Hadyn wrote over one hundred symphonies, Mozart about fifty, and Beethoven nine. Although Beethoven especially broke with many Classical traditions after his second symphony, all three of the Viennese masters essayed their own interpretations of the form. The movements described above are only general stylistic norms for the period. In reality, each composer experimented within the genre. Some Haydn symphonies, for example, use one theme only in the first movement, but present it within the traditional key relationships, whether tonic-dominant or minor-major, as if there were two themes. His development sections are often short, with very little "development" at all. Beethoven also changed the Classical proportions of the symphony, sometimes adding a third or fourth theme in the sonata-allegro movement or using tempestuous tempos and rhythms in what had been the stately minuet, and ultimately transforming it into a scherzo. Listen to Presto (scherzo) from Beethoven's Symphony no. 7 in A major, op. 92 *(supplemental listening)* (see pages 75–76, 257, 273–274). Beethoven, a Classicist in his earlier works, turned music into a personal means of expression that eventually became the source of inspiration for many composers of the nineteenth century.

Concerto

Concertos of the Classic Period are in three movements. The minuet movement is not used since it does not lend itself to virtuoso solo treatment, the essence of a concerto. The other movements follow forms described for the symphony and string quartet (see below). The final (third) movement of the concerto is typically in rondo form.

The penchant for contrast between concertino and tutti, typical of the concerto grosso, was adapted by Baroque composer Antonio Vivaldi (1678–1741) in his *solo concertos*. Since he was an excellent   SOLO CONCERTO

Ludwig van Beethoven.

From the Joseph Muller Collection. Courtesy of the New York Public Library.

violinist himself, Vivaldi wrote over three hundred concertos for the instrument. These subsequently became a model for the later Classicists, who composed them for solo piano, violin, viola, cello, flute, bassoon, horn, harp, and clarinet, all with orchestral accompaniment. The piano and violin works, of course, were clearly in the majority during the Classic period. Composers of solo concertos include J. S. Bach's sons, Johann Christian Bach (1735–1782) and Carl Philipp Emanuel Bach (1714–1788), as well as Haydn (20 for piano, 9 for violin, 6 for cello), Mozart (25 for piano, 8 for violin), and Beethoven (5 for piano, 1 for violin).

The solo concerto exemplifies the Classical ideal of duality and balance. Solo instrument and orchestra have equal roles, with themes tossed back and forth between like musical "ping pong." Only in the **CADENZA** brilliant *cadenza*, which sums up the first movement, does the soloist have the opportunity clearly to establish his or her technical superiority.

Although each movement is similar to the corresponding movement of a symphony or string quartet, the first movement, in sonata-allegro form, is slightly modified, since there is an obligatory double exposition. In the first Exposition the orchestra presents both themes in the tonic key, but in the second,where the soloist begins, the normal key relationship between themes is observed.

Exposition one	Exposition two		Development		Recapitulation
Tonic key	Theme one—tonic				Tonic key
	Theme two— modulation				

Selection no. 66 For a demonstration of this stylistic trait, listen to Allegro, the first movement of Mozart's Horn Concerto no. 3 in E♭ major, K. 447 *(listening selections)* (see pages 208–210).

CHAMBER MUSIC

Chamber music was popular in the Classic period and includes such forms as string quartet, solo sonata, mixed quartets (three strings plus either piano, flute, or oboe), string trios, mixed trios, string quintets, and **SERENADE** mixed quintets. Among larger instrumental genres were the *serenade* **DIVERTIMENTO** (Nachtmusik) and *divertimento*, compositions written for varied instrumental groups, such as strings with some winds, and consisting of between four and ten movements. These light and entertaining pieces

Wolfgang Amadeus Mozart.

Courtesy of the New York Public Library.

are similar to the Baroque suite and were used primarily for out-of-door performances. However, they were composed with the formal schemes found in the symphony, string quartet, or solo sonata. Listen to Rondo-Allegro from Mozart's Serenade in G, K. 525, *Eine kleine Nachtmusik (listening selections)* (see page 253).

Selection no. 72

String Quartet

The *string quartet,* consisting of first and second violin, viola, and cello, became the most important genre of chamber music during the Classic period. These instruments are able to play a combined range of seven octaves, with more homogeneity of sound than any other combination of instruments. A string quartet, which may be considered a sonata for four string instruments, uses the four-movement structure of the symphony. The length and scope of a quartet, of course, is smaller and more intimate. The major composers of quartets are Haydn (83), Luigi Boccherini (1743–1805) (91), Beethoven (16), and Mozart (26).

Solo Sonata

Although a solo sonata has the three-movement structure of the concerto, it is smaller in scale and less dramatic. Some were written in two movements, others in four. Piano sonatas are unaccompanied, while those for other instruments use piano accompaniment. Beethoven especially favored the genre and wrote thirty-two sonatas for the piano. Haydn composed forty-nine.

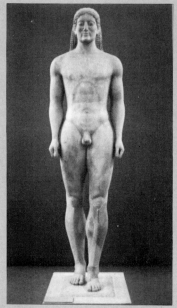

Chateau at Cheverny, a building with Classic form and symmetry.
Photo by Daniel E. Arthur.

An ancient statue with Classic proportions, restraint, and symmetry. Kroisos: Kouros from Anavysos, c. 525 B.C., marble.

National Museum, Athens. Photo by Daniel E. Arthur.

Sculptors of the eighteenth century were inspired by statues of the ancient world to produce works with elegance and simplicity that idealized humanity into almost god-like proportions. Symmetry and form became important attributes, manifested in statues with two gracefully matched and balanced sides. Neo-Classic sculptors include Canova (1757–1822), Flaxman (1755–1826), and the American, Hiram Powers (1805–1873). Painting, sculpture, and

Neo-Classical sculpture showed the restraint and emphasis on form also characteristic of music of the same period. *Bust of Voltaire,* Jean Antoine Houdon, French, 1776, marble.

architecture of eighteenth-century America also reflected Neo-Classic attitudes. Leaders and government figures were painted in godlike settings. Many of our government buildings show a Classic ordering of elements, including the use of triangular pediments, domes, and fluted columns typical of ancient Greek and Roman buildings. Neo-Classicism in the visual arts, however, was only a flicker between the exuberance of Baroque masters, like Rembrandt and Rubens, and Romantic painters who found Classical rules too restrictive for the post-French Revolution world.

VOCAL MUSIC

While instrumental music grew in importance during the eighteenth century, vocal music also flourished, with opera as its most important form.

Opera

In the first half of the eighteenth century, the focus of opera composition and innovation was in Naples. Here, opera had become a series of arias, the chorus seldom being used. Plots became stylized, artificial, dealing with complicated situations and impossible intrigues. Leading hero roles were portrayed by castrati. This type of Italian opera, called opera seria, was the favored form throughout Europe.

In the same period, a second type of opera developed from the practice of interpolating comic scenes within and between the acts of an opera seria. Secondary, low-life characters such as maids, servants, and merchants were placed in comic situations, with the intent of providing relief from the main drama. Fast singing and ensembles characterized these comic scenes. This developed into opera buffa, where there is less emphasis on solo arias and more on *parlando recitative*, a rapid delivery of dialogue in half-spoken, half-sung style. Women were eventually included in the casts and the bass voice also became popular.

PARLANDO RECITATIVE

Although Classical composers wrote both types of opera, seria and buffa, preference gradually shifted during the period to opera buffa.

Christoph Willibald Gluck (1714–1787) almost single-handedly reformed opera by returning to its dramatic integrity. Gluck specifically sought librettos of literary merit for his operas, with subjects including Greek myths, and wrote music that would enhance a dramatic situation rather than merely allow a singer to display his or her technical ability. He used the orchestra to provide dramatic unity, recitative to advance the plot. Solo singers were required to sing their written melodic lines instead of improvising ornaments at will. Gluck also wrote for chorus, and his overtures reflect the mood of the opera instead of providing only a fanfare. In a sense, Gluck brought back to opera much of the original vigor that had been lost since 1600, and anticipated the later "heroic" operas of the nineteenth century. Although his operas have not remained in the repertoire because of their rather stylized plots, he influenced his contemporaries, especially Mozart.

Of the twenty operas Mozart wrote, only two are considered opera seria; he preferred the vehicle of opera buffa, at least for his works in Italian. Mozart was a master of delineating characters through music. The plots of his operas are often complex, comic elements are almost

Scene from Mozart's *Don Giovanni*, with James Morris in the title role. The Don has many loves, all of which are cited in Leoporello's "Catalog Aria."

Photo by James Heffernan. Courtesy of the Metropolitan Opera Association.

always present, even in the more serious works, such as *Don Giovanni*. Recitative typically alternates with arias. Mozart's Italian operas include *The Marriage of Figaro, Così Fan Tutte,* and *Don Giovanni,* the last-named of which combines seria and buffa elements. Listen to

Selection no. 43 "Madamina, Il Catalogo" from Mozart's *Don Giovanni (listening selections)* (see pages 106–107). Although the subject, the Don's infidelity, is a serious matter, Leoporello portrays it rather comically.

Allegro

Pret - ty la - dy!   Here's a list   I would show you,
Ma - da - mi - na!   Il ca - ta - lo - go e que - sto,

Andante con moto

Is a____ maid - en   fair____ and slen - der
Nel - la____ bion - da   e - gli ha l'u - san - za

Mozart also wrote folk opera in German, called *Singspiel,* in which   SINGSPIEL
spoken dialogue is used instead of recitative. His best-known work in
this idiom is *The Magic Flute.*

Oratorios and Masses

In addition to opera, Classical composers continued to write oratorios,
Masses, and related church works. Haydn wrote two oratorios, *The
Creation* and *The Seasons,* as well as fourteen Masses. Mozart wrote
fifteen Masses as well as a *Requiem* (left incomplete at his death but
later finished by Süssmayr). These works combine chorus, soloists, and
orchestra, as in the Baroque period, but the preference, as with all
Classical music, is for homophony, blended timbres, and slower harmonic rhythms than in the Baroque.

SUMMARY

Classical music is known by its simplicity and restraint. Music written
between 1750 and 1825 often uses simple, folk-like melodies with
homophonic accompaniment, in which phrase structure and sections
are regular. A clear beat in either duple, triple, or quadruple meter is
common. Homogeneous instrumental families are preferred and
dynamic levels are equally restrained.

The symphony orchestra developed during this period and instrumental music generally became more important than vocal.
Among instrumental genres, the symphony, string quartet, solo concerto, and solo sonata are most important, all of which are multimovement works in either three or four movements. The first movement is
typically sonata-allegro form, while the second movement is a slow
ABA or theme and variations. A minuet and trio is used as the third
movement in symphonies and string quartets, and a rondo is typical
as the final movement in all sonatas.

Although vocal music is generally eclipsed in importance by instrumental, operas continued to be written in both seria and buffa
styles, and even oratorios and Masses were composed.

STUDY GUIDELINES

KEY TERMS AND CONCEPTS

Alberti Bass
Classicism
Crook
Double Exposition
Minuet and Trio
Opera Buffa
Opera Seria
Rococo
Rondo

Singspiel
Solo Concerto
Solo Sonata
Sonata
Sonata-allegro form
String Quartet
Style Galant
Symphony

CHAPTER REVIEW

Match items in the two columns. Answers in Appendix.

1. _____ Rococo
2. _____ Alberti bass
3. _____ crook
4. _____ symphony
5. _____ sonata-allegro form
6. _____ compound ternary form
7. _____ string quartet
8. _____ cadenza

A. sonata for orchestra
B. minuet and trio
C. brilliant solo passage at end of the first movement of a concerto
D. broken chord accompaniment
E. form for first movement of sonatas
F. sonata for two violins, viola, cello
G. style galant
H. additional tubing for a brass instrument

CHRONOLOGY OF MUSIC OF THE CLASSIC ERA (1750–1825)

*Louis Nicolas Clérambault	1676–1749
*Georg Philipp Telemann	1681–1767
*Jean Philippe Rameau	1683–1764

*Domenico Scarlatti	1685–1757
*François Couperin	1688–1733
*Giovanni Battista Sammartini	1701–1775
Christoph Willibald Gluck	1714–1787
*Georg Christoph Wagenseil	1715–1777
*Georg Matthias Monn	1717–1750
*Johann Stamitz	1717–1757
Carl Philipp Emanuel Bach	1714–1788
Franz Joseph Haydn	1732–1809
Johann Christian Bach	1735–1782
Michael Haydn	1737–1806
Karl Ditters von Dittersdorf	1739–1799
Luigi Boccherini	1743–1805
Wolfgang Amadeus Mozart	1756–1791
Luigi Cherubini	1760–1842
Ludwig von Beethoven	1770–1827

*Pre-Classic.

FOR FURTHER LISTENING

Beethoven	Piano Concerto no. 2 in B♭ major, op. 19
	Symphony no. 1 in C major, op. 21
Boccherini	String Quartets (91)
	String Quintets (125)
Clementi	Keyboard sonatas and sonatinas
Gluck	*Iphigénie en Aulide* (opera)
	Iphigénie en Tauride (opera)
Haydn	*The Seven Last Words*
	St. Cecilia's Mass
	Symphonies
	no. 45 in f♯ minor (*Farewell*)
	no. 101 in D major (*Clock*)
Mozart	*Così Fan Tutte*
	The Magic Flute (opera)
	Quintet in A major for Clarinet and String
	Quartet, K. 581
	Quartet in C major, K. 465
	Symphonies
	no. 39 in E♭ major, K. 543
	no. 41 in C major, K. 551

CHAPTER FIFTEEN

THE ROMANTIC ERA: 1825-1900

❖

GENERAL CHARACTERISTICS
INSTRUMENTAL MUSIC
VOCAL MUSIC

SUMMARY
STUDY GUIDELINES

The ideals of Classicism were short-lived, and the political and social upheavals of the late eighteenth century, manifest in the American, French, and Industrial Revolutions, ushered in a new order for the arts as well. This movement, which endured for all of the nineteenth century, and continues to some degree in the present, is called *Romanticism*. It was first apparent in the work of the German writers Goethe, Schiller, and Heine, but soon spread to England, especially in the literature of Byron, Scott, and Wordsworth. The painters Delacroix, Géricault, and Goya were seized by its spirit and even the late works of Mozart, such as *Don Giovanni*, allude to Romanticism. Many of Beethoven's works written after 1800 are clearly Romantic.

Romanticism in the arts grew out of the revolutionary spirit of the times. The word "romantic" derives from "romance" and deals with the emotional side of humanity. There was new freedom in the arts, freedom from the forms and restraints of Classicism. Romantic literature presented medieval tales of knights, damsels, and chivalry, when the world was full of strangeness, wonder, and even mysticism. Romantic artists avoided Classical subject matter and painted scenes drawn from historical and literary sources, including fantastic, shocking, and exotic subjects. They also began to portray current events, whether wars or massacres, in a realistic fashion. Satire was evident in the works of both writers and painters. Romantic artists in general portrayed a love for nature. In the second half of the century, nationalistic elements began to assert themselves.

Romantic composers similarly seized the new spirit, beginning gradually and then developing new musical genres, such as lieder and tone poems, while adapting the older Classical structures to fit this new age of personal expression. Although composers drew upon elements of the Classic and Baroque periods, they shaped these in the most personal manner yet found in music history.

All composers of the Baroque period sound somewhat alike, since style preferences were so universal. This was also true to a large extent in the Classic period. But in the Romantic period, composers began to sound unique. Chopin is not easily confused with Wagner, nor Tchaikovsky with Brahms. Each composer has an individual style and, as a result, generalizations concerning Romantic music have to

Dramatic treatment of scenes of turbulence were favored subjects of Romantic painters. *Arabs Skirmishing in the Mountains,* Eugene Delacroix, French, 1863, oil on canvas.

Courtesy of the National Gallery of Art, Washington, Chester Dale Fund.

cover a much greater range (and are perhaps more questionable) than those for earlier style periods.

GENERAL CHARACTERISTICS

When traits of Romantic music are discussed, a dichotomy frequently emerges regarding size of compositions. Some symphonies and operas grew to enormous proportions, but others, notably character pieces, short descriptive compositions usually for piano, and lieder, are miniature by comparison. Either extreme, whether a composition lasting five hours or one of two minutes, demonstrates the new freedom inherent in Romanticism. A composer could create a work that fulfilled his or her personal need, at whatever length or complexity that required. As a result, some Romantic music is simple, some quite virtuoso in nature. Despite this broad scope of personal choices possible in music of the Romantic era, the following generalizations may be observed.

Rhythm

Rhythm in early Romantic music was very little changed from the styles and practices already familiar from earlier eras, but grew more varied and distinctive as the century progressed. There are more fluctuations in tempo than are found in Classical and Baroque works. When quadruple meters were employed, composers frequently used syncopation and cross-rhythms to obscure the traditional arrangement of strong and weak beats, thus heightening tension. Composers preferred either extremely slow or fast tempos, often precisely noting these with metronomic markings. Style continued to be described in Italian (although later in the language of the composer, especially German or French) and many expressive terms were used, including:

Animato	animated
Canto espressivo	an expressive song
Cantabile	in a singing style
Dolce	sweetly
Maestoso	majestically
Poco f: poco rit.	somewhat loud and somewhat slowed down
Ritenuto	held back in tempo

Melody

Melody was especially emphasized in Romantic music, tending to be cast in longer phrase structures that were less symmetrical than those in Classical music. As a result, cadences are not as clear. Many melodies are warm, emotional, and memorable. Although major and minor scales are frequently the basis for melodies, chromaticism was favored after 1850. The chromatic scale, which uses all twelve pitches of an octave, made available added notes in a melody, as well as possibilities of richer harmonies and a variety of modulations.

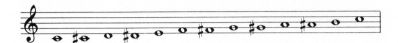

Tension and release, present to a degree in all style periods, was particularly heightened in melodies of the Romantic period. Listen to *In the Hall of the Mountain King* from Grieg's *Peer Gynt Suite II (listening selections)* (see page 43). This example uses one melody, but builds tension through the use of both accelerando and crescendo.

Selection no. 18

Harmony

The observations regarding harmony during the nineteenth century are similar to those concerning melody. Although major and minor tonalities predominated, modulation was increasingly favored, particularly to distant and unrelated keys, and tonality became less important as a structural device and more an expedient for providing color and tension. Chromatic and modal harmonies were used and triads were extended to sevenths, ninths, elevenths, and thirteenths, all of which add dissonance, color, and tension to the music. Although homophony generally predominated, all textures except heterophonic were in evidence.

Dynamics

Dynamics became both louder and softer. Composers used markings such as "ppp" or "fff," sometimes changing quickly between these extremes. Crescendo, diminuendo, and sforzando were all employed. In contrast to the restrained and graceful changes inherent in Classicism, music of the nineteenth century may change dramatically from one moment to the next. Romantic music is thus volatile and dramatic, since it expresses a constantly shifting variety of moods, temperaments, and personalities. Listen to Allegro Energico e Passionato, Più Allegro from Brahms's Symphony no. 4 in e minor, op. 98 *(supplemental listening)* (see pages 249–251).

Form

As was true in the classic period, form and timbre changed perhaps more than other elements during the Romantic era.

Anton Dvořák.

Drawing by Lupas. Courtesy of the New York Public Library.

Although composers of the early nineteenth century continued to use the forms of the late eighteenth century, especially theme and variation, rondo, and sonata-allegro, they were less rigidly structured and organized than before. Sectioning became less distinct, so that one section might receive more emphasis than another. Key relationships were no longer used to delineate these sections. The traditional forms were reshaped and molded to fit the individual style and expression of the composer. Listen to Allegretto grazioso from Dvořák's Symphony no. 8 in G major, op. 88 *(listening selections)* (see pages 47–48, 228). Although it was traditional to cast this movement in triple time, in the coda Dvořák changed to duple time in a spirited tempo, thus deviating from earlier (eighteenth-century) norms.

Selection no. 21

Similarly, new forms were created throughout the century to fit the spirit of the times. In addition to the symphony, other familiar forms were adapted and new ones evolved, including character pieces, lieder, suites, concert overtures, cycles, tone poems, and program symphonies. Compositions more frequently use extramusical associations than in the Classic and Baroque periods, when instrumental music was largely absolute.

Timbre

Tone color (timbre) available to the composer was also expanded considerably in the Romantic period through technological changes in many instruments. A new system of fingering (Boehm) for woodwinds allowed performers to play intricate melodies. The addition of valves on trumpet and French horn provided greater versatility. Improvements in percussion instruments, such as the pedal on timpani, and the addition of mallet instruments (xylophone, marimba), provided added color in the orchestra. In general, the symphony orchestra became bigger, with many traditional instrument families adding alto and tenor counterparts. Witness the makeup of the orchestra used by Hector Berlioz (1803–1869) in his compositions, which included:

first violins (in three sections)	two trumpets, two cornets
second violins	four French horns
violas	three trombones
cellos (often in two sections)	two tubas
double basses	four timpani
two harps	bass drum
two flutes, one piccolo	cymbals
two oboes, one English horn (alto oboe)	snare drum
two clarinets, one E♭ (sopranino) clarinet	tubular chimes
four bassoons	

Improvements in the concert harp (double-action pedals) and the invention of new instruments, such as the celesta, provided additional

Left, percussionist on xylophone; right, variety of mallets for percussion instruments. Romantic composers incorporated additional instruments in their orchestra, largely because of vast technological improvements. This included the percussion family, where a variety of playing techniques and mallets allowed increased variety in timbres produced.

Painters of the Romantic period turned to revolutionary themes that embodied the tenets of liberty, equality, and fraternity. Goya (1746–1828) recorded his impressions of Spanish rulers and the horrors of the French invasion of Spain during Napoleonic times, producing works often bordering on the bizarre and fantastic. Géricault's (1791–1824) works include *The Raft of the Medusa,* a painting of a sea disaster in 1818 that left survivors of the ship Medusa adrift on a raft for three weeks. Its exhibition in Paris in 1819 shocked traditional painters but was applauded by the Romanticists. Delacroix (1798–1863) used vivid color to bring emotion to his works. As with Romantic music, artists sought not only to portray their vision of reality, but to express themselves fully in the artistic process. As a result, form, balance, and symmetry were often subordinated to the sheer emotional impact of the work.

Romantic painters, such as Delacroix, portrayed emotionalism and passion in their canvases. *The Lion Hunt,* Eugene Delacroix, French, 1858, oil on canvas.

Courtesy of the Museum of Fine Arts, Boston, S.A. Denio Collection. Purchased from Sylvanus Adam Denio Fund.

ORCHESTRATION   color for the Romantic composer, and *orchestration* making use of this enlarged palette became a study in its own right. Both Berlioz and Nicolai Rimsky-Korsakov (1844–1908) wrote books on this burgeoning discipline.

Professionalism

The rise of conservatories and universities for training composers and musicians generally raised the overall professional level for both. The conductor, rarely present in Baroque ensembles and only incipient in Classic times, emerged as a larger-than-life performer whose instrument was the composite timbre of the gigantic Romantic orchestra. Listen to the Prelude to Act III of Wagner's *Lohengrin (listening selections)* (see pages 33–34, 313), a work whose complexities can be held together only by the strong hand of a dynamic conductor.

Selection no. 10

Social Changes

The role of the composer and musician changed in the nineteenth century. Whereas composers of earlier periods had been servants, employed by churches or nobility to produce and perform new music, the French Revolution and its aftermath ended this patronage system to a large extent. Composers now worked for themselves, seeking commissions from a variety of patrons rather than one prince or bishop. The emerging middle class began to demand music, a need met through public concerts and recitals supported by ticket sales. Since the public gradually became interested in older works as well as the new, the concept of historical masterpieces was established. Although the composer was freer in one sense, the newly commercial nature of musical performance entailed no assurance that a work would be heard or purchased. Unless they had been born into wealthy families, composers sometimes lived a hand-to-mouth existence. Others earned a living by teaching, performing, conducting, or by writing musical reviews for newspapers and magazines, rather than from musical composition. Although some composers found a rich patron, many had to scrape to survive in the brave new world of "free-lance" artists. Only in the twentieth century has a patronage system of sorts, in the form of government or university foundations and grants, been re-established for composers.

INSTRUMENTAL MUSIC

Symphonic Literature and the Concerto

Composers of the first half of the nineteenth century continued to write symphonies in the four-movement format favored by Classicists, but the results are often programmatic, as in Berlioz's *Symphonie Fantastique* or Mendelssohn's *Italian* Symphony. Listen to the Allegro Vivace from Mendelssohn's Symphony no. 4 *(Italian)* in A major, op. 90 *(supplemental listening)* (see pages 163–164). The spirit and vigor of this movement were Mendelssohn's method of describing the sunny, bright land of Italy.

Symphony. The symphony generally became longer during the Romantic era. Movements were added, often performed without a clear break between. Additional themes could be introduced when sonata-allegro form was used. The Classical minuet and trio evolved into scherzo and trio, an innovation for which Beethoven is responsible. Themes were used cyclically throughout and human voices sometimes were added to the symphonic sound.

Other Symphonic Forms. One innovation of the period is the *symphonic poem (tone poem)*, a programmatic work in one movement. Franz Liszt (1811–1886) is credited with inventing the genre. Since the tone poem either describes a setting or provides a narrative, changes of mood are inherent, creating variety and contrast among all of the musical elements. Listen to Smetana's *The Moldau (supplemental listening)* (see pages 160–162), which describes a river in Bohemia, from its source to its final flow into the ocean. The *concert overture* is similar to a tone poem except that its form, as described in Chapter 10, is stricter.

SYMPHONIC POEM

TONE POEM

CONCERT
OVERTURE

SYMPHONIC SUITE

Symphonic suites were popular during the era, but they are not necessarily based on dances, as were earlier versions of the form. Most consist of several short, programmatic movements, such as Mussorgsky's *Pictures at an Exhibition*. Others are adapted from the ballet, in which case there is more attention to the traditional forms. Listen to an example of the latter, the Trepak from Tchaikovsky's *Nutcracker Suite (listening selections)* (see pages 174–175).

Selection no. 58

Concerto. Romantic concertos utilize the full colors of the symphony. Although the three-movement scheme remained from earlier eras, the double exposition was generally abandoned, thus allowing the soloist to enter at the opening of the first movement. All solo concertos were written for virtuoso performances, emphasis being on technique and musical prowess. As a result, cadenzas became especially long and involved. The piano was the most favored solo instrument. The balance inherent between soloist and orchestra in the Classical concerto became a relationship of struggle, conflict, and battle between the two. As is true with all Romantic music, cyclic themes may occur between movements.

Solo Piano

The middle-class audience that emerged in the Romantic era enjoyed virtuoso performance, and the piano became a preferred medium. As a result, an extensive body of piano literature developed during the period, often written by composers who were also performers of their own works.

Niccolò Paganini (1782–1840) was perhaps the most renowned violinist of all time. As a youth, he displayed a musical talent so astounding he was recognized as a "wonderchild." To many, his amazing technique on the violin did not seem humanely possible. Paganini's power, tone control, Romantic passion, and intense performance style set him apart from other violin virtuosos of his time. Along with his rather diabolic features, such wondrous tricks as playing the entire *Witches' Dance* on one string often stirred rumors that he was in league with the devil, if not the devil himself. Although famous for his violin concerts and compositions, he was also an accomplished guitarist. His most famous work for violin is *Twenty-four Caprices*, a set of variations.

Technological Changes. Although the piano had been invented in the eighteenth century, it remained largely unchanged for the first one hundred years of its existence. The manufacturers began to incorporate new structures and inventions. Sébastien Érard (1752–1831) developed *double escapement* in 1821, a device that allows any key to be repeated rapidly, since the hammer does not need to return to its original position before it is struck again. In 1825 Alpheus Babcock invented a one-piece *cast-iron frame* that allowed thicker strings to be used. Since the frame could now support eighteen tons of tension, the piano's dynamic range and brilliance were increased. Babcock also patented *cross-stringing* in 1830. High and middle strings fan across the entire sounding board of the piano, the bass strings crossing over above them. This gave the piano a warmer, richer sound that added to its increasing popularity.

DOUBLE ESCAPEMENT

CAST-IRON FRAME

CROSS-STRINGING

Many virtuoso piano pieces were written during the period. The rising middle class also purchased pianos and they became an appropriate fixture in many nineteenth-century parlors, where they were used for amateur music making. Listen to Brahms's *Ballade* in g minor, op. 118 *(listening selections)* (see pages 42, 299).

Selection no. 17

Genres. Composers of Romantic piano music include Beethoven, Schubert, Schumann, Mendelssohn, and Brahms. Although Beethoven alone wrote thirty-two piano sonatas and twenty-one sets of variations, the spirit of time also led to new types of piano compositions, smaller and often nationalistically derived. The waltz, polonaise, and mazurka became the popular stylized dances of this century, maintaining the form, rhythm, and energy of the original dances as performed in the ballroom. New forms also developed, including the fantasy, ballade, and romance. The nocturne, a character piece in which the melody is heard over an arpeggiated accompaniment, became popular with the salon society. Although first written by John Field (1782–1837), an Irish

NOCTURNE

ETUDE   composer, it was Chopin who made the form his own. The etude, another admired type of character piece, was more virtuosic. Other character pieces include bagatelle, impromptu, capriccio, prelude, and intermezzo. Since character pieces are miniatures, they are usually performed in cycles or sets to provide an appropriate proportion of a recital.

Chopin and Liszt.   Chopin and Liszt represent the new style of piano writing. Chopin composed almost exclusively for the piano, preferring short character pieces to longer ones requiring extended development. His music is melodic and often encompasses daring harmonic modulations as well. Listen to Chopin's Etude no. 12 in c minor, op. 10

Selection nos. 4, 12   *(listening selections)* (see pages 8, 294–295) and Mazurka no. 24 in C major, op. 33, no. 3 *(listening selections)* (see pages 33, 299). Although technical ability is frequently required for its performance, Chopin's music also includes much that is lyric and poetic.

In contrast, Franz Liszt wrote piano compositions almost totally defined by their demands for great virtuosity. Modeling his approach to the piano on that of Niccolò Paganini to the violin, Liszt elevated piano technique to new levels. His music shows less concern for form, more for brilliance and show. He became a renowned concert artist, traveling extensively in Europe, where he played his own compositions as well as piano transcriptions of pieces originally composed by others for symphony orchestra. Many European villagers first heard the music of Bach, Paganini, and Wagner, as well as the symphonies of Beethoven, in these piano transcriptions.

Franz Liszt's (1811–1886) technical ability on the piano made him a legend in his own time. Born in Hungary, his talent was recognized early by his parents, and they moved to Vienna where young Franz was able to study piano and composition with celebrated teachers. Although he was a foreigner and therefore denied admission to the Paris Conservatory, he continued to study privately. Upon his debut in 1824, Liszt became a celebrity and with his prodigious technique remained one all his life. Often described as the "Paganini of the Piano," Liszt in his virtuosic performances was an actor on stage, moving at some concerts to a second piano so the entire audience could watch his hands. His programs sometimes included improvisations on a theme offered from musicians in the audience.

In addition to his fame as a concert pianist, Liszt was also a composer and reformer of modern piano technique. He created the tone poem—a one-movement symphonic work—most famously displayed in his composition, *Les Préludes*. He also composed piano concertos, numerous character pieces, and the brilliant *Hungarian Rhapsodies*.

Chamber Music

Chamber music, although heard less frequently than in the Classic period, continued to be part of the musical fabric of the Romantic era. One of the most significant composers in this category was Brahms. His works utilized many varying combinations of instruments, including horn trio, piano trios, string quartets, piano quintet, plus numerous sonatas. Musicians, dependent upon commissions for their livelihood, used a practical approach in composition. With the exception of the few who specialized in works for solo voice or piano, most produced in a variety of genres, including chamber music.

VOCAL MUSIC

The Solo Song

Solo song developed from the same impulse as did short piano compositions, the challenge of presenting a story, mood, or form in a compressed two or three minutes. The earlier development inspired composers, and cultivation of the piano as a viable accompanying instrument was also crucial.

Lieder.   Writing for voice can weight the relationship between text and music in favor of either element. In an operatic aria, for example, musical considerations generally predominate, whereas in recitative the text is more important. In *lieder*, however, a balance is achieved between text and music. Each is important and requires equal emphasis.

Lieder are for solo voice and piano (sometimes orchestra). The relationship between text and music is so important that translation is rarely appropriate. Lieder were not invented in the Romantic period. Classical composers such as Haydn and Beethoven wrote lieder, but it was not until the early nineteenth century that the genre became a popular mode of expression with both composers and audiences. Franz Schubert wrote over six hundred, each showing a remarkable sensitivity in balancing music and text. Listen to three examples of Schubert's art: *Gretchen Am Spinnrade*, op. 2 (see pages 44–45, 301–302), "Who Is Sylvia?," op. 106 (see pages 105, 243–244); and *Erlkönig*, op. 1 (see pages 257–259) *(listening selections)*. Although lieder written in earlier periods had been strophic, Schubert often modified the second or third strophe to fit the text, a form called *modified-strophic*. He also used *through-composed* settings, as in *Erlkönig*, in which the music varies throughout to fit the changing mood and text. Schubert's model ultimately became the standard for the entire century.

The other major composers of lied include Schumann (over one

Selection nos. 19, 42, 73

MODIFIED-STROPHIC
THROUGH-COMPOSED

hundred), Mendelssohn, and Brahms. Hugo Wolf (1860–1903) is the most important composer of lieder in the second half of the century. The form constituted almost his entire musical output.

Chansons.   Solo song literature developed in France during the same period for the same reasons as did German lied: the presence of excellent texts by French poets, especially Verlaine and Baudelaire. Somewhat more popular in nature than lieder, French solo songs are called *chansons.* French composers utilizing the form include Duparc (1848–1933), Fauré (1845–1924), Gounod (1818–1893), and Chausson (1855–1899). (Russian composers writing solo songs at this time include Glinka [1804–1857], Tchaikovsky, and Mussorgsky.)

LIEDERKREIS   ***Song Cycles.***   *Song Cycles (liederkreis)* also developed in this century. A cycle may include songs set to texts by a single poet, as Schumann's *Dichterliebe* (on Heine) or Faure's *La Bonne Chanson* (on Verlaine). Alternatively, a theme or subject, however sketchy, may unify the work. Schubert's *Winterreise,* twenty-four songs set to poems by Müller, describes the mental journey of a person approaching insanity.

Opera

Solo piano music is a sharp contrast to the monumental forms that developed in Romantic symphonies. The same parallel may be drawn between solo song and opera. Operas developed into gigantic productions, often with distinct regional and nationalistic flavors. Italy, the birthplace of opera, remained the most conservative during the century, but German and French opera became distinctive. After 1850, regional influences were felt as well in Russia and Bohemia (Czechoslovakia).

Italy.   Italian Romantic opera in the first half of the nineteenth century is typified by Rossini (1792–1868), Donizetti (1797–1848), and Bellini (1801–1835). The changes advocated by Gluck were incorporated to an extent in Italian opera, thus encouraging greater unity between the drama and music. Nonetheless, the emphasis continued to be on solo singers and arias, with the orchestra serving primarily as accompaniment. Listen to "Ecco Ridente" from Rossini's *The Barber*

Selection no. 41   *of Seville (listening selections)* (see pages 102–104).

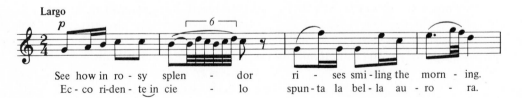

Courtesy of the New York Public Library.

Scene from Verdi's *Otello.* Some of Verdi's operas were based on plays of Shakespeare. Otello is seen in the lower left, Desdemona in the center.

In the second half of the century, Giuseppe Verdi (1813–1901) dominated Italian opera. In addition to basing his works on subjects of dramatic worth, he enlarged the orchestra, giving it a significant role in binding the drama together. His overtures introduced themes to be used in the opera; ballet was added, and choruses became integral. Verdi's operas show a lessened division between aria and recitative. The singing tends to be continuous. An aspect of many operas of the late Romantic period is their use of heightened realism or *verismo.* Giacomo Puccini (1858–1924), the most important Italian operatic composer in the years following Verdi, made use of some earthy verismo elements in his works, particularly in *La Bohème* and the one-act *Il Tabarro,* but the composers who embraced this style most completely were Pietro Mascagni (1863–1945), in *Cavalleria Rusticana,* and Ruggiero Leoncavallo (1858–1919), in *Pagliacci;* these two short works are often performed together on the same program.

Opera became, in a sense, a slice of life, with characters drawn from everyday events and situations. Listen to "Un Bel Di" from Puccini's *Madame Butterfly (listening selections)* (see pages 97–98). Although *Butterfly* can be regarded as part of the veristic movement because of its contemporary setting and realistically drawn characters, it can also be considered a descendant of the older operatic tradition

VERISMO

Selection no. 39

Winter scene from
Act III of Puccini's
La Bohème.

Courtesy of the Arizona Opera Company.

in view of its exotic Japanese locale and the passion and tragedy of its climax.

Andante molto calmo

One _____ fine day we'll no - tice   A thread _____ of smoke a - ris - ing
Un _____ bel di, ve - dre - mo   le - var - si un fil di fu - mo

France. French opera continued many of the traditions of opéra-comique but a parallel stream became grandiose, eventually developing into *grand opera* with continuous singing. Plots in the latter style are historical and characters are portrayed as being larger than life. These characteristics occur most notably in the works of Giacomo Meyerbeer (1791–1864). After 1850, the two traditions were merged in *lyric opera*, which has much pageantry. Composers include Charles Gounod, Jacques Offenbach (1819–1880), Jules Massenet (1842–1912), and Georges Bizet. Listen to "Habanera" from Bizet's *Carmen (listening selections)* (see pages 98–102). *Carmen* was originally conceived in the opera-comique tradition, with spoken dialogue, but the recitatives were later set to music by another composer to make it conform to the lyric opera image.

GRAND OPERA

LYRIC OPERA

Selection no. 40

Act IV of Bizet's *Carmen*. Viorica Cortez as Carmen, Lenus Carlson as Escamillo.

Photo by James Heffernan. Courtesy of the Metropolitan Opera Association.

Allegretto, quasi andantino

Gyp - sy love is a rov - ing rap - ture, A wan - ton bird___ that___none can tame.
L'a - mour est un oi - seau re - bel - le Que nul ne peut___ ap - pri - voi - ser.

Allegretto, quasi andantino

Oh, love is just a gyp - sy lad, He nev - er could and nev - er would play fair,
L'a - mour est en - fant de Bo - heme, Il n'a ja - mais, ja - mais con - nu de loi,

Germany.　German Romantic opera, widely performed in the first half of the century, follows the tradition of *Singspiel* in which dialogue is spoken. Arias were folk-like, a suitable complement to subject matter drawn from folk tradition, including fairy tales, supernatural characters and events, and mystic settings. In general, since it was used both to weave the drama together and to accompany, the orchestra was more important in German opera than it was in Italy or France. Carl Maria von Weber (1786–1826) is the leading composer of this genre.

SINGSPIEL

Although Richard Wagner (1813–1883) wrote operas in the German Romantic tradition early in his career (*Rienzi,* 1840; *The Flying Dutchman,* 1841), gradually he evolved new techniques with results that others labeled as *music-drama.* The subject matter is similar to that of German Romantic opera, but Wagner fused all elements into a new form. Music-drama uses *leitmotifs* (leading motive), musical themes that may symbolize ideas, characters, moods, emotions, or settings. A person or object may be represented on stage by a leitmotif without physically being present. Since Wagner prepared his own libretti, greater artistic unity was achieved. He even had a festival opera house built at Bayreuth to produce his works, which continue to be performed there to the present day.

Wagner's operas are written in a continuous flow of music, whether vocal or instrumental. The orchestra, which is large and colorful, becomes a character itself, presenting leitmotifs and conveying moods as well as accompanying. There is no division into aria and recitative. Tonality was stretched to new limits through Wagner's penchant for chromaticism. His works include *Tristan und Isolde* (1859), *Parsifal* (1882), and his most mystical work, the four-opera cycle *Der Ring des Nibelungen,* consisting of *Das Rheingold* (1854), *Die Walküre* (1856), *Siegfried* (1871), and *Götterdämmerung* (1874). There is often a religious overtone to Wagner's works, with particular emphasis on the idea of redemption. An articulate writer as well as composer, Wagner expressed views on opera in *Oper und Drama,* written in 1851. His influence on opera in the nineteenth century was paralleled only by that of Verdi.

Russia and Bohemia.   Nationalistic opera began to flourish in this same period in Russia and in Bohemia. The former school was represented by works of Glinka *(A Life for the Tsar)* and Mussorgsky *(Boris Godunov),* the latter by Smetana *(The Bartered Bride)* and Dvořák *(The Devil and Kate).*

Choral Music

Choral music continued to be written during the Romantic era, in forms including Masses, requiems, and Te Deums, as well as freer settings of scriptures. The difference from the Classic period was that most of these were grandiose conceptions, generally composed for concert, not church, use. The requiems by Berlioz, Verdi, Brahms, and Fauré, for example, are monumental works. Oratorios of the period include Mendelssohn's *St. Paul* and *Elijah.* Choral works of this time were usually performed with an orchestra, sometimes with the addition of an organ.

SUMMARY

Beethoven, whose later works began to display some of the traits identified with Romanticism, became a model for many composers of the nineteenth century. Romantic music is characterized by expressive melodies, rhythmic variety, and extended and rich harmonies, as well as the use of a richer and wider variety of timbres and dynamics. Older, Classical forms were expanded, but new forms and genres also developed, including the program symphony, tone poem, concert overture, character pieces (for piano), lieder (and chanson), and regional opera. Choral and chamber music, although relatively unimportant, continued to be composed. Perhaps more important than any stylistic trait is the increased difficulty in trying to generalize. Composers became quite personal in their writing style. Romantic music marks the beginning of the age of diversity, in which striking contrasts can be observed in the practice and use of all musical materials.

STUDY GUIDELINES

KEY TERMS AND CONCEPTS

Chanson
Concert overture
Cross-stringing (piano)
Cyclic theme
Double escapement (piano)
German Romantic opera
Grand opera
Leitmotif (Leading motive)
Lieder
Modified-strophic form

Music drama
Nationalistic opera
Opéra Comique
Orchestration
Romanticism
Song cycle (Liederkreis)
Symphonic poem (Tone poem)
Symphonic suite
Verismo

CHAPTER REVIEW

Match items in the two columns. Answers in Appendix.

1. _____ verismo
2. _____ tone poem
3. _____ cyclic themes
4. _____ leitmotif
5. _____ chanson
6. _____ lieder
7. _____ liederkreis
8. _____ double escapement
9. _____ music-drama
10. _____ grand opera

A. melodies used throughout a composition to unify it
B. song cycle
C. French spectacle opera
D. French solo song
E. invention that allows rapid repetition of a piano key
F. realism
G. term for Wagner's unification of opera
H. German solo song
I. one-movement orchestral work
J. leading motive in music-drama

CHRONOLOGY OF MUSIC OF THE ROMANTIC ERA (1825–1900)

Johann Adam Hiller	1728–1804
J. A. P. Schulz	1747–1800

Sébastien Érard	1752–1831
Ludwig van Beethoven	1770–1827
John Field	1782–1837
Niccolò Paganini	1782–1840
Alpheus Babcock	1785–1842
Carl Maria von Weber	1786–1826
Giacomo Meyerbeer	1791–1864
Gioacchino Rossini	1792–1868
Franz Schubert	1797–1828
Gaetano Donizetti	1797–1848
Vincenzo Bellini	1801–1835
Hector Berlioz	1803–1869
Michael Glinka	1804–1857
Felix Mendelssohn	1809–1847
Frédéric Chopin	1810–1849
Robert Schumann	1810–1856
Franz Liszt	1811–1886
Giuseppe Verdi	1813–1901
Richard Wagner	1813–1883
Charles Gounod	1818–1893
Jacques Offenbach	1819–1880
Bedřich Smetana	1824–1884
Anton Bruckner	1824–1896
Alexander Borodin	1833–1887
Johannes Brahms	1833–1897
Georges Bizet	1838–1875
Modest Mussorgsky	1839–1881
Peter Tchaikovsky	1840–1893
Anton Dvořák	1841–1904
Jules Massenet	1842–1912
Edvard Grieg	1843–1907
Nicolai Rimsky-Korsakov	1844–1908
Gabriel Fauré	1845–1924
Henri Duparc	1848–1933
Ernest Chausson	1855–1899
Giacomo Puccini	1858–1924
Hugo Wolf	1860–1903
Gustav Mahler	1860–1911
Richard Strauss	1864–1949

FOR FURTHER LISTENING

Romantic Works (in general)

Beethoven	Symphony no. 3 in E$^\flat$ major, op. 55
	Symphony no. 9 in d minor, op. 125
Berlioz	*Symphonie Fantastique*
Bizet	*L'Arlésienne* Suite No. 2
Chopin	Character pieces
	Concertos (2)
	Sonata no. 2 in b$^\flat$ minor, op. 35
Dvořák	Symphonies (9)
Fauré	*Après un Rève*
	La Bonne Chanson
Gounod	*Faust* (opera)
Liszt	*Étude de Concert* no. 3 in D$^\flat$ major
	Faust Symphony
	Les Préludes
Mendelssohn	*A Midsummer Night's Dream*
Mussorgsky	*Pictures at an Exhibition*
Puccini	*La Bohème*
	Madame Butterfly
	Tosca
Schubert	*Die Winterreise* (song cycle)
	Ländler, op. 171
Schumann	*Dichterliebe* (song cycle)
	Fantasiestücke (piano cycle)
Tchaikovsky	Concerto no. 1 in b$^\flat$ minor for Piano and Orchestra
	Marche Slave
	Nutcracker Suite
Verdi	*Aida*
	La Traviata
	Requiem
Wagner	*Siegfried-Idyll* (tone poem)
	Tristan und Isolde

Symphonic Variations

Brahms	*Variations on a Theme by Haydn,* op. 56a
Franck	*Symphonic Variations*

Symphony with Chorus
    Beethoven   Symphony no. 9 in d minor
    Mahler   Symphony no. 2 in c minor

Various Nationalistic Styles
    Dvořák (Bohemian)   *Slavonic Dances*
    Chopin (Polish)   Mazurkas and Polonaises
    Mussorgsky (Russian)   *Boris Godounov* (opera)
    Tchaikovsky (Russian)   Quartet no. 1 in D major, Second
                                   movement

Virtuoso Compositions
    Beethoven   Sonata no. 23 in f minor
                                   (*Appassionata*)
    Chopin   Etude in C major, op. 10, no. 1
    Liszt   *La Campanella*
                                   Concerto no. 1 in E$^\flat$ major for Piano
                                   and Orchestra
                                 Étude de Concert no. 3 in D$^\flat$ major
    Mendelssohn   *Capriccio Brillant*
    Paganini   *Caprice* no. 24

CHAPTER SIXTEEN

THE MODERN ERA: THE TWENTIETH CENTURY

◆

GENERAL CHARACTERISTICS	SUMMARY
COMPOSITIONAL TRENDS	STUDY GUIDELINES

No single, clearly delineated musical style has developed in the present century. Since the individualism and diversity noted in the Romantic period have become wider spread, not only does one composer not sound like another, frequently a composer does not sound like him/herself from one composition to the next. Without the advantage of hindsight, generalizations for this century are extremely difficult to draw. There has been such profusion of works that few clear trends emerge. Mass media and excellent communication systems have enabled audiences to hear more music of all time periods, and composers have been able to express and become cognizant of new ideas to an extent unheard of in the past. New technology has allowed them to expand their sound resources and to draw upon musical ideas from all world cultures and styles. In this century, music is omnipresent.

Romanticism, of course, did not end at the turn of the century, but continued along with new thoughts and procedures that were developing in composition. Around the time of World War I, many composers began to break with tradition.

Courtesy of the New York Public Library.

Stravinsky's position in twentieth-century music is much like Pablo Picasso's in the world of art. Igor Stravinsky's *Ragtime* (cover only). Drawing by Pablo Picasso.

GENERAL CHARACTERISTICS

Tonality

Tonality was one of the first elements to change in the twentieth century. Although late Romantic music had become chromatic, using both frequent and distant modulations, major and minor sounds still dominated, much as they had since Baroque times. The basic premise of tonality is that there are established relationships among pitches, providing certain expectations as one listens. Although chromaticism weakened these relationships, it did not destroy them. Composers in this century began to try different ways of dealing with tonality, including the option of eliminating it altogether. Different scales were used, including modes, whole-tone, and quarter-tone scales, as well as two or three scales simultaneously (bi- and poly-tonality). All of these require a new set of expectations from listeners.

ATONALITY   *Atonality*, which is the total negation of tonality, came into use by the 1920s. *Twelve-tone composition* is one of the structural principles **TONE-ROW** that can be used to achieve atonality. In twelve-tone music a *tone-row* that avoids expected tonal relationships is established and used as the basic unit of composition. All twelve tones in the chromatic scale are used in any order in constructing the row, the only restriction being that no tone can be repeated until all twelve are used. The musical work is then built on this row, again requiring that all twelve tones be used, in order, before the row can begin again. Variety is provided by the possibilities of using the row in *retrograde* (backwards), *inversion* (upside down), and *retrograde-inversion* (cancrizans—upside down and backwards), as well as in transposition and harmonically.

SERIALISM   This technique is also called *serialism*, since the twelve notes of the tone row are a "serial" arrangement of pitches used throughout a composition. This approach has been the most influential musical development of the twentieth century, with an effect on the techniques and practices of almost every composer. Arnold Schoenberg (1874–1951) focused thinking concerning serialism early in the century, and it was adapted and used extensively by his associates, Anton Webern (1883–1945) and Alban Berg (1885–1935), as well. Listen to the **Selection no. 54** Prelude from Schoenberg's *Suite* for piano, op. 25 *(listening selections)* (see pages 158, 232). The counterpoint that occurs in this selection results from the presence of various versions of tone row appearing simultaneously in the upper and lower parts.

More traditional composers, like Igor Stravinsky (1882–1971) and Aaron Copland (1900–   ), who studiously avoided serialism in the first part of the century, incorporated its techniques in some of their works later in the century, although they never used it exclusively.

Harmony

Other musical elements were naturally affected by changes in tonal concepts, especially harmony. The chromaticism of the late nineteenth century created harmony that was more complex than it had been previously. Instead of the simple triadic construction of the Classic period, Romanticists used sevenths and ninths, altering these chromati-

cally within the structure and thus contributing to overall tonal ambivalence.

normal
seventh
chord

chromatically
altered seventh
chords

Twentieth-century composers not only continued this practice but also
use chords less functionally than past periods. Whereas one chord (V₇,
for example) could normally be expected to progress to another (I):

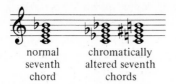

V^7 I

contemporary composers use chords as coloristic devices, not necessarily moving from one to another in a functional manner. This often
results in parallel and, thus, nonfunctional harmony, a practice with
roots in the nineteenth century, especially in the music of Claude
Debussy.

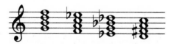

Some composers avoid triadic construction, preferring *quartal har-*
mony (built on fourths) and *clusters* (built on seconds):

QUARTAL
CLUSTER

Quartal   Cluster

as well as chords derived from tone rows.

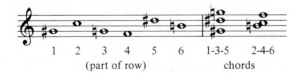

1   2   3   4   5   6   1-3-5   2-4-6

(part of row)   chords

In general, since chords now contain several pitch classes as well
as dissonant intervals, harmony has become more dissonant than in
earlier periods.

Texture

The texture of twentieth-century music is frequently polyphonic. Two or more melodies, based on one of the scale systems described above, generate their own harmony when sounded together, often resulting in harmonic dissonance. Since dissonance is treated more freely than in the past, it may never resolve to traditional consonance but, rather, be moderated only momentarily by a section with lessened dissonance. Thus, to a listener, a composition may sound totally dissonant. The change from the thick homophonic textures preferred in the nineteenth century to transparent polyphony has emphasized the clash between dissonant intervals.

Melody

Twentieth-century composers have frequently written disjunct melodies, using melodic intervals that are wide and tonally unrelated. Although singers must still perform them, melodies are less singable and memorable than in the past. Melody is simply not as important an element as it had been and one therefore hears melodies that are short, truncated, and motivic. The effect is of melodic fragments, instead of pitches closely arranged into phrases and periods. Some composers

PITCH SWEEP have replaced the traditional melodic units with *pitch sweeps* (glissandos) that provide indefinite tonal relationships and lessened stability.

Rhythm

Since the only memorable point about a melodic fragment may be its rhythmic vitality, rhythm receives more emphasis than melody in much twentieth-century music. Motives are frequently syncopated and the interplay between two or more simultaneous melodic lines can

ASYMMETRIC METER result in polyrhythms. *Asymmetric meters*, in five and seven, may be used, or meter may change for each measure. Composers commonly have preferred metric schemes other than duple and triple time. In addition, where traditional meters are written, accents are displaced by tying notes across the bar line or notating them with percussive accents (>). Music of the twentieth century generally exhibits great rhythmic variety and vitality.

Timbre

Timbre has been widely explored in this century, and its range is more diverse than ever before. Although the most obvious new sound source is the synthesizer, composers have exploited the timbral resources of traditional instruments, especially their percussive and noise-producing abilities. String players play with the wood of the bow

Strong lines and accents characterize Léger's painting, depicting the vitality and energy often heard in music of the same period. *Les Constructeurs*, Fernand Léger, French, 1950, gouache on paper.

University of Arizona Museum of Art, gift of Edward J. Gallagher, Jr.

(col legno), near the bridge *(sul ponticello)*, and with *harmonics* in addition to the traditional bowing and plucking (pizzicato) techniques. Wind players must produce double stops (two tones simultaneously), flutter-tongue, and click the keys or valves in some compositions. The piano has been played on the strings inside, on the soundboard, and on the pedals. The composer John Cage (1912–) inserted various objects inside the instrument, such as erasers, felts, and bolts, to alter the sound when a key is depressed. This is called a *prepared piano*. New notational devices have been invented by composers to indicate such innovations as harp pedal-sounds, timpani glissandos, clarinet harmonics, and flute flutter-tonguing.

Electronic amplification has changed acoustic sounds in many ways. In addition, the sound synthesizer is able to duplicate traditional sounds as well as to create new ones. Older instruments (harpsichord, guitar) have been rediscovered, and the human voice has been used much like an instrument rather than as a solo sound with accompaniment. In addition, speech intonation, *sprechstimme*, a cross between singing and speaking, has been used for some vocal compositions. Wind and percussive sounds have become equal to or more important than strings in the symphony. Despite the range of sounds now available to them, large ensembles are less favored by composers than are chamber groups with various instrumental combinations. This is due in part to the increased probability of a chamber work's being per-

COL LEGNO
SUL PONTICELLO

PREPARED PIANO

SPRECHSTIMME

formed publicly. By contrast, an avant-garde symphony might never reach the public ear because it lacks box office appeal. Listen to Varèse's *Ionisation (listening selections)* (see pages 128–131). This work shows the variety of effects that are possible with three classes of percussion instruments, those of definite, indefinite, and variable (i.e., siren) pitch.

Selection no. 50

Dynamics

The only musical elements that have not been drastically altered in the twentieth century are dynamics and form. Although Romantic composers frequently used a range of dynamics from loudest to softest within a single work, composers of this century have tended to avoid extreme internal contrasts, preferring to maintain fairly uniform levels for the duration of an individual composition. In general, dynamics have been used in objective ways. Some composers indicate the degree of loudness for each distinct pitch or phrase while others have created tension by using unchanging levels, i.e., the softest or the loudest dynamic possible. This creates a feeling of stasis, of "being" rather than the "progressing and becoming" forward motion evident in the Baroque through the Romantic periods.

Edgard Varèse in October 1957 working on the Varèse-Le Corbusier *Poème Électronique* to be presented at the 1958 Brussels World's Fair in the Phillips Pavillion designed by Le Corbusier.

Courtesy of the New York Public Library.

Form

Use of form in the twentieth century cannot be easily generalized. Although works have been written in all the established single- and multi-movement patterns of the past, composers have sought to avoid stereotypes and clichés. As a result, ternary and binary form have not been used exclusively, and additive form has been emphasized. There has also been renewed interest in the rather static quality of strophic form. In general, the length of works has been abbreviated from the monumental proportions favored in the late nineteenth century.

COMPOSITIONAL TRENDS

The diversity of all aspects of the twentieth century has led to categorization by broad social and political tendencies, including labels like capitalism, communism, and socialism. This is equally true in the arts, where a series of labels and "isms" has emerged to describe various tendencies. These have not necessarily developed chronologically or through the efforts of one composer or one country. Composers can often be placed into two or more of these categories. The remainder of this chapter will be devoted to examining, however fleetingly, some of these trends. The reader is advised that none of these trends developed in isolation. Rather, they have been source material for all composers of the late twentieth century.

Impressionism

Impressionism is a technique that developed near the end of the nineteenth century in France as a reaction to the heaviness of German Romanticism. Impressionism was first manifest in the paintings of a group of artists who had been inspired by Symbolist poetry, as well as by the advent of photography. Their paintings depict fleeting impressions—the sun rising or setting, light on a cathedral, wind blowing grass in a field. Impressionist painters lightened their palette and rendered everyday objects and events with soft edges, as impressions seen through a haze. Their atmosphere was slightly blurred since their interests were in portraying light and color on canvas, rather than clear contours and forms. Sculptors embraced a similarly unstructured style.

Debussy, a young student at the Paris Conservatory, saw the paintings of the Impressionists and was inspired to compose with the same purpose in mind: to lighten music and free it from the heaviness the French saw in late German Romanticism. Debussy is the major practitioner of Impressionism in music, but he inspired many future

Impressionistic painters applied small dabs of paint on the canvas, allowing the viewer's eye to mix the color. *Banks of the Seine, Vetheuil,* Claude Monet, French, 1880, oil on canvas.

Courtesy of the National Gallery of Art, Washington, Chester Dale Collection.

Impressionism in painting grew as a movement following an exhibit in the 1860s by a group of young painters at the Salon des Refusés in Paris. Somewhat influenced by the advent of photography, the painters emphasized light and color, unusual angles of view, and perceptions of the ephemeral, the changing, and the transient. Rejected by more traditional French artists, Impressionistic painters set up their easels outside and tried to capture the play of light and color on the surface of objects. They used tiny dabs of paint and small brush strokes, applying pure color to the canvas instead of blending the paints together. Close dabs of white and black paint, for example, from a distance created grey, blended by the viewer's perception rather than by the artist. Among Impressionistic painters are Manet (1832–1883), Monet (1840–1926), Degas (1834–1917), and Renoir (1841–1919).

French and American composers. Although the most productive period of musical Impressionism lasted only twenty years (1890–1910), as a point of view it has never disappeared.

In Impressionism, timbres are light and transparent. Woodwinds are favored over brass, muted violins and harp preferred over the entire string section. The piano was a favorite instrument of Debussy's, and his pieces evoke hazy atmospheres through the use of extreme registers of treble and bass, as well as the sustaining pedal, which allows sounds to blur together. Dynamics are generally quite soft, with only occasional louder sections occurring between softer passages.

Impressionistic sculpture. *Danaide*, Auguste Rodin, French, 1885, bronze.

University of Arizona Museum of Art, gift of the Gallagher family.

Although repetition and contrast are rarely literal in Impressionist compositions, external form is not a strongly controlling factor. Since Impressionist works are not rigidly structured, their organization is often influenced more by musical content and emotional program than

Claude Debussy.

Courtesy of the New York Public Library.

by an arbitrarily imposed format such as ABA or theme and variations.

Selection no. 27   Listen to Debussy's *Clair de Lune (listening selections)*(see pages 69–70).

Theme 1

Theme 2

Debussy often used the whole-tone scale to create the typical floating sensation of Impressionism. A whole-tone scale has no half-steps, no clear tendency tones. Its use invokes ambivalence.

Whole-tone scale

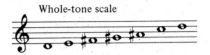

Debussy also employed harmony as a colorisitic device in his compositions. The voicing of chords is important, open positions being preferred. Chords are usually nonfunctional, with parallelism an important factor. His presentation is largely fragmentary, with musical ideas following one another swiftly in often unexpected patterns and combinations, rather than providing a smoothly synthesized surface and development. Although rhythm is notated traditionally, with an underlying beat governing time sequences, Debussy frequently obscured the beat by writing in long holds and pauses. Metric schemes are used, but the pervasive rubato provides very little feeling of strong and weak beats. The entire effect makes the passage of time seem somewhat amorphous. Listen to Debussy's "Fêtes" *(Nocturnes) (supplemental listening)*(pages 314–316). Impressionistic ideas were perpetuated in works of Debussy's younger colleague, Maurice Ravel (1875–1937), as well as by Paul Dukas (1865–1935). Other Impressionists include Ottorino Respighi (1879–1936) in Italy, Alexander Scriabin (1872–1915) in Russia, Isaac Albéniz (1860–1909) in Spain, Frederick Delius (1862–1934) in the United Kingdom, and Charles T. Griffes (1884–1920) in the United States.

Although Impressionism is not strictly a twentieth-century movement, it is pivotal in providing alternatives to German Romanticism. It has been a source of inspiration for many composers of the present century. Listen, for example, to Ravel's "Malagueña" *(Rapsodie Espag-*
Selection no. 88   *nole) (listening selections).*

Maurice Ravel.

Courtesy of the New York Public Library.

Neo-Classicism

Neo-Classicism is a trend that draws inspiration from music of the late seventeenth and eighteenth centuries, especially the works of the late Baroque masters as well as those of Haydn and Mozart, and is an ongoing consideration in this century. Like Impressionism, Neo-Classicism is a rejection of the ideals and emotionalism of Romantic music. Although composers of this movement preferred Classic restraint, moderation, and simplicity, there is one notable exception: the harmony (and thus tonality) is modern. Ferruccio Busoni (1866–1924) is credited with being the first Neo-Classicist because of his avowed dislike of Romanticism as well as his use of such titles as Sonatina,

Toccata, and Fantasia in his works. He was particularly inspired by the writing of Mozart and J. S. Bach. Other Neo-Classicists include Igor Stravinsky (in his so-called "middle period," the compositions between 1920–1940), Paul Hindemith (1895–1963), and the Russian Sergei Prokofiev (1891–1953), who wrote a work in this style called the Classical Symphony. Neo-Classicists were especially faithful to Baroque and Classical forms and genres, including the symphony, sonata, concerto grosso, toccata, sectional variations, passacaglia, and suite. They showed renewed interest in contrapuntal techniques and forms, including the fugue. Hindemith's *Ludus Tonalis* for piano, for example, is a study in Neo-Classical counterpoint. Listen to Stravinsky's "Gavotta con due Variazioni" (*Pulcinella* Suite) *(listening selections)* (see pages 22–23, 246). In addition to the use of sectional variations in this work, the clear phrase structure, lean harmony, and overall restraint display Neo-Classic traits.

Selection no. 9

A group of six composers in France, known as "Les Six," were vigorous defenders of Neo-Classicism. The most important members are Darius Milhaud (1892–1974), Francis Poulenc (1899–1963), and Arthur Honegger (1892–1955). Their music is thinner, leaner, and of briefer duration than Romantic works. They used well-defined timbres and preferred to write for chamber groups rather than full orchestra.

Music in Neo-Classic works is generally absolute, as it had been in the Classic period, rather than programmatic. Composers were especially attentive to the craft of their works, in balance and proportion, rather than in Romantic soul-searching and catharsis. This spirit of objectivity tends to be true for much music written in the twentieth century.

The balance, symmetry and restraint inherent in Neo-Classicism are also seen in many aspects of cubism. *Open Square,* Isamu Noguchi, American, 1962, granite.

University of Arizona Museum of Art, gift of Edward J. Gallagher, Jr.

attempted to provide a permanent order to objects by avoiding traditional treatment of perspective and modeling, instead rendering objects as geometric shapes. Cubistic art reflects the absolute qualities found in Neo-Classic music by emphasizing texture, color, line, and shape more than subject matter. Cubism thus marked the beginning of abstract art. Noted artists in this category include Braque (1882–1963), Picasso (1881–1973), Léger (1881–1955), and Gris (1887–1927).

A sculpture that depicts the ideals of cubism in three dimensions. *The Cellist,* Ossip Zadkine, Russian, 1890–1967.

Courtesy of the New York Public Library.

Cubism in painting and sculpture to some extent parallels Neo-Classicism in music. The Cubistic artist

Cubist painters reduced everyday objects to their most basic elements. *Still Life: The Table,* Georges Braque, French, 1928, oil on canvas.

Courtesy of the National Gallery of Art, Washington, Chester Dale Collection.

Expressionism

Musical Expressionism took its name from the philosophy associated with the writer Franz Kafka and the painters Paul Klee, Wassily Kandinsky, Oscar Kokoschka, and Franz Marc. Although it was not a clear-cut musical style like Impressionism or Neo-Classicism, it became manifest in compositions of certain composers from Germany and Austria: Schoenberg, Webern, Berg, and Ernst Krenek (1900–   ). Expressionism, in contrast to Impressionism, holds that validity is achieved through expression of the self, particularly the most personal inner self, the subconscious. Thus Expressionism is, at first glance, an extension of Romanticism, but taken to new extremes. Nineteenth-century composers used themes of strangeness and ecstasy, while Expressionists reached for the dreamlike, the irrational, and the bizarre in

Expressionism in the visual arts refers to works that express only the artist's inner feelings, whether faith, hate, anger, terror, love, or fear. Such a point of view releases the artist from all rules governing form and structure. Expressionism is contrasted with Impressionism, in which the artist tries to record the world in glowing colors without personal comment and feeling. Although works from many historical periods contain Expressionistic elements, in the twentieth century the term *Expressionism* applies to works that supplant objective reality with the expression of the artist's inner emotional state. The works represent an analog of the creator's thought process, rather than a picture of some tangible object or person. Notable Expressionistic artists include Kandinsky (1866–1944), Hofmann (1880–1966), and Pollack (1912–1956).

Abstract Expressionism. *Number 50*, Jackson Pollack, American, 1950, oil on masonite.

University of Arizona Museum of Art, gift of Edward J. Gallagher, Jr.

their musical programs. Distortion and symbolism predominate, bordering on the surrealistic, and there is little concern with Classic ideals of beauty and symmetry.

Expressionism in music is demonstrated in the use of extreme dissonance, angular, disjunct melodies, additive form, and atonality.

Timbre is presented in unconventional ways, particularly through extreme registers of instruments as well as Sprechstimme for the voice. Musical compositions that exemplify Expressionism include Schoenberg's *Erwartung*, an "opera" with one character (a woman who has been jilted and rambles through the woods at night, half-mad, searching for her lover), and *Pierrot Lunaire*, a musical recitation by a moonstruck clown.

Serialism

Arnold Schöenberg wrote atonal works before he formulated the principles of Serialism in the 1920s. Although Serialism is a compositional device that enables composers to create atonal works, atonal music is not necessarily serialistic. As explained earlier, the underlying principle is a tone row that is arranged to avoid conventional tonal relationships, such as outlining thirds and triads or resolving half-steps. (Tonal sounds can result if these relationships are permitted, and some composers have preferred these to the purity of Schoenberg's original principles.) Inevitably, to avoid tonal relationships, the tone row is often disjunct, since this helps avoid the preference for one tone, the basis of tonality.

The *tone-row* is a *serial*, or scale, used as source material for the composition. It may be played backwards or upside down; it may be transposed. Chords may be constructed for harmonic background, although polyphonic textures, two or more melodies derived from the tone row, are more common. Listen to Allegro misterioso—Trio estatico from Berg's *Lyric Suite*, Movement II *(listening selections)*. Although the exact row manipulations are seldom evident in this composition, the contrapuntal interplay among the various melodic lines here results from application of the serial techniques described above.

Selection no. 89

II

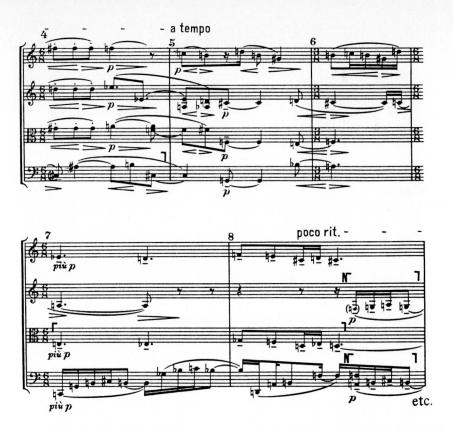

Music written in this way is usually dissonant. Schoenberg frequently used canonic and other imitative devices to provide unity. Schoenberg, however, serialized pitch only, while other composers who have followed this technique, notably Anton Webern, Olivier Messiaen (1908–), Milton Babbitt (1916–), and Pierre Boulez (1925–), have serialized other elements. Specific timbres may be assigned to each pitch in the row, in which case the composition becomes a flow of distinct instruments, each playing one or two pitches of the row.

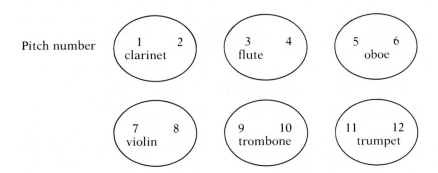

This is called *Klangfarbenmelodie,* "tone-color-melody." Similarly, durations of the row may be serialized, as may dynamics.

Serialization of pitch, timbre, duration, and dynamics gives the composer a great deal of control over a musical composition, but it also results in compositions that are difficult for a listener to appreciate. The normal syntax of music no longer exists and composition becomes a matter of mathematical manipulation. Music that is totally serialized, therefore, has no themes or melodies in the traditional sense, no development, few repetitions, and no punctuation in the form of phrases, periods, and sections. As with many art objects of this century, it is more "process" than "product."

Total serialization also results in music that is extremely difficult for musicians to perform, since traditional musical context does not exist. Each note designation must be considered, whether or not it falls into a pattern. Composers seeking total control of all musical elements and elimination of the variability and interpretation of the performer soon turned to electronic technology.

Electronic Music

Before the twentieth century, all instruments produced sound acoustically, by the vibration of strings, air, membranes, or themselves. Technological developments in this century have expanded the timbral resources available to composers. Although experimental electronic devices were used before 1950 (the Theremin and Trautonium, both incorporating *oscillators* or sound generators), electronic music became a viable means of composition only at mid-century with the development of magnetic tape.   OSCILLATOR

Electronic compositions of this period are *musique concrète,* sounds of acoustic instruments or of the environment that may have been taped, mutated, edited, and played on a tape recorder. Taped sound can be altered on a recorder by changing the speed, which also affects the pitch. Composers also re-recorded a tape played backwards, which affects the attack and release of each tone as well as its overall rhythm. *Tape loops* that provide continuous sounds (ostinatos) are common, as are *multiple tracking* (stereo), *reverberation* (echo), and *panning* (moving sound from one track to another). Musique concrète is, in a sense, laboratory music, a collage of sounds subjected to   MUSIQUE CONCRÈTE

TAPE LOOP
MULTIPLE TRACKING
REVERBERATION
PANNING

mechanical variation and spliced together in an editing room, resulting in a composition performed on tape recorder.

Soon after the first experiments in the form, composers began to incorporate live performance with tapes, providing the visual dimension so necessary for human interaction. Composers of musique concrète include Edgard Varèse (1883–1965, *Déserts* and *Poème électronique*), Karheinz Stockhausen (1928– , *Gesang der Jünglinge*), and Milton Babbitt *(Philomel).*

Development of the sound synthesizer after World War II expanded still further the resources available to composers. A sound synthesizer has one or more *sound generators (oscillators)* that may produce a *sine wave,* a sound devoid of overtones:

SOUND GENERATOR
SINE WAVE

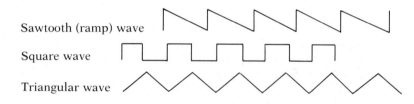

or another wave form such as:

Sawtooth (ramp) wave

Square wave

Triangular wave

WHITE NOISE   as well as *white noise,* a static-like sound that has all frequencies mixed together. These waves are circuited through electronic devices such as filters, enveloped shapers that affect the attack, sustaining quality, and decay of a tone, and amplitude and ring modulators that create bell-like effects and tremolo. The sounds are eventually mixed together and re-recorded on magnetic tape that becomes, by itself or in combination with live performers, a musical composition. Composers of synthesized music include Milton Babbitt *(Composition for Synthesizer, Ensemble for Synthesizer),* Luciano Berio (1925– , *Visages* and *Omaggio a Joyce*), Otto Luening (1900–), and Vladimir Ussachevsky (1911–).

Electronic music has been used to create new sounds as well as to fabricate electronic versions of masterworks (e.g., Tomita and Carlos). Although the elimination of live musicians is not the intention of most composers who turn to electronic means, this has happened at times purely for economic reasons. Synthesized sound is presently considered a new resource that provides an expanded palette for contemporary composers when it is added to traditional timbres.

A collage in art is much like musique concrète. Incorporating scraps of sand, string, paper, wire, wood, or other foreign materials, a collage emphasizes form, the materials used, and the arrangement of components on the canvas or piece of plywood. Sand may be mixed with the paint to create a variety of textures, and paint may be furrowed and ridged to enhance the surface. The arrangement possibilities for the materials in a collage are limited only by an artist's skill, an observation true also for musique concrète. Georges Braque (1882–1963) was one of the first artists to add texture to the canvas in this manner. Associated with Picasso in the Cubism school of painting, Braque transcended the common practice of the school with the introduction of various objects and textures into his visual presentations. Such techniques, considered radical earlier in this century, are now quite routine.

Collage, Kurt Schwitters, German, c. 1934, paper.

University of Arizona Museum of Art, gift of Edward J. Gallagher, Jr.

Experimentalism

Experimentalism is a broad category that includes all contemporary music that does not fall clearly into categories cited above. As a reaction to music that is totally controlled or totally serialized, some composers have experimented with *indeterminacy*. In this form of composition, instead of all elements being predetermined by the com-

INDETERMINACY

The variability inherent in a mobile is similar to the idea of indeterminancy in a musical composition. *Blue Moon Over the Steeple*, Alexander Calder, American, 1965, sheet metal, wire, and paint.

University of Arizona Museum of Art, gift of Edward J. Gallagher, Jr.

poser, the performer has control over some or many of the musical events. The composer may provide several pages of music and instruct the performer to play them in any order. A musical score may be written as a circle, with performers beginning at any point and then playing clockwise. Events in a composition may be specified according to game-like decisions, such as rolling dice or playing tic-tac-toe. Some scores have verbal directions only, with no standard musical notation. As a result of the employment of these variables, each performance of a given work is different. Composers of indeterminate works include John Cage *(Variations IV)*, Earle Brown (1926– , *Available Forms I*), and Lukas Foss (1922– , *Time Cycle and Echoi*).

Experimentalism also includes attempts by composers to explore the timbre, intensity, or some other aspect of the sound source, as Pauline Oliveros (1932–) does with the human voice in *Sound Patterns*. Listen to Oliveros's *Sound Patterns (listening selections)* (see pages 40–41). The composer has not used indeterminacy in this work. Events are rigidly controlled by traditional rhythmic notation, and each voice effect is specifically notated. It is interesting that the end result of works entailing either total control or qualities of indeterminacy—that

Selection no. 16

is, the composition as perceived by the listener—cannot always be predicted from the techniques used by the composer. Works in either mode can sound improvised or, conversely, highly structured.

Nationalism

Nationalism did not end at the outset of the twentieth century, but has continued throughout the modern era. Composers have used many of the contemporary techniques described in this chapter to evoke the music of their respective countries. This is often achieved by incorporating national rhythms and melodies as well as dance forms within the music. Béla Bartók (1881–1945) was notable for his accomplishments in this direction with Hungarian folk music. Listen, for example, to "Maruntel" from Bartók's *Rumanian Folk Dances (listening selections) (see pages 196–197).*

Selection no. 61

In the United States, Aaron Copland (1900–) has continued to compose with a strong nationalistic strain. Listen to "Hoedown" from Copland's *Rodeo (listening selections).*

Selection no. 90

Theme 1 (Strings)

Theme 2 (Trumpets)

Aaron Copland.

Courtesy of the New York Public Library.

The record list at the conclusion of this chapter includes many other composers pursuing nationalistic ideals.

SUMMARY

Generalizations are more difficult to draw about twentieth-century music than they were regarding past periods. Composers of this century have employed all of the varied techniques and compositional devices of the past. Although a great deal of diversity and individualism can be observed, it is generally true that music of this century has handled tonality in new ways, particularly through the use of serial techniques. Harmony is often dissonant, rhythms complex and syncopated. Timbre has also been used differently, especially in the variety of sound effects that can be produced on traditional acoustic instruments as well as by electronic means. Melodies are often fragmentary, and there has been renewed interest in older forms and genres, though twentieth-century versions are usually of shorter duration and not as fully elaborated as were earlier versions.

The twentieth century is a study in a variety of trends or "isms" that represent distinct schools of thought on composition. Impressionism, a French movement of the late nineteenth century, is a transitional style that leads to the twentieth century. The main composer is Debussy. Neo-Classicism finds inspiration in the ordering and structure of music of the eighteenth century, while Expressionism is a means of communicating personal feeling, especially despair. Serialism is a means of ordering musical events. Schoenberg was the first to serialize pitch, with serialism later being applied to timbre, duration, and dynamics as well. Electronic composition became important after 1950, first with tape collages called musique concrète and then with sounds produced entirely with electronic synthesizers, using sound generators as well as electronic devices that shape and modify sounds. Indeterminacy, a type of experimental music, offers the performer choices on what and how to perform a composition. Nationalism continues to be important throughout the twentieth century, with composers using many of the techniques described here and in earlier chapters.

STUDY GUIDELINES

KEY TERMS AND CONCEPTS

Asymmetric meters
Atonality
Cluster
Experimentalism
Expressionism
Impressionism
Indeterminacy
Musique Concrète
Nationalism
Neo-Classicism

Parallelism
Polyrhythm
Prepared piano
Quartal harmony
Serialism
Sound synthesizer
Total serialization
Twelve-tone
Wave forms
Whole-tone scale

CHAPTER REVIEW

Match items in the two columns. Answers in Appendix.

1. _____ indeterminacy
2. _____ retrograde
3. _____ *Klangfarbenmelodie*
4. _____ *musique concrète*
5. _____ restraint and form
6. _____ oscillator
7. _____ Oliveros
8. _____ sine wave
9. _____ Stravinsky (middle period)
10. _____ whole-tone scale

A. Impressionism
B. Neo-Classicism
C. Expressionism
D. Serialism
E. electronic music
F. Experimentalism
G. Nationalism
(you may use some twice)

CHRONOLOGY OF MUSIC OF THE TWENTIETH CENTURY

Issac Albéniz	1860–1909
Claude Debussy	1862–1918
Frederick Delius	1862–1934
Paul Dukas	1865–1935
Ferruccio Busoni	1866–1924

Alexander Scriabin	1872–1915
Arnold Schoenberg	1874–1951
Charles Ives	1874–1954
Maurice Ravel	1875–1937
Ottorino Respighi	1879–1936
Béla Bartók	1881–1945
Igor Stravinsky	1882–1971
Anton Webern	1883–1945
Edgard Varèse	1883–1965
Charles T. Griffes	1884–1920
Alban Berg	1885–1935
Sergei Prokofiev	1891–1953
Arthur Honneger	1892–1955
Darius Milhaud	1892–1974
Paul Hindemith	1895–1963
Francis Poulenc	1899–1963
Aaron Copland	1900–
Ernst Krenek	1900–
Otto Luening	1900–
Olivier Messiaen	1908–
Vladimir Ussachevsky	1911–
John Cage	1912–
Milton Babbitt	1916–
Lukas Foss	1922–
Luciano Berio	1925–
Pierre Boulez	1925–
Earle Brown	1926–
Karlheinz Stockhausen	1928–
Pauline Oliveros	1932–

FOR FURTHER LISTENING

Twentieth Century Works (in general)

Bartók	*Music for Strings, Percussion, and Celesta*
Berg	Concerto for Violin and Orchestra
Copland	*Appalachian Spring*
	Billy the Kid
Debussy	*La Mer*
	Trois Nocturnes
Hindemith	*Das Marienleben*
	Nobilissima Visione

Honegger	*King David*
	Pacific 231
Krenek	Pieces for Piano
Milhaud	*Le Boeuf sur le Toit*
	Suite Provençale
Prokofiev	*Classical Symphony*
	Toccata in d minor
Ravel	*Bolero*
	Daphnis et Chloé Suite no. 2
	La Valse
Schoenberg	*Drei Klavierstücke*
	Pierrot Lunaire
	Quartet no. 4
Stravinsky	*Dumbarton Oaks* Concerto
	L'Histoire du Soldat
	Octet for Wind Instruments
	Le Sacre du Printemps
Webern	Concerto for Nine Instruments

Various Nationalistic Styles
American

Copland	*Music for the Theater*
Creston	*Choric Dances*
Gershwin	*Porgy and Bess*
Grofé	*Grand Canyon Suite*
Ives	*Concord Sonata* (no. 2 for piano)
Piston	Quintet for Piano and Strings
Weill	*Down in the Valley*

Brazilian

| Villa-Lobos | *Bachianas Brasileiras* no. 5 |

English

| Vaughan Williams | Symphony no. 2 |

French

| Milhaud | *Suite Française* |

Hungarian

| Bartók | Rondos and Folk Dances |
| Kodály | *Galanta Dances* |

Jewish
  Bloch   *Schelomo*
  Bruch   *Kol Nidrei*
  Stein   *3 Hassidic Dances*

Mexican
  Chávez   *Sinfonia India*
  Revueltas   *Homage to Garcia Lorca*
                         Janitzio

Russian
  Khachaturian   *Sabre Dance* (from *Gayane* ballet)
  Prokofiev   Gavotte (Third movement, *Classical
                         Symphony)*

Spanish
  Albeniz   Spanish Dances
  Chabrier   *España:* Rhapsody for Orchestra
  Granados   *Spanish Dances*

THE STYLES OF JAZZ

❖

GENERAL CHARACTERISTICS

The term "jazz" was coined in the early twentieth century (c. 1915) to describe a style of music that had developed after the Civil War. Now the term is used to refer to several categories, including ragtime, blues, swing, boogie woogie, bop, cool, free form, third stream, funky, and fusion. Since jazz also denotes an individual style of playing music, even these categories do not adequately delineate all types. Jazz can be both a folk and art idiom, so its sounds are quite diverse. It may be simple or complex, vocal or instrumental, for dancing or purely for listening. Its performers can be untrained musicians or those with graduate degrees from prestigious conservatories.

All jazz, however, shares certain characteristics. Since it is not a style of composing music but, rather, of performing it, it is considered a "player's art." This means a jazz composition is shaped by the performers who improvise on the melody in performance, adding and deleting notes or changing rhythms. They can even give a personal interpretation to the sounds, interpolating growls, grunts, groans, slurs, unexpected accents, and other unique means of expression on their instruments. Although a jazz composition usually has a steady beat, the melody line often moves slightly ahead of or behind this beat. This SYNCOPATION is called *syncopation*, and it lends energy and rhythmic momentum. If one word characterizes jazz, it is *vitality*, apparent whether the tempo is slow, or fast, or the composition is improvised or notated.

Listening to jazz is not unlike listening to any type of music. Although there is a composer at its foundation, the performer assumes more importance and may have more freedom than in other musical styles. Jazz performers frequently use a popular song as the basis of a composition. Although the composer of such a song has provided melody and indicated basic harmonies, the jazz composition develops from the interpretation and treatment of the song by its performers. A jazz interpretation can be given to any melody, whether popular, classical, folk, or rock. In some categories of jazz the performers do not begin with a fixed tune but improvise freely, in which case they are both composer and performer. Conversely, some jazz compositions are "arranged," in which case the performers read notation somewhat strictly (although never as strictly as in a Mozart symphony, for example). The norm in most jazz is for the performer to have some degree of control over the musical events.

From the listener's standpoint, a jazz concert is often less formal than one of classical music. Applause occurs whenever a performer has improvised particularly well, not only at the conclusion of a composition. There is often more audience participation, including foot tapping, hand clapping, and even dancing, at least with some styles of jazz.

Miles Davis, a leading jazz innovator since the 1940s, when this picture was taken, has pursued numerous musical directions throughout his career. Here he performs with a cup-mute in his trumpet.

Courtesy of CBS Records.

ORIGIN OF JAZZ

Jazz is a combination of many traits, especially the rhythms of Afro-American peoples, the instruments of Europe, the harmonies of Protestant hymn tunes, and the timbre and soul of black voices, as well as overall American vitality and ingenuity. Jazz is uniquely American, and its birthplace was the American South.

Field Hollers

Before the Civil War, black slaves were allowed to sing work songs in the fields, since the overseers believed this would elevate the workers' mood and increase the capacity to work. *Field hollers*, as these worksongs are called, had a steady, slow beat. The leader often intoned one phrase, answered by a chorus of workers, resulting in *call-response* or an antiphonal effect. Lyrics of field hollers, which allude to a better life in the next world and were often improvised, had one meaning to the singers, another to the overseer.

CALL-RESPONSE

Spirituals

Although black slaves generally were not allowed to sing music from their African past, church hymns were permissible; the singing of *spirituals* developed from this practice. Like a field holler, a spiritual may use a call-response technique. Its overall feeling is often melancholic. Existing Protestant melodies were often shaped and molded to fit the feelings and needs of black singers. Since the lyrics were improvised, few were sung the same way twice.

Both spirituals and field hollers contributed to the genesis of jazz, showing such elements as improvisation, liberty in performance, call-response, and a means to express deep-seated emotions.

Blues

After the Civil War, the slaves were uprooted and a new type of music developed that, after 1900 came to be called *blues*. Blues allude to despair and frustration, but always have a bittersweet twist, a hope that things will get better. Listen to Lightnin' Hopkins's "Rainy Day Blues" *(listening selections)* (see pages 7, 222–223).

Selection no. 3

New Orleans, an "easy" and open city, became a mecca for many blacks after the Civil War. Since it was an international port, the city was tolerant of a variety of cultures and mores. Blacks were free to sing and dance in public and black musicians found employment in the brothels that were legal in New Orleans, especially in a designated red-light district called Storyville. Since wind instruments were manufactured in New Orleans, they could be purchased inexpensively. The emancipated black musicians began to adapt their soulful singing to instruments and gradually the form known as jazz emerged.

EARLY JAZZ STYLES

Ragtime

Two of the earliest designated jazz styles are *ragtime* and *classic blues*. Ragtime developed in the last decade of the nineteenth century and was popular until 1910, but it has re-emerged in popularity since the 1970s. It cannot be considered a strictly improvised form since arrangements were usually written out and published. Ragtime was written for the piano. Before the turn of the century, a ragtime player was often hired to provide music instead of an ensemble of four or five musicians. He was expected to sound like a full band on the one instrument. Therefore ragtime style uses a consistent bass-chord with melody, imitating on a single instrument the rhythm and harmony section of a jazz ensemble (left hand) as well as the melody instruments (right hand). The form is usually compound binary, which includes a modulation to subdominant key or relative major in the second section.

A   modulation   B

In addition, both A and B sections incorporate a design of their own, whether binary or ternary, this form being common:

A   B
aabba   ccdd

Four themes are typically used. Listen, for example, to Joplin's *Euphonic Sounds (listening selections)* (see pages 46–47).

Selection no. 20

Sedalia, Missouri, rather than New Orleans, was the main center for ragtime composition. The principal composers of rags are Scott Joplin (1868–1917), Eubie Blake (1884–1983), James Scott (1886–1938), Joseph F. Lamb (1887–1960), and Ben Harney (c. 1872–1938). With the introduction of ragtime to Chicago and New York, much public interest was created. Amateur pianists wanted to learn the new style, so instruction manuals, such as Joplin's *School of Ragtime* (1908), began to appear. Since these method books as well as the rags themselves were marketable, some composers were able to realize substantial financial return from royalties. The simplified and somewhat commercialized versions that appeared after 1910, however, generally signified the decline in the quality of ragtime composition.

Classic Blues

Blues, in contrast to rags, were improvised. In the late nineteenth and early twentieth centuries, the vocal blues evolved into a classic format, one stanza of blues consisting of a rhymed couplet over a standard chord progression. The rhythmic framework is twelve measures in $\frac{4}{4}$ time, four measures to each phrase, with the first line of the couplet repeated.

Phrase 1	I was with you, baby, when you didn't have a dime.
Phrase 2	I was with you, baby, when you didn't have a dime.
Phrase 3	Now since you got plenty money you have throwed your good gal down.

The chord progression is also standard.

Phrase 1	I	I	I	I_7
Phrase 2	IV	IV	I	I
Phrase 3	V_7	IV_7	I	I
	(or V_7)			

In classic blues, the lead singer improvises a melody over this underlying harmony, while the piano, harmonium (small reed organ), or guitar provides the basic harmony of I, IV, and V_7 chords. Rhythm instruments keep a steady beat. Typically, a lead instrument such as the cornet or saxophone provides a *fill-in* melody for the last part of each phrase, supplying an antiphonal answer to the singer.

FILL-IN

Voice (call)   Instrument (response)

I was with you, baby, when you didn't
have a dime.

Selection no. 8   Listen to "Lost Your Head Blues" *(listening selections)* (see pages 20–22). Each new stanza of blues follows the same harmonic structure, much like a chaconne, while the singer continues to improvise new lyrics, altering the melody slightly each time. The mood is one of melancholy and despair, and tempo slow and persistent.

BLUE TONES   The melodic scale used in blues has the third and seventh pitches flatted (infrequently the fifth as well). These so-called *blue tones* provide dissonance when sounded against the normal tones of the major scale used for the harmony.

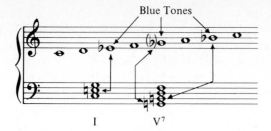

The blues became popular during the same era as ragtime but remained so throughout the 1920s. Mamie Smith (1890–1946) was the artist who made the first recording of blues "Crazy Blues" in 1920. Other blues stylists include Bessie Smith (c. 1894–1937), Gertrude "Ma" Rainey (1886–1939), and Billie Holiday (1915–1959). Since these singers first performed in touring tent shows, vocal blues did not develop in one centralized urban center. After 1920, sound recordings became the means through which they were circulated to the public.

Bessie Smith, who performs the *Lost Your Head Blues.*

Courtesy of CBS Records.

New Orleans Jazz

The instrumental style that derives from vocal blues is called *New Orleans jazz*, since its development prior to the 1920s was primarily in that city. Jazz ensembles that play New Orleans-style have three lead performers, cornet, trombone, and clarinet, plus a rhythm section of drums, piano, and guitar or banjo. Sometimes a bass tuba (Sousaphone) is added. Since early New Orleans groups often played in the back of a wagon or even marched, the piano was used only for indoor performance.

The framework for this style is the same as vocal blues: three phrases in twelve bars supported by a standard harmonic progression. Traditionally, the first stanza (chorus) is simultaneously improvised by the three lead performers. The cornet maintains the melody (or a slightly modified version of it) while the clarinet embellishes it with arpeggios based on the chord progression and the trombone plays a countermelody. Although the rhythm section may also play a stanza, most stanzas are passed among the lead instruments. The final stanza will use *simultaneous improvisation* once again, as a tutti section to round out and finish the composition. Listen to "Dead Man Blues" *(listening selections)* (see pages 194–195). This selection uses the standard twelve-bar chord progression shown above as well as simultaneous improvisation.

New Orleans jazz, whose main performers include Charles "Buddy" Bolden (1868–1931), Joe "King" Oliver (1885–1938), Louis Armstrong (1900–1971), and "Jelly Roll" Morton (1885–1941), was exported from the South when Storyville was closed down in 1917. As the pure New

SIMULTANEOUS IMPROVISATION

Selection no. 60

Louis Armstrong.

Courtesy of the New York Public Library.

Orleans style came into contact with outside forces during the 1920s, it gradually changed its nature and expanded the patterns that had been clearly evident in its original form.

JAZZ OF THE 1920s AND 1930s

Jazz ensembles became larger and more sophisticated in the period following World War I. Many black musicians moved to Chicago and made their living playing in clubs and hotels. White musicians with musical training began to hear and imitate these jazz sounds and a new style evolved, similar to the New Orleans style, called *Chicago jazz*.

Chicago Jazz

Chicago jazz uses a slightly larger ensemble than the New Orleans mode. The tenor saxophone often replaced the clarinet, while the cornet was replaced by the trumpet, the banjo by guitar, and the tuba by a string bass. The piano was typically included. Jazz became very popular during the 1920s, which have been called the jazz era, and the saxophone became the instrument most associated with the musical style. Jazz was heard in clubs and cabarets as well as on the radio, with the developing record industry also contributing to its popularity.

Solo improvisation receives more emphasis in Chicago jazz than it does in New Orleans jazz. Jazz selections often include allowance for intricate introductions, transitions (breaks), and codas. Simultaneous improvisation occurs less frequently since musical structure is generally "arranged" rather than being freely improvised. *Scat singing*, the rhythmic use of nonsense syllables by a singer, also became common. Perhaps most important, the framework of jazz gradually began to change. Instead of basing their performances on the twelve-bar blues, musicians preferred to use popular music of the day, either as a point of departure or in original compositions, in which the basic structure is usually AABA. Each section (e.g., A) is an eight-bar phrase, adding up to thirty-two bars per stanza. Although each A section uses primary chords, the B section *(bridge)* modulates to a new key, thus providing a more varied and sophisticated approach to harmonic structure and tonality. Modulation between stanzas also became quite typical.

Listen to "I Gotta Right to Sing the Blues" *(listening selections)* (see pages 226–228). "Blues" no longer refers to a classic structure but, rather, to a torchy song with sad lyrics. Leading musicians of the Chicago style included Louis Armstrong, a performer who was also adept in the New Orleans style, Leon "Bix" Beiderbecke (1903–1931), and Earl "Fatha" Hines (1905–1983).

SCAT SINGING

Selection no. 69

Boogie woogie was popular at the same time as Chicago Dixie in the 1920s and 1930s. A special type of piano jazz, boogie woogie, is characterized by a rhythmic "boogie" pattern or "walking" bass in the left hand while the player improvises a melody with the right hand (music at right). Boogie woogie was often improvised with harmonies borrowed from the twelve-bar blues. Similarly, popular songs of the period became the bases of other types of jazz, often in AABA form

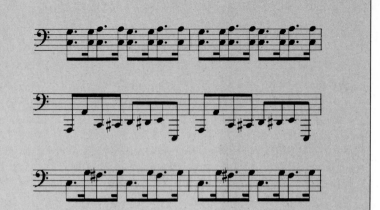

and using an expanded harmonic vocabulary. Boogie woogie was improvised by leading stylists, including "Pinetop" Clarence Smith (1904–1929), Jimmy Yancey (1898–1951), and Meade Lux Lewis (1905–1964).

Swing

Big band jazz, which developed in the 1930s, is called *swing.* Swing was for dancing, and instruments were treated both as soloists and members of sections. The saxophone section, for example, included alto, tenor, and baritone saxophones. Four trumpets and four trombones were typical, as well as double bass, guitar, piano, and drums. Special percussion instruments, such as conga and bongo drums, claves and maracas, were used by some groups, and some had vocalists, too. The typical swing accompanying figure is *riff,* an ostinato played by the entire group.

RIFF

Since collective improvisation was impossible for such a large group, stock arrangements were made, called *charts.* They outline the harmony and rhythm for each performer. Solos continued to be improvised over a given chord progression, and notation was therefore sketchy. Each swing band tried to obtain individuality in its arrangements, some of the better-known results being the so-called Glenn Miller or Tommy Dorsey sounds. These charts are still used by groups who want to re-create the sounds of these famous bands. Listen to "One O'Clock Jump" *(listening selections)* (see pages 124–125), an example of swing performed by Count Basie and his Orchestra.

CHART

Selection no. 48

Swing, which can be considered the popular music of the 1930s, was played in nightclubs and hotel ballrooms where people gathered to dance and to listen. The recording industry also grew during this

"Count" William Basie (1904–1984) was a top American jazz pianist. As a child he learned piano from his mother and studied with piano stylist Fats Waller. In his early professional career, Basie played drums and piano in vaudeville, at one point accompanying the Whitman sisters. In 1936 he formed his own band in Kansas City, playing in theatres, nightclubs, and hotels. The band played over radio station W9XBY in Kansas City, broadcasting from the Reno Club, where Basie was first dubbed the "Count." The group ultimately moved to New York City and played at the Roseland and Savoy Ballrooms during the period of his discovery by American jazz aficionados. He made his first recording with the group using the "Basie" name in 1937 and his group was featured in several Hollywood films, including "Choo-Choo Swing" and "Hit Parade of 1943."

Basie's musical career spanned a number of decades. He led a European tour with his group in the 1950s, including a performance for the Queen of England. In 1958 he was elected to the Down Beat Hall of Fame, and in 1974, honored on his seventieth birthday with a banquet at

Count Basie.
Photo by William Gottlieb. Courtesy of the New York Public Library.

the Waldorf-Astoria Hotel in New York City. In 1981 he was further honored for revolutionizing jazz at a special ceremony at the White House. He continued in his last years to appear as a backup for singers including Frank Sinatra and Tony Bennett.

Basie's music demonstrates the "riff," a repeated series of notes (ostinato) used in various sections of the group as background to a solo instrument or singer. Another characteristic is the light, tinkling piano sound, contrasted by sections with heavy brass or blended saxophones. Among his most famous songs are "One O'Clock Jump" and "Goin' to Chicago."

period, thus providing an additional outlet for musicians. Radio stations often used "live" performances, and swing was a regular feature of popular music broadcasts.

Popular bandleaders of the period included Glenn Miller (1904–44), Benny Goodman (1909–1986), the Dorsey brothers, Tommy (1905–1956) and Jimmy (1904–1957), Artie Shaw (1910–   ), Fletcher Henderson (1898–1952), Count Basie (1904–1984), and Lionel Hampton (1909–   ).

Selection no. 13   Listen to "When Lights Are Low" *(listening selections)* (see pages 37–38), also an example of swing performed with Lionel Hampton on vibes, Dizzy Gillespie on trumpet, and Coleman Hawkins on tenor saxophone (recorded in New York in 1939).

Swing gradually died out when World War II began. Gas rationing limited transportation and made tours of "one-night" stands difficult. The military draft also decimated the ranks of many ensembles, and a war-time cabaret tax, as well as the entire war effort, dampened enthusiasm for the carefree rhythms of swing.

Lionel Hampton.

Courtesy of the New York Public Library.

JAZZ OF THE 1940s AND 1950s

Bop

A reaction to the "sweet," homogeneous sound of swing set in during the 1940s, and many musicians began to feel jazz should be listened to as art music, not as commercialized entertainment. The new style of jazz that emerged is called *bop*. Bop is purely for listening, not dancing. Since many musicians were now classically trained, had excellent instrumental technique, and understood musical structure, especially harmony and form, they established an elite corps of musicians for this new kind of jazz.

A bop ensemble is small, three to six players, and may use amplified instruments, such as guitar or electric bass. Although bop is based on popular tunes, at least in its phrase structure and harmony, primary chords are not used. Bop musicians preferred *substitute* chords, extended triads used in place of basic chord progressions:

SUBSTITUTE
CHORD

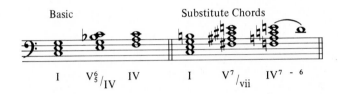

The harmonic structure is thus complex, with a fast harmonic rhythm. Since musicians improvise over the chords in a steady flow of eighth or sixteenth notes, both melody and tempo seem somewhat frantic. Dynamic accents are common and hard melodic articulations provide much contrast.

Although a well-known popular song was often used as the basis of improvisation, rarely was this "theme" presented clearly at the beginning. Rather, musicians immediately began to improvise on the theme, tending to obscure the original tune. Bop is often difficult to follow because the melody may not be identifiable to a listener. The selection "Koko," for example, uses chord progressions from "Cherokee," a popular song of the 1940s, but this is not generally recognized by most listeners. Listen to "Koko" *(listening selections),* performed by the Charlie Parker Quintet (1947).

Selection no. 91

Many bop compositions also use a unison melody in the first stanza, followed by individual variations on lead instruments. These can include statements by the piano or double bass as well as intricate drum solos. The composition is then concluded with another unison stanza.

Bop is frequently considered "overstated" jazz, busy and frantic. Bop musicians exemplified their individualism by wearing sunglasses

Charlie Parker.
From the Otto F. Hess Collection.
Courtesy of the New York Public Library.

Charlie Parker (1920–1955) was born in Kansas City. His mother gave him an alto saxophone when he was eleven because she did not like the baritone horn (euphonium) he had been assigned to play in his high school band. Largely through self-instruction, he mastered the instrument and left home at fifteen to become a professional musician.

He played in such swing groups as the Harlan Leonard band and the big band of Jay McShann, with which he made his first recordings. In 1943 Parker, along with Dizzy Gillespie and Billy Eckstine, left the Earl Hines group to play a new kind of jazz, bebop. He became a bebop master, renowned for his brilliant technique, breakneck speeds, stylistic complexity, driving rhythms, and florid melodies. He was a living legend but suffered from drug dependency and alcoholism, ultimately breaking down and dying at age thirty-five.

(shades), berets, beards, and goatees, as well as dasheekis (African shirts) and caftans. Musicians associated with this style include Charlie Parker (1920–1955), Dizzy Gillespie (1971–), and Thelonious Monk (1920–1982).

Cool Jazz

Cool Jazz emerged in the late 1940s and 1950s as a reaction to the excesses of bop. Performers continued to be technicians on their instruments, with sufficient knowledge of music history and theory to understand intellectually what they were trying to achieve in music. In contrast to bop, however, cool jazz is subtle and understated. Tempos are moderate, harmonic rhythm slow, and improvisation minimal. Performers avoided bold articulation and wide vibrato and favored restraint, thus justifying use of the term "cool." Listen to Miles

Selection no. 92

Davis's "So What" *(listening selections)*.

Many forms and structures of art music were employed by cool performers, including rondo or sonata-allegro. Many artists have used asymmetric meters, reminiscent of the rhythmic organization found in the works of Bartók or Stravinsky. Listen to "Unsquare Dance" *(listen-*

Selection no. 24

ing selections) (see page 52), which uses $\frac{7}{4}$ meter divided into 2 + 2 + 3.

Cool jazz harmonies included the use of extended chords, voiced to sound open. As with bop, cool ensembles are usually small, but include instruments normally not favored in bop, such as the flute and

Miles Davis in the 1950s.

Courtesy of CBS Records.

Dave Brubeck (b. 1920), an American jazz pianist, studied composition with Darius Milhaud and Arnold Schoenberg, and received a degree in music from College of the Pacific in 1942. In 1951 he formed the jazz quartet that made him famous. The group, including saxophonist Paul Desmond, first received attention in the San Francisco area, later gaining national recognition at the Newport Jazz Festival in 1958.

Brubeck also composed large-scale "classical" works, which include the oratorio "The Light in the Wilderness," written in 1968.

The original quartet disbanded, but in 1972 Brubeck and his three sons formed another group, Two Generations of Brubeck. He received an Honorary Doctorate from his alma mater in 1981, and actively continues his involvement in contemporary jazz circles.

Dave Brubeck.
Courtesy of the New York Public Library.

vibraphone (vibes). Leading cool performers include Miles Davis (1926–   ), Gerry Mulligan (1927–   ), Lester Young (1909–1959), George Shearing (1919–   ), and Dave Brubeck (1920–   ).

CONTEMPORARY JAZZ

All the jazz styles described continue to be performed and heard. Some musicians specialize in the blues, others in ragtime. Bop and cool can still be encountered in live performance and on records. Even the swing charts of the 1930s are used by some jazz combos. In a sense, no style of jazz has ever been relegated to the past.

Although more recent jazz styles are not as clearly delineated as those of earlier times, certain categories may be noted.

Free-Form

Free-form jazz developed in the 1960s as an offshoot of bop. Free-form uses pure improvisation, without a previously established foundation. A soloist typically improvises while the other musicians react by providing countermelodies, harmonies, and rhythms to complement the soloist. Free-form defies the usual rules of jazz in which the point of departure is a fixed tune and chords, with an underlying beat. By contrast, free-form implies total spontaneity, the improvisational process is the important thing, and the result is therefore frequently abstract and esoteric. Since there may be dissonance and free rhythms, free-form can sound much like an avant-garde, experimental composition. Modal scales have been used and some jazz artists even employ twelve-tone techniques. Some consider free-form an undisciplined form of jazz, while its most vehement critics refer to it as "noise."

Unlike most jazz styles, harmony follows the improvised melody in free-form. The soloist usually has a highly technical command of the instrument, as in bop, which allows the possibility of a flow of notes or "sheets of sound," punctuated by loud accents, cries, and dramatic

Selection no. 32 changes of register. Listen to "Alabama" *(supplemental listening)* (see pages 78–79).

Symphonic

The refinement of jazz techniques has led to experiments in combining it with the symphonic tradition. Symphonic jazz, scoring jazz or pseudo-jazz rhythms for a full symphony orchestra, was written in the 1920s and 1930s by George Gershwin *(Rhapsody in Blue)*, Aaron Copland *(Music for the Theater)*, Darius Milhaud *(Creation of the World)*, and George

Courtesy of the New York Public Library.

John Coltrane, a leading exponent of "free-form" jazz, as heard in *Alabama.*

Antheil *(Jazz Symphony),* to name a few. Although jazz rhythms and syncopation were adapted by both European and American composers during this period, this jazz was strictly written out, with no freedom for improvisation. Listen to Copland's "Dance" *(listening selections).*

Selection no. 93

Third-Stream
In the 1950s and 1960s, some composers experimented by combining symphonic and jazz traditions in a new strain of music called *third-stream.* Jazz techniques, particularly improvisation, were applied to orchestral settings. As with the cool style, forms common to art music were used, including theme and variation, rondo, and fugue. Some compositions were structured like a concerto grosso, the tutti being provided by a traditional music group with notated score, while the concertino was a jazz ensemble improvising on ideas presented by the tutti. Traditional orchestral instruments, such as oboe, French horn, and strings, were employed. Since harmony resulted from the converging contrapuntal lines, not from chord constructions, the effect is usually dissonant. Gunther Schuller (1925–) has been the leading exponent of third-stream jazz, but other practitioners include John Lewis (1920–), George Russell (1923–) and Larry Austin (1930–).

Funky

Free-form and third-stream were both attempts to bring more sophistication to jazz, but the results are often abstract and difficult to follow. Many jazz fans were repulsed by such esoteric experiments. A return to simpler expression, reminiscent of the soul and spirit of early times, resulted in *funky jazz,* beginning in the 1960s. Funky jazz uses the simple chords of early blues, the I, IV, and V₇. The sound is happier than bop, cool, or free-form, much in keeping with the spirit of the Chicago and Swing styles. A steady, bouncy beat is typical, and the basis of improvisation became again a well-known tune. There is gospel simplicity in funky, including the use of blue notes. After the esoteric excursions of the 1940s and 1950s, funky has attracted many listeners because of its simplicity. The style, in a sense, is a return to the "roots" of jazz. Listen to "Serenade to a Soul Sister" *(supplemental listening).* Horace Silver (1928–), Julian "Cannonball" Adderley (1928–1975), and Art Blakey (1919–) have been leaders in this style.

Fusion

The most recent jazz has been termed *fusion,* a synthesis of jazz with another tradition, such as East Indian, country-western, rock, or electronic music. As with third-stream, instruments of various traditions may be used. Improvisation is the basis for fusion, even with the incorporation of a country fiddle or synthesizer with a jazz ensemble. Jazz-rock, for example, is built on rock tunes and rhythms, resulting in a more sophisticated treatment than that achieved by most rock

Selection no. 52   ensembles. Listen to "Open Country Joy" *(listening selections)* (see page 136), in which the synthesis is between jazz and country-western music.

Some composers have used Indian ragas and talas as the basis for improvisation. Fusion musicians are numerous, but leading artists include John McLaughlin (1942–), Don Ellis (1934–1980), Chick Corea (1941–), Herbie Hancock (1940–), Stanley Clark (1951–), Chuck Mangione (1940–), and the musical groups Chicago and Blood, Sweat and Tears.

SUMMARY

Jazz is a style of composition and of playing that allows a high degree of personal interpretation in music. It developed from spirituals and field hollers and manifested itself immediately following the Civil War in a style called blues. Classic blues and ragtime are two of the earliest

John McLaughlin (b. 1942) is a guitarist from Yorkshire, England, whose dexterity on the piano, synthesizer, and guitar resulted from arduous self-study, not formal music lessons. He is renowned primarily as a guitarist and composer in the world of fusion.

McLaughlin immigrated to the United States in 1968 and played sideman for Miles Davis, a jazz trumpeter associated with the cool style, in the album, *Bitches Brew*. In 1971 he formed his own group, the Mahavishnu Orchestra, named after his guru and mixing elements of Hinduism with Baroque structure. Blues artists such as Leadbelly and Muddy Waters, and the jazz guitarist Django Reinhardt, have inspired McLaughlin, whose jazz style also electronically integrates influences of Indian music and sounds of Nashville. Notable sidemen who have played with McLaughlin include Billy Cobham, Tony Oxley, and Jean-Luc Ponty.

John McLaughlin (second from left) and Shakti. McLaughlin, a leading exponent of fusion jazz, is pictured here playing a Western guitar with an East Indian ensemble.
Courtesy of CBS Records.

identifiable types of jazz. Blues are vocal couplets improvised over set chord patterns in twelve-bar stanzas, while ragtime is jazz for piano using a syncopated right-hand melody over a steady left-hand accompaniment.

During the period before World War I, instrumental blues became popular in New Orleans. Jazz was popular during the 1920s in Chicago, where the basis for jazz became the popular song. Jazz ensembles became larger in size, especially during the 1930s, when the prevalent style was called swing.

During the 1940s, a reaction to swing occurred in bop, an esoteric type of jazz intended only for listening. Cool jazz of the 1950s was understated, scaled down in sound, often employing the forms and techniques of contemporary art music.

More recent types of jazz include free-form, in which the process of improvisation is more important than the end-product, the resulting sound, as well as third-stream, which blends symphonic and jazz traditions. Funky jazz is a return to the spirit and simplicity of early styles, while fusion is a blending between jazz improvisation and other styles, including rock, electronic, country-western, and raga.

Since jazz constantly combines and recombines various styles and techniques, it is truly a living art form. No style of jazz has ever been totally superseded by another, so one performer may often be able to play in several styles. Ultimately, jazz is neither a definable piece of music nor a delimited style but, rather, a manner of interpreting music.

STUDY GUIDELINES

KEY TERMS AND CONCEPTS

Blues
Blue tone
Boogie-woogie
Bop
Call-response
Chicago jazz
Classic blues
Cool jazz

Free-form jazz
Funky
Fusion
New Orleans jazz
Ragtime
Swing
Third-stream jazz

CHAPTER REVIEW

Match items in the two columns. Answers in Appendix.

1. _____ simultaneous improvisation
2. _____ piano jazz
3. _____ big band for dancing
4. _____ revolt against esoteric jazz
5. _____ jazz-rock
6. _____ rhymed couplet in twelve bars
7. _____ pure improvisation
8. _____ understated; no vibrato
9. _____ 1920s jazz
10. _____ revolt against swing

A. blues
B. ragtime
C. Chicago jazz
D. New Orleans jazz
E. swing
F. bop
G. cool
H. free-form
I. funky
J. fusion

CHRONOLOGY OF JAZZ

Scott Joplin	1868–1917
Charles "Buddy" Bolden	1868–1931
Ben Harney	c. 1872–1938
Eubie Blake	1884–1983
Joe "King" Oliver	1885–1938
"Jelly Roll" Morton	1885–1941
James Scott	1886–1938

Gertrude "Ma" Rainey	1886–1939
Joseph F. Lamb	1887–1960
Mamie Smith	1890–1946
Bessie Smith	c. 1894–1937
Jimmy Yancey	1898–1951
Fletcher Henderson	1898–1952
Louis Armstrong	1900–1971
Leon "Bix" Biederbecke	1903–1931
"Pinetop" Clarence Smith	1904–1929
Glenn Miller	1904–1944
Jimmy Dorsey	1904–1957
"Count" Basie	1904–1984
Tommy Dorsey	1905–1956
Earl "Fatha" Hines	1905–1983
Meade Lux Lewis	1905–1964
Lester Young	1909–1959
Benny Goodman	1909–1986
Artie Shaw	1910–
Lionel Hampton	1913–
Billie Holliday	1915–1959
"Dizzy" Gillespie (John Birks)	1917–
Art Blakey	1919–
George Shearing	1919–
Charlie Parker	1920–1955
Thelonious Monk	1920–1982
Dave Brubeck	1920–
John Lewis	1920–
George Russell	1923–
Earl "Bud" Powell	1924–1966
Gunther Schuller	1925–
John Coltrane	1926–1967
Miles Davis	1926–
Gerry Mulligan	1927–
Julian "Cannonball" Adderley	1928–1975
Horace Silver	1928–
Sonny Rollins	1929–
Larry Austin	1930–
Ornette Coleman	1930–
Don Ellis	1934–1980
"Herbie" Hancock (Herbert Jeffrey)	1940–

"Chuck" Mangione (Charles Frank)	1940–
"Chick" Corea (Armando Anthony)	1941–
John McLaughlin	1942–
Stanley Clark	1951–

FOR FURTHER LISTENING

Anthology
The Smithsonian Collection of Classic Jazz
The Smithsonian Associates
Washington, D.C. 20560

Blues
Billie Holliday, *The Golden Years*
Columbia Records, C3L 40

Roots of the Blues
Atlantic 1348

Jazz Singers
Folkway Records, FJ 2804

The Empress (Bessie Smith)
Columbia G-31093

Boogie Woogie
Boogie Woogie
Folkways Jazz, Vol. 10

Bop
The Be-Bop Era
RCA Victor Records, LPV-519

Chicago Jazz
Chicagoans
Decca Records, 79231

The Bix Beiderbecke Legend
RCA Victor Records, LMP 2323

Cool
Complete Birth of the Cool
Capitol M-11026

Cool Burnin'
Prestige Records, PR 7496

Out of the Cool (Gil Evans)
Impulse Records A-4

Free-Form
A Love Supreme (John Coltrane)
Impulse Records 77
Free Jazz (Ornette Coleman and Eric Dolphy)
Atlantic 1364

Funky
Horace Silver and the Jazz Messengers
Blue Note 81518
The Best of Cannonball Adderley
Capitol Records, SKA0 2939

Fusion
Jazz-Rock
Alfred's Music Records
Chicago
Columbia Records, KGP 24
The New Wave in Jazz
Impulse Records A-90

New Orleans Jazz
The Original Dixieland Jazz Band
Decca Records DXSF-7140 (Vol. I)
King of New Orleans Jazz
RCA Victor Records LPM-1649

Ragtime
Best of Scott Joplin and Others
Vanguard VSD-39/40

Swing
The Big Bands
Prestige 7645
This Is Duke Ellington
RCA Victor Records VPM-6042
Benny Goodman Carnegie Hall Concert
Columbia OSL-160

Third Stream
Jazz Abstractions (Gunther Schuller)
Atlantic Records S-1365

NON-WESTERN MUSICAL STYLES

❖

THE MEANING OF NON-WESTERN

"Non-Western" is a general classification encompassing music other than that based on European tradition, which is represented by those styles described in Chapters Eleven through Seventeen. Although Medieval music is somewhat different from Renaissance, as Baroque is different from Classical, in a global sense all Western styles are much more *alike* than they are different. Although non-Western styles also may be described through historical development, to a Western listener all music from India, for example, whose tradition is probably older than European-based music, may sound similar. In this chapter, generalizations concerning the music of India, Indonesia, Japan, China, and other select cultures will be discussed, without examining each in historical context.

Common Practice

The definition of music as "organized sound" applies equally to non-Western and European music. All Western music is organized similarly, with melodies based on scales, major and minor being the most common. Harmony is almost always present and there are well-established traditions for constructing chords and providing tension-release, and consonance-dissonance. The half-step is the smallest inter-

Standing Bodhisattva,
possibly Northern Ch'i
Dynasty, 550–557,
unknown artist, bronze.

University of Arizona Museum of Art, gift of Alfred
Messner.

val normally used in both melody and harmony. Rhythm is governed
by an underlying beat grouped into regular strong and weak patterns.
Timbres have evolved into the four families of the orchestra: strings,
woodwinds, brass, and percussion. Although various musical designs
may be identified, traditional Western art music has used return and
processive form almost to the exclusion of strophic and additive. These
traditions—the use of melody, harmony, rhythm, timbre, dynamics, and
form in normally expected ways—constitute the *common practice* usage
of Western music. Only early Medieval music and experimental works
of this century represent extreme departures from the Western tradition.

General Traits
Since the traditions of non-Western nations are different from one
another, it is impossible to generalize about common practice in non-
Western music. Nonetheless, one can discuss the broad variance between non-Western music and European music.

Harmony/Texture.   The most striking difference is the general absence of harmony as an expressive element. Non-Western music is almost totally devoid of harmony; when it occurs, it is either incidental or accidental. In Indian music, incidental harmony is provided by a *drone*, the constant sounding of one or two reference pitches against which the melody sounds.

DRONE

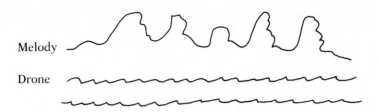

In music of Japan and China, two or three instruments play similar versions of a melody, resulting in a texture called *heterophonic*. At points where instruments deviate, the resulting harmony sounds almost accidental.

HETEROPHONIC

There are no established rules to govern harmony and chords such as those that developed in the Western world after 1000 A.D.

Melody.   Other elements have received heightened emphasis in non-Western music, especially melody and rhythm. In Indian music, melodies are based on pitch-like frameworks called *ragas*. A raga is somewhat like a scale in that five, six, or even seven pitches are used. However, the raga ascending is frequently different from its descending version. In addition, unlike Western diatonic scales in which intervals are generally limited to either half- or whole-steps, the Indian raga can be divided *microtonally*, that is, in increments of less than a half-step. Intervals can be smaller than a half-step—a quarter-tone or even an eighth of a tone—or larger than a whole step, all within the same raga. Each raga, and there are literally hundreds of possibilities handed down by tradition, is different. Melodies derived from ragas are thus more complicated and diverse than those found in Western music. Although the variability of intervals is especially noticeable in Indian music, pitch relationships in much non-Western music exhibit the same property. Intervals are not the same as found in Western tempered-scales, and may sound "out-of-tune" to the Western listener.

RAGA

MICROTONE

This, however, is a matter of context since such pitches are perfectly "in-tune" to people from those cultures involved.

Rhythm. Non-Western music often treats rhythm differently from the ways customary in the European tradition. Rhythmic development, building and progressing to a dramatic climax, is not usual. Rather, rhythm occurs in longer cycles, repeated again and again with little variation. In Indonesia the rhythmic cycle often consists of sixteen beats, punctuated by a large gong. In Indian music, the *tala* or rhythmic cycle is often asymmetric. A cycle of eight beats in a tala could be divided as:

TALA

    1 2 **3** 4 5 **6** 7 8   (2 + 3 + 3); or
    1 2 3 4 **5** 6 **7** 8   (3 + 2 + 3); or
    1 2 3 **4** 5 6 **7** 8   (3 + 3 + 2)

The regularly recurring accents of duple, triple, or quadruple meter are not as common in non-Western music.

Polyrhythm. *Polyrhythms* are frequently encountered in some non-Western cultures, especially in the music of Western Africa. Although a steady, inexorable beat is present, each performer may observe a different set of accents:

Instrument one **1** 2 3 **4** 5 6 **7** 8 9 **10** 11 12
Instrument two **1** 2 **3** 4 **5** 6 **7** 8 **9** 10 **11** 12

Heterorhythm. In Australian aboriginal music, each performer may observe a beat totally different from fellow performers, with accents of the various parts never really converging. This is called *heterorhythm*, and sounds like two or more solos being performed simultaneously and individually:

Performer one 1 2 3 4 5 6 7
Performer two 1 2 3 4 5 6 7 8 9 10
Performer three 1 2 3 4 5

It is difficult to generalize about rhythm in non-Western music, since rhythm is, by definition, the movement of sounds within a time frame. Some non-Western music has a rhythmic structure that is similar to Western usage, but in other cases, as noted here, the structure can be either simpler or more complicated. These differences will be further explored in the presentation of each specific style.

Timbre. Timbres are equally hard to generalize. Although non-Western instruments are either aerophones, chordophones, membranophones, or idiophones, rarely are these instruments ones that are known and used in the West. When the instrument is a familiar one, as with the violin in India or hammer dulcimer in China, the playing technique is usually quite different. Each culture has developed a special way to combine and use instruments. Indian ensembles consist of three or four musicians, the same number generally used in the orchestra for Japanese Noh drama, but the former is usually for listening, the latter as accompaniment for stage movements. Although instrument group-ings are large in Southeast Asia, Indonesia, Thailand, and Burma, rarely is the instrumentation rigidly set. Zairean or Kenyan groups freely add or delete members, often within the course of a single composition when a bystander is inspired to participate or a performer becomes exhausted. Tuning systems of instruments are compatible within the requirements of the culture. A primitive flute may have only three finger holes, since melodies used in that society are narrow in range. On a more sophisticated level, the frets of the Indian sitar are moveable to accommodate the variable pitch relationships of numerous ragas.

Voice. The human voice, the only universal instrument, is found in all musical cultures but, as with instruments, its uses are diverse. In some cultures vocal production is nasal, while others a deep and resonant sound is favored. In some cultures it may be important to convey words, in which case the voice is treated as a solo instrument. Other cultures, however, provide no special accommodation for sing-ing, and vocal sounds are simply added to the general fabric.

Scene from *Musume Dojoji,* one of the famous eighteen classic dramas of the Kabuki repertoire. Kabuki is one of Japan's dramatic art forms. Although it was developed in the late seventeenth century, it is still popular today. The Kabuki orchestra in the background uses several traditional Japanese instruments.

Courtesy of the Embassy of Japan.

Form. Although all music has form, the designs of non-Western are rarely the return forms that are so common in the West. Rather, strophic, processive, and additive occur more frequently.

Purpose. Finally, the purpose of music in non-Western societies is as varied as the musical elements cited above. In general, music is presented for reasons more practical than are found in the West. Villagers in Nigeria may sing and chant to celebrate the birth of a child, the passage of a teenager into adult society, a wedding, a death. Japanese instrumentalists accompany the signing and action in Kabuki theater or Noh drama, while the Indonesian gamelan provides music for dancing or puppetry. Even in India, where the environment for musical performance is similar to that of a Western concert, the performer attempts to evoke an atmosphere in which the listener can share. Non-Western music is rarely for listening alone. Rather, it is utilitarian and, because of its cultural significance, probably reaches a greater proportion of its population than is true for Western art music.

MUSIC OF INDIA

Indian "classical music" involves a small group of musicians, generally three or four. One performer leads the group, with the harmonic accompaniment (drone) provided by another and a third musician usually playing the drum. The optional fourth musician would share the leadership position. The music is largely improvised. Each composition begins with exploration of the melody and ends with a contest between lead performer and drums. Listen to *Rága Simhendra-Madhyamam (listening selections)* (see pages 50–51, 79).

Selection no. 23

Instruments

SITAR The timbres of Indian music include the North Indian *sitar*. A sitar is a chordophone with a long (hollow) neck and one or two resonators. Seven main strings are used as well as numerous sympathetic strings that pass through the hollow neck and under the main strings, thus reinforcing main pitches and providing resonance. The performer uses finger movement along the string as well as sideways to play the pitches and ornaments.

TAMBOURA The drone is provided by the *tamboura*, another chordophone held in an upright, vertical position. Its four strings are tuned to two pitches, the vadi (tonic) and samvadi (dominant). These two basic pitches serve as reference points for the lead performer, no matter how far afield his or her improvisation may wander.

TABLA
DAYA The rhythmic accompaniment is often played on *tabla*, the collective name for two drums. The smaller *daya* has a wooden shell, its head

Top, tamboura, Indian drone lute; bottom, tabla, Northern Indian paired drums (baya on left and daya on right).

Photos by K.H. Han. Northern Illinois University.

laced onto the body by leather straps that are also used in tuning. Fine tuning is accomplished by placing a blob of paste (manganese dust) on **BAYA** the head. The larger *baya* has a metal shell and is tuned similarly, but sounds an octave lower. The daya is played with the performer's right hand, the baya with the left. Sounds produced vary according to how as well as where the hand strikes the head or rim of each drum.

There are many additional Indian instruments. The violin has been used since Colonial days, but it is tuned to the two main pitches of the raga, not to four distinct pitches separated by fifths as in the West. It is also held lower, against the chest, and, since it is an unfretted chordophone, can play the microtones used in Indian ragas. Since instruments are still handcrafted in India, there are regional differences in size, number of strings, and method of usage, even among commonly known examples like the sitar, tamboura, or tabla. A singer or instrumentalist performs with other musicians whose ranges (and skill) are compatible. The degree of standardization found in a Western symphony orchestra is simply not necessary in a culture in which the musical ensembles are small and performances largely improvisatory.

Raga

The melodic basis of Indian music is called a *raga*. Although a raga is a catalog of pitches, it is less abstract than a scale. The raga has certain **RASA** intervals and ornaments that associate it with a given sentiment, a *rasa*. The rasa may allude to love, compassion, valor, or tranquillity, and it is the purpose of the lead performer to convey this sentiment to the audience. Ragas are classified by time of day and season, some appropriately played in morning, others in afternoon or evening. Some are suitable for the rainy season, others for the dry.

MELA Basically, a raga derives from a parent scale called a *mela*. Each **SWARA** mela uses eight pitches, or *swaras*.

Sa Ri Ga Ma Pa Dha Ni Sa'
└────────────octave────────────┘

The outer limit of the mela, like a Western scale, is an octave, Sa to Sa'. Sa, however, is not a fixed pitch like "C" or "F" but rather is set to any pitch suitable for the lead instrument or singer. Other pitches of the mela are then tuned relative to it, much like the other pitches of a major or minor scale are arranged in a set pattern once the tonic or keynote is established. The following melas and the ragas based on them are typical (note that Sa is shown as C only for convenience; as noted, it can be any pitch):

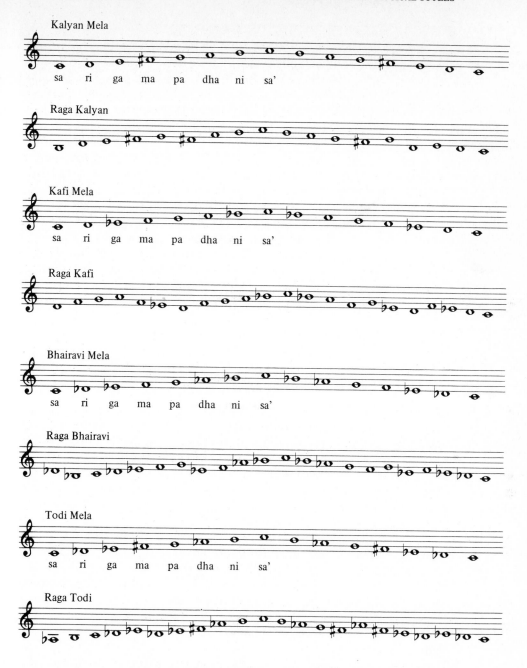

Many Indian compositions begin with two instruments. One, such as the tamboura, contributes to the drone, which provides two reference pitches, *vadi* and *samvadi*, similar to the tonic and dominant in Western composition. The lead instrument, such as the sitar, or the singer

VADI
SAMVADI

Pitches in the mela, with one exception, can vary within the limits of the mela. Pa, tuned approximately one fifth higher than Sa, is the only tone with a fixed position. But Ri, for example, the second pitch in the mela, may be as close to Sa as an eighth of a tone or as wide as a whole-step. Thus, pitch choices in setting a mela may be diagrammed as shown below.

There are twenty-two pitch choices, called *shrutis,* within the octave Sa to Sa'. Some intervals are narrow, others wide, and provide an infinite variety of available pitches when constructing a mela. Theoretically possible choices, however, do not result in concrete musical differences or add emotional impact. In practice, Indian musicians use few melas, about seventy-two in South India and ten in the North.

Once a parent scale or mela is established, several ragas may be based on it. Although 200 ragas are currently used, only thirty are considered popular and easily recognized. A raga derived from a mela does not necessarily use all seven pitches, but must use at least five. Similar to a tonic, one tone is designated the principle tonic note, the *vadi.* Ornaments such as slurs, glissandos, turns, and vibrato give a specific raga identity.

```
          ┌──── Perfect Fifth    Perfect Fourth ────┐
          │                                          │
       Sa—4—Ri—3—Ga—2—Ma—4—Pa—4—Dha—3—Ni—2—Sa'
          │                                          │
          └──────────── Perfect Octave ─────────────┘
```

introduces the raga, initially played within one octave, ascending and descending, to show its characteristic intervals and ornaments. This occurs at first in a free tempo with no underlying beat. As the raga is repeated, slight variations accompany reiteration of notes or addition of ornaments. The lower and higher octaves are gradually worked in. Eventually, the drum begins and the composition builds to a climax. Highly skilled performers may keep a composition going for several hours with intricate improvisation.

Since Indian music is not notated, a young performer learns the ragas by rote, serving as the tamboura player to a master performer in an apprenticeship role. Emotional and spiritual development are equally important in the training of a musician, and many apprentices simply live with their guru for a period of years.

Tala

The rhythmic structure of a performance is governed by a tala, the division of time into a set number of beats and accent groupings. This is not established until the drum begins; the earliest statements of the raga are performed without rhythmic underpinning. Each tala has a
MATRA   set number of *matra* or beats, which provide an indirect pulse for the variations. Although the rhythmic structure governs the second part

The talas identified at the right are the most popular and frequently used. Some, like teental, are symmetric; others, like tivratal, are asymmetric. The first beat of a rhythmic cycle is called the *sam* and it often coincides with the main note of the raga, the vadi, in performance. The following composition shows the use of both raga and tala:

jhaptal	10 matra $(2 + 3 + 2 + 3)$
jhumratal	14 $(3 + 4 + 3 + 4)$
tivratal	7 $(3 + 2 + 2)$
ektal	12 $(4 + 4 + 2 + 2)$
teental	16 $(4 + 4 + 4 + 4)$
dadratal	6 $(3 + 3)$
rupaktal	7 $(3 + 2 + 2)$

Gitam (song)

Raga: Mōhana

Tala: Rūpakam (2+4)

sa   ré   ga   pa   dha   sa   dha   pa   ga   ré   sa

Tala: 1 2 3 4 5 6

va ra vee na   mru-dhu pa ni   va na ru ha lo   cha nu ra-ah ni

su ru chi-ra pam   ba ra vay-yay ni   su ray nu te kal   ya-ah-ah-ah ni

ni ru pa ma su-bha   gu na lo la   ne ra ta je ya   pra-dha-shi-la

va-re da pre-ya   ren-ga na yeh-ki   va han chi-ta pa la   dha-ah-ah-ah yeh-ki

sa re si ja   sa na je na ni   je ya je ya je ya

of the composition, the matra and accent grouping are usually imperceptible to the listener. Rather, the drummer performs rhythm patterns to enhance variations being performed by the lead instrument.

Form

ALAP
GAT

The form of Indian music is processive, somewhat like a continuous variation. Nonetheless, two distinct sections may be noted in many Indian performances: (1) the beginning, called the *Alap*, in which the raga is first presented and developed, and (2) the *Gat*, in which the tala is established, and improvisation develops between drum and lead instrument.

MUSIC OF INDONESIA

Gamelan

The orchestra of Indonesia, the *gamelan*, may be either large or small. Palace gamelans of earlier times had as many as eighty performers, but gamelans heard in modern hotel lobbies or tourist centers are often limited to three or four. Each gamelan is unique because of the tuning. Since there is no pitch standard in Indonesia, instruments built for one gamelan are not usable in another. Nonetheless, there are many similarities among all gamelans on the many islands of Indonesia, especially on Java and Bali.

Instruments

METALLOPHONE

SARON
GENDER

A gamelan consists largely of xylophone-like instruments with metal keys. These are called *metallophones* and they have at least five keys made of bronze, brass, or iron. The keys are placed in a frame over either box or tube resonators. Those with a single box resonator for all keys are called *sarons*, those with a tube resonator for each individual key are *genders*. Sarons and genders are instruments of definite pitch, and the arrangement of keys represents the scale to which they are tuned. Both instruments are played with a wooden mallet. The technique requires the performer to hit the key in its center and then quickly damp the tone, a skill requiring much coordination.

Sarons and genders are built in families with bass, tenor, alto, and soprano models. Although all play a version of the same melody, generally the lower the instrument, the fewer notes it plays (see p. 499).

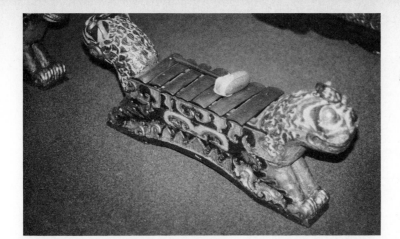

Top, saron; bottom, gender.

Photos by K.H. Han. Northern Illinois University.

Left, bonang; right, three colotomic instruments (left to right: rincik, 8-disk cymbals on back of a turtle; kempur, medium gong; kelenang, small time-beating kettle).

Photos by K.H. Han. Northern Illinois University.

BONANG
COLOTOMIC
INSTRUMENTS

Two additional families of instruments in the gamelan are: (1) *bonangs,* metal kettles suspended in rope frames, which are played by several musicians at once; and (2) *colotomic* instruments, the time keepers. The colotomic group includes drums, metal kettles, and gongs. The largest gong marks the ending of main sections of the composition, while the other percussive instruments keep a steady beat within the rhythm cycle.

Large gamelans often use chordophones, aerophones, and vocalists, but there is no dynamic adjustment to accommodate the additional

Kendang player.   Photo by K.H. Han. University of Wisconsin.

timbres. Rather, they are simply added to the original texture as another layer of sound.

The gamelan is usually led by a drummer. Since the music is not notated, it is his or her responsibility to teach each person's part by rote. The order in which instruments are added must be agreed upon, and gestures by the drummer usually indicate when to terminate a composition. Although it appears that the music is being improvised, in reality it is learned and is thus quite similar from one performance to the next. A new composition is created by the conductor who then teaches it to the entire group. In the same sense, compositions are created for a given gamelan and are not used by another group. Thus, each gamelan has both a unique tuning and repertoire. Listen to *Golden Rain Hudjan Mas (listening selections)* (see pages 205–207).   Selection no. 65

Unlike the musicians of India, who apprentice themselves to a guru for years in order to learn their craft, the gamelan performers, dancers, and puppeteers of Indonesia are all amateurs. They work in rice fields by day, gathering in clubs in evening hours to practice and perfect their craft. The instruments, owned by the village, are a source of civic pride.

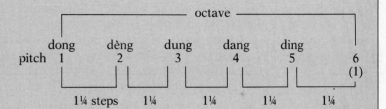

Indonesian music uses only two scales. The *slendro* scale has five equally spaced tones (pentatonic) and is bound by an octave, each divided slightly differently. Because there are six whole steps in one octave, each interval is slightly less than 1¼ steps, since 1¼ × 5 = 6¼ (see chart at right). In Bali the tones are called dong, dèng, dung, dang, and ding, but do not correspond to pitches used in Western music. One instrument builder may choose a certain pitch for 1 (dong) and may use wide or narrow intervals between adjacent tones, thus making a saron from one gamelan out-of-tune for another gamelan. Even within one gamelan, paired instruments usually have corresponding keys that are slightly out of tune with each other. This slight discrepancy creates "beats," a shimmering effect between the two instruments when identical keys are struck.

The second scale is seven-toned (heptatonic) and called the *pelog*. In contrast to the slendro in which all intervals are of similar size, intervals of the pelog are either 3/4 of a step (150 cents) or 1 1/8 of a step (225 cents). As with the slendro, the tones are not standardized between gamelans, and the pitches do not agree. For this reason, all but the largest gamelans are drawn from one scale or the other. Composers never modulate from pelog to slendro within one composition.

Melody and Form

CANTUS FIRMUS The main melody or *cantus firmus* is played by sarons and genders in a middle register, with the lower instruments playing a simplified version of the cantus firmus, the higher instruments an elaborated version. This results in simultaneous variations on the melody, that is,

HETEROPHONY *heterophony.*

Since the cantus firmus melody is repeated again and again, reinforced by instruments of the colotomic group, the form of Indonesian music is processive. At each repetition, additional instruments are added, resulting in an intensification of both timbre and rhythm, somewhat like a continuous variation.

Javanese music is linked to both drama (puppet plays) and dancing, so it is soft to enable the words to be heard. It is also quite regular in rhythm. By contrast, Balinese music is spirited and tends to change tempo. On the whole, the Balinese gamelan is louder and more brilliant than the Javanese group.

MUSIC OF JAPAN

Japanese music is especially difficult to characterize, since it is an art form that has evolved over centuries to include diverse traditions and instruments. Japan has often been called a storehouse of cultural influences, and the native music reflects the varied practices and instruments collected through the years.

Eight Views of the Hsaio-Hsiang Rivers in China, Unkoku Toyo, Japanese, c. 1600, six panels, ink on paper, mounted on silk, wood frame.

University of Arizona Museum of Art, gift of Alfred Messner.

Koto performer.

Courtesy of Sekai Bunka Photo.

Instruments

The most popular Japanese instruments are the ones used in the chamber trio called *Sankyoku*.

SANKYOKU

Koto. The *koto* has been used in Japan for over one thousand years. It is classified as a *zither*, a chordophone whose strings pass across the entire body. The koto is about six feet long and usually has thirteen strings, tuned by bridges that elevate the strings from the body. The performer kneels over the instrument and plucks the strings with picks worn on his or her fingers.

ZITHER

Samisen. The *samisen* is also a chordophone. Its hollow resonator is covered with animal skin, much like an American banjo, and the neck has no frets. The three strings are usually tuned to open fifths or fourths. The strings are plucked with a large pick that, when allowed to strike the skin, produces a percussive effect. Since the samisen is an easy instrument to learn, it has been used in Japan by both popular entertainers and amateurs.

Japanese theater has incorporated musical instruments for centuries. *Noh drama*, a theatrical form reaching its peak about 1500, uses an orchestra of four: flute, flat drum *(Taiko)*, Ko-tsuzumi drum (played on the shoulder) and O-tsuzumi drum (played on the lap). Tsuzumi drums are hour-glass shaped and laced so that pressure on the cords tightens the drum heads and raises the pitch.

Instruments were also used in *Kabuki*, a popular art form dating from the early seventeenth century. The *Koto* was considered an elegant addition to the home, often used by noble families to train their children. The *Samisen* served as a folk instrument, more suitable for street musicians.

The oldest form of theatrical entertainment in Japan is *Gagaku*, meaning "elegant" or "refined" music. Gagaku, adapted from the Chinese court music of the T'ang dynasty (seventh-ninth centuries A.D.), was presented only for the emperor of Japan. It incorporates dancers, masked actors, and musicians in colored robes. Performers of the Left, meaning their music is derived from China and India, wear red while those of the Right, with music from Korea and Manchuria, wear green. Two orchestras incorporate the instruments of either the Left or Right. The koto, for example, is derived from China and used in the orchestra of the Left, while tsuzumi drums are used in the orchestra of the Right.

Only in the nineteenth century did purely instrumental forms, such as the *Sankyoku*, evolve in Japan. As is true with many non-Western countries that Westernize rapidly, the traditional music of Japan has been superseded by the art and instruments of Europe.

Traditional Japanese percussion instruments. From left to right, ko-tsuzumi, o-tsuzumi, and taiko. The surface of the taiko is covered with cowhide, except for the small area in the center where deerskin is used. The o-tsuzumi has a head of cowhide, the ko-tsuzumi, horsehide. The tone of all three drums is adjusted by the tension of the linen cords.

Courtesy of the Embassy of Japan.

Courtesy of the Embassy of Japan.

Another musical group, Hayashi, differs from the Noh group in that the samisen replaces the flute. This ensemble consists of (from left to right), the taiko, a drum beaten with short thick drumsticks; the o-tsuzumi, placed on the lap or held under the left arm; the ko-tsuzumi, held on the right shoulder; and the samisen, a three-string chordophone with a resonator covered with catskin.

Courtesy of the Embassy of Japan.

Scene from *Kagami-Jishi*, one of the famous eighteen classic dramas of the Kabuki repertoire. Instrumentalists can be seen in the background.

Shakuhachi. The *shakuhachi,* an end-blown flute about 20" long, is played in a vertical position like a clarinet or oboe. There are four front finger holes and one thumb hole. The pitches are:

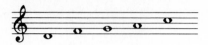

but overblowing allows the performer to produce notes in the two upper octaves. Ornaments and other pitches are produced by the performer's shaking his or her head slightly or by covering some holes only partially. The shakuhachi can be traced to the fourteenth century when it was used by priests and samurais, the latter using it for personal entertainment but also finding it suitable for personal defense when wielded like a billy club.

Characteristics

PENTATONIC Japanese music basically uses one of several possible five-toned *(pentatonic)* scales. It is common for these scales to have two half-steps and some wider intervals. In one tuning of the koto, the traditional chordophone, the scale is:

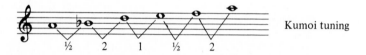

Kumoi tuning

In another:

Hira-Joshi tuning

Japanese music is heterophonic in texture. In order to distinguish the parts, each one is played by an instrument of contrasting timbre. In the chamber group called *Sankyoku,* the trio consists of the aforementioned *koto,* samisen, and shakuhachi. Each timbre can be heard distinctly in its separate version of the melody.

Japanese tempos are either slow or moderate, and the beat, whether direct or indirect, is steady. Quadruple time is most common.

The following excerpt has a vocal melody accompanied by an instrument. The scale is pentatonic:

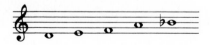

The accompaniment follows the vocal line very closely, with only the slight deviations in pitch and rhythm typical of heterophony.

十三の砂山
THE DUNE OF TOSA
(Bon - Songs of Tosa Gata)

Melody transcribed by Hattori

Piano part arranged by **M. Shiohara**

DAN Processive form is common in Japanese art music. The typical composition for koto is the *dan*. Before the seventeenth century, the dan was an instrumental accompaniment to the recitation of lyric poetry set in strophes. As this form evolved, the koto player frequently varied the accompaniment for each strophe, resulting in theme and variations. These variations are now performed without poetry, with forms identified according to the number of variations included. *Go-dan* means a theme with four variations, *Roku-dan*, a theme with five variations. *Rokudan-No-Shirabe* means music of six steps, that is, a theme with five variations. The term refers both to a form and specific **Selection no. 36** compositions. Listen to *Rokudan No Shirabe (listening selections)* (see pages 93–94).

MUSIC OF CHINA

The music of China antedates that of Japan by several centuries. During the Ch'in dynasty (255–206 B.C.), the feudal wars that had plagued the area ended and unification of China was achieved. Docu-

Performer on 21-string cheng, a Chinese zither.

Photo by K.H. Han. Northern Illinois University.

ments were thereafter maintained that show the importance of music to the well-being of the political structure.

In ancient times music was used for the worship of heaven, earth, and ancestors, for the recitation of poetry, at athletic contests, and as preparation for battle. The division was reflected in two titles: secular music *(su-yueh)* and ritual music *(ya-yueh)*. Instruments were known by the eight materials of which they could be made: earth (pottery), bamboo, leather, wood, gourd, stone, silk, and metal. China is one of the few cultures of the world that has used instruments made of stone, called *lithophones*.

LITHOPHONE

Instruments

Sheng. Among Chinese instruments is the *sheng,* an ancient wind instrument classified as a gourd. Although its wind-chest is made of gourd, the seventeen tubes are bamboo. When the performer sucks in, drawing air across the reed, sound is produced. The sheng is probably the oldest known instrument in the world based on the free-reed (organ) principle. Listen to "Old Monk Sweeping the Buddhist Temple" *(listening selections)* (see pages 91–92). This example has the solo sheng, one of the few Chinese instruments capable of playing melody and harmony simultaneously.

Selection no. 59

Music in China was important to politics, so a great deal of time was spent developing acoustically accurate instruments. Musical instruments were carefully constructed to maintain the stability of the government responsible for their manufacture. "Acoustically accurate" construction was achieved if the instrument could produce musical pitches from a fundamental tone called the *huang-chung* or *yellow bell.* The tone could be sounded on a bamboo tube, bronze bell, or stone chime. According to Chinese legend, in 2697 B.C. the reigning emperor, Huang-ti, the Yellow Emperor, sent a faithful servant to the Western mountains to cut bamboo that would serve to create the fundamental pitch and the musical tones. This suggests the twelve tones, called *lus,* were originally derived from bamboo pipes. A tube of bamboo cut two-thirds the size of a previous pipe produced a pitch one perfect fifth higher. Additional pitches, called the *gamut,* were produced in a ratio of 2:3 after the huang chung was established. Other pitches in the gamut were doubled to keep within one octave. If huang chung were synonymous with middle C (which it is not), the Chinese gamut would be:

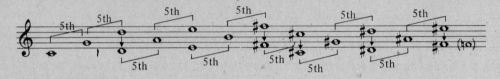

Since Chinese music is pentatonic, five notes were chosen from any five pitches in sequence. If C were huang chung, the scale would then be:

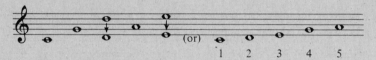

If G, the scale would be:

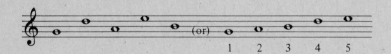

These five tones were known by proper names:

The resulting scale is much like an incomplete major scale:

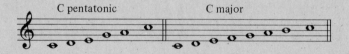

1   Kung
2   Shang
3   Chiao
4   Chih
5   Yu

Chinese music has less dissonance than Western music because it uses no half-steps in the basic scale. However, the Chinese also used two additional tones in the scale, adding two pitches to the preceding pentatonic series.

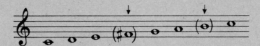

These are called *pien tones* and they were used as ornaments to main tones or as passing tones between, for example, e and g or a and c.

Pien-chung, Chinese chime bells.

Made by Chuang Pen-li. Photo by Chuang Pen-li.

Cheng. The *cheng* is a chordophone said to have originated in the Chin dynasty (221–209 B.C.). It is a forerunner of the Japanese koto. Some have six strings, others as many as twenty-one. Like the koto, the moveable bridges are used for tuning, but many chengs are only four feet in length. The strings, originally made of silk, are now of copper or stainless steel.

Hsiao. The *hsiao*, an end-blown flute, is similar to the Japanese shakuhachi. it is about 24" long. Hsiaos were once made of jade, copper, and even marble, but bamboo is now used most commonly. It has been said that the hsiao was invented in about 2700 B.C. Listen to "Flowers on Brocade" *(listening selections)* (see pages 5–6). Chinese music is almost always programmatic, its descriptive titles conveying a distinct mood or picture. This work uses both the cheng and the hsiao.

Selection no. 2

Sheng performer, cupping the base of the instrument in his hands as he draws in air to produce sound.

Courtesy of K.H. Han. Northern Illinois University.

Cheng, Chinese sixteen-string zither with bridges.

Photo by K.H. Han. Northern Illinois University.

Many Chinese instruments seem similar to Japanese instruments. The *san-hsien*, for example, a three-stringed chordophone, is an ancestor of the Japanese samisen. On the other hand, the *yang ch'in*, a butterfly harp, is similar to a Western hammer dulcimer.

Other Chinese instruments include the *hsuan*, an ocarina made of clay, the *yu-eh ch'in*, a moon-shaped guitar, and the *p'i-p'a*, a lute-like instrument with four strings.

The *pien-ch'ing* is a suspended set of stones arranged in a scale, and the *erh'hu* is a two-stringed Mongolian fiddle tuned in fifths and played by a bow permanently attached between the strings.

Left, san-hsien, Chinese three-string banjo; right, yang ch'in, Chinese hammer dulcimer.

Photos by K.H. Han. Northern Illinois University.

Left, hsuan, Chinese ocarina; right, p'i-p'a, Chinese four-string lute.

Photos by K.H. Han. Northern Illinois University.

Left, pien-ch'ing,
Chinese stone chimes;
right, erh-hu, Chinese
two-string fiddle with
attached bow.

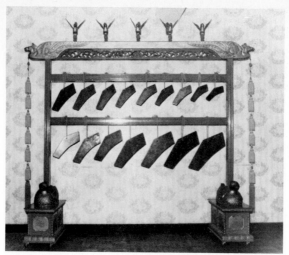 

Photos by K.H. Han and Chuang Pen-li. Northern Illinois University.

Peking Opera

KUO-CHÜ

The most important dramatic music in China is the *Peking opera*, a genre that includes more acrobatics than singing. In the twentieth century it has become known as *Kuo-chü* or national drama. The singing, acting, costuming, and movements are all stylized. Symbolism

Chinese opera. Left, a
young woman who
has an outgoing
character; right, a
young woman of
virtue.

Courtesy of the National Fu Hsing Dramatic Arts Academy, Taipei, Taiwan, Republic of China.

is a major factor; wearing red, for example, signifies dignity, gold means a celestial being, and white represents treachery.

The arias of Peking opera are derived from about thirty standardized melodies, each with a specific connotation. Although these are used in every opera, the lyrics are changed to suit the situation. Peking opera is rarely the work of one composer, but rather is "arranged" by a committee of artists. Singing is usually in a high range, constrained and nasal, with accompaniment provided by percussive instruments that enhance spoken dialogue and acrobatics. Melodic instruments double the melodic line in arias. Western instruments have been added recently to Chinese orchestras, part of a tendency away from traditional heterophony and toward homophony.

TRIBAL MUSIC

Since few regions have been untouched by Western influences, tribal music is rare in the late twentieth century. Young people of Africa probably prefer to hear music on their transistor radios rather than make it themselves. American Indian youth leave the reservations before they can learn the tribal music of their elders. Rarely is music of the corroboree in Australia presented for its original purpose—celebrating the hunt, the coming of rain, the miracle of birth; more often, it is offered as an entertainment for tourists.

Because tribal music is almost extinct, generalizations concerning it are particularly difficult to draw. The following represent what has been observed by ethnomusicologists in times past rather than what is necessarily presently true. The allusions are broad, in an effort to apply certain universal commonalities to a worldwide range of tribal music.

Tribal music is not primitive. It may be performed by persons of a primitive, undeveloped country or tribe, and its instruments may be simple, that is, crafted by hand. But the music itself is not simple, and in fact may be strikingly complicated. Listen to Murat Music of North Borneo *(listening selections)* (see pages 3–4). Selection no. 1

Tribal music is almost always utilitarian, serving societal needs. Through song and dance, a child learns the language of the tribe, traditions of family life, and the taboos, mores, history, and traditions of his or her people. Good music is not defined merely as that which is performed with precision and accuracy. Music is valued because it serves a purpose, and is considered "good" when it fulfills that purpose—if a healing song makes the patient get well, or a rain dance leads to the appearance of clouds. Since the community shapes and adapts the common musical heritage, music that serves no societal purpose is

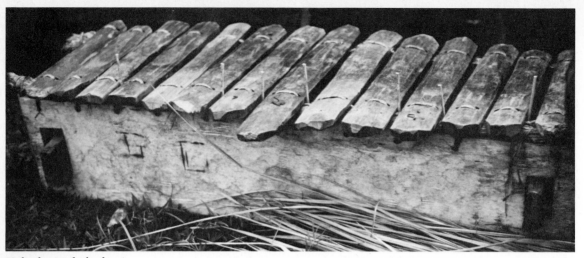

Xylophone (balaphon) from Zaire.

Selection no. 70

simply dropped from the repertoire. Listen to "Ahorohani" (work song), Music of the Black Caribs of Honduras *(listening selections)* (see pages 244–245).

The dual concept of producers and consumers of music rarely exists in tribal societies. All are music makers and all participate in musical endeavors openly and joyously. Although some societies have a medicine man who is responsible for music in general, as well as specialized instrumentalists, the entire tribe typically joins in a performance with singing, clapping, and dancing. People enter and leave the group at will; instruments are often exchanged between performers.

Although the elements of tribal music are the same as those in all music, Western and non-Western, the emphasis may be different. Instrumental timbres are diverse, and idiophones and membranophones occur more commonly than do chordophones and aerophones. The playing techniques are highly varied; a drum, for example, may be struck on various places on the head, rim, or shell to achieve a variety of sounds and effects. Listen to *Darubuka* (hand drum) *(listening selections)* (see page 56).

Selection no. 26

SANSA
MBIRA
Selection no. 94

Some unfamiliar instruments are employed, such as the thumb piano of Central and East Africa, known as the *sansa* or *mbira*. Listen to *Mbutu, mbira, sansa, bells, drums (listening selections)*. As in this example, singing is almost always a part of the fabric of sound, rather than a solo accompanied by supporting instruments.

Melodies are narrow in range, less than an octave, and the arrangement of pitches often is pentatonic. Most pitches are untempered and therefore not in tune with Western scales. A melody may be linked with tribal languages, many of which are inflected, at least in West Africa. In an inflected language, the meaning of a word changes

Zairean drummer,
Bakete Village.

according to the pitch levels invoked when it is pronounced. Instruments, such as the talking drum, can thus be said to "speak," since the two, three, four, and sometimes five pitch levels of inflection may be produced on them. Listen to *Talking Drum with Accompaniment (listening selections)* (see page 127).

Selection no. 49

Mbira from Zaire.

University of Arizona Museum of Art, gift of R. Vernon Hunter.

The rhythmic vitality and energy inherent in this painting are synonymous with those found in tribal music. *The Bow and Arrow Dance*, José Rey Toledo, American, 1940, tempera on paper.

Selection no. 55

Selection no. 6

Harmony is usually incidental in tribal music, occurring because one singer deviates from the melody. In some tribal societies, however, a constant interval, often a third, is used for harmony in singing.

Rhythmic vitality is also typical of much tribal music, polyrhythms prevailing especially in sub-Saharan Africa. Heterorhythms are common among Australian aboriginals. Listen to Cloud Chant (from Northeast Arnhem Land) *(listening selections)* (see pages 166–168). Form usually incorporates repetition, resulting in overall strophic design. Listen to "Navajo Hoop Dance" *(listening selections)* (see page 12).

SUMMARY

Non-Western music is that which is derived from other than the European tradition. It includes music of India, Indonesia, Japan, and China, as well as tribal music. Melodies and scales rarely follow the tempered major and minor sounds of the Western world, and the octave may be divided unevenly into additional pitches, as in India, or evenly into fewer, as in Indonesia. Harmony is rare, its use often incidental, and heterophonic texture is thus common. Rhythm includes the use of beats and accent groupings, but longer cycles may also occur, as in the music of India and Indonesia. In tribal music, poly-rhythms and heterorhythms are common. Timbre requires the most diverse classifications since it includes singing as well as playing instru-ments. Techniques for producing both vocal and instrumental sounds are especially varied in non-Western cultures. Finally, form is rarely return but, rather, processive and strophic.

In general, non-Western music is utilitarian. It is used for a specific purpose—e.g., to accompany dancing—or to produce a physical or emo-tional effect—to attempt control of the weather and environment, to bless, to curse, to heal. There is little "art for art's sake" but, rather, communal use, purpose, and sharing in the music.

STUDY GUIDELINES

KEY TERMS AND CONCEPTS

China
  Cheng
  Hsiao
  Peking Opera
  Sheng
Drone
Heterophony
Heterorhythm
India
  Microtone
  Raga
  Rasa
  Sitar
  Swara (sa, ri, ga, ma, pa, dha, ni)
  Tabla
  Tala
  Tambura

Indonesia
  Bonang
  Colotomic
  Gamelan
  Gender
  Saron
Japan
  Koto
  Samisen
  Shakuhachi
Non-Western music
Polyrhythm

CHAPTER REVIEW

Match items in the two columns. Answers in Appendix.

1. ＿＿＿ koto
2. ＿＿＿ sitar
3. ＿＿＿ gamelan
4. ＿＿＿ mbira
5. ＿＿＿ huang chung
6. ＿＿＿ tala
7. ＿＿＿ shakuhachi
8. ＿＿＿ shruti
9. ＿＿＿ raga
10. ＿＿＿ bonang
11. ＿＿＿ saron
12. ＿＿＿ samisen
13. ＿＿＿ tambura
14. ＿＿＿ sheng
15. ＿＿＿ gender

A. India
B. Indonesia
C. Japan
D. China
E. tribal

FOR FURTHER LISTENING

Africa

African Music
Folkways Records RW 8852

Anthology of Music of Black America
Everest Records 3254 (Three record set)

UNESCO collection—*An Anthology of African Music*
Barenreiter-Musicaphon (Eleven records, BM 30 L2301-2310)

Australia

Tribal Music of Australia
Folkways Records FE 4439

China

China's Instrumental Heritage
Lyrichord Discs LL 92

China's Treasures
Lyrichord Discs LLST 7227

Chinese Classical Instrumental Music
Folkways Records FW 6812

Chinese Folk Opera
Bruno Hi-Fi Records BR-50157

The Ruse of the Empty City (Peking opera)
Folkways Records FW 8882

India

Classical Music of India
Nonesuch Records H-72014

Music of India: Morning and Evening Ragas
Angel Records 35283

The Ragas of India
Folkway Records FL 8368

Three Ragas
Capital Records DT-2720

Indonesia

Golden Rain
Nonesuch Records H-72028

Jasmine Isle, The Javanese Gamelan Music
Nonesuch Records H-72031

Music for the Balinese Shadow Play
Nonesuch Records H-72037

Music of Indonesia
Folkways Records FE 4537 (double album)

Japan

Art of the Koto: The Music of Japan
Elektra Records EKS-7234

Folk Music of Japan
Folkways Records FE 4429

Gagaku: The Imperial Court Music of Japan
Lyrichord Discs LL 126

Japanese Kabuki Nagauta Music
Lyrichord Discs LLST 7134/LL 134

The Koto Music of Japan
Nonesuch Records H-2005/HS 72005

Noh Plays of Japan (double album)
Caedmon TC 2019

Native American

American Indians of the Southwest
Folkways Records FW 8850

Dances of the North American Indians
Folkways Records FD 6510

Music of the American Indians of the Southwest
Folkways Records P420

APPENDIX

ANSWERS FOR CHAPTER REVIEW

Answers for Chapter Review, Chapter One

1.	J	5.	D	8.	H	11.	K	14.	A
2.	F	6.	P	9.	I	12.	G	15.	N
3.	L	7.	B	10.	M	13.	C	16.	E
4.	O								

Answers for Tempos, Notes, and Meters, Chapter Two

1.	O	5.	A	9.	M	13.	I	17.	P
2.	C	6.	K	10.	H	14.	B	18.	N
3.	Q	7.	D	11.	T	15.	R	19.	G
4.	F	8.	S	12.	L	16.	J	20.	E

Answers for Terms and Concepts, Chapter Two

1.	H	4.	D	7.	J	10.	G
2.	E	5.	C	8.	F	11.	I
3.	A	6.	K	9.	B		

Answers for Note Values and Meters, Chapter Two

A. ♩, 𝅗𝅥   **D.** ♪. ♩.   **G.** $\frac{4}{4}$ **J.** $\frac{9}{8}$

B. ♩, ♪   **E.** ♩, 𝅗𝅥.   **H.** $\frac{3}{4}$ **K.** $\frac{5}{4}$ (2+3)

C. ♩, ♪   **F.** ♪, ♪, ♩   **I.** $\frac{6}{8}$

Answers for Chapter Review, Chapter Three

1.	F	4.	C	7.	E	10.	B
2.	I	5.	H	8.	L	11.	G
3.	J	6.	K	9.	A	12.	D

Answers for Chapter Review, Chapter Four

1. F	**5.** I	**9.** E	**13.** S	**17.** O
2. J	**6.** L	**10.** Q	**14.** H	**18.** G
3. N	**7.** B	**11.** C	**15.** M	**19.** P
4. A	**8.** D	**12.** R	**16.** K	

Answers for Chapter Review, Chapter Five

1. J	**5.** I	**9.** N	**13.** C	**17.** R
2. B	**6.** L	**10.** E	**14.** P	**18.** F
3. O	**7.** H	**11.** G	**15.** Q	
4. M	**8.** A	**12.** K	**16.** D	

Answers for Chapter Review, Chapter Six

1. A	**4.** B	**7.** I	**10.** D
2. J	**5.** K	**8.** C	**11.** H
3. F	**6.** G	**9.** E	

Answers for Chapter Review, Chapter Seven

1. G	**4.** I	**7.** D	**10.** J
2. K	**5.** L	**8.** F	**11.** H
3. C	**6.** A	**9.** E	**12.** B

Answers for Chapter Review, Chapter Eight

1. B	**4.** M	**7.** H	**10.** E	**13.** A
2. F	**5.** D	**8.** C	**11.** J	**14.** L
3. I	**6.** N	**9.** K	**12.** G	

Answers for Chapter Review, Chapter Nine

1. B	**4.** B	**7.** A	**10.** B
2. A	**5.** B	**8.** B	**11.** A
3. A	**6.** A	**9.** A	**12.** B

Answers for Chapter Review, Chapter Ten

1. E	**4.** F	**7.** L	**10.** H	**13.** M
2. C	**5.** B	**8.** D	**11.** A	
3. G	**6.** J	**9.** I	**12.** K	

Answers for Chapter Review, Chapter Eleven

1. H	**5.** B	**9.** M	**13.** O
2. L	**6.** I	**10.** A	**14.** P
3. N	**7.** K	**11.** E	**15.** G
4. J	**8.** C	**12.** F	**16.** D

Answers for Chapter Review, Chapter Twelve

1. J	**4.** B	**7.** D	**10.** F	**13.** K
2. A	**5.** I	**8.** L	**11.** H	
3. M	**6.** C	**9.** E	**12.** G	

Answers for Chapter Review, Chapter Thirteen

1. primary triads	**5.** monody
2. stile moderno	**6.** suite
3. ripieno	**7.** equal temperament
4. figured bass	**8.** terraced dynamics

Answers for Chapter Review, Chapter Fourteen

1. G	**4.** A	**7.** F
2. D	**5.** E	**8.** C
3. H	**6.** B	

Answers for Chapter Review, Chapter Fifteen

1. F	**4.** J	**7.** B	**10.** C
2. I	**5.** D	**8.** E	
3. A	**6.** H	**9.** G	

Answers for Chapter Review, Chapter Sixteen

1. F	**4.** E	**7.** F	**10.** A
2. D	**5.** B	**8.** E	
3. D	**6.** E	**9.** B	

Answers for Chapter Review, Chapter Seventeen

1. D	**4.** I	**7.** H	**10.** F
2. B	**5.** J	**8.** G	
3. E	**6.** A	**9.** C	

Answers for Chapter Review, Chapter Eighteen

1. C	**4.** E	**7.** C	**10.** B	**13.** A
2. A	**5.** D	**8.** A	**11.** B	**14.** D
3. B	**6.** A	**9.** A	**12.** C	**15.** B

GLOSSARY

absolute music abstract music not based on extramusical references.

a cappella literally in the style of the chapel—unaccompanied choral music in the Renaissance tradition.

accelerando to speed up.

accent stress: >.

accented beat a stressed beat, which creates strong and weak recurring patterns in meter.

accidentals sharp, flat, or natural occurring outside of the given key signature within a composition.

actual time time as measured by a clock.

adagio slow tempo, but not as slow as largo.

additive form musical design in which repetition does not occur, such as ABCD . . ., and so on.

aerophone wind instrument.

affections catalogued feelings used during the Baroque period.

agitato in an agitated manner or style.

Agnus Dei final movement of the Ordinary of the Mass—literally "Lamb of God."

alap opening, rhapsodic movement in Indian music, usually without a direct beat.

Alberti bass keyboard chordal pattern that treats the pitches of a chord in a rhythmical pattern. Named for Domenico Alberti (1710–1740), who used it extensively.

alla breve cut time, such as $\frac{2}{2}$.

allegretto a little slower than allegro.

allegro fast and lively tempo.

allemande opening dance movement of a suite in moderate $\frac{4}{4}$ time.

alto low female voice.

amplitude height of a sound wave that shows degree of loudness of the sound.

anacrusis pick-up beat or series of beats.

andante moderately slow—a walking tempo.

andantino slightly faster than andante.

animato animated.

antecedent first phrase in a period that asks a musical question and typically cadences on a chord other than the tonic.

antiphonal describing two musical groups that perform alternately in a call-response manner.

appassionato passionately.

aria solo song in opera, oratorio, or cantata that is usually accompanied by an orchestra.

arpeggio broken chord whose pitches are heard successively.

Ars Nova term referring to music of fourteen-century Italy and France in which counterpoint became more independent and duple time was incorporated.

art music music that requires study to understand its tradition and training to perform it—a type of music often referred to as "classical," as opposed to folk music.

art song fusion of poetry and melody to create a composition for solo singer and piano, such as lieder.

assai modifying term meaning "very."

associative listener one who sees visual images or makes up stories as while listening.

asymmetrical meter nonsymmetrical meter, grouped by accents into fives, sevens, and so on, with subdivisions such as 2 + 3 and 2 + 3 + 2.

527

a tempo return to the original tempo.

atonality absence of tonality or of a tonal center.

attentive listener one who listens for the mood and feeling and then analyzes through the musical elements of rhythm, melody, harmony, timbre, dynamics, and form.

audible frequency spectrum range of pitches humans are able to hear, 16 cycles per second to 16,000.

augmentation proportional lengthening of all note values.

augmented triad a three-pitch chord consisting of two major thirds, such as C-E-G sharp.

authentic mode medieval mode used from low to high, all pitches falling within the gamut of the octave, such as d to d' in the Dorian mode.

background underlying rhythm and harmony of a musical composition.

ballade character piece of the nineteenth century, often in ABA form, incorporating one heroic and one lyric theme.

balophon African xylophone.

baritone man's vocal range that falls between tenor and bass.

bar line vertical dividing line between measures on the musical staff.

Baroque stylistic period of music between 1600 and 1750.

bas instrument soft-sounding instrument used during the Renaissance, suitable for indoor performance.

bass lowest male vocal range.

bass clef F clef that indicates the placement of f below c_1.

basso continuo bass-line and accompanying chords for keyboard instruments, used extensively in Baroque period.

baya larger drum of the tabla, played with performer's left hand.

beam straight-line flags that join notes, such as eighths, when two or more are used in succession: ♫.

beat underlying pulsation of many types of music, which may be heard, in which case it is referred to as direct, or felt, in which case it is referred to as indirect.

binary form two-part form.

bithematic using two themes.

bitonality set in two tonalities or keys simultaneously.

blue tones lowered third, fifth, and seventh degrees of the major scale often used in some types of jazz.

bonang Indonesian instrument consisting of several metal kettles arranged in scale-like fashion.

boogie-woogie piano jazz and improvisation of the 1930s, incorporating a stylized ostinato in the left hand.

bop jazz of the 1940s.

bore diameter of the tubing in an aerophone.

brass family orchestral instruments using cup-shaped mouthpieces, including the trumpet, French horn, trombone, and tuba.

breve note value used in the Middle Ages and Renaissance and notated as □. It is now commonly referred to as a double-whole note.

broken consort instruments not of the same family.

Bugaku danced portions of Japanese Gagaku.

Burgundian school transitional period of music between the Middle Ages and the Renaissance, centered in the Burgundy region of present-day France. The innovations of this period, in the middle of the fifteenth century, include use of intervals of thirds and sixths, fauxbourdon, and melodic interest in the top voice.

caccia medieval hunting song using two upper voices in canon, with an accompanying lower part in slower-moving note values.

cadence punctuation or termination of a musical phrase.

cadenza solo, virtuoso display for the featured soloist often occurring near the end of the first movement of a solo concerto.

call-response a type of singing or performing in which one group or individual leads and a second group follows in direct (or at least similar) imitation.

cancrizans retrograde-inversion, central to twelve-tone music (contour is upside down and row is presented backwards).

canon composition or technique in which one melody is imitated by a second melody, either exactly or very closely. A round is an example of an exact canon.

cantabile in a singing style.

cantata literally a musical composition for voices, but usually incorporating aria and recitative for soloists with orchestral accompaniment.

cantus firmus a fixed melody, usually derived from Gregorian chant.

cantus firmus Mass a Mass setting that incorporates a fixed melody, derived from Gregorian chant, in each of its movements.

canzona multi-sectioned instrumental composition, often in additive form, of the late Renaissance.

castrato a neutered adult male who sings in the soprano range.

C clef clef that identifies middle c, c_1, on the staff: ‖𝄡.

chaconne continuous variations based on a harmonic progression.

chalumeau forerunner of the clarinet; the lowest register of the clarinet.

chamber music instrumental music with one or two performers on each part, as contrasted with symphonic music, in which several performers may perform each part.

changing meter descriptive term for rhythmic notation that frequently changes meter, often with every measure.

character cycle collection of character pieces performed in one unit as a longer composition.

character piece short piece for the piano, such as a waltz, mazurka, polonaise, etude, popular during the nineteenth century.

chart jazz score, often abbreviated.

cheng Chinese zither with moveable bridges, often incorporating 16 strings.

ch'in Chinese zither with seven strings.

chorale hymn-tune used for congregational singing.

chorale cantata a longer vocal composition based on a church chorale.

chord simultaneous combination of at least three different pitches.

chordophone instrument that produces its sound through the vibration of strings.

chromatic scale consisting entirely of half-steps or a melody based on such a scale.

clavichord early keyboard instrument in which the key action allows a metal tangent to hit the string in the case, thus producing a musical pitch. The strings are typically parallel to the keyboard.

clef symbol indicating pitch placement on the staff: 𝄞 , 𝄢 , ‖𝄡, g_1, f, c_1, respectively.

closed position pitches of a chord placed so that all tones are in the closest proximity possible one to another.

closely related keys tonalities that share numerous common pitches.

cluster chord built of seconds, half-steps and whole-steps.

coda ending, outside of standard forms, added to a musical composition.

codetta abbreviated coda.

col legno playing the strings of a violin (or other string instrument) with the wood of the bow.

color melodic unit in an isorhythmic motet.

coloratura florid, agile singing.

colotomic term referring to the group of rhythm-keepers in Indonesian music.

common practice term used to refer to European art music of the seventeenth through nineteenth centuries, in which certain conventions of harmonic usage, essentially triadic chords, as well as form and genres were consistent.

complete cadence cadence that terminates on the tonic triad, with the tonic tone appearing as the highest-sounding pitch.

compound meter meter in which the basic beat is a dotted note value and the movement of patterns and melodies over this basic beat is a division into triplets rather than duplets. Common compound meters include $\frac{6}{8}$, $\frac{9}{8}$, and $\frac{12}{8}$.

compound ternary large three-part form in which each main section has its own unique form, the total movement then reflecting both small- and large-scale form.

concertato style compositional style incorporating contrast through the use of small and large musical groups, as in a concerto grosso.

concert master/mistress leader of the violins in an orchestra, serving somewhat as second-in-command for the entire orchestra.

concerto composition for soloists and orchestra, often in three movements.

concerto grosso concerto using more than one soloist, such as a small group called a concertino, playing within and against the entire orchestral accompaniment, called a ripieno or tutti.

concert overture one-movement symphonic work that can be either programmatic or absolute. Concert overtures are often used as the opening composition in a concert.

conductus medieval composition in a homophonic style.

conjunct melodic movement with close pitches; stepwise movement.

con moto with motion.

consequent the answer phrase in a period, often terminated with a complete cadence, thus ending on the tonic chord.

consonance absence of tension or dischord in music.

consort group of instruments.

continuous variations type of processive form in which one variation runs over into the next without a clear-cut sectioning or cadencing. Chaconnes and passacaglias are examples of continuous variation.

contour melodic direction.

contrafactum vocal composition in which the original text is replaced by a new one, such as German for Latin, or secular for sacred.

contralto lowest female vocal range.

contrary motion movement of two melodies in opposite directions.

cool jazz jazz style of the 1950s.

cornett wood or ivory aerophone using a cup-shaped mouthpiece but with finger holes instead of valves or keys.

counterpoint movement of two or more melodies in a polyphonic texture.

countersubject contrasting theme used polyphonically against the statement of a fugal subject.

coupler mechanical or electronic device on an organ that allows the timbres available on one manual to be played on a second manual.

couplet two rhyming lines of poetry.

courante the second traditional dance in a suite, often in triple time and with a faster tempo than the opening allemande.

course on lute-like instruments, two or more strings tuned in unison or at the octave and played together to reinforce the level of dynamics.

cps cycles per second, referring to frequency of a vibrating sound. A = 440 cps means a_1 above middle c (c_1) vibrates at 440 cycles per second. CPS is equivalent to hertz.

Credo third movement of the Ordinary of the Mass, stating the church beliefs.

crescendo to become louder gradually: $<$.

critical listener one who judges aspects of performance quality while listening.

crook piece of tubing inserted into a brass instrument to change its harmonic spectrum.

cross stringing a means of allowing some of the strings of a grand piano to fan across others, thus reducing the need for a long piano case and also reinforcing the resonance of the sound because of overtones.

cyclic theme melody used in more than one movement of a larger work, such as a symphony or mass.

da capo aria solo vocal piece in two sections (AB) in which the B section is followed by repetition of the A though observation of the written directions D.C. al Fine—return to the "head" (Capo) of the music and continue to the "finish" (Fine). In Baroque practice, the repeat of the A section is usually accomplished with added ornamentation.

dan a set theme of 108 beats in Japanese music that is used as the basis of variations.

daya the smaller drum of the Indian *tabla*, played with the performer's right hand.

decibel unit for measuring volume of sound.

decrescendo to become softer gradually: $>$.

definite pitch referring to pitched percussion instruments, such as the xylophone or glockenspiel, as well as those that can produce a set pitch, such as tympani.

descant melody of only a few pitches added above a given, perhaps well-known melody; a countermelody.

development the middle section of a sonata-allegro form in which thematic material is worked out by being subjected to various modulations and treatments of timbre and dynamics.

diatonic eight-pitch scale incorporating five whole-steps and two half-steps. Major scales are diatonic. In a diatonic scale, each pitch name is used in sequence within an octave.

didjeridu Australian aerophone.

diminuendo to become softer gradually; decrescendo.

diminution proportionally shortening all note values.

disjunct melodic movement by skips and leaps.

dissonance dischord in music, suggesting a state of tension or "seeking."

distant keys tonalities that do not share common pitches.

divertimento light instrumental composition with numerous short movements, written for mixed groups of instrumentation.

division variation form in which activity of melody is continually divided into smaller note values.

dodecaphony twelve-tone music.

dolce sweetly.

dominant the fifth pitch and/or chord of a diatonic scale.

dominant seventh chord extended chord built on the fifth note of a major or minor scale and incorporating a triad plus an added seventh.

dot notational device that lengthens a given duration by half: ♩. = ♩ ♪, for example.

double bar two bar lines used to signal the end of a song or section.

double escapement a mechanism incorporated into the action of a piano that allows rapid reiteration of a key.

double flat symbol that lowers a pitch by two half-steps: ♭♭.

double fugue fugue that uses two subjects.

double sharp symbol which raises a pitch by two half-steps: ✗.

double stop   playing two strings, such as on a violin, at once.

drone   repeated or held pitch, such as occurs in Indian music or on the bagpipes.

duet   composition for two performers.

duple time   rhythm that has an accent every other beat.

duplum   the voice added above the tenor in medieval music.

dynamics   degree of loudness in music, including the change from one level to another.

electrophone   musical instrument that produces sounds through electrical energy or voltage, such as with a sound generator or oscillator.

embouchure   position and application of the lips and muscles of the face to the mouthpiece of an aerophone.

enharmonic   two pitches that sound the same but are spelled differently, such as C sharp and D flat.

entr'acte   an instrumental composition to be performed between the acts of a staged production.

episode   transition section in a composition that contains secondary material heard between statements of main themes.

equal temperament   an accepted way of tuning that equalizes half-steps, thus making some intervals within an octave narrower or wider than they actually occur. Equal temperament allows the performer to play in any tonality on a keyboard instrument (or on most fixed-pitch instruments).

erh-hu   Chinese two-stringed bowed fiddle.

espressivo   expressively.

etude   a musical study; a type of character piece for piano, a form used extensively by Chopin.

euphonium   baritone horn, a brass instrument.

even pattern   rhythmic pattern that either moves exactly with the underlying beat or evenly divides two or four notes over the beat.

exposition   first section of a sonata-allegro movement in which two themes are typically introduced, contrasted by key as well as contour and timbre.

extended chord   triad to which additional thirds have been added, making it a seventh chord, a ninth chord, and so on.

familiar style   in homophonic style.

fantasia   mood-piece based on somewhat free play of the composer's ideas, resulting in a free form; a type of character piece.

fauxbourdon   false bass, so called from the use of triads in first inversion by composers of the Burgundian court.

fermata   a hold: ⌢.

field holler   work song of southern blacks in pre–Civil War days.

fifth   in a triad, the second pitch added above the root and after the third. In the triad C-E-G, G is the fifth (so called because it is the interval of a fifth higher than the root).

figured bass   musical shorthand for keyboard players who provided the continuo during the Baroque period. Various figurations indicate to the performer what harmonies are to be added.

flag   appendage on certain note stems that distinguishes their value. Eighth notes have one flag (♪), sixteenth notes two (♬), thirty-second notes, three (♬).

flat   symbol that lowers a pitch by one half-step: ♭.

folk music   simple music of national origin, usually not requiring advanced musical training and technique to perform.

foreground   the prominent features of a musical composition, such as the melody and main motives, as distinguished from the background of accompaniment and harmony.

form musical design, incorporating repetition and contrast, unity and variety.

forte loud.

fortissimo very loud.

forzato forced or accented.

free-form jazz jazz of recent times that does not use a set tune as the basis of improvisation, but rather allows the performers to interact and to generate their own composition through this musical interaction.

fret thin strip of metal or wood dividing the neck of lute-like instruments, such as the guitar or sitar, marking a place to stop the string for raising the pitch progressively.

French overture musical composition in one movement that typically begins slow, has a middle section in a faster tempo, and then returns, even if only briefly, to the opening slower tempo.

frequency speed with which a tone vibrates, such as $a_1 = 440$ cps, a standard of tuning in the Western world.

frottola Italian song c. 1500 in strophic form, harmonized with the melody in the uppermost part.

fugue polyphonic composition for a set number of parts or voices (two to four being common), in which a subject (theme) is imitated by each part, entering in one and then in another. Each voice or part may present the subject several times. A fugue is typically a processive form.

fundamental a main pitch or the first harmonic heard in an overtone series.

funky jazz jazz of recent times that returns to simple chords and driving rhythms in a gospel-like interpretation.

fusion jazz jazz of recent times that combines jazz techniques, particularly improvisation, with another type of music, such as rock, country-western, or Indian.

gagaku Japanese theatrical form dating from the eighth century that incorporates music and dance.

gamelan Indonesian orchestra, consisting largely of metallophones.

gamut range or compass of pitches.

gangsa Balinese metallophone.

gat concluding portion of a presentation of Indian music in which the tala is introduced by drums and becomes the basis for coordinating improvisations by the melodic instrument, such as the sitar, and the drums, such as the tabla.

gaukler medieval minstrel, especially from German regions.

gavotte a dance, often heard in the suite as an optional inclusion, in moderate quadruple time, such as $\frac{4}{4}$.

gender Indonesian metallophone characterized by having an individual tube resonator for each metal key.

gigue concluding dance of a suite in a quick tempo, usually set in compound duple or quadruple time, such as $\frac{6}{8}$ or $\frac{12}{8}$.

gleeman medieval minstel, especially from English regions.

glissando fast, uninterrupted sweep of pitches up or down an instrument, such as piano or harp.

Gloria second movement of the Ordinary of the Mass, celebrating the glory of God.

goliards students who became minstrels during the Middle Ages and sang songs based on Latin poems.

gong ageng large gong used in the gamelan to punctuate the ending of each rhythmic cycle by the colotomic group of instruments.

grand opera nineteenth-century opera that became somewhat grandiose in design, incorporating a larger orchestra, continuous singing, and a large cast.

grand staff name given to the joining of the treble and bass staffs to create a continuous range of pitches.

grave very slow and solemn.

grazioso gracefully.

ground bass   short musical phrase repeated as a bass line, over which melodic variations occur, as in a passacaglia.

half-step   the closest pitch above or below any given pitch on the keyboard, such as c to c♯ or e to f.

harmonic rhythm   actual movement of chord changes underlying a melody.

harmony   simultaneous sound of two or more different pitches.

haut instrument   a loud instrument during the Renaissance, suitable for out-of-door performance.

heptatonic   seven-toned, as a heptatonic scale.

hertz   cycles per second.

heterophony   texture characterized by similar melodies occurring simultaneously.

heterorhythm   rhythmic structure in which two or more different and noncoordinated pulses each support a variety of patterns or melodies above them.

homophony   texture characterized by one melody supported by chordal accompaniment.

hsiao   Chinese vertical notched flute.

hsuan   Chinese ocarina made of pottery.

huang chung   the beginning pitch in Chinese music theory for deriving all additional pitches or lus.

idiophone   a self-vibrating instrument, that is, one that produces its sound by its inherent material, such as wood or metal.

imitative canon   canon whose second melody follows the first in contour and motion, but does not necessarily use each pitch exactly as found in the first melody.

impromptu   character piece with an improvisatory flavor.

improvisation   the art of creating a composition or ornamenting a melody extemporaneously.

incomplete cadence   punctuation point at the end of a phrase that does not sound finished, since it may pause on the subdominant or dominant seventh chord. Incomplete cadences are often used at the end of an antecedent phrase.

indeterminancy   term referring to music that has elements of chance or a great deal of freedom.

inflected language   language in which the meanings of words are determined by how they are pitched as well as what is actually said.

intensity   degree of loudness; dynamics.

intermezzo   character piece of casual creation and importance.

interval   the measured distance between two pitches.

introduction   short section of a composition that precedes the main musical theme or section. It may contrast in tempo with the main material.

invention   short keyboard piece in two-part counterpoint, based on a single motive.

inversion   arranging the tones of a chord in an order different from the way they are derived; performing a melody by turning the contour upside down.

isorhythm   late medieval compositional technique for providing greater unity in a composition by incorporating two repeating elements—a color, or melody, and talea, or rhythmic pattern.

Italian overture   instrumental composition in one movement but divided into three sections, the first and third of which are in a fast tempo, the middle of which is slow.

jegogan   a Balinese metallophone

jongleur   medieval minstrel, especially from French regions.

Kabuki   Japanese theatrical form incorporating music, dancing, and acting. Men portray all characters in Kabuki.

kalungu   African talking-drum.

key   the basic scale and tonality of a composition.

keynote   the tonic pitch, number one of the scale.

key signature   designation of sharps or flats at the beginning of a composition to indicate its basic scale and tonality.

khali   silent beat.

klangfarbenmelodie   serialized melody in which timbre is also a leading factor, especially in twelve-tone music.

klavier   generic name for keyboard instruments.

koto   Japanese zither with thirteen strings and moveable bridges.

ko-tsuzumi   Japanese hourglass drum used in Noh drama, held on the shoulder while being played.

krummhorn   medieval double-reed aerophone.

Kuo-Chü   Chinese national drama.

Kyrie Eleison   opening movement of the Ordinary of the Mass, using the text, "Lord Have Mercy."

largo   very slow.

leading tone triad   triad constructed on the seventh note of a diatonic major or minor scale.

ledger line   short line added above or below a staff to allow notation of a pitch that does not occur on the main staff.

legato   smooth and flowing.

leitmotif   leading motive; use of a theme to identify a character, emotion, or topic in a musical composition, notably in the music-drama of Richard Wagner.

libretto   text of an opera, oratorio, or cantata.

lied   German art song (pl., *lieder*).

liederkreis   cycle of art songs.

lithophone   musical instrument that uses stone as the source of sound.

lu   Chinese pitches.

lute   chordophone used during the Renaissance, characterized by a rounded body shaped like a halved pear, incorporating several strings (often eleven) and frets. Its sound is produced by the plucking of the performer's fingers.

lyre   chordophone with a yoke, characterized by numerous strings attached at one end to a crossbar, at the other to the resonating body. Each string is able to produce only one pitch.

madrigal   secular vocal composition in the vernacular or "mother" tongue, popular during the Renaissance.

maestoso   majestically.

Magnificat   vocal composition in Latin considered a canticle to the Virgin, since it uses the text "My soul doth magnify the Lord" (Magnificat anima mea Dominum).

major diatonic scale   scale built on the formula of two whole steps, one half-step, three whole steps, one half-step.

major triad   triad built of one major third and one minor third, such as C E G. In a major key, the tonic, subdominant, and dominant chords are all major triads.

mallet   stick or beater with a padded end used to strike a percussion instrument.

manual   a keyboard.

Mass   musical work used to celebrate the most solemn ritual of the Catholic church, Holy Eucharist. The Ordinary of the Mass is used for most occasions and includes five parts or movements: Kyrie, Gloria, Credo, Santus-Benedictus, and Agnus Dei. The Proper of the Mass changes according to church season, and includes portions such as the Introit, Gradual, and Offertory.

matra   beat in Indian tala.

mazurka   character piece, based on a Polish dance of the same name, in triple time with an accent on the second beat of each grouping.

mbira African idiophone commonly known as the "thumb" piano.

measure division of accented beats into set groups in musical notation. A measure is denoted by a bar line.

mela parent scale or set of pitches from which a raga is derived.

melismatic text setting in which each syllable has several pitches.

melody the tune in music; pitch that is organized into a logical and recognizable unit by rhythm.

membranophone class of instruments that produce sound by a vibrating membrane, such as the head of a drum.

meno modifying word meaning "less."

Messa Brevis abbreviated, often spoken Mass.

Messa Pro Defunctis funeral or requiem Mass.

metallophone xylophone-like instrument with metal keys.

meter signature written indication in a musical composition that specifies accent groupings and the type of note that will receive the beat throughout the composition. For example ¾ means triple time with the quarter note receiving one beat.

metronome mechanical or electronic device that sounds beats and can be adjusted to indicate a variety of tempos.

mezzo medium.

mezzo forte medium loud (mf).

mezzo piano medium soft (mp).

mezzo soprano a medium soprano; one who sings in the lower part of the soprano range.

microtone pitch division smaller than a half-step, such as a quarter-tone.

Minnesinger medieval poet-musician of noble birth in Germany who composed secular songs.

minor diatonic scale scale built on the formula of one whole step, one half-step, two whole steps, one half-step, two whole steps.

minor triad triad built with one minor third and one major third, such as C E flat G. In a minor key, the tonic, subdominant, and dominant triads are minor, although the dominant is frequently altered to make it a major triad so a seventh tone can be added to allow its use as a dominant seventh chord.

mixed meter changing meter.

mode diatonic scale other than major or minor, especially the dorian, phrygian, lydian, and mixolydian, used extensively in the Middle Ages and Renaissance.

moderato moderately.

modified-strophic form used in art song in which one or more strophes (repetitions) may be slightly altered or changed to conform more closely to text or to provide contrast.

modulation changing from one tonality to another within a composition.

molto modifying term meaning "very" or "much."

monody a single melody accompanied with sparse harmony.

monophonic texture characterized by a single melody without accompaniment.

monothematic using one theme only, as in many fugues.

mordent type of melodic ornamentation.

mosso motion.

motet polyphonic vocal composition in one movement.

motive rhythmic or melodic idea used as a building block for a melody or phrase.

movement one part of a larger composition that is relatively complete and independent, much like one chapter of a novel. Symphonies and sonatas are often cast in three or four movements that are contrasted by tempo and meter.

multiple-tracking more than one track of

sound in an electronic system, such as stereo (two) or quadriphonic (four).

music-drama Wagnerian approach to grand opera that uses continuous singing, orchestral commentary, leitmotifs, and plots derived from Teutonic mythology.

musique concrète system of electronic composition in which natural sounds are taped, edited, and shaped into a composition recorded on magnetic tape.

mute device attached to string instruments or placed in the bell of brass instruments to alter the timbre by restricting or changing the overtones produced.

natural mark that cancels out a sharp or a flat: ♮.

neume notational symbol used in Gregorian chant during the Middle Ages: ◆.

nocturne character piece, invented by John Field but popularized by Frédéric Chopin, in which a languid melody is accompanied by an arpeggiated harmonic structure, reminiscent of melancholy and thus suitable for performance in evening (although it may be performed at any time).

Noh drama Japanese theatrical form originating in fourteenth century for the entertainment of feudal lords.

non-harmonic tone pitch that is outside a given chord.

non-transposing instrument that sounds C when it reads C, thus, a concert pitch instrument. The flute, oboe, violin, and bassoon are all non-transposing instruments.

non troppo not too much.

non-Western music world music that does not follow the traditions and structures of Western or European-based music.

oblique motion type of counterpoint in which one melody remains momentarily on one pitch while the second melody moves either up or down in relationship to it.

octave an interval of eight pitch names, such as c to c_1; a distance of twelve half-steps.

octet composition for eight performers.

open position pitches of a chord placed so that they are not in the closest proximity that is possible.

opera staged drama that is predominantly sung, often incorporating aria and recitative, with orchestral accompaniment.

opus a term meaning "works," referring to a chronological ordering of a composer's compositions during his/her lifetime of production.

oratorio a quasi-religious vocal production that is similar in musical construction to opera, but is neither staged nor acted out.

Ordinary those parts (movements) of the Mass that remain the same regardless of the church season. These are Kyrie, Gloria, Credo, Sanctus-Benedictus, and Agnus Dei.

ordo one statement of a medieval rhythmic mode. Iambic in fourth ordo would indicate a weak-strong-weak-strong-weak-strong-weak strong arrangement of each single phrase in a composition.

organum an early appearance of harmony in Gregorian chant in which a second melody (vox organalis) was added to the existing plainsong (vox principalis). Although its early manifestations were in parallel organum, it eventually became somewhat freed from the vox principalis and developed into free and melismatic organum, which eventually developed into the motet.

ornament melodic decoration, such as a trill, turn, or mordent.

oscillator electronic sound generator.

ostinato repeated rhythmic, melodic, or harmonic pattern that becomes part of the accompaniment.

o-tsuzumi Japanese hour-glass drum used in Noh drama; it is held and played on the lap.

overture extended orchestral introduction to an opera, ballet or similar type of musical presentation.

paired dances grouping of two contrasting dances arranged for instruments for concert purposes, such as the pavanne (slow) and galliard (fast).

paired phrases a period with two phrases, an antecedent and consequent.

panning moving the sound electronically from one track (speaker) to another, much like panning with a movie camera.

parallel keys tonalities that have the same tonic pitch, such as C major and c minor, but different key signatures.

parallel motion counterpoint in which melodies move in the same direction at the same time, whether up or down.

parlando a manner of singing that approximates speaking.

parody Mass mass that uses as its basis material derived from another source, such as secular song, including its melody, rhythm, and harmony.

partita a suite.

passacaglia continuous variations on a bass melody (ground bass).

passing tone nonharmonic tone that literally moves between two chordal tones.

Passion a musical setting of the events leading to Christ's crucifixion, performed the week prior to Easter.

pelog Indonesian heptatonic scale.

pentatonic any five-tone scale.

period double phrase paired into antecedent (question) and consequent (answer).

phrase melodic unit ending with a cadence, often analogous to a "breath" length.

pianissimo very soft (pp).

piano soft (p).

piccolo trumpet a smaller version of the trumpet that plays in a higher register. It usually has four piston valves.

pien-ch'ing Chinese lithophone using tuned pieces of stone, such as jade.

pien-chung Chinese idiophone using tuned bronze bells.

pien tone passing tone in Chinese scale, used in addition to the five basic tones.

p'i-p'a Chinese lute

pitch the highness or lowness of sound determined by its frequency of vibration.

pitch class pitches that share the same name but may occur in different octaves, such as CC, c, c_3.

pitch sweep an electronic glissando.

più more.

pivot chord chord that is common to two tonalities or keys and is used as the basis of modulating from one to the other.

pizzicato playing string instruments by plucking with the fingers rather than bowing.

plagal mode an arrangement of the pitches of a mode so that the interval a fifth above the final and a fourth below are used, thus resulting in a different contour from melodies based on an authentic mode. The pitches used in a plagal mode are the same as those used in an authentic of similar name (Hypodorian and Dorian, for example), but the octave in which they occur may be different.

plainsong Gregorian chant.

plectrum pick.

poco little.

polonaise character piece derived from the Polish dance of the same name, typically in triple time and often stately.

polychoral antiphonal music for two or more groups.

polyphonic lied contrapuntal setting of a folk song.

polyphony texture in which two or more independent melodies occur simultaneously, thus generating their own harmony.

polyrhythm two or more rhythms occurring simultaneously, resulting in shifting accents and cross-rhythms.

polytonality based on two or more tonalities or keys simultaneously.

portative organ small, portable medieval organ.

prelude composition that precedes another composition, often as the opening work; a short character piece based on one theme or motive.

prepared piano mutation of a traditional piano's timbre by the insertion of various devices and paraphernalia among and between the strings.

prestissimo faster than presto.

presto very fast; faster than allegro.

primary chord the tonic, subdominant, and dominant chords of a major or minor key; I, IV, and V chords.

processive form repetition of a musical section or idea with variation.

program music music that conveys a narrative or visual setting.

program symphony symphonic composition in several movements that has an extra-musical reference, whether story or picture.

Proper those portions of the Mass that change according to church calendar and season, such as the Introit, Gradual, and Offertory.

psychic time perception of the passage of time, in contrast to actual clock time.

pulse beat.

quadruple time rhythm that has an accent every fourth beat.

quadruplum fourth voice of polyphony of a motet, added above the cantus firmus and after the duplum and triplum have been added.

quartal harmony chords built on the interval of a fourth.

quarter tone one-half of a half-step.

quarter tone scale scale of twenty-four pitches, each separated by a quarter tone.

quartet composition for four instruments, voices, or family of instruments.

quintet composition for five instruments, voices, or family of instruments.

quatrain four lines of poetry; a strophe of four phrases.

raga Indian melodic material; a traditional melodic pattern or mode, or the improvisation based on it.

ragtime piano jazz popular at the end of the nineteenth and beginning of the twentieth century in which a syncopated right-hand melody is accompanied by straight bass-chord ostinati in the left hand.

range distance between the highest and lowest pitches used in a melody, that is, its outer limits.

rank set of organ pipes producing one timbre.

rasa feeling.

realization performing bass line and filling in the harmonies implied in a figured bass on a keyboard instrument.

recapitulation third section of a sonata-allegro movement in which both themes appear in the opening tonality; a return.

recitative type of speech-song used in opera, oratorio, and cantata to convey text on a pitch. It is usually performed without a rigid beat and accompanied sparsely, such as with a harpsichord and cello.

refrain chorus of music repeated at intervals in a song, especially following each verse.

regal small reed organ.

register given pitch compass of an instrument or voice that is identifiable by a slightly different timbre. The clarinet, for example, has three registers, the chalumeau, the clarion, and the altissimo.

relative keys   tonalities that share the same key signature, such as C major and a minor, but have different tonics.

Requiem   funeral Mass.

responsorial   style of singing or reciting in which one leader alternates with a chorus.

retrograde   backwards.

retrograde-inversion   backwards with a contour turned upside down; cancrizans.

return form   musical form in which one or several musical ideas are heard between contrasting sections or ideas, such as ABA or ABACA.

reverberation   echo.

rhythm   the movement and distribution of music in a time framework, including its tempo, beat, accent, and pattern.

ricercar(e)   instrumental equivalent of the vocal motet, that is, a Renaissance instrumental composition that is largely polyphonic, each phrase or section being a point of imitation.

riff   jazz ostinato.

ripieno   the large group (tutti) in a concerto grosso.

ritardando   a decrease in tempo.

ritenuto   held back.

Rococo   an eighteenth-century style of art, somewhat transitional between the Baroque and Classical styles, characterized by a high degree of decoration and ornamentation.

rondo   spirited and lively return form, frequently cast in ABABA, ABACA, or ABACABA, and often used as a final movement in symphonies, sonatas, and concertos.

root   the pitch which is the foundation or building block of a chord.

root position   the position of a chord whose root is the lowest sounding pitch. In a C major chord, it would be C.

round   a strict canon in which each part performs the same melody, entering in turn at a different but set time, such as one measure, two measures, and so on.

rubato   deviation in tempo characterized by a slight increase followed immediately by a slight decrease, resulting in a subtle pushing and pulling of the basic beat and tempo.

sackbut   medieval trombone.

sam   the main matra in a tala; downbeat.

samisen   Japanese chordophone with three strings, held and played like a guitar.

samvadi   pitch in a raga a fifth higher than the vadi, acting as a dominant.

Sanctus   fourth movement of the Ordinary of the Mass, meaning "Holy, holy, holy."

Sankyoku   Japanese trio of samisen, koto, and shakuhachi.

sansa   mbira (African "thumb" piano).

sarabande   third dance of a suite in slow, triple time.

saron   Indonesian metallophone in which metal keys are placed over a wooden trough that acts as a resonator.

SATB   soprano, alto, tenor, and bass.

scale   catalog of pitches arranged from low to high.

scat singing   style of vocal jazz improvisation in which nonsense syllables are used to imitate the sound of an instrument.

score order   arrangement of an open orchestral score in a standard format, with woodwind instruments appearing at the top arranged from high to low, followed by brass and percussion, with the string family at the very bottom.

secondary dominant   a dominant seventh to a triad other than the tonic, such as the dominant of the dominant.

secondary triad   a triad other than the tonic (I), subdominant (IV), or dominant (V).

sectional variation   processive form in which

a theme with a set phrase structure is used as the basis for subsequent variations, all of which follow the same phrase structure.

semibreve whole note: ◇ or ○.

sempre always.

sensuous listener one who bathes in the sound without really listening.

senza battuta without beat.

septet composition for seven instruments, voices, or family of instruments.

sequence repetition of a melodic idea or phrase at a higher or lower pitch level.

serenade instrumental composition for a small group of performers, often more for entertainment than formal concert presentation. A serenade, like a divertimento, may be in several short movements.

serialism use of a set sequence of pitches as the basis for a musical composition, such as the ordering of the twelve chromatic tones, which are then transposed, inverted, presented retrograde, and so on.

sextet composition for six instruments, voices, or family of instruments.

7-6-1 cadence frequently used by Burgundian composers in which the melody resolved to 1 (or 8) at the cadence, not directly after the leading tone was sounded, but after sounding the submediant (6), thus resolving in order of 7-6-1.

seventh the added tone that distinguishes a dominant chord from a dominant seventh, so called because the added fourth pitch forms an interval of a seventh with the root.

sforzato played with special emphasis; a forced accent (also called sforzando) (sfz).

shakuhachi Japanese vertical notched flute.

sharp symbol that raises a pitch by one half-step: ♯.

shawm medieval double-reed aerophone considered a forerunner of the modern oboe.

sheng Chinese mouth organ.

sho Japanese mouth organ.

shruti microtonic division of the Indian gamut into twenty-two possible intervals.

simple binary AB.

simple meter meter signature in which the top number is 2, 3, or 4, designating division of measures into, respectively, duple, triple, or quadruple time. The bottom number in such a signature designates the type of duration used for the beat; for example, 4 stands for quarter note, 8 for eighth note.

simultaneous improvisation type of improvisation used in some styles of jazz, notably dixieland, in which two or three performers improvise at the same time, following a given harmonic progression. In dixieland, the trumpet usually carries the main melody, the clarinet elaborates around the trumpet part, and the trombone fills in the harmonies.

sine wave representation (on an oscilloscope) of a sound devoid of all overtones, only the fundamental thus being present.

sinfonia generic name for an orchestral composition during the Baroque period.

Singspiel German folk opera.

sitar Indian chordophone.

slendro Indonesian pentatonic scale.

slide trumpet trumpet equipped with a slide mechanism, not unlike that used on the trombone, that enables the performer to fill in the missing notes of the harmonic series by lengthening the instrument's tubing.

solo composition for one performer.

sonata instrumental composition in several movements, typically three or four.

sonata-allegro form return form consisting of three sections: exposition, development, and recapitulation.

sonatina abbreviated sonata.

song cycle series of art songs grouped by composer, poet, or performer.

song form ternary form in ABA.

soprano highest female vocal range.

sostenuto sustained.

sound generator electronic means of producing sound.

spinet wing-shaped harpsichord.

Sprechstimme speech-song.

Stabat Mater choral work based on the devotional poem concerning Mary's vigil at the Cross. It uses a Latin text.

staccato detached, sharply cut off.

staff five equidistant horizontal lines on which notes are placed to indicate pitch.

stile antico religious style of musical composition associated with the Renaissance that continued into the Baroque period.

stile moderno secular, theatrical style of composition that developed in the early Baroque period.

stop mechanical or electrical device for engaging/disengaging an organ rank; also refers to the actual set of pipes.

string quartet a chamber group consisting of first and second violin, viola, and cello. The term also refers to the literature for this instrumental grouping.

strophic exact repetition.

style galant gallant style.

subdominant fourth pitch of a diatonic scale as well as the triad built upon that pitch.

subject fugal theme.

submediant sixth pitch of a diatonic scale.

substitute chord a chord other than the basic primary and secondary triads, such as an extended chord, that can be used to harmonize a given melody or section of melody. Substitute chords are frequently used in jazz accompaniments.

suite extended instrumental composition in which each movement is typically based on a dance in binary form. In the Baroque suite the usual dances were allemande, courante, sarabande, and gigue, with optional dances frequently inserted between the last two, including minuet, gavotte, passepied, and bourrée.

sul ponticello bowing a string instrument near its bridge to produce a harsh timbre.

supertonic second pitch of a diatonic scale.

swara the pitches actually used in a raga, which are sa, ri, ga, ma, pa, dha, and ni. Swara are chosen from the twenty-two shrutis available for use, following rather restrictive rules.

swing big band jazz of the 1930s.

syllabic textual setting in which each syllable of text receives one pitch in the melody.

symphonic poem synonym for tone poem, referring to a one-movement orchestral work that is most typically programmatic.

syncopation shifting a strong beat to a weak or eliminating it altogether.

tabla Northern Indian set of drums that includes the baya and daya.

tablature notational scheme that shows the position of the performer's fingers on strings or holes rather than the actual pitches and durations.

tabor small medieval drum with two heads.

tala Indian time cycle.

talea rhythmic unit in an isorhythmic structure.

tamboura Indian chordophone that plays the drone.

tape loop use of a magnetic tape that is connected to itself to provide a continuous surface and create an electronic ostinato.

Te Deum Latin hymn of Thanksgiving to the glory of God.

tempo speed or pace of the music, especially its underlying beat.

tempus imperfectum division of the breve (sometimes the semibreve) into two equal parts; generally, the expression refers to the division of any value into two equal parts.

tempus perfectum division of the breve (sometimes the semibreve) into three equal parts; generally, the expression refers to the division of any value into three equal parts.

tenor highest male vocal range.

ternary form three-part form that is typically return, such as ABA.

terraced dynamics layering of dynamic levels within a composition, change occurring without gradual transition.

tertian harmony chords based on the interval of a third.

tessitura the average position of the majority of pitches within a melody; an average pitch level.

texture relationship of a melody or melodies to the background accompaniment.

theme a melody that assumes importance in the development of a composition because of its central and continued use.

theme and variations presentation of a given theme, followed by transformations of the theme. Variations may be sectional or continuous.

third middle pitch of a triad, which is a third higher than the root. In the triad C-E-G, E is the third.

through-composed nonrepeating music; additive form.

tie connecting line between two or more notes of the same pitch name, used to lengthen the value of the first note by the duration of all the following ones.

timbre tone color of sound.

timpani kettle drums.

toccata keyboard piece (usually) that displays the performer's manual dexterity; typically in one movement.

tonality a feeling in melody and harmony that one pitch, the tonic, is the pulling force or center.

tone poem one-movement orchestral work, typically programmatic.

tonic first pitch of a diatonic scale or the triad built on such a pitch.

transition passage in a musical composition that occurs between important sections or statements of themes. It is synonymous with episode.

transposing instrument an instrument that does not sound at concert pitch when it reads a pitch of the same name. A B-flat instrument sounds B-flat when it reads C, an E-flat instrument sounds E-flat when it reads C. Common transposing instruments are the trumpet, clarinet, saxophone, and French horn.

transposition to play, read, or write a composition in a different key from its original.

transverse a position for holding a woodwind instrument (notably the flute) so it is parallel to the floor.

Trecento period fourteenth century.

triad chord with three pitches, each separated from the next by the interval of a third.

trill melodic ornament in which there is rapid alternation between a given pitch and the one above it, whether half-step or whole-step.

trio composition for three performers.

trio sonata composition in which two melody instruments play in counterpoint, accompanied by continuo (harpsichord plus cello or viola da gamba). Trio sonatas are frequently in three or four movements.

triplet three notes in the time of two.

triple time rhythm in which every third beat is accented.

triplum the third voice in organum, added above the cantus firmus, and after the duplum.

trope textual interpolation within the melismatic passages of plainsong.

troubadour minstrel of noble birth in southern France during the eleventh to thirteenth centuries.

trouvère   minstrel of noble birth in northern France during the eleventh to thirteenth centuries.

turn   melodic ornament in which the main pitch is adorned by also playing the one above and the one below in quick succession, such as CDCBC.

tutti   the large group of performers in a concerto grosso.

twelve-bar blues   jazz form based on three phrases of four measures each in $\frac{4}{4}$ time, using a set progression of I, IV, and V_7 chords.

twelve-tone music   twentieth-century system of writing music in which the twelve tones of the chromatic scale are arranged into a series (number 1 to 12), and subsequently used as the basis of melodic and harmonic variation.

uneven pattern   rhythmic pattern that maintains the underlying accent grouping of the music but does not move exactly with the underlying beat. Rather, notes of uneven length follow one another. A dot is frequently used in simple meters to create uneven patterns.

vadi   tonic pitch of a raga.

verismo   realism.

vertical   referring to a woodwind that is played in a forward position, parallel to the performer's body, as compared to a transverse woodwind (flute), which is held parallel to the floor.

viol   medieval and Renaissance bowed chordophone, used in consorts, with six strings and a fretted neck. Viols were used in soprano, tenor, and bass (viola da gamba) sizes.

viola da gamba   bass viol.

virelai   a type of medieval French song.

virginal   small Renaissance harpsichord.

vivace   lively.

voicing   arrangement of the pitches of a chord within the pitch spectrum.

vox organalis   the added voice of organum that parallels the vox principalis at the interval of a fifth.

vox principalis   the main Gregorian melody used in organum, usually as the lowest sounding part.

white noise   static; the presence of all frequencies.

whole-step   distance of two half-steps in the same direction, such as between C and D or E and F sharp.

whole-tone scale   scale in which all intervals are whole steps, such as C D E F sharp G sharp A sharp C'.

wind quintet   chamber group consisting of flute, oboe, clarinet, bassoon, and French horn.

yang ch'in   Chinese hammer dulcimer.

zither   chordophone whose strings pass the entire length of its body, such as the koto, cheng, or ch'in.

INDEX